Masterworks of Literature Series

William S. Osborne, *editor*
Southern Connecticut State University

Essays on American Life and Letters

D1546381

Essays on American Life and Letters

by MARGARET FULLER

Edited for the Modern Reader by
Joel Myerson
University of South Carolina

N C U P, Inc.
(formerly New College and University Press, Inc.)
Albany, NY 12203

New Material, Introduction, Notes and Textual Commentary by
JOEL MYERSON

Printed by:
Communication Marketing Services, Inc.
74 Yardboro Avenue, Albany NY 12205

Contents

Introduction*

At Sarah Margaret's birth on 23 May 1810, her father, Timothy Fuller, was disappointed that his first child was a girl. He had wanted a boy to educate to his own manner of intellectual life. Nevertheless, he soon began to assign his daughter the same intellectual tasks young men of a comparable age would have undertaken; and, as a result, Margaret was raised to take full advantage of an excellent education. By age fifteen her schedule included reading literary and philosophical works in four languages during a day that lasted from five in the morning until eleven at night. The only break in this scholarly routine was the few hours reserved for walking, singing, and playing the piano. She was an omnivorous reader, her interest in German literature bringing her to the attention of the new religious and philosophical dissenters, the Transcendentalists. When her family moved to Cambridge in the early 1830s, she soon met most of the people who would become involved with the Transcendental Club and the *Dial*. Already well on her way to that "predetermination to *eat* this big universe as her oyster or her egg," which Thomas Carlyle later noticed in her,[1]

* Portions of this introduction were delivered as lectures before the Canadian Association of American Studies convention in Ottawa, Ontario, 11 October 1974; and the Thoreau Lyceum, Concord, Massachusetts, 14 May 1975. I would like to thank Thomas Blanding, Amy Boyd Daigle, Robert N. Hudspeth, Cameron Northouse, William S. Osborne, Thomas Jackson Rice, and especially Robert Burkholder and Robert A. Morace for their help. I am grateful to the Boston Public Library and the Houghton Library of Harvard University for permission to quote from manuscripts in their possession.

[1] Carlyle to Emerson, 7 May 1852, *The Correspondence of Emerson and Carlyle*, ed. Joseph Slater (New York: Columbia University Press, 1964), p. 478.

7

Fuller realized that her position in life would have been different and much higher had she been a man. Bothered by her own physical shortcomings, which included nearsightedness, complexion problems, and a tendency to robustness, Fuller concentrated on cultivating her mental powers. Therefore, she set for herself, with her father's tacit approval, the task of competing with men on purely intellectual terms, hoping that by showing her attainments in that area she would be accepted as an equal. She nearly succeeded in her plan but at a cost; many felt she had sacrificed the traditional concept of femininity, and Fuller's ego sometimes showed to others "the presence of a rather mountainous ME."[2]

The death of her father in October 1835 changed the course of her action. Plans for a European trip were cancelled, and Fuller took up teaching to support herself and her family. A brief stint at Bronson Alcott's progressive Temple School in Boston proved informative but unremunerative, and in June 1837 she went to Providence, Rhode Island. The post was a good one: the new Green Street School was liberal-minded, Emerson gave the dedication address, and the yearly salary of $1,000 was generous.

At Providence, Fuller continued to develop her literary powers. Beginning in 1835, she had been an occasional contributor of poems and reviews of foreign literature to the *Western Messenger*, a liberal Unitarian journal in the Ohio valley edited chiefly by her friend, James Freeman Clarke. When George Ripley began his *Specimens of Foreign Standard Literature* series in 1838, Fuller proposed to write a life of Goethe for it. Indeed, one reason for her taking the job at Providence had been that it allowed her time for scholarly pursuits. Her continuing study of German literature bore results; for when John Sullivan Dwight solicited aid from his friends for his edition of *Select Minor Poems, Translated from the German of Goethe and Schiller* in Ripley's series, Fuller contributed two translations.

Teaching school for Fuller was a means and not an end. She keenly felt her separation from Boston, and only in her correspondence with the Transcendentalists did she feel

---

[2] [R.W. Emerson, W.H. Channing, and J.F. Clarke], *Memoirs of Margaret Fuller Ossoli* (Boston: Phillips, Sampson, 1852), I, 236.

close to the center of activity. She began to believe that she had not yet really accomplished anything, not yet left her mark on the world, and that her time to do so was rapidly running out. Accordingly, she left Providence in December 1838 for Boston, where she supported herself by giving private language lessons while working on her biography of Goethe.

Fuller had first given classes in German, Italian, and French literature in 1836 in Boston, and her purposes this time were the same: to enable her students, "with ease and pleasure, to appropriate some part of the treasures of thought, which are contained in the classical works of foreign living languages."[3] The biography of Goethe soon proved a greater task than she had anticipated; and the only product of her labors was a translation of Eckermann's *Conversations with Goethe in the Last Years of His Life*, which was published in May 1839 as Volume IV of Ripley's *Specimens* series.

Living in Boston again placed Fuller close to the center of things, and she quickly renewed her acquaintance with the Transcendentalists. This group expressed their disagreement with the current state of affairs on three fronts: in literature, they championed English and continental writers such as Carlyle and Goethe; in philosophy, they followed Kant in believing that man had an innate ability to perceive that his existence transcended mere sensory experience, as opposed to the prevailing Lockean sensationalism; and in religion, unlike the conservative Unitarians, they denied the existence of miracles, preferring Christianity to rest upon the teachings rather than upon the deeds of Christ. Fuller was in agreement with them and gladly accepted an invitation to attend the meetings of the Transcendental Club.[4]

---

[3] See her prospectus for the language classes in Joel Myerson, *Margaret Fuller: A Descriptive Primary Bibliography*, A1, forthcoming from the University of Pittsburgh Press.

[4] Emerson wrote Fuller that the "rules" of the Club might be let down and "who knows but the . . . more timid or more gracious may crave the aid of wise & blessed women at their session." During the four years of the Club's existence, Fuller attended eight meetings, an excellent record considering that she was absent from Boston for two of those years (17 August 1837, *The Letters of Ralph Waldo Emerson*, ed. Ralph L. Rusk [New York: Columbia University Press, 1939], II, 95; see Joel Myerson, "A Calendar of

On 18 September 1839 the Transcendental Club met to discuss "the subject of a Journal designed as the organ of views in accordance with the Soul."[5] After the meeting, Fuller was urged by Emerson to "conduct a magazine" which should offer her "space" and "occasion" to do anything she wished; and in early October, when she hinted to Emerson that she would be available for the editor's job, he invited her to his home in Concord to "talk of these things."[6]

When Fuller went to Concord, she also spoke with Alcott, who had been approached by Orestes A. Brownson about the possibility of merging the yet unpublished journal with his own magazine, the *Boston Quarterly Review*. Emerson and Fuller agreed with Alcott that Brownson's journal was too narrow and dogmatic in its views of philosophy and literature, and that a truly Transcendental journal was needed, one in which "the purest thought and tastes may be represented."[7] They having decided to reject Brownson's offer, Fuller volunteered to be editor of the journal, which was to be called the *Dial*, after the name Alcott had given a collection of his thoughts on the Soul he had been assembling from his journals.[8] And in November, Emerson announced to friends that Fuller would edit the *Dial* and that Ripley would act as business manager.[9]

Fuller officially assumed her editorial duties in January 1840 and tried for two years to fairly present "all kinds of people" in her journal. The *Dial*'s contributors indeed had "freedom to say their say, for better, for worse";[10] but the

---

Transcendental Club Meetings," *American Literature*, XLIV [May 1972], 197-207).

[5] Alcott, "Diary July-December 1839," p. 249, Houghton Library, Harvard University.

[6] Emerson to Fuller, 16 October 1839, *Letters*, II, 229.

[7] Alcott, 19 October, "Diary July-December 1839," p. 320.

[8] Joel Myerson, "Bronson Alcott's 'Scripture for 1840,' " Entry LXXXI, February, *ESQ: A Journal of the American Renaissance*, XX (IV Quarter 1974), 242.

[9] Emerson to Elizabeth Hoar, 4 November, *Letters*, II, 231.

[10] Fuller to Emerson, 9 April 1842, *Letters*, III, 45n. Earlier, Fuller had herself declined to contribute to periodicals because she feared that what she did write would be "mutilated"; she refused to have what she wanted to write "dictated to suit the public taste" (letter dated 1836, *Memoirs*, I, 168).

reviewers, choosing the *Dial* as a convenient scapegoat for all the unpopular aspects of Transcendentalism, abused the new journal, while the public, unable to grasp or to digest the disparate articles, declined to buy the magazine.[11] In March 1842, hampered by ill health and upset that none of her promised salary had been paid, Fuller resigned. Despite Emerson's assuming the editorship, the *Dial* failed in 1844. The experience was valuable for Fuller, though, in teaching her to write review articles and in providing her with a ready outlet for literary productions.

While editing the *Dial*, Fuller had supported herself by holding Conversations on various topics, including Greek mythology. She believed women had been educated solely for display and not to think, and she wished to rectify this mistake.[12] By March 1841 the course had become so popular—even though it was one of the most expensive series in Boston—that men were admitted. She also continued her study of German literature, and in 1842 she translated part of Bettina's correspondence with Günderode for the press of Elizabeth Peabody. It was easy for Fuller to identify with Günderode, who, in Fuller's words, threw herself "into the river because the world is all too narrow."[13] The book was published in March, just as Fuller left the chore of editing the *Dial* behind her.

During the spring and summer of 1842, Fuller travelled a great deal, stopping in Concord for the month of September as Emerson's houseguest.[14] That November she began her fourth annual series of winter Conversations in Boston and used the proceeds to embark the following May on a tour

[11] See Joel Myerson, "The Contemporary Reception of the Boston *Dial*," *Resources for American Literary Study*, III (Autumn 1973), 203-20; and Myerson, "A Union List of the *Dial* and Some Information About Its Sales," *Papers of the Bibliographical Society of America*, LXVII (III Quarter 1973), 325-28.

[12] Fuller's description of her aims can be found in her letters to Albert G. Greene, [1839], Brown University Library; and to Sophia Ripley, Autumn 1839, *Memoirs*, I, 324-28.

[13] 19 February 1841, *Memoirs*, II, 58.

[14] Her record of this visit is printed in Joel Myerson, "Margaret Fuller's 1842 Journal: At Concord with the Emersons," *Harvard Library Bulletin*, XXI (July 1973), 320-40.

through the mid-west. She returned to Boston in September, started another round of Conversations, contributed some reviews to the *Dial*, and worked at writing up the record of her travels in book form. After the Conversations ended in April 1844, she concentrated on her book—which she researched at the usually all-male sanctuary of the Harvard University Library—and on 4 June her account was published as *Summer on the Lakes, in 1843*.[15]

Fuller's first book was typical of all her writings: its best parts were superb, which made the poorer sections seem even more so. The value of *Summer on the Lakes* lies not in its factual matter, for Fuller had aimed at giving her "poetic impression of the country at large." It lies in its commentary on the people and their manners. She immediately sympathized with the plight of the Indian and wondered why he had not murdered the white man outright after the latter's territorial imperative was made manifest. Throughout her trip she was amazed at the beauty of the country, a beauty often overlooked by the local residents, as she remarked of a boat captain who "presented a striking instance how men, for the sake of getting a living, forget to live." Fuller saw that the desire of some to imitate European and Eastern standards would cause a basic conflict: "If the little girls grow up strong, resolute, able to exert their faculties, their mothers mourn over their want of fashionable delicacy." To prevent this, parents sent their children to schools, the result of which was "most likely to make them useless and unhappy at home." These concerns were to be echoed fifty years later by such regional writers as Hamlin Garland, especially in *Crumbling Idols* and *Rose of Dutcher's Coolly*. The artistic success of *Summer on the Lakes* was hampered, though, by

---

[15] *Summer on the Lakes* was published by Charles C. Little and James Brown of Boston and sold for seventy-five cents, with Fuller receiving 10% royalties after publication costs had been met (Little and Brown to Emerson, 29 May 1844, Houghton Library, Harvard University). Inserted in some copies were seven etchings executed by Sarah Clarke, who had accompanied Fuller on her trip to the west. Although Fuller wrote her brother Richard that "near 700" copies were sold, 400 copies, bound in blue wrappers, were remaindered in New York by W.H. Graham the following year (9 January 1845, Houghton Library, Harvard University; *New-York Daily Tribune*, 13 May 1845, p. 2).

an unconscionable padding, as Fuller included large excerpts
from and summaries of her reading—one extending over
thirty-five pages—so that less than half the book actually
dealt with the subject matter promised by its title.

While the book was in press Fuller worried about its reception. This was her first extended piece of original writing,
and she wrote Emerson: "I feel a little cold at the idea of
walking forth alone to meet that staring sneering Pit critic,
the Public at large, when I have always been accustomed to
confront it from amid a group of liberally educated and respectable gentlemen."[16] She must have been satisfied, then,
when the critics praised her. The *New-York Weekly Tribune*
(15 June 1844) called attention to the book's "broad, general,
truthful criticism of common life"; and James Clarke called
Summer on the Lakes a "very interesting" book, marked by
its author's "keen perception, profound reflection and constructive imagination," in the *Christian World* (6 July
1844).[17] In the influential *Christian Examiner* (September
1844), Caleb Stetson praised *Summer on the Lakes* as "a
work of varied interest, rich in fine observation, profound
reflection and striking anecdote," though he did complain
about the "stiffness" and "unnaturalness" of her style: "we
find something cold, stately, almost *statuesque*, in her language."

Fuller's association with the Transcendentalists was commented on by most reviewers but for different reasons.
Graham's Magazine (September 1844) found *Summer on the
Lakes* "very agreeable," and a pleasant surprise, since Fuller
was usually associated with "a literary sect, the members of
which are prophets to themselves and heretics to others, and
whose excellencies and oddities are both distasteful to a considerable portion of the 'reading public.'"[18] Orestes A.

---

[16] 9 May [1844], Houghton Library, Harvard University.

[17] Complete bibliographical citations for review may be found in Joel
Myerson, *Margaret Fuller: An Annotated Secondary Bibliography* (New
York: Burt Franklin, 1977).

[18] Fuller herself had once said that she would only be called a Transcendentalist if the word meant that she had "an active mind" and that she was
"honored by the friendship" of such men as Alcott, Emerson, and Ripley
(Fuller to Caroline Sturgis, 16 November 1837, Houghton Library, Harvard
University).

Brownson, in his new journal, *Brownson's Quarterly Review* (October 1844), complained about this book by "the high-priestess of American Transcendentalism," with its "slipshod style" and a "certain toss of the head" which he found "exceedingly" offending. But the English *People's Journal* (February 1847) saw things differently. Fuller's writing was similar to that of the Transcendentalists in that both attempted to "counteract the prevalent materialism" in America, yet she differed from them in one important respect: "her habit of writing intelligibly to ordinary readers."

Summer on the Lakes was important for Fuller's career: it not only hurried recognition of her as a literary figure, but also brought her to the attention of Horace Greeley, editor of the *New-York Tribune*. He invited her to become the literary critic for his newspaper and offered to publish her next book, which would be an expansion and revision of her "The Great Lawsuit. Man *versus* Men. Woman *versus* Women," from the July 1843 *Dial*. Fuller accepted both offers, finished the book in November, and began boarding with the Greeley family the next month. Her first review for the *Tribune*—one of Emerson's *Essays*—appeared on 7 December 1844, and *Woman in the Nineteenth Century* was published in early February 1845.[19]

Woman in the Nineteenth Century is Fuller's most important work and is a major document in the history of American feminism. Fuller recognized the significance of her statement about woman's position in society and wrote a friend that if she were to die suddenly, "the measure of my footprint would be left on the earth."[20] The book is striking,

---

[19] *Woman in the Nineteenth Century* was published by Greeley & McElrath of New York in both cloth and wrappers, and sold for fifty cents. Earlier, Fuller had considered the possibility of financing an edition of 1,000 copies herself if it could be done for under $150, but her employer on the *Tribune* quickly secured it for his own press (Fuller to [W.H. Channing], 17 November 1844, Boston Public Library). Approximately 1,500 copies were printed and Greeley "sold them out very soon," with Fuller receiving an immediate $85 profit on the edition (Greeley to Richard Fuller, 30 July 1855, and Fuller to Eugene Fuller, 9 March 1845, Houghton Library, Harvard University). A pirated edition of *Woman in the Nineteenth Century* was published in England the following year by H.G. Clarke.

[20] Fuller to [W.H. Channing], 17 November 1844, Boston Public Library.

sometimes pedantic but more often impassioned and hard-hitting. Fuller especially attacked the hypocrisy of men, an hypocrisy that allowed them to campaign to free the black man while simultaneously legislating restrictions on women; an hypocrisy which complained of woman's physical and emotional unsuitability for positions of high responsibility in public life, yet which saw nothing inconsistent with allowing her the "killing labors" of the sempstress or the field hand, or assigning to her the role of raising children. She also felt that man had separated himself from woman with disastrous results for both sexes. Man had "educated woman more as a servant than a daughter, and found himself a king without a queen." As woman became less equal, man had lost respect for her. Fuller wanted a time when there would be equality, when "man and woman may regard one another as brother and sister, the pillars of one porch, the priests of one worship." When this happened, woman could live for "God's sake" and not sink into "weakness and poverty" through idolatry, with "imperfect man her god."

In its earlier form, as "The Great Lawsuit" in the *Dial*, Fuller's work had drawn many positive responses. Henry Thoreau called it "a noble piece, rich extempore writing";[21] the wife of George Ripley, who had helped her husband found the Brook Farm community, discovered it "rich in all good things";[22] and a friend told the well-known Transcendentalist minister Theodore Parker that he considered it "the best piece that has seen the light in the Dial."[23] Ellery Channing, Fuller's brother-in-law and an aspiring poet, recommended it "without qualification," and Emerson felt it to be "quite an important fact in the history of Woman."[24] The radical woman's rights advocate Mary Gove earnestly praised Emerson, as the *Dial's* editor, for printing Fuller's

---

[21] Thoreau to the Emersons, 8 July 1843, *The Correspondence of Henry David Thoreau*, ed. Walter Harding and Carl Bode (New York: New York University Press, 1958), pp. 124-25.

[22] Sophia Ripley to Emerson, 5 July [1843], Houghton Library, Harvard University.

[23] Parker to Emerson, 2 August 1843, Houghton Library, Harvard University.

[24] Emerson to Fuller, 11 July 1843, *Letters*, III, 183.

call-to-arms.[25] Only Sophia Hawthorne disliked "the speech which Queen Margaret has made"; it seemed to her that if Fuller were "married truly, she would no longer be puzzled about the rights of woman," since marriage, to Sophia, was "woman's true destiny and place."[26] And the *New-York Daily Tribune* (10 July 1843), the only publication to review the July 1843 *Dial*, declared that Fuller's contribution "sparkles with striking thoughts and noble sentiments," and reprinted in subsequent issues two selections from it.

When Fuller revised the *Dial* article and published it separately, it naturally received much more public attention. Women writers in 1845 were more tolerated than accepted, but only so long as they stayed within their proper sphere; Fuller, as the *Tribune*'s literary critic and therefore as a professional author with definite critical standards, broke the mould of the conventional woman writer who wrote for the family and women's magazines of the day.

These family and ladies' magazines tended to attack what they called "light literature," not because of its inherent mediocrity but because of its moral uselessness. Literature which did not teach a lesson was bad literature; it would "lead the young into vain and unsatisfying amusements."[27] The main audience for this type of reasoning was children and their mothers. Not surprisingly, then, magazines for the young consisted of moral tales, articles on manners and taste, and Poor Richard-esque sayings. Mothers were considered only children of an advanced age, and the real world was shielded from them, too. Copper and steel engravings of the latest fashions were the high points of the women's magazines; the publishers often paid more for one plate than for all their literary contributions. Just as the plates drew attention from the bland contents, the contents themselves drew attention from harsh reality. To "amuse and instruct" was the goal of these magazines, and they did both with a

---

[25] Gove to Emerson, 15 August 1843, Houghton Library, Harvard University.

[26] Undated, cited in Julian Hawthorne, *Nathaniel Hawthorne and His Wife* (Boston: Houghton, Mifflin, 1884), I, 257.

[27] [D. Newell], "The Influence of Light Literature Upon the Family Circle," *Christian Family Magazine*, II (January 1843), 110.

vengeance. Instruction consisted of preparing the woman to act out with perfection that station which life had assigned her. Reform movements were mostly ignored—they hurt circulation too much. Amusement was provided by maudlin, sentimental verses and stories of love, in which the heroine, by following the advice given elsewhere in the magazine, walked along the primrose path of life to a lovely marriage and lived happily ever afterwards.[28]

Even though *Woman in the Nineteenth Century* attacked many of the foundations that these magazines had built upon, nearly all the reviewers praised Fuller herself and expressed agreement with the need to discuss the questions which she had raised. It was with her solutions and the way in which she presented them that much consternation was created.[29]

Almost no one had a bad word to say about the author of *Woman in the Nineteenth Century.* In the *Boston Courier* (8 February 1845), Fuller's friend, Lydia Maria Child, called her "a woman of more vigorous intellect and comprehensive thought, than any other among the writers of this country," a sentiment echoed by the *New-York Daily Tribune* (13 February 1845), which called Fuller "a woman, second to none among us for generous character, strong and disciplined intellect, and varied experience." Horace Greeley, her editor on the *Tribune*, writing in *Graham's Magazine* (March 1845), called Fuller "one of the most independent, free-spoken and large-souled of her sex. . . a gifted, earnest and thoroughly informed woman—an embodied Intellect."[30] Only Brownson, in his *Quarterly Review* (April 1845), dissented, as he

---

[28] For a further discussion of this class of periodicals, see Caroline John Garnsey, "Ladies' Magazines to 1850: The Beginnings of an Industry," *Bulletin of the New York Public Library*, LVIII (February 1954), 74-88; and Bertha Monica Stearns, "Philadelphia Magazines for Ladies: 1830-1860," *Pennsylvania Magazine of History and Biography*, LXIX (July 1945), 207-19.

[29] As Fuller wrote her brother Eugene: "Abuse public and private is lavished upon its views, but respect expressed for me personally" (9 March 1845, Houghton Library, Harvard University).

[30] Privately, Greeley wrote Rufus Griswold, the editor of *Graham's:* "Margaret's book is going to *sell.* I tell you it has the real stuff in it" (15 January 1845, *Passages from the Correspondence and Other Papers of Rufus W. Griswold*, [ed. W.M. Griswold], [Cambridge: W.M. Griswold, 1898], p. 163).

sarcastically designated her "the chieftainess" of the Transcendentalists. To the *Ladies' National Magazine* (April 1845), Fuller's "bold opinions" showed that she "is no common woman," but rather "is a scholar and thinker, is earnest and high-souled, and longs, with almost a poet's yearning, for the amelioration of mankind."

The publication of the book itself—as opposed to the dissemination of the ideas it embodied—was also generally seen as good. *Graham's* decided it should be "widely read and cherished," and the *New-York Tribune* recommended it to "all who are interested in the advancement of humanity." Charles Lane, an English Transcendentalist now in America and writing for the *Herald of Freedom* (5 September 1845), a New Hampshire anti-slavery paper, gave *Woman in the Nineteenth Century* this encomium: "The book is strengthening to candid minds, and must be formidable to the nervous conservative of old notions and hereditary lusts from its well-selected array of pure and unquestionable evidence." Mrs. Child voiced a similar opinion in her comments in the *Boston Courier:* "Portions of the book will be considered very bold; for it speaks somewhat plainly on subjects which men generally do not wish to have spoken of, and of which women dare not speak." But to the *Spectator* (27 September 1845), apparently the only periodical in England to review Fuller's book, "it scarcely seems worth the reprinting in this country."

It was with Fuller's style and organization—or lack thereof—that reviewers became tough. The comment of the *Knickerbocker* (March 1845) that *Woman in the Nineteenth Century* was "a well-reasoned and well-written treatise" was definitely in the minority. The *Spectator* declared that Fuller had "imitated to exaggeration" Emerson's "peculiarities of style and manner," but "without reaching the searching depth of thought he occasionally exhibits." Even the partisan Mrs. Child told her readers that Fuller's "noble and beautiful thoughts" failed to "flow into orderly harmonious arrangement." Writing in the *Broadway Journal*, Charles Frederick Briggs reviewed *Woman in the Nineteenth Century* in three installments (1, 8, 22 March 1845), complaining of Fuller's "want of distinctness," and gave this advice:

TIME FLIES, should be inserted on the door–posts of every author's dwelling . . . the author who writes to instruct, cannot write too briefly, for we have much to learn, and but little time to learn in. . . . The time that the best of us can devote to reading, is but short, and therefore, we cannot afford to read books which lack method, or which contain more words than are necessary to convey the author's meaning, provided he have any. That Miss Fuller is justly chargeable with wasting the time of her reader, her most devout admirer cannot deny.

Brownson was more direct as he wrote about Fuller's "interminable prattle":

Nothing is or can be less artistic than the book before us, which, properly speaking, is no book, but a long talk on matters and things in general, and men and women in particular. It has neither beginning, middle, nor end, and may be read backwards as well as forwards, and from the centre outwards each way, without affecting the continuity of the thought or the succession of ideas. We see no reason why it should stop where it does, or why the lady might not keep on talking in the same strain till doomsday, unless prevented by want of breath.

And one writer included Fuller and her book in his novel of New York society as "the authoress of 'Woman in the Present Day,' a work which, to understand properly, you must commence at the middle, read backwards to the beginning, then jump to the end and read backwards to the middle."[31]

Even compliments on Fuller's style were backhanded ones. F. D. Huntington, writing in the *Christian Examiner* (May 1845), said he had expected to find in *Woman in the Nineteenth Century* "a considerable amount of mannerism, affectation, eccentricity and pedantry," but was rather pleasantly surprised to discover that the "number of inverted sentences, *outré* ideas, far-fetched comparisons and foreign idioms, is more limited than we had feared." Still, he concluded, "the book lacks method sadly," being "rather a collection of clever sayings and bright intimations, than a logical treatise, or a profound examination of the subject it discusses."

---

[31] Thomas Dunn English, *1844; or, the Power of the "S.F."* (New York: Burgess, Stringer, 1847), p. 125.

It was on the subject of Fuller's book, on the position and role of woman in the nineteenth century, that most of the adverse, as well as the genuinely positive, criticism centered; and it is through this aspect of the contemporary reviews that one can see the general concepts of women and of marriage that Fuller was arguing against.

In a listing of the "peculiarities of the female temperament" in its article on "The Condition of Woman," the *Southern Quarterly Review* (July 1846) outlined the qualities of the mid-nineteenth-century American woman. She was marked by "much more excitability and enthusiasm than men"; "a nicer perception of minute circumstances" which showed itself in modesty and also made her "often incapable of appreciating bolder and more striking points"; "boundless humanity," as seen in "her glowing compassion for the unfortunate, her unwearied attention to the sick, and her active benevolence to the destitute"; and "feebleness of muscle." Also, women were incurably romantic: "Love which is, but an episode with man, forms the whole story of a woman's life." And to preserve these traits, women must not, as Fuller proposes, be allowed to enter man's sphere of action. This is for her own sake, lest she lose, in the words of the *Ladies' National Magazine* (April 1845)

> reverence for things not of this earth, a longing for supernal happiness, and a treasure of comfort in the darkest hours of sorrow, which would be unknown, if woman, as well as man, mingled promiscuously in the world, and lost, in its hard wear and tear, its knavery, its deceit, its meanness, the heavenly purity of character which now forms her brightest gem.

In short, by keeping woman within her particular, and, one might add, her God-given sphere, man is actually keeping her in a place of great position and importance, a place that she would no longer occupy if granted an equal opportunity to become sullied through contact with the harsh real world. On this last point Brownson had also commented:

> ... Miss Fuller thinks ... men have the advantage; with them it is not so bad. ... Men are not much more easily satisfied than women; and if women are forced to take to tea, scandal, philanthropy, evening-meetings, and smelling bottles, men are forced

to take to trade, infidelity, sometimes the pistol, and even to turn *reformers*, the most desperate resort of all.[32]

Rather than making women share the trials and tribulations of men, they should perfect their womanly attributes, as Briggs had written in the *Broadway Journal*:

> To make sailors of women and milliners of men is to have imperfect sailors and imperfect milliners. . . . Men labor for little else than to make women happy; the cream of every enjoyment is skimmed for their express use, while the sour milk is drank by their lords. . . . The restraints which Miss Fuller complains of as hindering women from becoming blacksmiths, sailors, and soldiers, are the restraints which Nature has imposed, and which can never be overcome.

The *Southern Quarterly Review* had pursued this point at length, describing how woman's power is actually what many foolish people consider to be her weakness:

> Imaginative and susceptible, weak, timid and dependent, she looks up to and leans upon man, as the being who is to cherish, to support and to defend her, and . . . she adds, by the claims of her dependence, a charm to the existence of her protector, and by the sweet influence of her virtues, leads him to better deeds and purer thoughts.

Woman, then, should take comfort in the knowledge that only by her weakness is man able to be strong.

The point which disturbed most reviewers was Fuller's comments on marriage. Perhaps the best statement of this, quoted by her from "one of the ripe thinkers of the times," is "We must have units before we can have union." Marriage was a partnership between two people, each respecting the other's individuality, each sharing in the success of the pair. Because of this, Fuller decried the traditional stereotyped

---

[32] Three months later, in an article on "Transcendentalism, or the latest Form of Infidelity," Brownson continued his tirade: "Miss Fuller, in her *Woman in the Nineteenth Century*, patronizes several renowned courtesans; and the chief ground of her complaint against our *masculine* social order seems to be, that it imposes undue restraints on woman's nature, and does not permit her to follow her natural sentiments and affections" (*Brownson's Quarterly Review*, VII [July 1845], 312).

roles for men and women, saying that individuals should express themselves and not be merely what others think they should be because of their sex. Briggs, for one, had disagreed:

> She is offended that women should esteem it a compliment to be called masculine, while men consider it a reproach to be called feminine. . . . It is the law that woman shall reverence her husband, and that he shall be her head. We may love those whom we protect, but we can never wish ourselves in their place . . . .

Briggs had also rebuked Fuller's endorsement of the suggestion by "a profound thinker" that, since "no married woman can represent the female world, for she belongs to her husband," the "idea of woman must be represented by a virgin":

> It would be as reasonable to say that none but a deaf man could give a true idea of music. Woman is nothing but as a wife. How, then, can she truly represent the female character who has never filled it? No woman can be a true woman, who has not been a wife and a mother . . . they are the natural destiny of woman, and if she is kept from them, her nature is distorted and unnatural; and she sees things through a false medium.

Seizing on a tale related by Fuller, Briggs had made another point:

> "A party of travellers lately visited a lonely hut on a mountain. There they found an old woman that told them she and her husband had lived there forty years; why, they said, did you choose so barren a spot? She did not know, it was the man's notion . . . I would not have it so"; says Miss Fuller. In the name of all that is monstrous, what would she have? Would she have the woman to leave her husband, or would she have the husband abandon what he believed to be for his interest to do, to satisfy a whim of his wife? She is not bound to provide for him, but he is bound to provide for her, and therefore he must be allowed the privilege of following his own business in his own way, unless she can advise him better: but he must be the judge of the advice. The old woman was a true woman and a good wife, who had no thought but to please her husband. Women who have any other thoughts have no business with a husband. If

there is anything clear in revealed and natural law, it is that man is the head of the woman.[33]

Clearly Fuller did not understand that woman's position as wife and mother is the highest role she could aspire to. It was so high, in fact, that to grant her equality would be a demotion. To support Fuller, therefore, was to demean and to endanger woman's natural superiority.

A few reviewers did endorse Fuller's ideas. F. D. Huntington, in the *Christian Examiner*, had applauded the "deserved contempt" she cast upon the condescending way in which men treated women in conversation. The most favorable review of *Woman in the Nineteenth Century* had been Lane's in the *Herald of Freedom*, which Fuller herself considered "the only notice that ever appeared of the book, I thought worth keeping."[34] Lane's first sentence had made his position clear at once: "The misfortune in almost every endeavor for Woman's enfranchisement and elevation is the sentiment, that she is to attain them somehow by the gift, or at least, the sufferance of Man." A believer in celibacy, Lane alone among the reviewers dealt with sexual enslavement: "Freedom, peace, salvation, cannot be expected for woman while she permits herself to be the instrument of man's lowest gratifications, and tolerates a degree of unchastity in him, which in her he would utterly condemn." But what most appalled Lane was that man dared believe he could rescue woman from the pedestal upon which he had placed her:

Man, a fallen, an erring, a corrupt creature, as he confesses, is proposed to be the instrument of woman's elevation, the donor of her goodness and purity. Monstrous absurdity. He who is so lost a being; he who enslaves black women in the field, and white women in the factory, for whom the royal palace and the peasant's cottage are alike scenes for the gratification of his lowest lust, is to bestow on woman her just rights. Cruel delusion!

[33] Fuller told this story to demonstrate why women need "a much greater range of occupation than they have, to rouse their latent powers."
[34] Fuller to Richard Fuller, 10 December 1845, Houghton Library, Harvard University.

Seeing *Woman in the Nineteenth Century* through the press had exhausted Fuller ("really," she wrote a friend, "the work seems but half done when your book is *written*"); but its reception was gratifying.[35] Fuller was also pleased with the opportunities which life in New York was opening to her. She took in its cultural attractions and interested herself in various reform movements. Of special interest to her were the female convicts of the city; and she had passed Christmas Day 1844 in the company of these women, including prostitutes whom Fuller described as having been "trampled in the mud to gratify the brute appetites of men."[36]

However, her tenure as the *Tribune*'s literary critic took its toll. She continued to be plagued by headaches (the result of her nearsightedness), an infirmity made worse by the pressure to meet deadlines.[37] Greeley wanted someone who could write copy on demand, and he grew impatient when Fuller instead waited for the mood to strike her. What he considered an inconsistency between her insistence on the one hand for the equality of sexes, and her desire on the other hand to be treated with the traditional courtesy extended women, sometimes led to "sharpish sparring" between them. On occasions when Fuller implied that Greeley should treat her with "the courtesy and protection of Manhood," he would reply, quoting from *Woman in the Nineteenth Century*, "Let them be sea-captains if they will," a response which did little to ripen their acquaintance.[38] Fuller's energies were also drained by an unsuccessful ro-

[35] Fuller to [Mary Rotch], [15 January 1845], Houghton Library, Harvard University.
[36] Fuller to [Mary Rotch], [15 January 1845], Houghton Library, Harvard University; see also the account of her visit, "Christmas in State Prisons," *New-York Daily Tribune*, 26 December 1844, p. 2.
[37] An interesting study of Fuller's "ill health" is in George M. Gould, *Biographic Clinics* (Philadelphia: Blakiston, 1904), II, 271-81.
[38] *Memoirs*, II, 156. Fuller also had little success in cultivating Mrs. Greeley's acquaintance. Beman Brockway recounts an incident when Mrs. Greeley, who had an antipathy for kid gloves, met Fuller in the street and, touching Fuller's kid gloves, shuddered and said, "Skin of a beast, skin of a beast!" Fuller, not to be outdone, touched Mrs. Greeley's silk gloves and exclaimed, "Entrails of a worm!" (*Fifty Years in Journalism* [Watertown, N.Y.: Daily Times Printing and Publishing House, 1891], p. 157).

mance which left her feeling used and hurt.[39] Still, she managed to write nearly 250 reviews and occasional essays for the *Tribune* over the next year and a half. By the summer of 1846 she had saved enough money to plan a trip to Europe; and in August she sailed for England, just a few weeks before a collection of her reviews, *Papers on Literature and Art*, was published in New York the next month.[40]

At the urging of Evert Duyckinck, who had hailed *Summer on the Lakes* as the only genuine American book he had read,[41] Fuller had selected enough of her periodical and newspaper essays to fill two volumes. She had considered doing such a collection as early as January 1846, concluding that whether she would "depends on how far M[argaret]. may win the favor of the public (without making it her object as most of the others do!)."[42] *Papers on Literature and Art* was published in Wiley and Putnam's Library of American Books, a series which included Nathaniel Hawthorne's *Mosses from an Old Manse*, Herman Melville's *Typee*, and Edgar Allan Poe's *Tales*. The final collection contained critical reviews on English, American, and continental literature and art. Fuller's comments on American authors were uncannily accurate in an age that saw in Henry Wadsworth Longfellow the best that American poetry could offer: William Cullen Bryant's "range is not great, nor his genius fertile"; James Russell Lowell, "to the grief of some friends, and the disgust of more," was found "absolutely wanting in the true spirit and tone of poesy"; Longfellow was "a man of cultivated taste, delicate though not deep feeling, and some, though not much, poetic force." Emerson, to Fuller, took "the highest

---

[39] See *Love-Letters of Margaret Fuller* (New York: D. Appleton, 1903).

[40] Wiley and Putnam sold *Papers on Literature and Art* for fifty cents apiece for the two parts issued in wrappers or $1.25 for both parts bound in one volume, with Fuller receiving 12% after the publisher's expenses had been made (Fuller to Richard Fuller, n.d., Houghton Library, Harvard University). The book evidently sold well and a second printing was done in 1848.

[41] Diary entry, quoted in Perry Miller, *The Raven and the Whale: The War of Words and Wits in the Era of Poe and Melville* (New York: Harcourt, Brace, 1956), p. 170.

[42] Fuller to Mary Rotch, 9 January 1846, Houghton Library, Harvard University.

rank" among her contemporaries.

The general reception of *Papers on Literature and Art* was quite good. The *Democratic Review* (September 1846) saw it as formally opening "a new era of candor and plain speaking on a subject which has certainly had more than its fair share of nonsense and impertinence." The *New-York Mirror* (19 September 1846), also praised Fuller's candor in discussing the low quality of the periodical press: "Her estimate of our magazine literature is not very flattering, but we should not care to be so ungallant as to say it was not just." Other reviewers were generous in their praise. The *Albion* (12 September 1846) noticed the "keen perceptions of the beautiful" and the "critical acuteness" Fuller possessed; the *New-York Daily Tribune* (12 September 1846) called attention to "the lucid and vigorous outpouring of a clear, cultivated, lofty, human intellect, enriched by a thoughtful observation of life and the amplest acquaintance with literature"; the English *Spectator* (26 September 1846) praised Fuller's "full and discerning mind"; the *Harbinger* (26 September 1846), at the Brook Farm community, called it "penetrating and catholic criticism"; *Godey's Magazine and Lady's Book* (November 1846) pointed out its "learning, ability and taste"; and the London *Athenæum* (19 December 1846) expressed its "gratification" with the book. A young New York newspaperman, Walter Whitman, welcomed *Papers on Literature and Art* "right heartily" in the Brooklyn *Daily Eagle* (9 November 1846); and Frederic Henry Hedge, an old friend of Fuller's, gave her this encomium in the *Christian Examiner* (January 1847): "They bear marks throughout of a vigorous mind, discriminating thought, varied and ever ready power, with candid and fearless expression." In New York, a friend wrote Poe to comment favorably on Fuller's book and placed her next to Poe on his own list of best critics.[43] In fact, the *Democratic Review* had hit on Fuller's aim exactly when it said that "The peculiarity of these papers has been their representation of the individual life of the author." However,

[43] 27 July 1847, Thomas Ollive Mabbott, "The Letters of George W. Eveleth to Edgar Allan Poe," *Bulletin of the New York Public Library*, XXVI (March 1922), 183-84.

even many of these otherwise favorable reviews complained of Fuller's treatment of Longfellow[44] and Lowell.[45]

All the reviews of *Papers on Literature and Art* were not complimentary. In a mixed review, the English *Critic* (3 October 1846) praised Fuller's "quickness of apprehension," "sound judgment," and "discriminating taste," but also complained of "a tendency to philosophise beyond her powers." The same problem disturbed the *New-York Illustrated Magazine of Literature and Art* (November 1846), which called some essays "very able and justly written," while others were "weak and partial." Fuller's style had also bothered the *Harbinger.* The complaint was of an "occasional streak of grandiloquence" which left "a certain disagreeable impression." *Graham's* (October 1846) was more pointed: Fuller's style was "half petulant, half oracular, often inexpressibly amusing rather than particularly edifying," and marked by "a

[44] Privately, Longfellow noted in his journal this "furious onslaught" and "bilious attack" by Fuller, "a dreary woman" (11 December 1845, *The Letters of Henry Wadsworth Longfellow*, ed. Andrew Hilen [Cambridge: Harvard University Press, 1966-   ], III, 93n). Earlier, in the January 1843 *Dial*, Fuller had reviewed Longfellow's *Poems on Slavery* thus: "The thinnest of all Mr. Longfellow's thin books; spirited and polished, like its forerunners; but the topic would warrant a deeper tone" (III, 415; the book is thirty-one pages long).

[45] This notice was probably in Lowell's mind when he drew Fuller as Miranda, with an "I-turn-the-crank-of-the-Universe air," three years later in his *A Fable for Critics.* That same year, Lowell drew this other, less well known, picture of Fuller:

> Her eye,—it seems a chemic test,
> And drops upon you like an acid;
>
> . . . .
>
> There, you are classified: she's gone
> Far, far away into herself;
> Each with its Latin label on,
> Your poor components, one by one,
> Are laid upon their proper shelf
> In her compact and ordered mind,
>
> . . . .
>
> One problem still defies thy art;—
> Thou never canst compute . . .
> The distance and diameter
> Of any simple human heart.

"Studies for Two Heads," *Poems, Second Series* [Cambridge: George Nichols; New York: B.B. Mussey, 1847], pp. 136-37).

certain dogmatism of tone." The only completely negative
response was in the *American Review* (November 1846),
which complained of the "transcendental bombast" and
"outre phraseology," and concluded that one may as well call
the book "Eulogistic essays, showing the effects produced
upon a feminine spirit of the transcendental-Boswell world,
by reading the memoirs of great writers and artists, and the
praises bestowed upon them." But these were definitely
minority views, and the total contemporary reception of *Papers on Literature and Art* must be considered favorable. As
word of this reaction caught up with Fuller in Europe, it
pleased her as much as the trip itself.

It had been over ten years since Fuller had been forced to
cancel her European trip when her father had died, a post-
ponement which doubtless made her journey at this time
even more appreciated. She met the literary lions of the
British Isles, including Carlyle ("He does not converse,—
only harangues") and Wordsworth ("I had found no Apollo,
flaming with youthful glory . . . but, instead, a reverend old
man clothed in black, and walking with cautious step along
the level garden-path").[46] In November she settled at Paris,
where she stayed until the following February. *La Revue
Indépendante* had translated and published her essay on
"American Literature" from *Papers on Literature and Art*,
and had asked her to be its American correspondent. The
American public, too, was kept aware of her during this time;
as one of the *Tribune's* foreign correspondents, she contributed some three dozen travel letters to that paper. In April
she took up residence at Rome and in the summer of 1847
made an extended tour through northern Italy, including
Florence, Bologna, Venice, Milan, and Lake Como, a trip
reported on to the *Tribune's* readers. What she did not report,
even to her private correspondents, was that she had met and
had been captivated by an Italian count, Giovanni Ossoli,
eleven years her junior.

[46] Letters dated [1847] and 27 August 1846, *At Home and Abroad* (Boston: Crosby, Nichols, 1856), pp. 184, 131-32. On the other hand, Carlyle
told a friend he found her to be "a strange lilting lean old maid" who was
"not nearly such a bore as I expected" (8 October 1846, James Anthony
Froude, *Thomas Carlyle: A History of His Life in London 1834-1881*
[London: Longmans, Green, 1884], I, 401).

Rome, as seen by Fuller when she returned in October, was in a state of turmoil. The revolution was in full swing and she was caught up by it: "I am deeply interested in this public drama, and wish to see it *played out*. Methinks I have *my part* therein, either as actor or historian."[47] It was under these conditions that Fuller accepted Ossoli as her lover. Since it was already known that Ossoli supported the republicans, his marriage to this foreigner—and a non-Catholic at that—would have ended in his being disowned by his aristocratic family. As a result, though the affair was soon physically consummated, the marriage itself was delayed for nearly a year.

Fuller spent a miserable winter, bothered by headaches and the interminable rains; and in July she removed to Rieti, near Rome, to await the birth of their child. At first she was unhappy, for the local people saw her as "an ignorant *Inglese*, and they fancy all *Inglesi* have wealth untold";[48] but she came to be accepted by the villagers. On 5 September 1848 a boy, named Angelo, was born. Fuller spent the winter at Rieti, visiting Rome and Ossoli, a sergeant in the Civic Guard, only for short periods of time. In April 1849 she came to Rome, leaving her child behind with a wet nurse, and served well on hospital duty during the tumultuous and decisive months that followed. But Rome fell in July and the hopes of the Revolution with it. Both Ossoli, discredited by his support for the losing side, and Fuller, as a foreigner sympathetic with the rebels, were declared *personae non gratae* and were forced to leave. They returned to Rieti where they found Angelo ill, and, after nursing him back to health, journeyed to Florence in November.

Police pressures continued at Florence; and these, combined with a diminishing amount of funds and Fuller's growing homesickness, forced another move. The Ossolis planned to return to the United States, where she planned to arrange for the publication of her account of the Roman revolution, then in manuscript. They sailed in May, despite her premonitions that the voyage would be ill-fated. It certainly began that way: the captain died of smallpox off Gibraltar, and

---

[47] Fuller to Emerson, 19 May 1848, *Memoirs*, II, 239.
[48] Letter undated, *Memoirs*, II, 281.

Angelo was almost a victim of the same disease during the crossing. On 18 July land was sighted; but, as the ship approached, a storm rose, causing the inexperienced acting captain to run the vessel aground off shore, near Fire Island, where she remained fast. The storm subsided and attempts were made to swim to the nearby beach. Fuller would not be separated from her husband; and though she encouraged others to make for shore, she resolutely resigned herself to death. The next day, after the storm resumed, she gave Angelo to a sailor in a last rescue effort; but she and Ossoli stayed aboard and, as the ship was finally pulled apart under the pounding of the sea, they drowned. The body of Angelo was washed ashore but the Ossolis—and her Roman manuscript—were never found.

Her death shocked all who knew her. Thoreau was sent to the scene of the wreck to collect whatever he could find of her belongings; only one trunk, containing her and Ossoli's letters to each other, and a few other manuscripts and books, was saved from the sea and from the scavengers who had gathered.[49]

[49] A facsimile reproduction of "Thoreau's Notes on the Shipwreck at Fire Island" is printed by Kenneth Walter Cameron in *Emerson Society Quarterly*, No. 52 (III Quarter 1968), 97-99.

Bibliographical Note

The standard bibliography of writings by Fuller is Joel Myerson, *Margaret Fuller: A Descriptive Primary Bibliography* (forthcoming from the University of Pittsburgh Press). Of the nearly 350 articles, essays, and poems Fuller contributed to newspapers and periodicals, most remain uncollected. An edition of Fuller's *Tribune* pieces is currently being prepared by Wilma R. Ebbitt and Robert N. Hudspeth.

Fuller published five books during her life: *Conversations with Goethe in the Last Years of His Life* (Boston: Hilliard, Gray, 1839); *Günderode* (Boston: Elizabeth Peabody, 1842); *Summer on the Lakes, in 1843* (Boston: Charles C. Little and James Brown, 1844); *Woman in the Nineteenth Century* (New York: Greeley & McElrath, 1845); and *Papers on Literature and Art* (New York: Wiley & Putnam, 1846). The first two, translations from the German, have not been reprinted since 1852 and 1861 respectively. Arthur B. Fuller took up the task of editing his sister's writings after her death: his edited text of *Woman in the Nineteenth Century*, a few dozen uncollected *Tribune* essays, and many previously unpublished extracts from letters and journals appeared as *Woman in the Nineteenth Century, and Kindred Papers* (Boston: John P. Jewett, 1855); his edited texts of *Summer on the Lakes* and the travel letters from Europe to the *Tribune* were published as *At Home and Abroad* (Boston: Crosby, Nichols, 1856); reviews and miscellaneous writings from the *Western Messenger*, *Dial*, and *Tribune*, along with a generous selection of poetry, were collected as *Life Without and Life Within* (Boston: Brown, Taggard, and Chase, 1860). Fuller's translation of *Tasso* was added to the contents of *Papers on Literature and Art* to form *Art, Literature, and the Drama* (Boston: Brown, Taggard, and Chase, 1860). None of

Arthur Fuller's texts are faithful to his sister's original intentions, since he attempted to polish her style and eliminate matter he believed unnecessary. An unrecovered and abortive work by Fuller is discussed in Alexander E. Jones, "Margaret Fuller's Attempt to Write Fiction," *Boston Public Library Quarterly*, VI (April 1954), 67-73.

An edition of Fuller's letters—nearly 800—is being done by Robert N. Hudspeth and when completed will provide a much-needed single and reliable text. An annotated calendar of the letters Hudspeth has located will be printed by him in *Studies in the American Renaissance*. At present, most of Fuller's manuscript letters are at the Boston Public Library and the Houghton Library at Harvard University. A glimpse of the Boston Public Library's holdings is given in Margaret Munsterberg, "Margaret Fuller Centenary," *Boston Public Library Quarterly*, II (July 1950), 245-68. Published texts are generally untrustworthy. Many letters are printed in the *Memoirs of Margaret Fuller Ossoli* (Boston: Phillips, Sampson, 1852); but the editors—William Henry Channing, James Freeman Clarke, and Emerson—took great liberties in transcription and lost many of the manuscripts as well. Most of Fuller's letters to Emerson are accurately printed in *The Letters of Ralph Waldo Emerson*, ed. Ralph L. Rusk (New York: Columbia University Press, 1939); those to James Nathan during the New York period are printed with less accuracy in *Love-Letters of Margaret Fuller* (New York: D. Appleton, 1903). Three important collections of letters to Fuller are: *The Letters of James Freeman Clarke to Margaret Fuller*, ed. John Wesley Thomas (Hamburg: Cram, de Gruyter, 1957); Leona Rostenberg, "Mazzini to Margaret Fuller, 1847-1849," *American Historical Review*, XLVII (October 1941), 73-80; and Leopold Wellisz, *The Friendship of Margaret Fuller D'Ossoli and Adam Mickiewicz* (New York: Polish Book Importing Company, 1947). Extensive selections from Fuller's European correspondence are given in Emma Detti, *Margaret Fuller Ossoli E I Suoi Corrispondenti* (Firenze: Félice Le Monnier, 1942 [Italian and English]).

There is no edition of Fuller's journals. Sections of them are printed inaccurately and at random in the *Memoirs*. Two journals have been edited with care: Joel Myerson, "Margaret Fuller's 1842 Journal: At Concord with the Emersons,"

Harvard Library Bulletin, XXI (July 1973), 320-40; and Leona Rostenberg, "Margaret Fuller's Roman Diary," *Journal of Modern History*, XII (June 1940), 209-20.

The standard bibliography of writings about Fuller is Joel Myerson, *Margaret Fuller: An Annotated Secondary Bibliography* (New York: Burt Franklin, 1977). The bibliography in Madeleine B. Stern, *The Life of Margaret Fuller* (New York; Dutton, 1942) is excellent for material published through 1942 on the people and events surrounding Fuller.

Biographical information on Fuller is available in the many accounts of the Fuller family. Of general interest are [Arthur B. Fuller], "Historical Notices and Genealogy of the Fuller Family," *New England Historic and Genealogical Register*, XIII (October 1859), 351-63, revised and expanded as *Historical Notices of Thomas Fuller and His Descendants, with a Genealogy of the Fuller Family, 1638-1902* (Cambridge, Mass.: n.p., 1902); and Arthur B. Nichols, "Thomas Fuller and His Descendants," *Publications of the Cambridge Historical Society*, XXVIII (1943), 11-28. Fuller's father is the subject of Leona Rostenberg, "The Diary of Timothy Fuller in Congress, January 12-March 15, 1818," *New England Quarterly*, XII (September 1939), 521-29. For information on Arthur B. Fuller, see "Arthur Buckminster Fuller," in *Heralds of a Liberal Faith*, ed. Samuel A. Eliot (Boston: American Unitarian Association, 1910), III, 128-31; Richard F. Fuller, *Chaplain Fuller* (Boston: Walker, Wise, 1864); and [Thomas Wentworth Higginson], "Arthur Buckminster Fuller," in *Harvard Memorial Biographies*, [ed. T. W. Higginson] (Cambridge: Sever and Francis, 1866), I: 79-94. Richard Fuller's impressions of his sister and their contemporaries are given in *Recollections of Richard F. Fuller* (Boston: Privately printed, 1936) and in "The Younger Generation in 1840 from the Diary of a New England Boy," *Atlantic Monthly Magazine*, CXXXVI (August 1925), 216-224; also Walter Harding, "Visit to the Wachusett, July 1842 by Richard Fuller," *Thoreau Society Bulletin*, No. 121 (Fall 1972), 1-4. The Fuller Family Papers are at the Houghton Library at Harvard University.

There are a number of full-length biographies of Fuller. The *Memoirs* greatly influenced the public's picture of her for years to come: a picture of an egotistic, intellectually aloof person.[1] An overly sympathetic portrait of Fuller by one who knew her is Julia Ward Howe, *Margaret Fuller (Marchesa Ossoli)* (Boston: Roberts, 1883). The best nineteenth-century biography is Thomas Wentworth Higginson, *Margaret Fuller Ossoli* (Boston: Houghton, Mifflin, 1884), which quotes extensively from her journals and letters in an attempt to correct the picture of Fuller as "a little too much in the clouds," the impression given in the *Memoirs*. The narrow focus of Katherine Anthony, *Margaret Fuller. A Psychological Biography*. (New York: Harcourt, Brace and Howe, 1920), and the semi-fictional approach of Margaret Bell, *Margaret Fuller* (New York: Charles Boni, 1930), limit their usefulness today. Mason Wade, *Margaret Fuller: Whetstone of Genius* (New York: Viking, 1940), is a good general biography but lacks annotation, as does Faith Chipperfield, *In Quest of Love: The Life and Death of Margaret Fuller* (New York: Coward-McCann, 1957), a thesis-ridden book of little scholarly use. A psycho-biography of Fuller is attempted in Margaret Ross McGavran, "Mary [Wollstonecraft] and Margaret: The Triumph of Woman," Ph.D. dissertation, Cornell University, 1973. Fuller's last years are discussed in detail by Joseph Jay Deiss, *The Roman Years of Margaret Fuller* (New York: Crowell, 1969). The best introductory book on Fuller is Arthur W. Brown, *Margaret Fuller* (New York: Twayne, 1964), a conscientiously researched and concisely stated overview of Fuller's life and writings. Stern's *The Life of Margaret Fuller*, remains today as the most valuable biography. It is the most detailed and best researched life, and it is especially strong in describing Fuller's environment.

Certain aspects of Fuller's life have attracted scholars more than others. Her stay in Providence is the subject of an anonymous, untitled article in *Book Notes*, X (23 September 1893), 217-18; Charles R. Crowe, "Transcendentalism and the Providence Literati," *Rhode Island History*, XIV (July 1955), 65-78; Henry L. Green, "The Greene-St. School, of Providence, and Its Teachers," *Publications of the Rhode*

---

[1] Or as Carlyle put it, the book was "dreadfully longwinded and indistinct;—as if one were telling a story not in words, but in *symbolical* tunes on the bagpipe!" (19 June 1852, *New Letters of Thomas Carlyle*, ed. Alexander Carlyle [London: John Lane, 1904], II, 130-31).

Island Historical Society, n.s. VI (January 1899), 199-219;
Edward A. Hoyt and Loriman S. Brigham, "Glimpses of Margaret Fuller: The Green Street School and Florence," *New England Quarterly*, XXIX (March 1956), 87-98; Harriet Hall Johnson, "Margaret Fuller as Known by her Scholars," *Christian Register*, 21 April 1910, pp. 426-29; and Annie Russell Marble, "Margaret Fuller as Teacher," *Critic*, XLIII (October 1903), 334-45. Manuscript journals kept by students at Fuller's school are located at the American Antiquarian Society, Brown University, and the University of South Carolina.

Fuller was best known for her conversational powers; unfortunately, the only extended account of her Conversations is in Caroline Healey Dall, *Margaret and Her Friends* (Boston: Roberts, 1895). Granville Hicks, "A Conversation in Boston," *Sewanee Review*, XXXIX (April-June 1931), 129-43, writes an imaginative reconstruction of a Conversation by Fuller in November 1840.

Fuller's role as editor of the *Dial* can be traced in George Willis Cooke, *An Historical and Biographical Introduction to Accompany THE DIAL* (Cleveland: Rowfant Club, 1902); Joel Myerson, "A History of the *Dial*," Ph.D. dissertation, Northwestern University, 1971; and Myerson, "An Annotated List of Contributions to the Boston *Dial*," *Studies in Bibliography*, XXVI (1973), 133-66. Her critical principles as editor are discussed in Helen Hennessy, "The *Dial*: Its Poetry and Poetic Criticism," *New England Quarterly*, XXXI (March 1958), 66-87; and Donald F. Warders, " 'The Progress of the Hour and the Day': A Critical Study of *The Dial*," Ph.D. dissertation, University of Kansas, 1973. A more general view of Fuller's periodical career is provided in Clarence L. F. Gohdes, *The Periodicals of American Transcendentalism* (Durham: Duke University Press, 1931).

A general account of Fuller's relations with Brook Farm is Karl Knortz, *Brook Farm und Margaret Fuller* (New York: Druck von Hermann Bartsch, 1886 [German]). An excellent picture of her life in New York is in Constance Penta, "Fuller's Folly: The Eccentric World of Margaret Fuller and the Greeleys," M.A. thesis, Columbia University, 1960.

Much of Fuller's reputation lies not with her writings but rather with the effect she had upon those who knew her.

Martha Ann Tull, "Contemporary Portraiture of Margaret Fuller," M.A. thesis, George Peabody College, 1929, presents a general survey of published comments by Fuller's contemporaries. Her relationship with Emerson—with Fuller unsuccessfully attempting to force him from his usual aloof position—has always fascinated scholars. Most of their correspondence is printed in *The Letters of Ralph Waldo Emerson*, ed. Rusk. Fuller's comments in Myerson, "Fuller's 1842 Journal," are valuable, as are Emerson's comments on her in *The Correspondence of Emerson and Carlyle*, ed. Joseph Slater (New York: Columbia University Press, 1964), and *The Journals and Miscellaneous Notebooks of Ralph Waldo Emerson*, ed. William H. Gilman *et al.* (Cambridge: Harvard University Press, 1960-   ), 12 volumes to date. Interesting studies of their friendship are Mary Amanda Lucas, "Emerson and Margaret Fuller: A Transcendental Adventure in Friendship," M.A. thesis, University of Washington, 1933; John Bard McNulty, "Emerson's Friends and the Essay on Friendship," *New England Quarterly*, XIX (September 1946), 390-94; Ralph L. Rusk, *The Life of Ralph Waldo Emerson* (New York: Scribners, 1949); and Harry R. Warfel, "Margaret Fuller and Ralph Waldo Emerson," *Publications of the Modern Language Association*, L (June 1935), 576-94.

No less intriguing is Fuller's relationship with Hawthorne, whose possible use of her in his writings is discussed by Francis E. Kearns, "Margaret Fuller as a Model for Hester Prynne," *Jahrbuch für Amerikastudien*, X (1965), 191-97; and Kelly Thurman, "Margaret Fuller in Two American Novels: *The Blithedale Romance* and *Elsie Venner*," M.A. thesis, University of Kentucky, 1945. Hawthorne's comments in *The American Notebooks*, ed. Claude M. Simpson (Columbus: Ohio State University Press, 1972), are important. General studies of the two are Oscar Cargill, "Nemesis and Nathaniel Hawthorne," *Publications of the Modern Language Association*, LII (September 1937), 848-62; Anne Elizabeth Gushee, "Nathaniel Hawthorne and Margaret Fuller," M.A. thesis, Columbia University, 1955; William Peirce Randel, "Hawthorne, Channing, and Margaret Fuller," *American Literature*, X (January 1939), 472-76; and Austin Warren, "Hawthorne, Margaret Fuller, and 'Nemesis,'" *Pub-*

lications of the Modern Language Association, LIV (June 1939), 615-18.

Information concerning Fuller and Alcott can be found in *The Journals of Bronson Alcott*, ed. Odell Shepard (Boston: Little, Brown, 1938); *The Letters of A. Bronson Alcott*, ed. Richard L. Herrnstadt (Ames: Iowa State University Press, 1969); F. B. Sanborn and William T. Harris, *A. Bronson Alcott: His Life and Philosophy* (Boston: Roberts, 1893); and Odell Shepard, *Pedlar's Progress: The Life of Bronson Alcott* (Boston: Little, Brown, 1937). Thoreau's relationship with Fuller can be followed in *The Correspondence of Henry David Thoreau*, ed. Walter Harding and Carl Bode (New York: New York University Press, 1958); Walter Harding, *The Days of Henry Thoreau* (New York: Knopf, 1965); and Charles Thomas Waller, "A Contrast of the Religious Thought of Henry David Thoreau and Margaret Fuller," M.A. thesis, University of Georgia, 1959.

Studies of other figures of the time who knew Fuller well are also informative. Among the most useful are Helene G. Baer, "Mrs. Child and Miss Fuller," *New England Quarterly*, XXVI (June 1953), 249-55; Charles E. Blackburn, "James Freeman Clarke: An Interpretation of the Western Years (1833-40)," Ph.D. dissertation, Yale University, 1952; Arthur S. Bolster, Jr., *James Freeman Clarke: Disciple to Advancing Truth* (Boston: Beacon, 1954); George Willis Cooke, *John Sullivan Dwight: Brook-Farmer, Editor, and Critic of Music* (Boston: Small, Maynard, 1898); Charles Crowe, *George Ripley: Transcendentalist and Utopian Socialist* (Athens: University of Georgia Press, 1967); Jane Ball Davidson, "Margaret Fuller and Edgar Allan Poe: A Relationship Between Literati," M.A. thesis, American University, 1968; Edwin Gittleman, *Jones Very: The Effective Years 1833-1840* (New York: Columbia University Press, 1967); Horace Greeley, "Margaret Fuller," in *Recollections of a Busy Life* (New York: J. B. Ford, 1868), pp. 169-91; William Harlan Hale, *Horace Greeley: Voice of the People* (New York: Harpers, 1950); Robert N. Hudspeth, *Ellery Channing* (New York: Twayne, 1973); Georgiana Bruce Kirby, *Years of Experience: An Autobiographical Narrative* (New York: Putnam, 1887); Frederick T. McGill, Jr., *Channing of Concord: A Life of William Ellery Channing II* (New Brunswick, N.J.: Rutgers

University Press, 1967); Joel Myerson, "Caroline Dall's Reminiscences of Margaret Fuller," *Harvard Library Bulletin*, XXII (October 1974), 414-28; *The Journals of Charles King Newcomb*, ed. Judith Kennedy Johnson (Providence: Brown University Press, 1946); F. B. Sanborn, *Recollections of Seventy Years* (Boston: Richard G. Badger, 1909); John Wesley Thomas, *James Freeman Clarke: Apostle of German Culture to America* (Boston: John W. Luce, 1949); and David Alec Wilson, "Margaret Fuller Has to Listen (1846)," in *Carlyle on Cromwell and Others (1837-1848)* (London: Kegan, Paul, Trench, Trubner, 1925), pp. 346-51. The background to Lowell's devastating satire of Fuller in *A Fable for Critics* can be pieced together from *Letters of James Russell Lowell*, ed. Charles Eliot Norton (New York: Harpers, 1894); Martin Duberman, *James Russell Lowell* (Boston: Houghton Mifflin, 1966); and Leon Howard, *Victorian Knight-Errant: A Study of the Early Literary Career of James Russell Lowell* (Berkeley and Los Angeles: University of California Press, 1952).

Critical studies of Fuller's writings have centered either on her comments on foreign literature or on her criticism in general. The most inclusive study of Fuller and foreign literature is Russell E. Durning, *Margaret Fuller, Citizen of the World. An Intermediary Between European and American Literatures* (Heidelberg: Carl Winter, 1969). Particular areas of her interest are discussed in Lucy Gregory, "The Influence of George Sand on Margaret Fuller," M.A. thesis, Columbia University, 1918; Ursula Kearns, "The Translations of Margaret Fuller," M.A. thesis, Columbia University, 1949; Mary Ruth Miller, "Margaret Fuller's Part in the Language Interests of American Transcendentalism," M.A. thesis, University of North Carolina, 1946; Maud Cannell Quayle, "Margaret Fuller's Attitude Toward France," M.A. thesis, University of California, 1913; and William Silas Vance, "Margaret Fuller," in "Carlyle and the American Transcendentalists," Ph.D. dissertation, University of Chicago, 1941, pp. 329-55.

German Literature exerted the greatest influence on Fuller; good general studies in this area are Henry A. Pochmann, *German Culture in America* (Madison: University of Wisconsin Press, 1957); Arthur R. Schultz, "Margaret Fuller—

Transcendentalist Interpreter of German Literature," *Monatschefte für Deutschen Unfericht*, XXXIV (April 1942), 169-82; and Stanely M. Vogel, *German Literary Influences on the American Transcendentalists* (New Haven: Yale University Press, 1955). Probably the author who exerted the most influence on Fuller was Goethe, and not surprisingly much has been published on this subject: Frederick Augustus Braun, *Margaret Fuller and Goethe* (New York: Henry Holt, 1910); Frederick A. Braun, "Margaret Fuller's Translation and Criticism of Goethe's *Tasso*," *Journal of English and Germanic Philology*, XIII (April 1914), 202-13; Russell E. Durning, "Margaret Fuller's Translation of Goethe's 'Prometheus,' " *Jahrbuch für Amerikastudien*, XII (1967), 240-45; Harry Slochower, "Margaret Fuller and Goethe," *Germanic Review*, VII (April 1932), 130-44; and J. Wesley Thomas, "New Light on Margaret Fuller's Projected 'Life of Goethe,' " *Germanic Review*, XXIV (October 1949), 216-23.

The most worked-over area of Fuller scholarship is that of her published criticism. Her theoretical ideas are examined in Roland Crozier Burton, "Margaret Fuller's Criticism: Theory and Practice," Ph.D. dissertation, University of Iowa, 1941; and Wilma R. Ebbitt, "Margaret Fuller's Ideas on Criticism," *Boston Public Library Quarterly*, III (July 1951), 171-87. Fuller's literary criticism is discussed by Patrick Frederick Berger, "Margaret Fuller: Critical Realist as Seen in Her Works," Ph.D. dissertation, St. Louis University, 1972; Wilma R. Ebbitt, "The Critical Essays of Margaret Fuller from the New York *Tribune*," Ph.D. dissertation, Brown University, 1943; Josephine J. Fay, "Margaret Fuller, Literary Critic," Ph.D. dissertation, St. John's University, 1951; Henry Lawrence Golemba, "The Balanced View in Margaret Fuller's Literary Criticism," Ph.D. dissertation, University of Washington, 1971; Vivian C. Hopkins, "Margaret Fuller: American Nationalist Critic," *Emerson Society Quarterly*, No. 55 (II Quarter 1969), 24-41; Helen Neill McMaster, "Margaret Fuller as a Literary Critic," *University of Buffalo Studies*, VII (December 1928), 35-100; and Margaret Wallace, "Margaret Fuller: Critic," *Bookman*, LXIX (March 1929), 60-67. Specific areas of Fuller's criticism are covered in Roland Crozier Burton, "Margaret Fuller's Criticism of the Fine Arts," *College English*, VI (October 1944), 18-23;

Elizabeth F. Shore, "Margaret Fuller and Welfare Journalism," M.S.W. thesis, University of California, 1956. Other aspects of Fuller's thoughts and writings are discussed by Margaret V. Allen, "The Political and Social Criticism of Margaret Fuller," *South Atlantic Quarterly*, LXXII (Autumn 1973), 560-73; Margaret V. Allen, " 'This Impassioned Yankee': Margaret Fuller's Writing Revisited," *Southwest Review*, LVIII (Spring 1973), 162-71; Elsie Furbush Brickett, "Studies in the Poets and Poetry of New England Transcendentalism," Ph.D. dissertation, Yale University, 1937; Lawrence Buell, *Literary Transcendentalism: Style and Vision in the American Renaissance* (Ithaca: Cornell University Press, 1973); Vivian C. Hopkins, "Margaret Fuller: Pioneer Women's Liberationist," *American Transcendental Quarterly*, No. 18 (Spring 1973), 29-35; Francis E. Kearns, "Margaret Fuller and the Abolition Movement," *Journal of the History of Ideas*, XXV (January-March 1964), 120-27; Francis Edward Kearns, "Margaret Fuller's Social Criticism," Ph.D. dissertation, University of North Carolina, 1960; Mary Maxine, "Margaret Fuller: From Liberal to Radical, a Foreshadowing of the Feminist Movement," Ph.D. dissertation, University of New Mexico, 1973; Kathryn A. Pippin, "Margaret Fuller's Views on Education," M.A. thesis, University of North Carolina, 1972; and Daniel Edgar Rider, "The Musical Thought and Activities of the New England Transcendentalists," Ph.D. dissertation, University of Minnesota, 1964.

Only two of Fuller's books have been studied in detail. *Summer on the Lakes* is the subject of Richard V. Carpenter, "Margaret Fuller in Northern Illinois," *Journal of the Illinois State Historical Society*, II (January 1910), 7-22; Madeleine B. Stern in her "Introduction" to the B. De Graff facsimile reprinting of *Summer* (Nieuwkoop, the Netherlands, 1972). An able study of Fuller's feminist book is Marie Mitchell Olesen Urbanski, "Margaret Fuller's *Woman in the Nineteenth Century*," Ph.D. dissertation, University of Kentucky, 1973. Fuller's reception in Britain is incompletely surveyed by Frances M. Barbour, "Margaret Fuller and the British Reviewers," *New England Quarterly*, IX (December 1936), 618-25. For a more complete listing of contemporary reviews of Fuller's writings, consult Myerson, *Margaret Fuller: An Annotated Secondary Bibliography.* Despite the amount of material published on Fuller, much good scholarship needs to be done: an accurate and complete edition of her writings; a new biography built upon the large amount of material made available since Stern's book in 1942; studies of Fuller and her contemporaries; and more detailed examinations of *Summer on the Lakes* and *Woman in the Nineteenth Century.* An instructive article in this respect is Madeleine B. Stern, "A Biographer's View of Margaret Fuller," *AB Bookman's Weekly,* LIII (4 February 1974), 427-28, 430.

J.M.

Textual Note

The texts of Fuller's works as edited by her brother in 1855, 1856, and 1860 have no textual authority; indeed, Arthur Fuller made a conscious effort to tidy up and "improve" his sister's writing for his audience. The present edition, therefore, presents the texts Fuller herself prepared for publication. Emendations have been made in cases of obvious typographical errors or misspellings, or when clarity of thought is disturbed. No attempt has been made to regularize Fuller's spelling and punctuation practices, or to modernize archaic spellings. The text is as close to Fuller's intentions as is possible.

The four book reviews by Fuller in the *Dial* were not collected by her; they are reprinted from the *Dial* texts, with the following emendation (page.line numbers to the present edition):

61.10   Quest] Guest

"A Short Essay on Critics" is reprinted from its first appearance in the *Dial*, even though Fuller later included it in *Papers on Literature and Art*. A comparison of the two texts shows numerous changes in punctuation and capitalization (accidentals), and three instances where wording (substantives) has been changed. Since Fuller, as editor of the *Dial* when "A Short Essay on Critics" appeared, carefully read proof, the earlier text is undoubtedly closer to her own practice with accidentals than the later text, which was probably subjected to rules of house styling. Therefore, the *Dial* text is reprinted in this edition with the following emendations adopted from the *Papers on Literature and Art* text:

52.19   with a] with the
53.32   should] would
55.37   and all living influence] and living influences

43

The chapter from *Summer on the Lakes, in 1843* is re-printed from the first edition, with the following emenda-tions:

65.19	Mendelssohn] Mendelsohn
72.26	mine."] mine.
77.9	milliners'] milliner's
79.17	Boone] Boon
80.22	gazers'] gazers

Woman in the Nineteenth Century presents a text that dif-fers markedly from Fuller's "The Great Lawsuit" in the *Dial*. Her changes show an attempt to clarify her thought, the addi-tion of more examples, an attempt to regularize punctuation practices (probably imposed upon her by the printer, follow-ing rules of house styling), the substitution of more exact words and phrases, and the addition of appendices. The text following in this edition is that of the first edition of *Woman in the Nineteenth Century*, with the following emendations:

82.13	even] evea
85.3	reward.] reward
93.17	We] "We
104.29	mind.' '] mind.'
109.9	improvvisatrici] improvisatrici
120.3	Du Barry] Dubarry
126.1	find] fiud
139.11	the first] he first
140.25	"Thus] Thus
140.31	"Having] Having
141.2	me,'] me,
141.3	'has] has
146.10	reformation.] reformation.'
150.7	Vittoria] Victoria
150.35	Southcott] Southcote
152.27	*hérissé*] *herissé*
153.1	Rochefoucauld] Rochefoucoult
157.36	Kelley] Kelly
158.5	Kelley] Kelly
160.10	reform-growth.] reform-growth,
161.3	vow."] vow.
169.36	mother.] mother,

169.37	reason, was] reason,
176.24	wrong.' "] wrong."
181.7	"You] You
186.17	bases] basis
191.3	English] English,
195.6	Valkyrie] Walkyrie
195.28	Necker's] Neckar's
204.34	spot?"] spot?
205.29	employments] employements
210.8	the conspicuous] conspicuous
216.10	largest] argest
222.37	Mother] mother
227.8	Aulis] Anlis
229.38	friends."] friends.'
237.31	Iolaus."] Iolaus.

Fuller's articles in the *New-York Tribune* are reprinted from their original appearance, with the following emendations:

240.20	necessarily] neces-/arily
251.12	thou] thous
254.3	Year's] Years'
254.29	requires] require
256.36	Whittington] Wittington
258.18	Immanuel] Emanuel
264.7	with] with,
265.12	view] veiw
274.35	Grimes's] Grime's
275.20	headache] headach
280.12	power] powe
284.20	others] others.
286.9	manifested.] manifested
287.1	Sargent] Sargeant
288.8	poetic faculty] poeticfaculty
288.8	broad] bread
290.9	Mississippi] Mississipi
293.41	others'] others
294.20	Soule] Soulie
294.23	Soule] Soulie
295.3	Kinmont] Kinment

295.14	Soule] Soulie
298.22	does] do
305.37	as Nature] a Nsature
307.4	professions] profession
309.11	value] valne
310.15	such] sueh
310.24	American] Americen
310.24	Women] Woman
312.15	especially] expecially
315.10	harmonious] haamonious
316.10	intersperse] instersperse
318.32	future.] future,
319.20	ungenerous.] ungenerous,
320.29	literature] literatue
327.34	without] with /out
333.38	literature] literatare
339.17	Christ] Chrlst
354.6	dilettanti's] dillettanti's
370.7	frivolity] frivality
373.6	Rappaccini's] Rapaccini's
374.9	Concord] Ciacord
377.1	been] heen
378.17	intercourse] intercouse

Capitalization of and periods in article titles are considered matters of styling and are not followed in this edition. The book reviews usually begin with a bibliographical citation for the work; in this edition these are eliminated and full bibliographical information is given in notes. Fuller usually signed her articles with an asterisk (*); this signature mark is not reproduced in this edition.

"American Literature," written especially for *Papers on Literature and Art*, is reprinted from that book with the following emendations:

381.14	literature] literatnre
392.26	pantomime] pantomine
396.38	to do this] to this
397.4	bold,] bold

Possible compound words hyphenated at the end of lines in the original text and their treatment in this edition are as follows:

76.41	torch-flower] torch-/flower
79.28	guide-book] guide-/book
84.25	universe-spirit] universe-/spirit
85.12	heart-strings] heart-/strings
86.2	candlestick] candle-/stick
119.37	shopkeeper's] shop-/keeper's
120.32	manlike] man-/like
134.12	writing-desk] writing-/desk
136.10	fellow-pilgrim] fellow-/pilgrim
147.34	twilight] twi-/light
153.2	*over*-flowed] *over*-/flowed
165.25	over-flow] over-/flow
174.29	lurking-places] lurking-/places
179.12	hard-hearted] hard-/hearted
207.15	world-year] world-/year
217.32	sweethearts] sweet-/hearts
242.17	deep-rooted] deep-/rooted
253.14	many-voiced] many-/voiced
264.27	backsliders] back-/sliders
268.4	well-meant] well-/meant
292.28	washerwoman] washer-/woman
299.15	upbearing] up-/bearing
311.17	newborn] new-/born
327.12	short-sighted] short-/sighted
337.3	shoemakers] shoe-/makers
340.15	spy-glasses] spy-/glasses
353.2	horse-racing] horse-/racing
366.22	hairbreadth] hair-/breadth
380.21	topmost] top-/most
381.20	schoolmasters] school-/masters
390.11	second-hand] second-/hand
397.26	off-spring] off-/spring

Possible compound words hyphenated at the end of lines in this edition and their appearance in the original text are as follows:

61.14	common-/sense-philosophy] common-sense-philosophy
64.7	hare-/bell] harebell
64.8	flower-/world] flower-world
69.24	sun-/beams] sunbeams

95.33	*Frauen-/emancipation*] *Frauen-emancipation*
96.24	house-/top] house-top
128.26	house-/keeper] housekeeper
157.20	stage-/coach] stage-coach
197.20	under-/clothes] under-clothes
202.5	hand-/maid] hand-maid
248.14	twelfth-/night] twelfth-night
268.16	farm-/house] farm-house
268.18	cup-/board] cupboard
271.17	canker-/worms] canker-worms
279.19	bel-/esprit] bel-esprit
326.36	clear-/sighted] clear-sighted
328.20	to-/day] to-day
330.24	money-/making] money-making
337.17	waste-/times] waste-times
350.15	travel-/worn] travel-worn
359.2	apple-/woman] apple-woman
369.17	house-/keeper] housekeeper
383.17	soul-/less] soulless

The following words are hyphenated at the end of lines in both this edition and in the original text:

76.4	wild-/wood (wild-wood)
182.21	grand-/mother (grandmother)
312.24	Truth-/tellers (Truth-tellers)

Margaret Fuller:
Essays on American Life and Letters

A Short Essay On Critics.*

An essay on Criticism were a serious matter; for, though this age be emphatically critical, the writer would still find it necessary to investigate the laws of criticism as a science, to settle its conditions as an art. Essays entitled critical are epistles addressed to the public through which the mind of the recluse relieves itself of its impressions. Of these the only law is, "Speak the best word that is in thee." Or they are regular articles, got up to order by the literary hack writer, for the literary mart, and the only law is to make them plausible. There is not yet deliberate recognition of a standard of criticism, though we hope the always strengthening league of the republic of letters must ere long settle laws on which its Amphictyonic council may act.[1] Meanwhile let us not venture to write on criticism, but by classifying the critics imply our hopes, and thereby our thoughts.

First, there are the subjective class, (to make use of a convenient term, introduced by our German benefactors.) These are persons to whom writing is no sacred, no reverend employment. They are not driven to consider, not forced upon investigation by the fact, that they are deliberately giving their thoughts an independent existence, and that it may live to others when dead to them. They know no agonies of conscientious research, no timidities of self-respect. They see no Ideal beyond the present hour, which makes its mood an uncertain tenure. How things affect them now they know; let the future, let the whole take care of itself. They state their impressions as they rise, of other men's spoken, written, or acted thoughts. They never dream of going out of them-

---

* In *Dial*, I (July 1840), 5-11.
[1] Of the several Amphictyonic Leagues in ancient Greece, the most famous was Delphi, which controlled the oracle there.

selves to seek the motive, to trace the law of another nature. They never dream that there are statures which cannot be measured from their point of view. They love, they like, or they hate; the book is detestable, immoral, absurd, or admirable, noble, of a most approved scope;—these statements they make with authority, as those who bear the evangel of pure taste and accurate judgment, and need be tried before no human synod. To them it seems that their present position commands the universe.

Thus the essays on the works of others, which are called criticisms, are often, in fact, mere records of impressions. To judge of their value you must know where the man was brought up, under what influences,—his nation, his church, his family even. He himself has never attempted to estimate the value of these circumstances, and find a law or raise a standard above all circumstances, permanent against all influence. He is content to be the creature of his place, and to represent it by his spoken and written word. He takes the same ground with a savage, who does not hesitate to say of the product of a civilization on which he could not stand, "It is bad," or "It is good."

The value of such comments is merely reflex. They characterize the critic. They give an idea of certain influences on a certain act of men in a certain time or place. Their absolute, essential value is nothing. The long review, the eloquent article by the man of the nineteenth century are of no value by themselves considered, but only as samples of their kind. The writers were content to tell what they felt, to praise or to denounce without needing to convince us or themselves. They sought not the divine truths of philosophy, and she proffers them not, if unsought.

Then there are the apprehensive. These can go out of themselves and enter fully into a foreign existence. They breathe its life; they live in its law; they tell what it meant, and why it so expressed its meaning. They reproduce the work of which they speak, and make it better known to us in so far as two statements are better than one. There are beautiful specimens in this kind. They are pleasing to us as bearing witness of the genial sympathies of nature. They have the ready grace of love with somewhat of the dignity of disinterested friendship. They sometimes give more pleasure than the original production of which they treat, as melodies will sometimes ring sweetlier in the echo. Besides there is a peculiar pleasure in a true response; it is the assurance of equipoise in the universe. These, if not true critics, come nearer the standard than the subjective class, and the value of their work is ideal as well as historical.

Then there are the comprehensive, who must also be apprehensive. They enter into the nature of another being and judge his work by its own law. But having done so, having ascertained his design and the degree of his success in fulfilling it, thus measuring his judgment, his energy, and skill, they do also know how to put that aim in its place, and how to estimate its relations. And this the critic can only do who perceives the analogies of the universe, and how they are regulated by an absolute, invariable principle. He can see how far that work expresses this principle as well as how far it is excellent in its details. Sustained by a principle, such as can be girt within no rule, no formula, he can walk around the work, he can stand above it, he can uplift it, and try its weight. Finally he is worthy to judge it.

Critics are poets cut down, says some one by way of jeer; but, in truth, they are men with the poetical temperament to apprehend, with the philosophical tendency to investigate. The maker is divine; the critic sees this divine, but brings it down to humanity by the analytic process. The critic is the historian who records the order of creation. In vain for the maker, who knows without learning it, but not in vain for the mind of his race.

The critic is beneath the maker, but is his needed friend. What tongue could speak but to an intelligent ear, and every noble work demands its critic. The richer the work, the more severe should be its critic; the larger its scope, the more comprehensive must be his power of scrutiny. The critic is not a base caviller, but the younger brother of genius. Next to invention is the power of interpreting invention; next to beauty the power of appreciating beauty.

And of making others appreciate it; for the universe is a scale of infinite gradation, and below the very highest, every step is explanation down to the lowest. Religion, in the two modulations of poetry and music, descends through an infinity of waves to the lowest abysses of human nature. Nature is the literature and art of the divine mind; human literature and art the criticism on that; and they, too, find their criticism within their own sphere.

The critic, then, should be not merely a poet, not merely a philosopher, not merely an observer, but tempered of all three. If he criticize the poem, he must want nothing of what constitutes the poet, except the power of creating forms and speaking in music. He must have as good an eye and as fine a sense; but if he had as fine an organ for expression also, he would make the poem instead of judging it. He must be inspired by the philosopher's spirit of inquiry and need of generalization, but he must not be constrained by the hard cemented masonry of method to which philosophers are prone. And he must have the organic acuteness of the observer, with a love of ideal perfection, which forbids him to be content with mere beauty of details in the work or the comment upon the work.

There are persons who maintain, that there is no legitimate criticism, except the reproductive; that we have only to say what the work is or is to us, never what it is not. But the moment we look for a principle, we feel the need of a criterion, of a standard; and then we say what the work is *not*, as well as what it *is*; and this is as healthy though not as grateful and gracious an operation of the mind as the other. We do not seek to degrade but to classify an object by stating what it is not. We detach the part from the whole, lest it stand between us and the whole. When we have ascertained in what degree it manifests the whole we may safely restore it to its place, and love or admire it there ever after.

The use of criticism in periodical writing is to sift, not to stamp a work. Yet should they not be "sieves and drainers for the use of luxurious readers," but for the use of earnest inquirers, giving voice and being to their objections, as well as stimulus to their sympathies. But the critic must not be an infallible adviser to his reader. He must not tell him what books are not worth reading, or what must be thought of them when read, but what he read in them. Wo to that coterie where some critic sits despotic, intrenched behind the infallible "We." Wo to that oracle who has infused such soft sleepiness, such a gentle dulness into his atmosphere, that when he opes his lips no dog will bark. It is this attempt at

dictatorship in the reviewers, and the indolent acquies-
cense of their readers, that has brought them into disrepute.
With such fairness did they make out their statements, with
such dignity did they utter their verdicts, that the poor
reader grew all too submissive. He learned his lesson with
such docility, that the greater part of what will be said at any
public or private meeting can be foretold by any one who
has read the leading periodical works for twenty years back.
Scholars sneer at and would fain dispense with them altogether; and the public, grown lazy and helpless by this constant use of props and stays, can now scarce brace itself even
to get through a magazine article, but reads in the daily
paper laid beside the breakfast plate a short notice of the last
number of the long established and popular review, and
thereupon passes its judgment and is content.

Then the partisan spirit of many of these journals has
made it unsafe to rely upon them as guide-books and expurgatory indexes. They could not be content merely to stimulate and suggest thought, they have at last become power-
less to supersede it.

From these causes and causes like these, the journals
have lost much of their influence. There is a languid feeling
about them, an inclination to suspect the justice of their
verdicts, the value of their criticisms. But their golden age
cannot be quite past. They afford too convenient a vehicle
for the transmission of knowledge; they are too natural a
feature of our time to have done all their work yet. Surely
they may be redeemed from their abuses, they may be turned
to their true uses. But how?

It were easy to say what they should *not* do. They should
not have an object to carry or a cause to advocate, which
obliges them either to reject all writings which wear the
distinctive traits of individual life, or to file away what does
not suit them, till the essay, made true to their design, is
made false to the mind of the writer. An external consistency
is thus produced, at the expense of all salient thought, all
genuine emotion of life, in short, and all living influence.
Their purpose may be of value, but by such means was no
valuable purpose ever furthered long. There are those, who
have with the best intention pursued this system of trimming
and adaptation, and thought it well and best to

"Deceive their country for their country's good."

But their country cannot long be so governed. It misses the pure, the full tone of truth; it perceives that the voice is modulated to coax, to persuade, and it turns from the judicious man of the world, calculating the effect to be produced by each of his smooth sentences to some earnest voice which is uttering thoughts, crude, rash, ill-arranged it may be, but true to one human breast, and uttered in full faith, that the God of Truth will guide them aright.

And here, it seems to me, has been the greatest mistake in the conduct of these journals. A smooth monotony has been attained, an uniformity of tone, so that from the title of a journal you can infer the tenor of all its chapters. But nature is ever various, ever new, and so should be her daughters, art and literature. We do not want merely a polite response to what we thought before, but by the freshness of thought in other minds to have new thought awakened in our own. We do not want stores of information only, but to be roused to digest these into knowledge. Able and experienced men write for us, and we would know what they think, as they think it not for us but for themselves. We would live with them, rather than be taught by them how to live; we would catch the contagion of their mental activity, rather than have them direct us how to regulate our own. In books, in reviews, in the senate, in the pulpit, we wish to meet thinking men, not schoolmasters or pleaders. We wish that they should do full justice to their own view, but also that they should be frank with us, and, if now our superiors, treat us as if we might some time rise to be their equals. It is this true manliness, this firmness in his own position, and this power of appreciating the position of others, that alone can make the critic our companion and friend. We would converse with him, secure that he will tell us all his thought, and speak as man to man. But if he adapts his work to us, if he stifles what is distinctively his, if he shows himself either arrogant or mean, or, above all, if he wants faith in the healthy action of free thought, and the safety of pure motive, we will not talk with him, for we cannot confide in him. We will go to the critic who trusts Genius and trusts us, who knows that all good writing must be spontaneous, and who will write out the bill of fare for the public as he read it for himself,—

> "Forgetting vulgar rules, with spirit free
> To judge each author by his own intent,
> Nor think one standard for all minds is meant."

Such an one will not disturb us with personalities, with sectarian prejudices, or an undue vehemence in favor of petty plans or temporary objects. Neither will he disgust us by smooth obsequious flatteries and an inexpressive, lifeless gentleness. He will be free and make free from the mechanical and distorting influences we hear complained of on every side. He will teach us to love wisely what we before loved well, for he knows the difference between censoriousness and discernment, infatuation and reverence; and, while delighting in the genial melodies of Pan, can perceive, should Apollo bring his lyre into audience, that there may be strains more divine than those of his native groves.

Hawthorne's *Grandfather's Chair**

We are glad to see this gifted author employing his pen to raise the tone of children's literature; for if children read at all, it is desirable that it should be the production of minds able to raise themselves to the height of childhood's innocence, and to the airy home of their free fancy. No one of all our imaginative writers has indicated a genius at once so fine and rich, and especially with a power so peculiar in making present the past scenes in our own history. There is nothing in this volume quite equal to the sketch of "Endicott and his Men," in one of the Tokens.[1] But the ease with which he changes his tone from the delicate satire that characterizes his writings for the old, to the simpler and more vulnerable tone appropriate to his earnest *little* auditors, is an earnest of the perfect success which will attend this new direction of his powers. We are glad to learn that he is engaged in other writings for the little friends, whom he has made in such multitudes by Grandfather's Chair.[2] Yet we must demand from him to write again to the older and sadder, and steep them in the deep well of his sweet, humorsome musings.

* Nathaniel Hawthorne, *Grandfather's Chair: A History for Youth.* Boston: E.P. Peabody, 1841. In *Dial*, I (January 1841), 405; titled supplied.
[1] "Endicott and the Red Cross" appeared in *The Token and Atlantic Souvenir* for 1838.
[2] Also in 1841 Elizabeth Peabody's press published two more volumes in this series: *Famous Old People: Being the Second Epoch of Grandfather's Chair* and *Liberty Tree: With the Last Words of Grandfather's Chair.*

Lowell's *A Year's Life**

We are late in a notice of this volume. But not only do we consider this delay complimentary as intimating that we suppose the book still fresh in the public mind, but, in truth, we are timid with regard to all comments upon youthful bards. We doubt the utility whether of praise or blame. No criticism from without is of use to the true songster; he sings as the bird sings, for the sake of pouring out his eager soul, and needs no praise. If his poetic vein be abundant enough to swell beyond the years of youthful feeling, every day teaches him humility as to his boyish defects; he measures himself with the great poets; he sighs at the feet of beautiful Nature; his danger is despair. The proper critic of this book would be some youthful friend to whom it has been of real value as a stimulus. The exaggerated praise of such an one would be truer to the spiritual fact of its promise, than accurate measurement of its performance. To us it has spoken of noble feelings, a genuine love of beauty, and an uncommon facility of execution. Neither the imagery nor the music are original, but the same is true of the early poems of Byron; there is too much dwelling on minute yet commonplace details, so was it with Coleridge before he served a severe apprenticeship to his art. The great musicians composed much that stands in the same relation to their immortal works that those productions perhaps may to those of Mr. Lowell's riper age; superficial, full of obvious cadences and obvious thoughts; but sweet, fluent, in a large style, and breathing the life of religious love.

* James Russell Lowell, *A Year's Life*. Boston: Charles C. Little and James Brown, 1841. In *Dial*, II (July 1841), 133-34; title supplied. For more on Lowell and Fuller, see p. 27 above.

Hawthorne's *Twice-Told Tales**

Ever since the "Gentle Boy" first announced among us the presence of his friend and observer, the author of the "Twice-Told Tales" has been growing more and more dear to his readers, who have now the pleasure of seeing all the leaves they had been gathering up here and there collected in these two volumes.[1]

It is not merely the soft grace, the playfulness, and genial human sense for the traits of individual character, that have pleased, but the perception of what is rarest in this superficial, bustling community, a great reserve of thought and strength never yet at all brought forward. Landor says, "He is not over-rich in knowledge who cannot afford to let the greater part lie fallow, and to bring forward his produce according to the season and the demand." We can seldom recur to such a passage as this with pleasure, as we turn over the leaves of a new book. But here we may. Like gleams of light on a noble tree which stands untouched and self-sufficing in its fulness of foliage on a distant hill-slope,—like slight ripples wrinkling the smooth surface, but never stirring the quiet depths of a wood-embosomed lake, these tales distantly indicate the bent of the author's mind, and the very frankness with which they impart to us slight outward details and habits shows how little yet is told. He is a favorite writer with children, with whom he feels at home, as true manliness always does; and the "Twice-Told Tales" scarce

* Nathaniel Hawthorne, *Twice-Told Tales*. Boston: James Munroe, 1842. In *Dial*, III (July 1842), 130-31; title supplied.

[1] "The Gentle Boy" was first published in *The Token* for 1832. A separate edition of the story was published in 1839 with an illustration by Sophia Peabody, later Hawthorne's wife.

calls him out more than the little books for his acquaintance of fairy stature.

In the light of familar letters, written with ready hand, by a friend, from the inns where he stops, in a journey through the varied world-scenes, the tales are most pleasing; but they seem to promise more, should their author ever hear a voice that truly calls upon his solitude to ope his study door.

In his second volume, "The Village Uncle," "Lily's Quest," "Chippings with a Chisel," were new to us, and pleasing for the same reasons as former favorites from the same hand. We again admired the sweet grace of the little piece, "Footprints on the Sea-shore."

"Chippings with a Chisel," from its mild, common-sense-philosophy, and genial love of the familiar plays of life, would have waked a brotherly smile on the lips of the friend of Dr. Dry-as-dust.

It is in the studies of familar life that there is most success. In the mere imaginative pieces, the invention is not clearly woven, far from being all compact, and seems a phantom or shadow, rather than a real growth. The men and women, too, flicker large and unsubstantial, like "shadows from the evening firelight," seen "upon the parlor wall." But this would be otherwise, probably, were the genius fully roused to its work, and initiated into its own life, so as to paint with blood-warm colors. This frigidity and thinness of design usually bespeaks a want of deeper experiences, for which no talent at observation, no sympathies, however ready and delicate, can compensate. We wait new missives from the same hand.

From *Summer on the Lakes, in 1843**

In the afternoon of this day we reached the Rock river, in whose neighborhood we proposed to make some stay, and crossed at Dixon's ferry.

This beautiful stream flows full and wide over a bed of rocks, traversing a distance of near two hundred miles, to reach the Mississippi. Great part of the country along its banks is the finest region of Illinois, and the scene of some of the latest romance of Indian warfare. To these beautiful regions Black Hawk returned with his band "to pass the summer," when he drew upon himself the warfare in which he was finally vanquished. No wonder he could not resist the longing, unwise though its indulgence might be, to return in summer to this home of beauty.

Of Illinois, in general, it has often been remarked that it bears the character of country which has been inhabited by a nation skilled like the English in all the ornamental arts of life, especially in landscape gardening. That the villas and castles seem to have been burnt, the enclosures taken down, but the velvet lawns, the flower gardens, the stately parks, scattered at graceful intervals by the decorous hand of art, the frequent deer, and the peaceful herd of cattle that make picture of the plain, all suggest more of the masterly mind of man, than the prodigal, but careless, motherly love of nature. Especially is this true of the Rock river country. The river flows sometimes through these parks and lawns, then betwixt high bluffs, whose grassy ridges are covered with fine trees, or broken with crumbling stone, that easily assumes the forms of buttress, arch and clustered columns.

* Chapter III of *Summer on the Lakes, in 1843* (Boston: Charles C. Little and James Brown, 1844), pp. 43-69.

Along the face of such crumbling rocks, swallows' nests are clustered, thick as cities, and eagles and deer do not disdain their summits. One morning, out in the boat along the base of these rocks, it was amusing, and affecting too, to see these swallows put their heads out to look at us. There was something very hospitable about it, as if man had never shown himself a tyrant near them. What a morning that was! Every sight is worth twice as much by the early morning light. We borrow something of the spirit of the hour to look upon them.

The first place where we stopped was one of singular beauty, a beauty of soft, luxuriant wildness. It was on the bend of the river, a place chosen by an Irish gentleman, whose absenteeship seems of the wisest kind, since for a sum which would have been but a drop of water to the thirsty fever of his native land, he commands a residence which has all that is desirable, in its independence, its beautiful retirement, and means of benefit to others.

His park, his deer-chase, he found already prepared; he had only to make an avenue through it. This brought us by a drive, which in the heat of noon seemed long, though afterwards, in the cool of morning and evening, delightful, to the house. This is, for that part of the world, a large and commodious dwelling. Near it stands the log-cabin where its master lived while it was building, a very ornamental accessory.

In front of the house was a lawn, adorned by the most graceful trees. A few of these had been taken out to give a full view of the river, gliding through banks such as I have described. On this bend the bank is high and bold, so from the house or the lawn the view was very rich and commanding. But if you descended a ravine at the side to the water's edge, you found there a long walk on the narrow shore, with a wall above of the richest hanging wood, in which they said the deer lay hid. I never saw one, but often fancied that I heard them rustling, at daybreak, by these bright clear waters, stretching out in such smiling promise, where no sound broke the deep and blissful seclusion, unless now and then this rustling, or the plash of some fish a little gayer than the others; it seemed not necessary to have any better heaven, or fuller expression of love and freedom than in the mood of nature here.

Then, leaving the bank, you would walk far and far through long grassy paths, full of the most brilliant, also the most delicate flowers. The brilliant are more common on the prairie, but both kinds loved this place.

Amid the grass of the lawn, with a profusion of wild strawberries, we greeted also a familiar love, the Scottish harebell, the gentlest, and most touching form of the flowerworld.

The master of the house was absent, but with a kindness beyond thanks had offered us a resting place there. Here we were taken care of by a deputy, who would, for his youth, have been assigned the place of a page in former times, but in the young west, it seems he was old enough for a steward. Whatever be called his function, he did the honors of the place so much in harmony with it, as to leave the guests free to imagine themselves in Elysium.[1] And the three days passed here were days of unalloyed, spotless happiness.

There was a peculiar charm in coming here, where the choice of location, and the unobtrusive good taste of all the arrangements, showed such intelligent appreciation of the spirit of the scene, after seeing so many dwellings of the new settlers, which showed plainly that they had no thought beyond satisfying the grossest material wants. Sometimes they looked attractive, the little brown houses, the natural architecture of the country, in the edge of the timber. But almost always when you came near, the slovenliness of the dwelling and the rude way in which objects around it were treated, when so little care would have presented a charming whole, were very repulsive. Seeing the traces of the Indians, who chose the most beautiful sites for their dwellings, and whose habits do not break in on that aspect of nature under which they were born, we feel as if they were the rightful lords of a beauty they forbore to deform. But most of these settlers do not see it at all; it breathes, it speaks in vain to those who are rushing into its sphere. Their progress is Gothic, not Roman, and their mode of cultivation will, in

---

[1] Elysium, in mythology, a place where the souls of the good and of heroes exempt from death resided.

the course of twenty, perhaps ten, years, obliterate the natural expression of the country.

This is inevitable, fatal; we must not complain, but look forward to a good result. Still, in travelling through this country, I could not but be struck with the force of a symbol. Wherever the hog comes, the rattlesnake disappears; the omnivorous traveller, safe in its stupidity, willingly and easily makes a meal of the most dangerous of reptiles, and one whom the Indian looks on with a mystic awe. Even so the white settler pursues the Indian, and is victor in the chase. But I shall say more upon the subject by-and-by.

While we were here we had one grand thunder storm, which added new glory to the scene.

One beautiful feature was the return of the pigeons every afternoon to their home. Every afternoon they came sweeping across the lawn, positively in clouds, and with a swiftness and softness of winged motion, more beautiful than anything of the kind I ever knew. Had I been a musician, such as Mendelssohn, I felt that I could have improvised a music quite peculiar, from the sound they made, which should have indicated all the beauty over which their wings bore them. I will here insert a few lines left at this house, on parting, which feebly indicate some of the features.

> Familiar to the childish mind were tales
>   Of rock-girt isles amid a desert sea,
> Where unexpected stretch the flowery vales
>   To soothe the shipwrecked sailor's misery.
> Fainting, he lay upon a sandy shore,
> And fancied that all hope of life was o'er;
> But let him patient climb the frowning wall,
> Within, the orange glows beneath the palm tree tall,
> And all that Eden boasted waits his call.
>
> Almost these tales seem realized to-day,
> When the long dullness of the sultry way,
> Where "independent" settlers' careless cheer
> Made us indeed feel we were "strangers" here,
> Is cheered by sudden sight of this fair spot,
> On which "improvement" yet has made no blot,
> But Nature all-astonished stands, to find
> Her plan protected by the human mind.

Blest be the kindly genius of the scene;
   The river, bending in unbroken grace.
The stately thickets, with their pathways green,
   Fair lonely trees, each in its fittest place.
Those thickets haunted by the deer and fawn;
Those cloudlike flights of birds across the lawn;
The gentlest breezes here delight to blow,
And sun and shower and star are emulous to deck the
   show.

Wondering, as Crusoe, we survey the land;
Happier than Crusoe we, a friendly band;
Blest be the hand that reared this friendly home,
The heart and mind of him to whom we owe
Hours of pure peace such as few mortals know;
May he find such, should he be led to roam;

Be tended by such ministering spirites—
Enjoy such gaily childish days, such hopeful nights!
And yet, amid the goods to mortals given,
To give those goods again is most like heaven.

    Hazelwood. Rock River, June 30th, 1843.

   The only really rustic feature was of the many coops of
poultry near the house, which I understood it to be one of
the chief pleasures of the master to feed.

   Leaving this place, we proceeded a day's journey along
the beautiful stream, to a little town named Oregon. We
called at a cabin, from whose door looked out one of those
faces which, once seen, are never forgotten; young, yet
touched with many traces of feeling, not only possible, but
endured; spirited, too, like the gleam of a finely tempered
blade. It was a face that suggested a history, and many histories, but whose scene would have been in courts and
camps. At this moment their circles are dull for want of that
life which is waning unexcited in this solitary recess.

   The master of the house proposed to show us a "short
cut," by which we might, to especial advantage, pursue our
journey. This proved to be almost perpendicular down a hill,
studded with young trees and stumps. From these he proposed, with a hospitality of service worthy an Oriental, to
free our wheels whenever they should get entangled, also,
to be himself the drag, to prevent our too rapid descent. Such
generosity deserved trust; however, we women could not

be persuaded to render it. We got out and admired, from afar, the process. Left by our guide—and prop! we found ourselves in a wide field, where, by playful quips and turns, an endless "creek," seemed to divert itself with our attempts to cross it. Failing in this, the next best was to whirl down a steep bank, which feat our charioteer performed with an air not unlike that of Rhesus, had he but been as suitably furnished with chariot and steeds![2]

At last, after wasting some two or three hours on the "short cut," we got out by following an Indian trail,—Black Hawk's! How fair the scene through which it led! How could they let themselves be conquered, with such a country to fight for!

Afterwards, in the wide prairie, we saw a lively picture of nonchalance, (to speak in the fashion of dear Ireland.) There, in the wide sunny field, with neither tree nor umbrella above his head, sat a pedler, with his pack, waiting apparently for customers. He was not disappointed. We bought, what hold in regard to the human world, as unmarked, as mysterious, and as important an existence, as the infusoria to the natural, to wit, pins. This incident would have delighted those modern sages, who, in imitation of the sitting philosophers of ancient Ind, prefer silence to speech, waiting to going, and scornfully smile in answer to the motions of earnest life,

> "Of itself will nothing come,
> That ye must still be seeking?"

However, it seemed to me to-day, as formerly on these sublime occasions, obvious that nothing would come, unless something would go; now, if we had been as sublimely still as the pedler, his pins would have tarried in the pack, and his pockets sustained an aching void of pence!

Passing through one of the fine, park-like woods, almost clear from underbrush and carpeted with thick grasses and flowers, we met, (for it was Sunday,) a little congregation just returning from their service, which had been performed in a rude house in its midst. It had a sweet and peaceful air,

---

[2] Rhesus, an ally of the Trojans who was killed and had his white horses taken in order to help defeat Troy.

as if such words and thoughts were very dear to them. The parents had with them all their little children; but we saw no old people; that charm was wanting, which exists in such scenes in older settlements, of seeing the silver bent in reverence beside the flaxen head.

At Oregon, the beauty of the scene was of even a more sumptuous character than at our former "stopping place." Here swelled the river in its boldest course, interspersed by halcyon isles on which nature had lavished all her prodigality in tree, vine, and flower, banked by noble bluffs, three hundred feet high, their sharp ridges as exquisitely definite as the edge of a shell; their summits adorned with those same beautiful trees, and with buttresses of rich rock, crested with old hemlocks, which wore a touching and antique grace amid the softer and more luxuriant vegetation. Lofty natural mounds rose amidst the rest, with the same lovely and sweeping outline, showing everywhere the plastic power of water,—water, mother of beauty, which, by its sweet and eager flow, had left such lineaments as human genius never dreamt of.

Not far from the river was a high crag, called the Pine Rock, which looks out, as our guide observed, like a helmet above the brow of the country. It seems as if the water left here and there a vestige of forms and materials that preceded its course, just to set off its new and richer designs.

The aspect of this country was to me enchanting, beyond any I have ever seen, from its fullness of expression, its bold and impassioned sweetness. Here the flood of emotion has passed over and marked everywhere its course by a smile. The fragments of rock touch it with a wildness and liberality which give just the needed relief. I should never be tired here, though I have elsewhere seen country of more secret and alluring charms, better calculated to stimulate and suggest. Here the eye and heart are filled.

How happy the Indians must have been here! It is not long since they were driven away, and the ground, above and below, is full of their traces.

"The earth is full of men."

You have only to turn up the sod to find arrowheads and

Indian pottery. On an island, belonging to our host, and nearly opposite his house, they loved to stay, and, no doubt, enjoyed its lavish beauty as much as the myriad wild pigeons that now haunt its flower-filled shades. Here are still the marks of their tomahawks, the troughs in which they prepared their corn, their caches.

A little way down the river is the site of an ancient Indian village, with its regularly arranged mounds. As usual, they had chosen with the finest taste. It was one of those soft shadowy afternoons when we went there, when nature seems ready to weep, not from grief, but from an overfull heart. Two prattling, lovely little girls, and an African boy, with glittering eye and ready grin, made our party gay; but all were still as we entered their little inlet and trod those flowery paths. They may blacken Indian life as they will, talk of its dirt, its brutality, I will ever believe that the men who chose that dwelling-place were able to feel emotions of noble happiness as they returned to it, and so were the women that received them. Neither were the children sad or dull, who lived so familiarly with the deer and the birds, and swam that clear wave in the shadow of the Seven Sisters. The whole scene suggested to me a Greek splendor, a Greek sweetness, and I can believe that an Indian brave, accustomed to ramble in such paths, and be bathed by such sunbeams, might be mistaken for Apollo, as Apollo was for him by West. Two of the boldest bluffs are called the Deer's Walk, (not because deer do *not* walk there,) and the Eagle's Nest. The latter I visited one glorious morning; it was that of the fourth of July, and certainly I think I had never felt so happy that I was born in America. Wo to all country folks that never saw this spot, never swept an enraptured gaze over the prospect that stretched beneath. I do believe Rome and Florence are suburbs compared to this capital of nature's art.

The bluff was decked with great bunches of a scarlet variety of the milkweed, like cut coral, and all starred with a mysterious-looking dark flower, whose cup rose lonely on a tall stem. This had, for two or three days, disputed the ground with the lupine and phlox. My companions disliked, I liked it.

Here I thought of, or rather saw, what the Greek expresses under the form of Jove's darling, Ganymede, and the following stanzas took form.

GANYMEDE TO HIS EAGLE.

SUGGESTED BY A WORK OF THORWALDSEN'S.[3]

Composed on the height called the Eagle's Nest, Oregon,
Rock River, July 4th, 1843.

Upon the rocky mountain stood the boy,
    A goblet of pure water in his hand,
His face and form spoke him one made for joy,
    A willing servant to sweet love's command,
But a strange pain was written on his brow,
And thrilled throughout his silver accents now—

"My bird," he cries, "my destined brother friend,
    O whither fleets to-day thy wayward flight?
Hast thou forgotten that I here attend,
    From the full noon until this sad twilight?
A hundred times, at least, from the clear spring,
    Since the full noon o'er hill and valley glowed,
I've filled the vase which our Olympian king
    Upon my care for thy sole use bestowed;
That at the moment when thou should'st descend,
A pure refreshment might thy thirst attend.

Hast thou forgotten earth, forgotten me,
    Thy fellow bondsman in a royal cause,
Who, from the sadness of infinity,
    Only with thee can know that peaceful pause
In which we catch the flowing strain of love,
Which binds our dim fates to the throne of Jove?

Before I saw thee, I was like the May,
    Longing for summer that must mar its bloom,
Or like the morning star that calls the day,
    Whose glories to its promise are the tomb;
And as the eager fountain rises higher
    To throw itself more strongly back to earth,
Still, as more sweet and full rose my desire,
    More fondly it reverted to its birth,

[3] Zeus, in the form of an eagle, made his cupbearer Ganymede immortal; Albert Thorwaldsen (1770-1844), Danish sculptor whose classical subjects included a statue of Ganymede.

For, what the rosebud seeks tells not the rose,
The meaning foretold by the boy the man cannot disclose.

I was all Spring, for in my being dwelt
  Eternal youth, where flowers are the fruit,
Full feeling was the thought of what was felt,
  Its music was the meaning of the lute;
But heaven and earth such life will still deny,
For earth, divorced from heaven, still asks the question
    Why?

Upon the highest mountains my young feet
  Ached, that no pinions from their lightness grew,
My starlike eyes the stars would fondly greet,
  Yet win no greeting from the circling blue;
Fair, self-subsistent each in its own sphere,
  They had no care that there was none for me;
Alike to them that I was far or near,
  Alike to them, time and eternity.

But, from the violet of lower air,
  Sometimes an answer to my wishing came,
Those lightning births my nature seemed to share,
  They told the secrets of its fiery frame,
The sudden messengers of hate and love,
The thunderbolts that arm the hand of Jove,
And strike sometimes the sacred spire, and strike the
    sacred grove.

Come in a moment, in a moment gone,
They answered me, then left me still more lone,
They told me that the thought which ruled the world,
As yet no sail upon its course had furled,
That the creation was but just begun,
New leaves still leaving from the primal one,
But spoke not of the goal to which *my* rapid wheels
    would run.

Still, still my eyes, though tearfully, I strained
To the far future which my heart contained,
And no dull doubt my proper hope profaned.

At last, O bliss, thy living form I spied,
  Then a mere speck upon a distant sky,
Yet my keen glance discerned its noble pride,
  And the full answer of that sun-filled eye;
I knew it was the wing that must upbear
My earthlier form into the realms of air.

Thou knowest how we gained that beauteous height,
Where dwells the monarch of the sons of light,
Thou knowest he declared us two to be
The chosen servants of his ministry,
Thou as his messenger, a sacred sign
Of conquest, or with omen more benign,
To give its due weight to the righteous cause,
To express the verdict of Olympian laws.

And I to wait upon the lonely spring,
    Which slakes the thirst of bards to whom 'tis given
The destined dues of hopes divine to sing,
    And weave the needed chain to bind to heaven.
Only from such could be obtained a draught
For him who in his early home from Jove's own cup has
        quaffed.

To wait, to wait, but not to wait too long,
Till heavy grows the burthen of a song;
O bird! too long hast thou been gone to-day,
My feet are weary of their frequent way,
The spell that opes the spring my tongue no more can say.

If soon thou com'st not, night will fall around,
My head with a sad slumber will be bound,
And the pure draught be spilt upon the ground.

Remember that I am not yet divine,
Long years of service to the fatal Nine
Are yet to make a Delphian vigor mine."

O, make them not too hard, thou bird of Jove,
Answer the stripling's hope, confirm his love,
Receive the service in which he delights,
And bear him often to the serene heights,
Where hands that were so prompt in serving thee,
Shall be allowed the highest ministry,
And Rapture live with bright Fidelity.

The afternoon was spent in a very different manner. The
family, whose guests we were, possessed a gay and graceful
hospitality that gave zest to each moment. They possessed
that rare politeness which, while fertile in pleasant ex-
pedients to vary the enjoyment of a friend, leaves him perfectly free the moment he wishes to be so. With such hosts,
pleasure may be combined with repose. They lived on the
bank opposite the town, and, as their house was full, we

slept in the town, and passed three days with them, passing to and fro morning and evening in their boats. (To one of these, called the Fairy, in which a sweet little daughter of the house moved about lighter than any Scotch Ellen ever sung, I should indite a poem, if I had not been guilty of rhyme on the very last page.) At morning this was very pleasant; at evening, I confess I was generally too tired with the excitements of the day to think it so.

Their house—a double log cabin—was, to my eye, the model of a Western villa. Nature had laid out before it grounds which could not be improved. Within, female taste had veiled every rudeness—availed itself of every sylvan grace.

In this charming abode what laughter, what sweet thoughts, what pleasing fancies, did we not enjoy! May such never desert those who reared it and made us so kindly welcome to all its pleasures!

Fragments of city life were dexterously crumbled into the dish prepared for general entertainment. Ice creams followed the dinner drawn by the gentlemen from the river, and music and fireworks wound up the evening of days spent on the Eagle's Nest. Now they had prepared a little fleet to pass over to the Fourth of July celebration, which some queer drumming and fifing, from the opposite bank, had announced to be "on hand."

We found the free and independent citizens there collected beneath the trees, among whom many a round Irish visage dimpled at the usual puffs of Ameriky.

The orator was a New Englander, and the speech smacked loudly of Boston, but was received with much applause, and followed by a plentiful dinner, provided by and for the Sovereign People, to which Hail Columbia served as grace.

Returning, the gay flotilla hailed the little flag which the children had raised from a log-cabin, prettier than any president ever saw, and drank the health of their country and all mankind, with a clear conscience.

Dance and song wound up the day. I know not when the mere local habitation has seemed to me to afford so fair a chance of happiness as this. To a person of unspoiled tastes, the beauty alone would afford stimulus enough. But with it would be naturally associated all kinds of wild sports, experiments, and the studies of natural history. In these regards, the poet, the sportsman, the naturalist, would alike rejoice in this wide range of untouched loveliness.

Then, with a very little money, a ducal estate may be purchased, and by a very little more, and moderate labor, a family be maintained upon it with raiment, food and shelter. The luxurious and minute comforts of a city life are not yet to be had without effort disproportionate to their value. But, where there is so great a counterpoise, cannot these be given up once for all? If the houses are imperfectly built, they can afford immense fires and plenty of covering; if they are small, who cares?—with such fields to roam in. In winter, it may be borne; in summer, is of no consequence. With plenty of fish, and game, and wheat, can they not dispense with a baker to bring "muffins hot" every morning to the door for their breakfast?

Here a man need not take a small slice from the landscape, and fence it in from the obtrusions of an uncongenial neighbor, and there cut down his fancies to miniature improvements which a chicken could run over in ten minutes. He may have water and wood and land enough, to dread no incursions on his prospect from some chance Vandal that may enter his neighborhood. He need not painfully economise and manage how he may use it all; he can afford to leave some of it wild, and to carry out his own plans without obliterating those of nature.

Here, whole families might live together, if they would. The sons might return from their pilgrimages to settle near the parent hearth; the daughters might find room near their mother. Those painful separations, which already desecrate and desolate the Atlantic coast, are not enforced here by the stern need of seeking bread; and where they are voluntary, it is no matter. To me, too, used to the feelings which haunt a society of struggling men, it was delightul to look upon a scene where nature still wore her motherly smile and seemed to promise room not only for those favored or cursed with the qualities best adapting for the strifes of competition, but for the delicate, the thoughtful, even the indolent or eccentric. She did not say, Fight or starve; nor even, Work or cease to exist; but, merely showing that the apple was a finer fruit than the wild crab, gave both room to grow in the garden.

A pleasant society is formed of the families who live along the banks of this stream upon farms. They are from various parts of the world, and have much to communicate to one another. Many have cultivated minds and refined manners, all a varied experience, while they have in common the interests of a new country and a new life. They must traverse some space to get at one another, but the journey is through scenes that make it a separate pleasure. They must bear inconveniences to stay in one another's houses; but these, to the well-disposed, are only a source of amusement and adventure.

The great drawback upon the lives of these settlers, at present, is the unfitness of the women for their new lot. It has generally been the choice of the men, and the women follow, as women will, doing their best for affection's sake, but too often in heartsickness and weariness. Beside it frequently not being a choice or conviction of their own minds that it is best to be here, their part is the hardest, and they are least fitted for it. The men can find assistance in field labor, and recreation with the gun and fishing-rod. Their bodily strength is greater, and enables them to bear and enjoy both these forms of life.

The women can rarely find any aid in domestic labor. All its various and careful tasks must often be performed, sick or well, by the mother and daughters, to whom a city education has imparted neither the strength nor skill now demanded.

The wives of the poorer settlers, having more hard work to do than before, very frequently become slatterns; but the ladies, accustomed to a refined neatness, feel that they cannot degrade themselves by its absence, and struggle under every disadvantage to keep up the necessary routine of small arrangements.

With all these disadvantages for work, their resources for pleasure are fewer. When they can leave the housework, they have not learnt to ride, to drive, to row, alone. Their culture has too generally been that given to women to make them "the ornaments of society." They can dance, but not draw; talk French, but know nothing of the language of flowers; neither in childhood were allowed to cultivate them, lest they should tan their complexions. Accustomed to the pavement of Broadway, they dare not tread the wildwood paths for fear of rattlesnakes!

Seeing much of this joylessness, and inaptitude, both of body and mind, for a lot which would be full of blessings for those prepared for it, we could not but look with deep interest on the little girls, and hope they would grow up with the strength of body, dexterity, simple tastes, and resources that would fit them to enjoy and refine the western farmer's life.

But they have a great deal to war with in the habits of thought acquired by their mothers from their own early life. Everywhere the fatal spirit of imitation, of reference to European standards, penetrates, and threatens to blight whatever of original growth might adorn the soil.

If the little girls grow up strong, resolute, able to exert their faculties, their mothers mourn over their want of fashionable delicacy. Are they gay, enterprising, ready to fly about in the various ways that teach them so much, these ladies lament that "they cannot go to school, where they might learn to be quiet." They lament the want of "education" for their daughters, as if the thousand needs which call out their young energies, and the language of nature around, yielded no education.

Their grand ambition for their children, is to send them to school in some eastern city, the measure most likely to make them useless and unhappy at home. I earnestly hope that, ere long, the existence of good schools near themselves, planned by persons of sufficient thought to meet the wants of the place and time, instead of copying New York or Boston, will correct this mania. Instruction the children want to enable them to profit by the great natural advantages of their position; but methods copied from the education of some English Lady Augusta, are as ill suited to the daughter of an Illinois farmer, as satin shoes to climb the Indian mounds. An elegance she would diffuse around her, if her mind were opened to appreciate elegance; it might be of a kind new, original, enchanting, as different from that of the city belle as that of the prairie torch-flower from the shopworn article that touches the cheek of that lady within her bonnet.

To a girl really skilled to make home beautiful and comfortable, with bodily strength to enjoy plenty of exercise, the woods, the streams, a few studies, music, and the sincere and familiar intercourse, far more easily to be met here than elsewhere, would afford happiness enough. Her eyes would not grow dim, nor her cheeks sunken, in the absence of parties, morning visits, and milliners' shops.

As to music, I wish I could see in such places the guitar rather than the piano, and good vocal more than instrumental music.

The piano many carry with them, because it is the fashionable instrument in the eastern cities. Even there, it is so merely from the habit of imitating Europe, for not one in a thousand is willing to give the labor requisite to ensure any valuable use of the instrument.

But, out here, where the ladies have so much less leisure, it is still less desirable. Add to this, they never know how to tune their own instruments, and as persons seldom visit them who can do so, these pianos are constantly out of tune, and would spoil the ear of one who began by having any.

The guitar, or some portable instrument which requires less practice, and could be kept in tune by themselves, would be far more desirable for most of these ladies. It would give all they want as a household companion to fill up the gaps of life with a pleasant stimulus or solace, and be sufficient accompaniment to the voice in social meetings.

Singing in parts is the most delightful family amusement, and those who are constantly together can learn to sing in perfect accord. All the practice it needs, after some good elementary instruction, is such as meetings by summer twilight, and evening firelight naturally suggest. And, as music is an universal language, we cannot but think a fine Italian duet would be as much at home in the log cabin as one of Mrs. Gore's novels.[4]

The sixth July we left this beautiful place. It was one of

[4] Mrs. Catherine Gore (1799-1861), prolific English novelist and playwright.

those rich days of bright sunlight, varied by the purple
shadows of large sweeping clouds. Many a backward look
we cast, and left the heart behind.

Our journey to-day was no less delightful than before,
still all new, boundless, limitless. Kinmont says, that limits are sacred; that the Greeks were in the right to worship
a god of limits.[5] I say, that what is limitless is alone divine,
that there was neither wall nor road in Eden, that those who
walked there lost and found their way just as we did, and
that all the gain from the Fall was that we had a wagon to
ride in. I do not think, either, that even the horses doubted
whether this last was any advantage.

Everywhere the rattlesnake-weed grows in profusion.
The antidote survives the bane. Soon the coarser plantain,
the "white man's footstep," shall take its place.

We saw also the compass plant, and the western tea
plant. Of some of the brightest flowers an Indian girl afterwards told me the medicinal virtues. I doubt not those students of the soil knew a use to every fair emblem, on which
we could only look to admire its hues and shape.

After noon we were ferried by a girl, (unfortunately not
of the most picturesque appearance) across the Kishwaukie,
the most graceful stream, and on whose bosom rested many
full-blown water-lilies, twice as large as any of ours. I was
told that, *en revanche*, they were scentless, but I still regret
that I could not get at one of them to try.

Query, did the lilied fragrance which, in the miraculous
times, accompanied visions of saints and angels, proceed
from water or garden lilies?

Kishwaukie is, according to tradition, the scene of a
famous battle, and its many grassy mounds contain the
bones of the valiant. On these waved thickly the mysterious
purple flower, of which I have spoken before. I think it
springs from the blood of the Indians, as the hyacinth did
from that of Apollo's darling.[6]

The ladies of our host's family at Oregon, when they

---

[5] Alexander Kinmont (1799-1838), best known for his *Twelve Lectures on
the Natural History of Man, and the Rise and Progress of Philosophy* (1839).

[6] After Hyacinth's death, the grieving Apollo caused a flower to blossom
from his blood which today is named after him.

first went there, after all the pains and plagues of building and settling, found their first pastime in opening one of these mounds, in which they found, I think, three of the departed, seated in the Indian fashion.

One of these same ladies, as she was making bread one winter morning, saw from the window a deer directly before the house. She ran out, with her hands covered with dough, calling the others, and they caught him bodily before he had time to escape.

Here (at Kishwaukie) we received a visit from a ragged and barefoot, but bright-eyed gentleman, who seemed to be the intellectual loafer, the walking Will's coffeehouse of the place. He told us many charming snake stories; among others, of himself having seen seventeen young ones reënter the mother snake, on the intrusion of a visiter.

This night we reached Belvidere, a flourishing town in Boone county, where was the tomb, now despoiled, of Big Thunder. In this later day we felt happy to find a really good hotel.

From this place, by two days of very leisurely and devious journeying, we reached Chicago, and thus ended a journey, which one at least of the party might have wished unending.

I have not been particularly anxious to give the geography of the scene, inasmuch as it seemed to me no route, nor series of stations, but a garden interspersed with cottages, groves and flowery lawns, through which a stately river ran. I had no guide-book, kept no diary, do not know how many miles we travelled each day, nor how many in all. What I got from the journey was the poetic impression of the country at large; it is all I have aimed to communicate.

The narrative might have been made much more interesting, as life was at the time, by many piquant anecdotes and tales drawn from private life. But here courtesy restrains the pen, for I know those who received the stranger with such frank kindness would feel ill requited by its becoming the means of fixing many spy-glasses, even though the scrutiny might be one of admiring interest, upon their private homes.

For many of these, too, I was indebted to a friend, whose property they more lawfully are. This friend was one of those rare beings who are equally at home in nature and with man. He knew a tale of all that ran and swam, and flew, or only grew, possessing that extensive familiarity with things which shows equal sweetness of sympathy and playful penetration. Most refreshing to me was his unstudied lore, the unwritten poetry which common life presents to a strong and gentle mind. It was a great contrast to the subtleties of analysis, the philosophic strainings of which I had seen too much. But I will not attempt to transplant it. May it profit others as it did me in the region where it was born, where it belongs. The evening of our return to Chicago the sunset was of a splendor and calmness beyond any we saw at the West. The twilight that succeeded was equally beautiful; soft, pathetic, but just so calm. When afterwards I learned this was the evening of Allston's death,[7] it seemed to me as if this glorious pageant was not without connection with that event; at least, it inspired similar emotions,—a heavenly gate closing a path adorned with shows well worthy Paradise.

> Farewell, ye soft and sumptuous solitudes!
> Ye fairy distances, ye lordly woods,
> Haunted by paths like those that Poussin knew,[8]
> When after his all gazers' eyes he drew;
> I go,—and if I never more may steep
> An eager heart in your enchantments deep,
> Yet ever to itself that heart may say,
> Be not exacting; thou hast lived one day;
> Hast looked on that which matches with thy mood,
> Impassioned sweetness of full being's flood,
> Where nothing checked the bold yet gentle wave,
> Where nought repelled the lavish love that gave.
> A tender blessing lingers o'er the scene,
> Like some young mother's thought, fond, yet serene,
> And through its life new-born our lives have been.
> Once more farewell,—a sad, a sweet farewell;
> And, if I never must behold you more,
> In other worlds I will not cease to tell
> The rosary I here have numbered o'er:

[7] Washington Allston (1779-1843), the noted American painter, died on 9 July.

[8] Nicholas Poussin (1594-1665), French historical and landscape painter.

And bright-haired Hope will lend a gladdened ear,
And Love will free him from the grasp of Fear,
And Gorgon critics, while the tale they hear,
Shall dew their stony glances with a tear,[9]
If I but catch one echo from your spell;—
And so farewell,— a grateful, sad farewell!

[9] The Gorgons, in Greek mythology, were three sisters with snakelike hair whose gaze could turn onlookers to stone.

Woman in the Nineteenth Century

"Frei durch Vernunft, stark durch Gesetze,
Durch Sanftmuth gross, and reich durch Schätze,
Die lange Zeit dein Busen dir verschweig."[1]

"I meant the day-star should not brighter rise,
Nor lend like influence from its lucent seat;
I meant she should be courteous, facile, sweet,
Free from that solemn vice of greatness, pride;
I meant each softest virtue there should meet,
Fit in that softer bosom to reside;
Only a (heavenward and instructed) soul
I purposed her, that should, with even powers,
The rock, the spindle, and the shears control
Of destiny, and spin her own free hours."[2]

Preface

The following essay is a reproduction, modified and expanded, of an article published in "The Dial, Boston, July, 1843," under the title of "The Great Lawsuit. Man versus Men: Woman versus Women."

This article excited a good deal of sympathy, and still more interest. It is in compliance with wishes expressed from many quarters, that it is prepared for publication in its present form.

[1] "Free through understanding, strong through principles,
Great through gentleness, and enriched by loved ones,
This long time your bosom has concealed you."
I have been unable to identify Fuller's source.

[2] Ben Jonson (*c.* 1573-1637), English essayist and dramatist, quoted from Epigram No. 76, "On Lucy, Countess of Bedford." See also p. 104 below.

Objections having been made to the former title, as not sufficiently easy to be understood, the present has been substituted as expressive of the main purpose of the essay; though, by myself, the other is preferred, partly for the reason others do not like it, *i. e.*, that it requires some thought to see what it means, and might thus prepare the reader to meet me on my own ground. Beside, it offers a larger scope, and is, in that way, more just to my desire. I meant, by that title, to intimate the fact that, while it is the destiny of Man, in the course of the Ages, to ascertain and fulfil the law of his being, so that his life shall be seen, as a whole, to be that of an angel or messenger, the action of prejudices and passions, which attend, in the day, the growth of the individual, is continually obstructing the holy work that is to make the earth a part of heaven. By Man I mean both man and woman: these are the two halves of one thought. I lay no especial stress on the welfare of either. I believe that the development of the one cannot be effected without that of the other. My highest wish is that this truth should be distinctly and rationally apprehended, and the conditions of life and freedom recognized as the same for the daughters and the sons of time; twin exponents of a divine thought.

I solicit a sincere and patient attention from those who open the following pages at all. I solicit of women that they will lay it to heart to ascertain what is for them the liberty of law. It is for this, and not for any, the largest, extension of partial privileges that I seek. I ask them, if interested by these suggestions, to search their own experience and intuitions for better, and fill up with fit materials the trenches that hedge them in. From men I ask a noble and earnest attention to any thing that can be offered on this great and still obscure subject, such as I have met from many with whom I stand in private relations.

And may truth, unpolluted by prejudice, vanity, or selfishness, be granted daily more and more, as the due inheritance, and only valuable conquest for us all!

November, 1844.

Woman in the Nineteenth Century

> "Frailty, thy name is WOMAN."[3]
>
> "The Earth waits for her Queen."[4]

The connection between these quotations may not be obvious, but it is strict. Yet would any contradict us, if we made them applicable to the other side, and began also

> Frailty, they name is MAN.
>
> The Earth waits for its King.

Yet man, if not yet fully installed in his powers, has given much earnest of his claims. Frail he is indeed, how frail! how impure! Yet often has the vein of gold displayed itself amid the baser ores, and Man has appeared before us in princely promise worthy of his future.

If, oftentimes, we see the prodigal son feeding on the husks in the fair field no more his own, anon, we raise the eyelids, heavy from bitter tears, to behold in him the radiant apparition of genius and love, demanding not less than the all of goodness, power and beauty. We see that in him the largest claim finds a due foundation. That claim is for no partial sway, no exclusive possession. He cannot be satisfied with any one gift of life, any one department of knowledge or telescopic peep at the heavens. He feels himself called to understand and aid nature, that she may, through his intelligence, be raised and interpreted; to be a student of, and servant to, the universe-spirit; and king of his planet, that as an angelic minister, he may bring it into conscious harmony with the law of that spirit.

In clear triumphant moments, many times, has rung through the spheres the prophecy of his jubilee, and those moments, though past in time, have been translated into eternity by thought; the bright signs they left hang in the heavens, as single stars or constellations, and, already, a thickly sown radiance consoles the wanderer in the darkest night. Other heroes since Hercules have fulfilled the zodiac

---

[3] *Hamlet*, I, ii, 1. 146.
[4] Unidentified; possibly by Fuller.

of beneficent labors, and then given up their mortal part to
the fire without a murmur; while no God dared deny that
they should have their reward.

> Siquis tamen, Hercule, siquis
> Forte Deo doliturus erit, data præmia nollet,
> Sed meruise dari sciet, invitus que probabit,
> Assensere Dei.[5]

Sages and lawgivers have bent their whole nature to the
search for truth, and thought themselves happy if they could
buy, with the sacrifice of all temporal ease and pleasure,
one seed for the future Eden. Poets and priests have strung
the lyre with the heart-strings, poured out their best blood
upon the altar, which, reared anew from age to age shall at
last sustain the flame pure enough to rise to highest heaven.
Shall we not name with as deep a benediction those who, if
not so immediately, or so consciously, in connection with the
eternal truth, yet, led and fashioned by a divine instinct,
serve no less to develope and interpret the open secret of
love passing into life, energy creating for the purpose of
happiness; the artist whose hand, drawn by a pre-existent
harmony to a certain medium, moulds it to forms of life more
highly and completely organized than are seen elsewhere,
and, by carrying out the intention of nature, reveals her
meaning to those who are not yet wise enough to divine it;
the philosopher who listens steadily for laws and causes,
and from those obvious, infers those yet unknown; the historian who, in faith that all events must have their reason
and their aim, records them, and thus fills archives from
which the youth of prophets may be fed. The man of science
dissects the statements, tests the facts, and demonstrates
order, even where he cannot its purpose.

[5] If any God dissent, and judge too great
The sacred honors of the heavenly seat,
Even he shall own his deeds deserve the sky,
Even he, reluctant, shall at length comply.
Th' assembled powers assent.
[Fuller's note, *Dial*, IV (July 1843), 2, from "Ovid, Apotheosis of Hercules,
translated into clumsy English by Mr. Gay".] John Gay (1685-1732) trans-
lated Book IX of Ovid's "Metamorphoses" for Dr. Samuel Garth's Ovid in
1717.

Lives, too, which bear none of these names, have yielded tones of no less significance. The candlestick set in a low place has given light as faithfully, where it was needed, as that upon the hill. In close alleys, in dismal nooks, the Word has been read as distinctly, as when shown by angels to holy men in the dark prison. Those who till a spot of earth scarcely larger than is wanted for a grave, have deserved that the sun should shine upon its sod till violets answer.

So great has been, from time to time, the promise, that, in all ages, men have said the gods themselves came down to dwell with them; that the All-Creating wandered on the earth to taste, in a limited nature, the sweetness of virtue; that the All-Sustaining incarnated himself to guard, in space and time, the destinies of this world; that heavenly genius dwelt among the shepherds, to sing to them and teach them how to sing. Indeed

"Der stets den Hirten gnadig sich bewies."

"He has constantly shown himself favorable to shepherds."

And the dwellers in green pastures and natural students of the stars were selected to hail, first among men, the holy child, whose life and death were to present the type of excellence, which has sustained the heart of so large a portion of mankind in these later generations.

Such marks have been made by the footsteps of *man*, (still alas! to be spoken of as the *ideal* man,) wherever he has passed through the wilderness of *men*, and whenever the pigmies stepped in one of those they felt dilate within the breast somewhat that promised nobler stature and purer blood. They were impelled to forsake their evil ways of decrepit scepticism, and covetousness of corruptible possessions. Conviction flowed in upon them. They, too, raised the cry; God is living, now, to-day; and all beings are brothers, for they are his children. Simple words enough, yet which only angelic nature, can use or hear in their full free sense.

These were the triumphant moments, but soon the lower nature took its turn, and the era of a truly human life was postponed.

Thus is man still a stranger to his inheritance, still a pleader, still a pilgrim. Yet his happiness is secure in the

end. And now, no more a glimmering consciousness, but assurance begins to be felt and spoken, that the highest ideal
man can form of his own powers, is that which he is destined
to attain. Whatever the soul knows how to seek, it cannot
fail to obtain. This is the law and the prophets. Knock and it
shall be opened, seek and ye shall find. It is demonstrated;
it is a maxim. Man no longer paints his proper nature in
some form and says, "Prometheus had it; it is God-like;"
but "Man must have it; it is human." However disputed by
many, however ignorantly used, or falsified by those who do
receive it, the fact of an universal, unceasing revelation has
been too clearly stated in words to be lost sight of in thought,
and sermons preached from the text, "Be ye perfect," are
the only sermons of a pervasive and deep-searching influence.

But, among those who meditate upon this text, there is
a great difference of view, as to the way in which perfection
shall be sought.

Through the intellect, say some. Gather from every
growth of life its seed of thought; look behind every symbol
for its law; if thou canst *see* clearly, the rest will follow.

Through the life, say others. Do the best thou knowest
to-day. Shrink not from frequent error in this gradual frag-
mentary state. Follow thy light for as much as it will show
thee, be faithful as far as thou canst, in hope that faith presently will lead to sight. Help others, without blaming their
need of thy help. Love much and be forgiven.

It needs not intellect, needs not experience, says a third.
If you took the true way, your destiny would be accomplished in a purer and more natural order. You would not
learn through facts of thought or action, but express through
them the certainties of wisdom. In quietness yield thy soul
to the causal soul. Do not disturb thy apprenticeship by
premature effort; neither check the tide of instruction by
methods of thy own. Be still, seek not, but wait in obedience. Thy commission will be given.

Could we indeed say what we want, could we give a description of the child that is lost, he would be found. As soon
as the soul can affirm clearly that a certain demonstration
is wanted, it is at hand. When the Jewish prophet described

the Lamb, as the expression of what was required by the coming era, the time drew nigh.[6] But we say not, see not as yet, clearly, what we would. Those who call for a more triumphant expression of love, a love that cannot be crucified, show not a perfect sense of what has already been given. Love has already been expressed, that made all things new, that gave the worm its place and ministry as well as the eagle; a love to which it was alike to descend into the depths of hell, or to sit at the right hand of the Father.

Yet, no doubt, a new manifestation is at hand, a new hour in the day of man. We cannot expect to see any one sample of completed being, when the mass of men still lie engaged in the sod, or use the freedom of their limbs only with wolfish energy. The tree cannot come to flower till its root be free from the cankering worm, and its whole growth open to air and light. While any one is base, none can be entirely free and noble. Yet something new shall presently be shown of the life of man, for hearts crave, if minds do not know how to ask it.

Among the strains of prophecy, the following, by an earnest mind of a foreign land, written some thirty years ago, is not yet outgrown; and it has the merit of being a positive appeal from the heart, instead of a critical declaration what man should *not* do.

"The ministry of man implies, that he must be filled from the divine fountains which are being engendered through all eternity, so that, at the mere name of his master, he may be able to cast all his enemies into the abyss; that he may deliver all parts of nature from the barriers that imprison them; that he may purge the terrestrial atmosphere from the poisons that infect it; that he may preserve the bodies of men from the corrupt influences that surround, and the maladies that afflict them; still more, that he may keep their souls pure from the malignant insinuations which pollute, and the gloomy images that obscure them; that he may restore its serenity to the Word, which false words of men fill with mourning and sadness; that he may satisfy the desires of the angels, who await from him the development

---

[6] Possibly Hosea 4:16: "For Israel slideth back as a backsliding heifer: now the Lord will feed them as a lord in a large place."

of the marvels of nature; that, in fine, his world may be filled with God, as eternity is."*

Another attempt we will give, by an obscure observer of our own day and country, to draw some lines of the desired image. It was suggested by seeing the design of Crawford's Orpheus,[7] and connecting with the circumstance of the American, in his garret at Rome, making choice of this subject, that of Americans here at home, showing such ambition to represent the character, by calling their prose and verse "Orphic sayings"—"Orphics."[8] We wish we could add that they have shown that musical apprehension of the progress of nature through her ascending gradations which entitled them so to do, but their attempts are frigid, though sometimes grand; in their strain we are not warmed by the fire which fertilized the soil of Greece.

Orpheus was a law-giver by theocratic commission. He understood nature, and made her forms move to his music. He told her secrets in the form of hymns, nature as seen in the mind of God. His soul went forth toward all beings, yet could remain sternly faithful to a chosen type of excellence. Seeking what he loved, he feared not death nor hell, neither could any shape of dread daunt his faith in the power of the celestial harmony that filled his soul.

It seemed significant of the state of things in this country, that the sculptor should have represented the seer at the moment when he was obliged with his hand to shade his eyes.

> Each Orpheus must to the depths descend,
> For only thus the Poet can be wise,
>   Must make the sad Persephone his friend,
> And buried love to second life arise;
>   Again his love must lose through too much love,
> Must lose his life by living life too true,
>   For what he sought below is passed above,
> Already done is all that he would do;

---

* St. Martin. [Fuller's note.] Unidentified.

[7] Thomas Crawford (1813-1857), American sculptor working in Rome.

[8] Fuller is probably referring to the "Orphic Sayings" by Goethe in the August 1836 *Western Messenger* or those by A. Bronson Alcott which she had published in the July 1840 and January 1841 *Dials*.

Must tune all being with his single lyre,
Must melt all rocks free from their primal pain,
Must search all nature with his one soul's fire,
Must bind anew all forms in heavenly chain.
If he already sees what he must do,
Well may he shade his eyes from the far-shining view.[9]

A better comment could not be made on what is required
to perfect man, and place him in that superior position for
which he was designed, than by the interpretation of Bacon
upon the legends of the Syren coast. When the wise Ulysses
passed, says he, he caused his mariners to stop their ears
with wax, knowing there was in them no power to resist the
lure of that voluptuous song. But he, the much experienced
man, who wished to be experienced in all, and use all to the
service of wisdom, desired to hear the song that he might
understand its meaning. Yet, distrusting his own power to
be firm in his better purpose, he caused himself to be bound
to the mast, that he might be kept secure against his own
weakness. But Orpheus passed unfettered, so absorbed in
singing hymns to the gods that he could not even hear those
sounds of degrading enchantment.[10]

Meanwhile not a few believe, and men themselves
have expressed the opinion, that the time is come when
Eurydice is to call for an Orpheus, rather than Orpheus for
Eurydice: that the idea of Man, however imperfectly
brought out, has been far more so than that of Woman, that
she, the other half of the same thought, the other chamber
of the heart of life, needs now to take her turn in the full
pulsation, and that improvement in the daughters will best
aid in the reformation of the sons of this age.

It should be remarked that, as the principle of liberty
is better understood, and more nobly interpreted, a broader
protest is made in behalf of Woman. As men become aware
that few men have had a fair chance, they are inclined to say
that no women have had a fair chance. The French Revolu-

[9] The poem is by Fuller.
[10] Francis Bacon (1561-1626), English essayist and philosopher. The Sirens, in Greek mythology, were sea nymphs whose singing lured sailors to death upon the rocks of their island. Ulysses (Odysseus) was the hero of Homer's *Odyssey*.

tion, that strangely disguised angel, bore witness in favor of woman, but interpreted her claims no less ignorantly than those of man. Its idea of happiness did not rise beyond outward enjoyment, unobstructed by the tyranny of others. The title it gave was citoyen, citoyenne, and it is not unimportant to woman that even this species of equality was awarded her. Before, she could be condemned to perish on the scaffold for treason, not as a citizen, but as a subject. The right with which this title then invested a human being, was that of bloodshed and license. The Goodess of Liberty was impure. As we read the poem addressed to her not long since, by Beranger, we can scarcely refrain from tears as painful as the tears of blood that flowed when "such crimes were committed in her name."[11] Yes! man, born to purify and animate the unintelligent and the cold, can, in his madness, degrade and pollute no less the fair and the chaste. Yet truth was prophesied in the ravings of that hideous fever, caused by long ignorance and abuse. Europe is conning a valued lesson from the blood-stained page. The same tendencies, farther unfolded, will bear good fruit in this country.

Yet, by men in this country, as by the Jews, when Moses was leading them to the promised land, every thing has been done that inherited depravity could do, to hinder the promise of heaven from its fulfilment. The cross here as elsewhere, has been planted only to be blasphemed by cruelty and fraud. The name of the Prince of Peace has been profaned by all kinds of injustice toward the Gentile whom he said he came to save. But I need not speak of what has been done towards the red man, the black man. Those deeds are the scoff of the world; and they have been accompanied by such pious words that the gentlest would not dare to intercede with "Father, forgive them, for they know not what they do."[12]

Here, as elsewhere, the gain of creation consists always in the growth of individual minds, which live and aspire, as

[11] Pierre–Jean de Béranger (1780-1857), French lyric poet known for his "La Liberte." The quotation is attributed to Madame Roland (1754-1793), a French revolutionist and follower of Rousseau's idealistic philosophy; see also note 67, p. 129 below.

[12] Luke 23:34.

flowers bloom and birds sing, in the midst of morasses; and in the continual development of that thought, the thought of human destiny, which is given to eternity adequately to express, and which ages of failure only seemingly impede. Only seemingly, and whatever seems to the contrary, this country is as surely destined to elucidate a great moral law, as Europe was to promote the mental culture of man.

Though the national independence be blurred by the servility of individuals, though freedom and equality have been proclaimed only to leave room for a monstrous display of slave-dealing and slave-keeping; though the free American so often feels himself free, like the Roman, only to pamper his appetites and his indolence through the misery of his fellow beings, still it is not in vain, that the verbal statement has been made, "All men are born free and equal." There it stands, a golden certainty wherewith to encourage the good, to shame the bad. The new world may be called clearly to perceive that it incurs the utmost penalty, if it reject or oppress the sorrowful brother. And, if men are deaf, the angels hear. But men cannot be deaf. It is inevitable that an external freedom, an independence of the encroachments of other men, such as has been achieved for the nation, should be so also for every member of it. That which has once been clearly conceived in the intelligence cannot fail sooner or later to be acted out. It has become a law as irrevocable as that of the Medes in their ancient dominion; men will privately sin against it, but the law, as expressed by a leading mind of the age,

> "Tutti fatti a sembianza d'un Solo,
> Figli tutti d'un solo riscatto,
> In qual'ora, in qual parte del suolo
> Trascorriamo quest'aura vital,
> Siam fratelli, siam stretti ad un patto:
> Maladetto colui che lo infrange,
> Che s'innalza sul fiacco che piange
> Che contrista uno spirto immortal."*

* Manzoni. [Fuller's note.] Alessandro Manzoni (1785-1873), Italian romantic novelist, quoted from "Coro Dell' Atto Secondo," *Il Conte di Carmagnola*, canto 45.

"All made in the likeness of the One,
All children of one ransom,
In whatever hour, in whatever part of the soil,
We draw this vital air,
We are brothers; we must be bound by one compact,
Accursed he who infringes it,
Who raises himself upon the weak who weep,
Who saddens an immortal spirit."

This law cannot fail of universal recognition. Accursed
be he who willingly saddens an immortal spirit, doomed to
infamy in later, wiser ages, doomed in future stages of his
own being to deadly penance, only short of death. Accursed
be he who sins in ignorance, if that ignorance be caused by
sloth.

We sicken no less at the pomp than the strife of words.
We feel that never were lungs so puffed with the wind of dec-
lamation, on moral and religious subjects, as now. We are
tempted to implore these "word-heroes," these word-Catos,
word-Christs, to beware of cant* above all things; to remember that hypocrisy is the most hopeless as well as the
meanest of crimes, and that those must surely be polluted by
it, who do not reserve a part of their morality and religion
for private use. Landor says that he cannot have a great deal
of mind who cannot afford to let the larger part of it lie fallow, and what is true of genius is not less so of virtue. The
tongue is a valuable member, but should appropriate but a
small part of the vital juices that are needful all over the
body. We feel that the mind may "grow black and rancid in
the smoke" even "of altars." We start up from the harangue
to go into our closet and shut the door. There inquires the
spirit, "Is this rhetoric the bloom of healthy blood or a false
pigment artfully laid on?" And yet again we know where is
so much smoke, must be some fire; with so much talk about

---

* Dr. Johnson's one piece of advice should be written on every door;
"Clear your mind of cant." But Byron, to whom it was so acceptable, in
clearing away the noxious vine, shook down the building. Sterling's emendation is worthy of honor:
          "Realize your cant, not cast it off."
[Fuller's note.] Samuel Johnson (1709-1784), English lexicographer and
essayist, quoted from James Boswell, *The Life of Samuel Johnson* (1791),
dated 15 May 1783; John Sterling (1806-1844), English poet and dramatist.

virtue and freedom, must be mingled some desire for them; that it cannot be in vain that such have become the common topics of conversation among men, rather than schemes for tyranny and plunder, that the very newspapers see it best to proclaim themselves Pilgrims, Puritans, Heralds of Holiness. The king that maintains so costly a retinue cannot be a mere boast, or Carabbas fiction.[13] We have waited here long in the dust; we are tired and hungry, but the triumphal procession must appear at last.

Of all its banners, none has been more steadily upheld, and under none have more valor and willingness for real sacrifices been shown, than that of the champions of the enslaved African. And this band it is, which, partly from a natural following out of principles, partly because many women have been prominent in that cause, makes, just now, the warmest appeal in behalf of woman.

Though there has been a growing liberality on this subject, yet society at large is not so prepared for the demands of this party, but that they are and will be for some time, coldly regarded as the Jacobins of their day.[14]

"Is it not enough," cries the irritated trader, "that you have done all you could to break up the national union, and thus destroy the prosperity of our country, but now you must be trying to break up family union, to take my wife away from the cradle and the kitchen hearth to vote at polls, and preach from a pulpit? Of course, if she does such things, she cannot attend to those of her own sphere. She is happy enough as she is. She has more leisure than I have, every means of improvement, every indulgence."

"Have you asked her whether she was satisfied with these *indulgences*?"

"No, but I know she is. She is too amiable to wish what would make me unhappy, and too judicious to wish to step beyond the sphere of her sex. I will never consent to have our peace disturbed by any such discussions."

" 'Consent—you?' it is not consent from you that is in

---

[13] Carabbas, character in Perrault's *Le Chat Botté* (*Puss in Boots*), whose name is synonymous with aristocratic pretension.

[14] Jacobins, name given to a radical organization in the French Revolution and usually associated with the Reign of Terror under Robespierre.

question, it is assent from your wife."

"Am not I the head of my house?"

"You are not the head of your wife. God has given her a mind of her own."

"I am the head and she the heart."

"God grant you play true to me another then. I suppose I am to be grateful that you did not say she was only the hand. If the head represses no natural pulse of the heart, there can be no question as to your giving your consent. Both will be of one accord, and there needs but to present any question to get a full and true answer. There is no need of precaution, of indulgence, or consent. But our doubt is whether the heart does consent with the head, or only obeys its decrees with a passiveness that precludes the exercise of its natural powers, or a repugnance that turns sweet qualities to bitter, or a doubt that lays waste the fair occasions of life. It is to ascertain the truth, that we propose some liberating measures."

Thus vaguely are these questions proposed and discussed at present. But their being proposed at all implies much thought and suggests more. Many women are considering within themselves, what they need that they have not, and what they can have, if they find they need it. Many men are considering whether women are capable of being and having more than they are and have, *and*, whether, if so, it will be best to consent to improvement in their condition.

This morning, I open the Boston "Daily Mail," and find in its "poet's corner," a translation of Schiller's "Dignity of Woman." In the advertisement of a book on America, I see in the table of contents this sequence, "Republican Institutions. American Slavery. American Ladies."

I open the *"Deutsche Schnellpost,"* published in New-York, and find at the head of a column, *Judenund Frauenemancipation in Ungarn.* Emancipation of Jews and Women in Hungary.[15]

The past year has seen action in the Rhode-Island legislature, to secure married women rights over their own

[15] Items from the *Deutsche Schnellpost*, a German-language newspaper, were often translated by Fuller for the *New-York Tribune* during her tenure as its literary critic.

property, where men showed that a very little examination of the subject could teach them much; an article in the Democratic Review on the same subject more largely considered, written by a woman, impelled, it is said, by glaring wrong to a distinguished friend having shown the defects in the existing laws, and the state of opinion from which they spring;[16] and an answer from the revered old man, J. Q. Adams, in some respects the Phocion of his time, to an address made him by some ladies. To this last I shall again advert in another place.[17]

These symptoms of the times have come under my view quite accidentally: one who seeks, may, each month or week, collect more.

The numerous party, whose opinions are already labelled and adjusted too much to their mind to admit of any new light, strive, by lectures on some model-woman of bride-like beauty and gentleness, by writing and lending little treatises, intended to mark out with precision the limits of woman's sphere, and woman's mission, to prevent other than the rightful shepherd from climbing the wall, or the flock from using any chance to go astray.

Without enrolling ourselves at once on either side, let us look upon the subject from the best point of view which to-day offers. No better, it is to be feared, than a high housetop. A high hill-top, or at least a cathedral spire, would be desirable.

It may well be an Anti-Slavery party that pleads for woman, if we consider merely that she does not hold property on equal terms with men; so that, if a husband dies without making a will, the wife, instead of taking at once his place as head of the family, inherits only a part of his fortune, often brought him by herself, as if she were a child, or ward only, not an equal partner.

We will not speak of the innumerable instances in which profligate and idle men live upon the earnings of industrious wives; or if the wives leave them, and take with them the

[16] "The Legal Wrongs of Women," *United States Magazine and Democratic Review*, XIV (May 1844), 477-483.

[17] John Quincy Adams (1767-1848), sixth president of the United States; Phocion (c. 402-317 B.C.), leader of the aristocratic party in Athens. For Adams' speech, see p. 181 below.

children, to perform the double duty of mother and father, follow from place to place, and threaten to rob them of the children, if deprived of the rights of a husband, as they call them, planting themselves in their poor lodgings, frightening them into paying tribute by taking from them the children, running into debt at the expense of these otherwise so overtasked helots. Such instances count up by scores within my own memory. I have seen the husband who had stained himself by a long course of low vice, till his wife was wearied from her heroic forgiveness, by finding that his treachery made it useless, and that if she would provide bread for herself and her children, she must be separate from his ill fame. I have known this man come to instal himself in the chamber of a woman who loathed him and say she should never take food without his company. I have known these men steal their children whom they knew they had no means to maintain, take them into dissolute company, expose them to bodily danger, to frighten the poor woman, to whom, it seems, the fact that she alone had borne the pangs of their birth, and nourished their infancy, does not give an equal right to them. I do believe that this mode of kidnapping, and it is frequent enough in all classes of society, will be by the next age viewed as it is by Heaven now, and that the man who avails himself of the shelter of men's laws to steal from a mother her own children, or arrogate any superior right in them, save that of superior virtue, will bear the stigma he deserves, in common with him who steals grown men from their mother land, their hopes, and their homes.

I said, we will not speak of this now, yet I have spoken, for the subject makes me feel too much. I could give instances that would startle the most vulgar and callous, but I will not, for the public opinion of their own sex is already against such men, and where cases of extreme tyranny are made known, there is private action in the wife's favor. But she ought not to need this, nor, I think, can she long. Men must soon see that, on their own ground, that woman is the weaker party, she ought to have legal protection, which would make such oppression impossible. But I would not deal with "atrocious instances" except in the way of illustration, neither demand from men a partial redress in some one matter, but go to the root of the whole. If principles could be established, particulars would adjust themselves aright. Ascertain the true destiny of woman, give her legitimate hopes, and a standard within herself; marriage and all other relations would by degrees be harmonized with these.

But to return to the historical progress of this matter. Knowing that there exists in the minds of men a tone of feeling towards women as towards slaves, such as is expressed in the common phrase, "Tell that to women and children," that the infinite soul can only work through them in already ascertained limits; that the gift of reason, man's highest prerogative, is allotted to them in much lower degree; that they must be kept from mischief and melancholy by being constantly engaged in active labor, which is to be furnished and directed by those better able to think, &c. &c.; we need not multiply instances, for who can review the experience of last week without recalling words which imply, whether in jest or earnest, these views or views like these; knowing this, can we wonder that many reformers think that measures are not likely to be taken in behalf of women, unless their wishes could be publicly represented by women?

That can never be necessary, cry the other side. All men are privately influenced by women; each has his wife, sister, or female friends, and is too much biased by these relations to fail of representing their interests, and, if this is not enough, let them propose and enforce their wishes with the pen. The beauty of home would be destroyed, the delicacy of the sex be violated, the dignity of halls of legislation degraded by an attempt to introduce them there. Such duties are inconsistent with those of a mother; and then we have ludicrous pictures of ladies in hysterics at the polls, and senate chambers filled with cradles.

But if, in reply, we admit as truth that woman seems destined by nature rather for the inner circle, we must add that the arrangements of civilized life have not been, as yet, such as to secure it to her. Her circle, if the duller, is not the quieter. If kept from "excitement," she is not from drudgery. Not only the Indian squaw carries the burdens of the camp, but the favorites of Louis the Fourteenth accompany him in his journeys,[18] and the washerwoman stands at her tub

---

[18] Louis XIV (1638-1715), ruler of France for all but five years of his life. His court was known for its sycophants.

and carries home her work at all seasons, and in all states of health. Those who think the physical circumstances of woman would make a part of the affairs of national government unsuitable, are by no means those who think it impossible for the negresses to endure field work, even during pregnancy, or the semptstresses to go through their killing labors.

As to the use of the pen, there was quite as much opposition to woman's possessing herself of that help to free agency, as there is now to her seizing on the rostrum or the desk; and she is likely to draw, from a permission to plead her cause that way, opposite inferences to what might be wished by those who now grant it.

As to the possibility of her filling with grace and dignity, any such position, we should think those who had seen the great actresses, and heard the Quaker preachers of modern times, would not doubt, that woman can express publicly the fulness of thought and creation, without losing any of the peculiar beauty of her sex. What can pollute and tarnish is to act thus from any motive except that something needs to be said or done. Women could take part in the processions, the songs, the dances of old religion; no one fancied their delicacy was impaired by appearing in public for such a cause.

As to her home, she is not likely to leave it more than she now does for balls, theatres, meetings for promoting missions, revival meetings, and others to which she flies, in hope of an animation for her existence, commensurate with what she sees enjoyed by men. Governors of ladies' fairs are no less engrossed by such a change, than the Governor of the state by his; presidents of Washingtonian societies no less away from home than presidents of conventions. If men look straitly to it, they will find that, unless their lives are domestic, those of the women will not be. A house is no home unless it contain food and fire for the mind as well as for the body. The female Greek, of our day, is as much in the street as the male to cry, What news? We doubt not it was the same in Athens of old. The women, shut out from the market place, made up for it at the religious festivals. For human beings are not so constituted that they can live without expansion. If they do not get it one way, they must another, or perish.

As to men's representing women fairly at present, while we hear from men who owe to their wives not only all that is comfortable or graceful, but all that is wise in the arrangement of their lives, the frequent remark, "You cannot reason with a woman," when from those of delicacy, nobleness, and poetic culture, the contemptuous phrase "women and children," and that in no light sally of the hour, but in works intended to give a permanent statement of the best experiences, when not one man, in the million, shall I say? no, not in the hundred million, can rise above the belief that woman was made *for man*, when such traits as these are daily forced upon the attention, can we feel that man will always do justice to the interests of woman? Can we think that he takes a sufficiently discerning and religious view of her office and destiny, *ever* to do her justice, except when prompted by sentiment, accidentally or transiently, that is, for the sentiment will vary according to the relations in which he is placed. The lover, the poet, the artist, are likely to view her nobly. The father and the philosopher have some chance of liberality; the man of the world, the legislator for expediency, none.

Under these circumstances, without attaching importance, in themselves, to the changes demanded by the champions of woman, we hail them as signs of the times. We would have every arbitrary barrier thrown down. We would have every path laid open to woman as freely as to man. Were this done and a slight temporary fermentation allowed to subside, we should see crystallizations more pure and of more various beauty. We believe the divine energy would pervade nature to a degree unknown in the history of former ages, and that no discordant collision, but a ravishing harmony of the spheres would ensue.

Yet, then and only then, will mankind be ripe for this, when inward and outward freedom for woman as much as for man shall be acknowledged as a right, not yielded as a concession. As the friend of the negro assumes that one man cannot by right, hold another in bondage, so should the friend of woman assume that man cannot, by right, lay even well-meant restrictions on woman. If the negro be a soul, if the woman be a soul, appareled in flesh, to one Master only are they accountable. There is but one law for souls, and if there is to be an interpreter of it, he must come not as man, or son of man, but as son of God.

Were thought and feeling once so far elevated that man should esteem himself the brother and friend, but nowise the lord and tutor of woman, were he really bound with her in equal worship, arrangements as to function and employment would be of no consequence. What woman needs is not as a woman to act or rule, but as a nature to grow, as an intellect to discern, as a soul to live freely and unimpeded, to unfold such powers as were given her when we left our common home. If fewer talents were given her, yet if allowed the free and full employment of these, so that she may render back to the giver his own with usury, she will not complain; nay I dare to say she will bless and rejoice in her earthly birth-place, her earthly lot. Let us consider what obstructions impede this good era, and what signs give reason to hope that it draws near.

I was talking on this subject with Miranda, a woman, who, if any in the world could, might speak without heat and bitterness of the position of her sex.[19] Her father was a man who cherished no sentimental reverence for woman, but a firm belief in the equality of the sexes. She was his eldest child, and came to him at an age when he needed a companion. From the time she could speak and go alone, he addressed her not as a plaything, but as a living mind. Among the few verses he ever wrote was a copy addressed to this child, when the first locks were cut from her head, and the reverence expressed on this occasion for that cherished head, he never belied. It was to him the temple of immortal intellect. He respected his child, however, too much to be an indulgent parent. He called on her for clear judgment, for courage, for honor and fidelity; in short, for such virtues as he knew. In so far as he possessed the keys to the wonders of this universe, he allowed free use of them to her, and by the incentive of a high expectation, he forbade, as far as possible, that she should let the privilege lie idle.

[19] Miranda, Fuller's name for herself. Her description of Miranda's upbringing accurately describes her own youth; see also the Mariana section of *Summer on the Lakes*, pp. 81-102.

Thus this child was early led to feel herself a child of the spirit. She took her place easily, not only in the world of organized being, but in the world of mind. A dignified sense of self-dependence was given as all her portion, and she found it a sure anchor. Herself securely anchored, her relations with others were established with equal security. She was fortunate in a total absence of those charms which might have drawn to her bewildering flatteries, and in a strong electric nature, which repelled those who did not belong to her, and attracted those who did. With men and women her relations were noble, affectionate without passion, intellectual without coldness. The world was free to her, and she lived freely in it. Outward adversity came, and inward conflict, but that faith and self-respect had early been awakened which must always lead at last, to an outward serenity and an inward peace.

Of Miranda I had always thought as an example, that the restraints upon the sex were insuperable only to those who think them so, or who noisily strive to break them. She had taken a course of her own, and no man stood in her way. Many of her acts had been unusual, but excited no uproar. Few helped, but none checked her, and the many men, who knew her mind and her life, showed to her confidence, as to a brother, gentleness as to a sister. And not only refined, but very coarse men approved and aided one in whom they saw resolution and clearness of design. Her mind was often the leading one, always effective.

When I talked with her upon these matters, and had said very much what I have written, she smilingly replied: "and yet we must admit that I have been fortunate, and this should not be. My good father's early trust gave the first bias, and the rest followed of course. It is true that I have had less outward aid, in after years, than most women, but that is of little consequence. Religion was early awakened in my soul, a sense that what the soul is capable to ask it must attain, and that, though I might be aided and instructed by others, I must depend on myself as the only constant friend. This self dependence, which was honored in me, is deprecated as a fault in most women. They are taught to learn their rule from without, not to unfold it from within.

"This is the fault of man, who is still vain, and wishes

to be more important to woman than, by right, he should be."

"Men have not shown this disposition toward you," I said.

"No! because the position I early was enabled to take was one of self-reliance. And were all women as sure of their wants as I was, the result would be the same. But they are so overloaded with precepts by guardians, who think that nothing is so much to be dreaded for a woman as originality of thought or character, that their minds are impeded by doubts till they lose their chance of fair free proportions. The difficulty is to get them to the point from which they shall naturally develope self-respect, and learn self-help.

"Once I thought that men would help to forward this state of things more than I do now. I saw so many of them wretched in the connections they had formed in weakness and vanity. They seemed so glad to esteem women whenever they could.

"The soft arms of affection," said one of the most discerning spirits, "will not suffice for me, unless on them I see the steel bracelets of strength."

But early I perceived that men never, in any extreme of despair, wished to be women. On the contrary they were ever ready to taunt one another at any sign of weakness, with,

"Art thou not like the women, who"—

The passage ends various ways, according to the occasion and rhetoric of the speaker. When they admired any woman they were inclined to speak of her as "above her sex." Silently I observed this, and feared it argued a rooted scepticism, which for ages had been fastening on the heart, and which only an age of miracles could eradicate. Ever I have been treated with great sincerity; and I look upon it as a signal instance of this, that an intimate friend of the other sex said, in a fervent moment, that I "deserved in some star to be a man." He was much surprised when I disclosed my view of my position and hopes, when I declared my faith that the feminine side, the side of love, of beauty, of holiness, was now to have its full chance, and that, if either were better, it was better now to be a woman, for even the slight-

est achievement of good was furthering an especial work of
our time. He smiled incredulous. "She makes the best she
can of it," thought he. "Let Jews believe the pride of Jewry,
but I am of the better sort, and know better."

Another used as highest praise, in speaking of a character
in literature, the words "a manly woman."

So in the noble passage of Ben Jonson:

> "I meant the day-star should not brighter ride,
>   Nor shed like influence from its lucent seat;
> I meant she should be courteous, facile, sweet,
>   Free from that solemn vice of greatness, pride;
> I meant each softest virtue there should meet,
>   Fit in that softer bosom to abide,
> Only a learned and a *manly* soul,
>   I purposed her, that should with even powers,
> The rock, the spindle, and the shears control
>   Of destiny, and spin her own free hours."[20]

"Methinks," said I, "you are too fastidious in objecting to
this. Jonson in using the word 'manly' only meant to height-
en the picture of this, the true, the intelligent fate, with
one of the deeper colors." 'And yet,' said she, 'so invariable
is the use of this word where a heroic quality is to be described, and I feel so sure that persistence and courage are
the most womanly no less than the most manly qualities,
that I would exchange these words for others of a larger
sense at the risk of marring the fine tissue of the verse. Read,
'a heavenward and instructed soul,' and I should be satisfied. Let it not be said, wherever there is energy or creative
genius, 'She has a masculine mind.' '

This by no means argues a willing want of generosity
toward woman. Man is as generous toward her, as he knows
how to be.

Wherever she has herself arisen in national or private
history, and nobly shone forth in any form of excellence,
men have received her, not only willingly, but with triumph.
Their encomiums indeed, are always, in some sense, mortifying; they show too much surprise. Can this be you? he
cries to the transfigured Cinderella; well I should never

[20] Ben Jonson; see note 2, p. 82.

have thought it, but I am very glad. We will tell every one
that you have "*surpassed your sex.*"

In every-day life the feelings of the many are stained
with vanity. Each wishes to be lord in a little world, to be
superior at least over one; and he does not feel strong enough
to retain a life-long ascendancy over a strong nature. Only
a Theseus could conquer before he wed the Amazonian
Queen. Hercules wished rather to rest with Dejanira, and
received the poisoned robe, as a fit guerdon.[21] The tale
should be interpreted to all those who seek repose with the
weak.

But not only is man vain and fond of power, but the same
want of development, which thus affects him morally, prevents his intellectually discerning the destiny of woman.
The boy wants no woman, but only a girl to play ball with
him, and mark his pocket handkerchief.

Thus, in Schiller's Dignity of Woman, beautiful as the
poem is, there is no "grave and perfect man," but only a
great boy to be softened and restrained by the influence of
girls. Poets, the elder brothers of their race, have usually
seen farther; but what can you expect of every-day men, if
Schiller was not more prophetic as to what women must be?
Even with Richter, one foremost thought about a wife was
that she would "cook him something good." But as this is a
delicate subject, and we are in constant danger of being accused of slighting what are called "the functions," let me
say in behalf of Miranda and myself, that we have high respect for those who cook something good, who create and
preserve fair order in houses, and prepare therein the shining raiment for worthy inmates, worthy guests. Only these
"functions" must not be a drudgery, or enforced necessity,
but a part of life. Let Ulysses drive the beeves home while
Penelope there piles up the fragrant loaves; they are both
well employed if these be done in thought and love, willingly. But Penelope is no more meant for a baker or weaver
solely, than Ulysses for a cattle-herd.

The sexes should not only correspond to and appreciate,

---

[21] Dejanira, wife of Hercules, gave her husband a robe smeared with the
blood of a centaur thinking it would help win back his love, but it was poisoned and lead to his death.

but prophesy to one another. In individual instances this happens. Two persons love in one another the future good which they aid one another to unfold. This is imperfectly or rarely done in the general life. Man has gone but little way; now he is waiting to see whether woman can keep step with him, but instead of calling out, like a good brother, "you can do it, if you only think so," or impersonally; "any one can do what he tries to do;" he often discourages with school-boy brag: "Girls can't do that; girls can't play ball." But let any one defy their taunts, break through and be brave and secure, they rend the air with shouts.

This fluctuation was obvious in a narrative I have lately seen, the story of the life of Countess Emily Plater, the heroine of the last revolution in Poland.[22] The dignity, the purity, the concentrated resolve, the calm, deep enthusiasm, which yet could, when occasion called, sparkle up a holy, an indignant fire, make of this young maiden the figure I want for my frontispiece. Her portrait is to be seen in the book, a gentle shadow of her soul. Short was the career—like the maid of Orleans, she only did enough to verify her credentials, and then passed from a scene on which she was, probably, a premature apparition.[23]

When the young girl joined the army where the report of her exploits had preceded her, she was received in a manner that marks the usual state of feeling. Some of the officers were disappointed at her quiet manners; that she had not the air and tone of a stage-heroine. They thought she could not have acted heroically unless in buskins; had no idea that such deeds only showed the habit of her mind. Others talked of the delicacy of her sex, advised her to withdraw from perils and dangers, and had no comprehension of the feelings within her breast that made this impossible. The gentle irony of her reply to these self-constituted tutors, (not one of whom showed himself her equal in conduct or reason,) is as good as her indignant reproof at a later period

---

[22] "Emily Plater, the Polish Heroine," *United States Magazine and Democratic Review*, XI (July 1842), 23-33.

[23] A reference to Joan of Arc (*c.* 1412-1431), French national heroine who was led by supernatural voices to help Charles VII gain the throne. She was later burned as a heretic.

to the general, whose perfidy ruined all.

But though, to the mass of these men, she was an embarrassment and a puzzle, the nobler sort viewed her with a tender enthusiasm worthy of her. "Her name," said her biographer, "is known throughout Europe. I paint her character that she may be as widely loved."

With pride, he shows her freedom from all personal affections; that, though tender and gentle in an uncommon degree, there was no room for a private love in her consecrated life. She inspired those who knew her with a simple energy of feeling like her own. We have seen, they felt, a woman worthy the name, capable of all sweet affections, capable of stern virtue.

It is a fact worthy of remark, that all these revolutions in favor of liberty have produced female champions that share the same traits, but Emily alone has found a biographer. Only a near friend could have performed for her this task, for the flower was reared in feminine seclusion, and the few and simple traits of her history before her appearance in the field could only have been known to the domestic circle. Her biographer has gathered them up with a brotherly devotion.

No! man is not willingly ungenerous. He wants faith and love, because he is not yet himself an elevated being. He cries, with sneering skepticism, Give us a sign. But if the sign appears, his eyes glisten, and he offers not merely approval, but homage.

The severe nation which taught that the happiness of the race was forfeited through the fault of a woman, and showed its thought of what sort of regard man owed her, by making him accuse her on the first question to his God; who gave her to the patriarch as a handmaid, and by the Mosaical law, bound her to allegiance like a serf;[24] even they greeted, with solemn rapture, all great and holy women as heroines, prophetesses, judges in Israel; and if they made Eve listen to the serpent, gave Mary as a bride to the Holy Spirit. In other nations it has been the same down to our day. To the woman who could conquer, a triumph was awarded. And

[24] These legal, moral, and ceremonial laws may be found in the last four books of the Pentateuch.

not only those whose strength was recommended to the heart by association with goodness and beauty, but those who were bad, if they were steadfast and strong, had their claims allowed. In any age a Semiramis, an Elizabeth of England, a Catharine of Russia, makes her place good, whether in a large or small circle.[25] How has a little wit, a little genius, been celebrated in a woman! What an intellectual triumph was that of the lonely Aspasia, and how heartily acknowledged! She, indeed, met a Pericles.[26] But what annalist, the rudest of men, the most plebeian of husbands, will spare from his page one of the few anecdotes of Roman women—Sappho! Eloisa![27] The names are of threadbare celebrity. Indeed they were not more suitably met in their own time than the Countess Colonel Plater on her first joining the army. They had much to mourn, and their great impulses did not find due scope. But with time enough, space enough, their kindred appear on the scene. Across the ages, forms lean, trying to touch the hem of their retreating robes. The youth here by my side cannot be weary of the fragments from the life of Sappho. He will not believe they are not addressed to himself, or that he to whom they were addressed could be ungrateful. A recluse of high powers devotes himself to understand and explain the thought of Eloisa; he asserts her vast superiority in soul and genius to her master; he curses the fate that cast his lot in another age than hers. He could have understood her: he would have been to her a friend, such as Abelard never could. And this one woman he could have loved and reverenced, and she, alas! lay cold in her grave hundreds of years ago. His sorrow is truly pathetic. These responses that come too late to give joy are as tragic as any thing we know, and yet the tears of later ages glitter as they fall on Tasso's prison bars.[28] And we

[25] Semiramis, legendary Assyrian queen who built Babylon.

[26] Aspasia, mistress of Pericles in ancient Athens, was highly regarded by Socrates.

[27] Sappho (fl. 600 B.C.), Greek lyric poet whose home on the island of Lesbos formed the center of a literary coterie of women; Eloisa refers to Héloise, whose affair with her teacher, the French theologian Peter Abelard (1079-1142), resulted in her family's castrating him.

[28] Torquato Tasso (1544-1595), Italian Renaissance poet imprisoned by Duke Alfonso II after he flew into an unprovoked rage at his wedding.

know how elevating to the captive is the security that some-where an intelligence must answer to his.

The man habitually most narrow towards women will be flushed, as by the worst assault on Christianity, if you say it has made no improvement in her condition. Indeed, those most opposed to new acts in her favor, are jealous of the re-putation of those which have been done.

We will not speak of the enthusiasm excited by actresses, improvvisatrici, female singers, for here mingles the charm of beauty and grace; but female authors, even learned wom-en, if not insufferably ugly and slovenly, from the Italian professor's daughter, who taught behind the curtain, down to Mrs. Carter and Madame Dacier, are sure of an admiring audience, and what is far better, chance to use what they have learned, and to learn more, if they can once get a plat-form on which to stand.[29]

But how to get this platform, or how to make it of rea-sonably easy access is the difficulty. Plants of great vigor will almost always struggle into blossom, despite impedi-ments. But there should be encouragement, and a free genial atmosphere for those of more timid sort, fair play for each in its own kind. Some are like the little, delicate flowers which love to hide in the dripping mosses, by the sides of moutain torrents, or in the shade of tall trees. But others re-quire an open field, a rich and loosened soil, or they never show their proper hues.

It may be said that man does not have his fair play either; his energies are repressed and distorted by the interposition of artificial obstacles. Ay, but he himself has put them there; they have grown out of his own imperfections. If there *is* a misfortune in woman's lot, it is in obstacles being inter-posed by men, which do *not* mark her state; and, if they express her past ignorance, do not her present needs. As every man is of woman born, she has slow but sure means of redress, yet the sooner a general justness of thought makes smooth the path, the better.

Goethe's play, *Torquato Tasso* (1790), is based on his life, as is Byron's poem "The Lament of Tasso."

[29] Elizabeth Carter (1717-1806), English translator, scholar, and poet; Anne Dacier (1654-1720), French classical scholar.

Man is of woman born, and her face bends over him in
infancy with an expression he can never quite forget. Eminent men have delighted to pay tribute to this image, and it
is an hacknied observation, that most men of genius boast
some remarkable development in the mother. The rudest tar
brushes off a tear with his coat-sleeve at the hallowed name.
The other day, I met a decrepit old man of seventy, on a
journey, who challenged the stage-company to guess where
he was going. They guessed aright, "To see your mother."
"Yes," said he, "she is ninety-two, but has good eye-sight
still, they say. I have not seen her these forty years, and I
thought I could not die in peace without." I should have
liked his picture painted as a companion piece to that of a
boisterous little boy, whom I saw attempt to declaim at a
school exhibition—

> "O that those lips had language. Life has passed
> With me but roughly since I heard thee last."[30]

He got but very little way before sudden tears shamed
him from the stage.

Some gleams of the same expression which shone down
upon his infancy, angelically pure and benign, visit man
again with hopes of pure love, of a holy marriage. Or, if not
before, in the eyes of the mother of his child they again are
seen, and dim fancies pass before his mind, that woman may
not have been born for him alone, but have come from heav-
en, a commissioned soul, a messenger of truth and love; that
she can only make for him a home in which he may lawfully
repose, in so far as she is

> "True to the kindred points of Heaven and home."[31]

In gleams, in dim fancies, this thought visits the mind
of common men. It is soon obscured by the mists of sensuality, the dust of routine, and he thinks it was only some
meteor, or ignis fatuus[32] that shone. But, as a Rosicrucian

---

[30] William Cowper (1731-1800), "On the Receipt of My Mother's Picture
Out of Norfolk."

[31] William Wordsworth (1770-1850), English poet laureate, quoted from
"To a Skylark" (1842).

[32] "ignis fatuus," a light appearing over a marshy ground; used to indicate a false or misleading influence.

lamp, it burns unwearied, though condemned to the solitude of tombs;[33] and to its permanent life, as to every truth,
each age has in some form borne witness. For the truths,
which visit the minds of careless men only in fitful gleams,
shine with radiant clearness into those of the poet, the priest,
and the artist.

Whatever may have been the domestic manners of the
ancients, the idea of woman was nobly manifested in their
mythologies and poems, where she appears as Sita in the
Ramayana, a form of tender purity, as the Egyptian Isis,*
of divine wisdom never yet surpassed.[34] In Egypt, too, the
Sphinx, walking the earth with lion tread, looked out upon
its marvels in the calm, inscrutable beauty of a virgin's face,
and the Greek could only add wings to the great emblem.
In Greece, Ceres and Proserpine, significantly termed "the
great goddesses," were seen seated, side by side. They
needed not to rise for any worshipper or any change; they
were prepared for all things, as those initiated to their mysteries knew. More obvious is the meaning of these three
forms, the Diana, Minerva, and Vesta. Unlike in the expression of their beauty, but alike in this,—that each was self-
sufficing. Other forms were only accessories and illustrations, none the complement to one like these. Another
might, indeed, be the companion, and the Apollo and Diana
set off one another's beauty. Of the Vesta, it is to be observed,
that not only deep-eyed, deep-discerning Greece, but ruder
Rome, who represents the only form of good man, (the always busy warrior,) that could be indifferent to woman, confided the permanence of its glory to a tutelary goddess, and
her wisest legislator spoke of meditation as a nymph.

---

[33] Rosicrucian, a mystical philosophy originating in Northern Europe,
whose founder's body was allegedly discovered in excellent preservation,
surrounded by magical unextinguished lamps, some 120 years after his tomb
had been first sealed.

* For an adequate description of the Isis, see Appendix A. [Fuller's note.]
Appendix A is printed on pp. 209-10.

[34] Sita, regarded by the Hindus as the goddess of wifely chastity be-
cause she preserved her virtue when captured by the evil demon Rāvana;
Ramayana, one of India's two great epics, dating from the second century
B.C.; Isis, most famous of Egyptian goddesses, the female counterpart of
Osiris.

Perhaps in Rome the neglect of woman was a reaction on the manners of Etruria, where the priestess Queen, warrior Queen, would seem to have been so usual a character.

An instance of the noble Roman marriage, where the stern and calm nobleness of the nation was common to both, we see in the historic page through the little that is told us of Brutus and Portia.[35] Shakspeare has seized on the relation in its native lineaments, harmonizing the particular with the universal; and, while it is conjugal love, and no other, making it unlike the same relation, as seen in Cymbeline, or Othello, even as one star differeth from another in glory.

> "By that great vow
> Which did incorporate and make us one,
> Unfold to me, yourself, your half,
> Why you are heavy. *   *   *
>   Dwell I but in the suburbs
> Of your good pleasure? If it be no more,
> Portia is Brutus' harlot, not his wife."[36]

Mark the sad majesty of his tone in answer. Who would not have lent a life-long credence to that voice of honor?

> "You are my true and honorable wife,
> As dear to me as are the ruddy drops
> That visit this sad heart."

It is the same voice that tells the moral of his life in the last words—

> "Countrymen,
> My heart doth joy, that yet in all my life,
> I found no man but he was true to me."

It was not wonderful that it should be so.

Shakspeare, however, was not content to let Portia rest her plea for confidence on the essential nature of the marriage bond;

[35] Marcus Junius Brutus (c. 84-42 B.C.), chief assassin of Julius Caesar, fell on his sword after being defeated by Marc Antony. As a result, his wife, Portia, killed herself, supposedly by swallowing burning coals.

[36] This and the lines following are from *Julius Caesar*.

"I grant I am a woman; but withal,
A woman that lord Brutus took to wife.
I grant I am a woman; but withal,
A woman well reputed—Cato's daughter.
Think you I am *no stronger than my sex*,
Being so fathered and so husbanded?"

And afterwards in the very scene where Brutus is suffering under that "insupportable and touching loss," the death of his wife, Cassius pleads—

"Have you not love enough to bear with me,
When that rash humor which my mother gave me
Makes me forgetful?
Brutus.—Yes, Cassius; and henceforth,
When you are over-earnest with your Brutus,
He'll think your mother chides and leave you so."

As indeed it was a frequent belief among the ancients, as with our Indians, that the *body* was inherited from the mother, the *soul* from the father. As in that noble passage of Ovid, already quoted, where Jupiter, as his divine synod are looking down on the funeral pyre of Hercules, thus triumphs—

Nic nisi *maternâ* Vulcanum parte potentem.
Sentiet. Aeternum est, à me quod traxit, et expers
At que immune necis, nullaque domabile flamma
Idque ego defunctum terrâ cœlestibus oris
Accipiam, cunctisque meum lætabile factum
Dis fore confido.
"The part alone of gross *maternal* frame
Fire shall devour, while that from me he drew
Shall live immortal and its force renew;
That, when he's dead, I'll raise to realms above;
Let all the powers the righteous act approve."

It is indeed a god speaking of his union with an earthly woman, but it expresses the common Roman thought as to marriage, the same which permitted a man to lend his wife to a friend, as if she were a chattel.

"She dwelt but in the suburbs of his good pleasure."

Yet the same city as I have said leaned on the worship of Vesta, the Preserver, and in later times was devoted to that of Isis. In Sparta, thought, in this respect as in all others, was expressed in the characters of real life, and the women of Sparta were as much Spartans as the men.[37] The citoyen, citoyenne of France was here actualized. Was not the calm equality they enjoyed as honorable as the devotion of chivalry? They intelligently shared the ideal life of their nation. Like the men they felt

> "Honor gone, all's gone,
> Better never have been born."[38]

They were the true friends of men. The Spartan, surely, would not think that he received only his body from his mother. The sage, had he lived in that community, could not have thought the souls of "vain and foppish men will be degraded after death, to the forms of women, and, if they do not there make great efforts to retrieve themselves, will become birds."

(By the way it is very expressive of the hard intellectuality of the merely *mannish* mind, to speak thus of birds, chosen always by the *feminine* poet as the symbols of his fairest thoughts.)

We are told of the Greek nations in general, that woman occupied there an infinitely lower place than man. It is difficult to believe this when we see such range and dignity of thought on the subject in the mythologies, and find the poets producing such ideals as Cassandra, Iphiginia, Antigone, Macaria, where Sibylline priestesses told the oracle of the highest god, and he could not be content to reign with a court of fewer than nine muses.[39] Even victory wore a female form.[40]

---

[37] Sparta, ancient Greek city known for its strict discipline.

[38] Unidentified.

[39] Cassandra, legendary Trojan princess given the gift of prophecy by Apollo but, because she resisted him, he caused everyone to disbelieve her; Iphigenia, daughter of Agamemnon and Clytemnestra: see p. 225 below; Antigone, daughter of Oedipus and his mother, Jocasta; Macaria, in Goethe's *Wilhelm Meister's Travels* (1821-1829), described by Fuller on p. 170 below as "a pure and perfected intelligence embodied in feminine form"; Sibylline priestesses, mythological women capable of prophecy.

[40] Nike and Victoria were, respectively, the Greek and Roman goddesses of victory.

But whatever were the facts of daily life, I cannot com- plain of the age and nation, which represents its thought by such a symbol as I see before me at this moment. It is a zodiac of the busts of gods and goddesses, arranged in pairs. The circle breathes the music of a heavenly order. Male and female heads are distinct in expression, but equal in beauty, strength and calmness. Each male head is that of a brother and a king—each female of a sister and a queen. Could the thought, thus expressed, be lived out, there would be noth- ing more to be desired. There would be unison in variety, congeniality in difference.

Coming nearer our own time, we find religion and poetry no less true in their revelations. The rude man, just disen- gaged from the sod, the Adam, accuses woman to his God, and records her disgrace to their posterity. He is not ashamed to write that he could be drawn from heaven by one beneath him, one made, he says, from but a small part of himself. But in the same nation, educated by time, instructed by a succes- sion of prophets, we find woman in as high a position as she has ever occupied. No figure that has ever arisen to greet our eyes has been received with more fervent reverence than that of the Madonna. Heine calls her the *Dame du Comptoir* of the Catholic church, and this jeer well expresses a serious truth.

And not only this holy and significant image was worship- ped by the pilgrim, and the favorite subject of the artist, but it exercised an immediate influence on the destiny of the sex. The empresses who embraced the cross, converted sons and husbands. Whole calendars of female saints, heroic dames of chivalry, binding the emblem of faith on the heart of the best-beloved, and wasting the bloom of youth in separation and loneliness, for the sake of duties they thought it religion to assume, with innumerable forms of poesy, trace their line- age to this one. Nor, however imperfect may be the action, in our day, of the faith thus expressed, and though we can scarcely think it nearer this ideal, than that of India or Greece was near their ideal, is it in vain that the truth has been rec- ognized, that woman is not only a part of man, bone of his bone, and flesh of his flesh, born that men might not be lonely, but that women are in themselves possessors of and possessed by immortal souls. This truth undoubtedly received a greater outward stability from the belief of the church that the earthly parent of the Saviour of souls was a woman.

The assumption of the Virgin, as painted by sublime artists, Petrarch's Hymn to the Madonna,* cannot have spoken to the world wholly without result, yet, oftentimes those who had ears heard not.

See upon the nations the influence of this powerful example. In Spain look only at the ballads. Woman in these is "very woman;" she is the betrothed, the bride, the spouse of man, there is on her no hue of the philosopher, the heroine, the savante, but she looks great and noble; why? because she is also, through her deep devotion, the betrothed of heaven. Her upturned eyes have drawn down the light that casts a radiance round her. See only such a ballad as that of "Lady Teresa's Bridal."[41]

Where the Infanta, given to the Moorish bridegroom, calls down the vengeance of Heaven on his unhallowed passion, and thinks it not too much to expiate by a life in the cloister, the involuntary stain upon her princely youth.† It was this constant sense of claims above those of earthly love or happiness that made the Spanish lady who shared this spirit, a guerdon to be won by toils and blood and constant purity, rather than a chattel to be bought for pleasure and service.

Germany did not need to *learn* a high view of woman; it was inborn in that race. Woman was to the Teuton warrior his priestess, his friend, his sister, in truth, a wife. And the Christian statues of noble pairs, as they lie above their graves in stone, expressing the meaning of all the by-gone pilgrimage by hands folded in mutual prayer, yield not a nobler sense of the place and powers of woman, than belonged to the altvater day. The holy love of Christ which summoned them, also, to choose "the better part, that which could not be taken from them," refined and hallowed in this nation a native faith, thus showing that it was not the warlike spirit alone that left the Latins so barbarous in this respect.

---

* Appendix, B. [Fuller's note.] Appendix B is printed on pp. 210-14.
[41] Lady Teresa (1515-1582), Spanish saint, author, and Carmelite nun.
† Appendix, C. [Fuller's note.] Appendix C is printed on pp. 214-16.

But the Germans, taking so kindly to this thought, did it the more justice. The idea of woman in their literature is expressed both to a greater height and depth than elsewhere.

I will give as instances the themes of three ballads.

One is upon a knight who had always the name of the Virgin on his lips. This protected him all his life through, in various and beautiful modes, both from sin and other dangers, and, when he died, a plant sprang from his grave, which so gently whispered the Ave Maria that none could pass it by with an unpurified heart.

Another is one of the legends of the famous Drachenfels.[42] A maiden, one of the earliest converts to Christianity, was carried by the enraged populace to this dread haunt of "the dragon's fabled brood," to be their prey. She was left alone, but unafraid, for she knew in whom she trusted. So, when the dragons came rushing towards her, she showed them a crucifix and they crouched reverently at her feet. Next day the people came, and seeing these wonders, are all turned to to the faith which exalts the lowly.

The third I have in mind is another of the Rhine legends. A youth is sitting with the maid he loves on the shore of an isle, her fairy kingdom, then perfumed by the blossoming grape vines, which draped its bowers. They are happy; all blossoms with them, and life promises its richest wine. A boat approaches on the tide; it pauses at their feet. It brings, perhaps, some joyous message, fresh dew for their flowers, fresh light on the wave. No! it is the usual check on such great happiness. The father of the Count departs for the crusade; will his son join him, or remain to rule their domain, and wed her he loves? Neither of the affianced pair hesitate a moment. "I must go with my father." "Thou must go with thy father." It was one thought, one word. "I will be here again," he said, "when these blossoms have turned to purple grapes." "I hope so," she sighed, while the prophetic sense said "no."

And there she waited, and the grapes ripened, and were gathered into the vintage, and he came not. Year after year passed thus, and no tidings; yet still she waited.

[42] Drachenfels, literally the "Dragon's Rock," a mountain range in western Germany, home of the legendary dragon slain by Siegfried.

He, meanwhile, was in a Moslem prison. Long he lan-
guished there without hope, till, at last, his patron saint appeared in vision and announced his release, but only on condition of his joining the monastic order for the service of the
saint.

And so his release was effected, and a safe voyage home
given. And once more he sets sail upon the Rhine. The maid-
en, still watching beneath the vines, sees at last the object
of all this patient love approach. Approach, but not to touch
the strand to which she, with outstretched arms, has rushed.
He dares not trust himself to land, but in low, heart-broken
tones, tells her of heaven's will; and that he, in obedience
to his vow, is now on his way to a convent on the river bank,
there to pass the rest of his earthly life in the service of the
shrine. And then he turns his boat, and floats away from her
and hope of any happiness in this world, but urged, as he believes, by the breath of heaven.

The maiden stands appalled, but she dares not murmur,
and cannot hesitate long. She also bids them prepare her
boat. She follows her lost love to the convent gate, requests
an interview with the abbot, and devotes her Elysian isle,
where vines had ripened their ruby fruit in vain for her, to
the service of the monastery where her love was to serve.
Then, passing over to the nunnery opposite, she takes the
veil, and meets her betrothed at the altar; and for a life long
union, if not the one they had hoped in earlier years.

Is not this sorrowful story of a lofty beauty? Does it not
show a sufficiently high view of woman, of marriage? This
is commonly the chivalric, still more the German view.

Yet, wherever there was a balance in the mind of man of
sentiment, with intellect, such a result was sure. The Greek
Xenophon has not only painted as a sweet picture of the domestic woman, in his Economics, but in the Cyropedia has
given, in the picture of Panthea,[43] a view of woman which
no German picture can surpass, whether lonely and quiet
with veiled lids, the temple of a vestal loveliness, or with
eyes flashing, and hair flowing to the free wind, cheering on

---

[43] Xenophon (c. 430-354 B.C.), Greek historian and essayist. His *Cyropædia* traces the life of Cyrus, ruler of Persia; for the story of Panthea, see
p. 139.

the hero to fight for his God, his country, or whatever name
his duty might bear at the time. This picture I shall copy by
and by. Yet Xenophon grew up in the same age with him who
makes Iphigenia say to Achilles—

"Better a thousand women should perish than one man cease to
see the light."[44]

This was the vulgar Greek sentiment. Xenophon, aiming at
the ideal man, caught glimpses of the ideal woman also.
From the figure of a Cyrus, the Pantheas stand not afar. They
do not in thought; they would not in life.

I could swell the catalogue of instances far beyond the
reader's patience. But enough have been brought forward
to show that, though there has been great disparity betwixt
the nations as between individuals in their culture on this
point, yet the idea of woman has always cast some rays and
often been forcibly represented.

Far less has woman to complain that she has not had her
share of power. This, in all ranks of society, except the lowest, has been hers to the extent that vanity would crave, far
beyond what wisdom would accept. In the very lowest, where
man, pressed by poverty, sees in woman only the partner of
toils and cares, and cannot hope, scarcely has an idea of, a
comfortable home, he often maltreats her, and is less influenced by her. In all ranks, those who are gentle and un-
complaining, too candid to intrigue, too delicate to encroach,
suffer much. They suffer long, and are kind; verily, they
have their reward. But wherever man is sufficiently raised
above extreme poverty or brutal stupidity, to care for the
comforts of the fireside, or the bloom and ornament of life,
woman has always power enough, if she choose to exert it,
and is usually disposed to do so, in proportion to her ignorance and childish vanity. Unacquainted with the importance
of life and its purposes, trained to a selfish coquetry and
love of petty power, she does not look beyond the pleasure
of making herself felt at the moment, and governments are
shaken and commerce broken up to gratify the pique of a
female favorite. The English shopkeeper's wife does not
vote, but it is for her interest that the politician canvasses by

[44] Euripides, *Iphigenia at Aulis*.

the coarsest flattery. France suffers no woman on her throne, but her proud nobles kiss the dust at the feet of Pompadour and Du Barry;[45] for such flare in the lighted foreground where a Roland would modestly aid in the closet.[46] Spain, (that same Spain which sang of Ximena and the Lady Teresa,) shuts up her women in the care of duennas, and allows them no book but the Breviary, but the ruin follows only the more surely from the worthless favorite of a worthless queen.[47] Relying on mean precautions, men indeed cry peace, peace, where there is no peace.

It is not the transient breath of poetic incense that women want; each can receive that from a lover. It is not life-long sway; it needs but to become a coquette, a shrew, or a good cook, to be sure of that. It is not money, nor notoriety, nor the badges of authority that men have appropriated to themselves. If demands, made in their behalf, lay stress on any of these particulars, those who make them have not searched deeply into the need. It is for that which at once includes these and precludes them; which would not be forbidden power, lest there be temptation to steal and misuse it; which would not have the mind perverted by flattery from a worthiness of esteem. It is for that which is the birthright of every being capable to receive it,—the freedom, the religious, the intelligent freedom of the universe, to use its means; to learn its secret as far as nature has enabled them, with God alone for their guide and their judge.

Ye cannot believe it, men; but the only reason why women ever assume what is more appropriate to you, is because you prevent them from finding out what is fit for themselves. Were they free, were they wise fully to develop the strength and beauty of woman; they would never wish to be men, or manlike. The well-instructed moon flies not from her orbit to seize on the glories of her partner. No; for she knows that one law rules, one heaven contains, one universe replies to them alike. It is with women as with the slave.

[45] Marquise de Pompadour (1721-1764) and Comtesse du Barry (1746-1793), mistresses and influential counsels of Louis XV of France.

[46] Madam Roland; see note 11, p. 91.

[47] Ximena, wife of the heroic Cid of Spanish legend; Lady Teresa, see p. 116 above and Appendix C, pp. 214-16; the Breviary of Alaric, a sixth-century law code.

"Vor dem Sklaven, wenn er die Kette bricht,
Vor dem freien Menschen erzittert nicht."[48]

Tremble not before the free man, but before the slave who has chains to break.

In slavery, acknowledged slavery, women are on a par with men. Each is a work-tool, an article of property, no more! In perfect freedom, such as is painted in Olympus, in Swedenborg's angelic state, in the heaven where there is no marrying nor giving in marriage, each is a purifed intelligence, an enfranchised soul,—no less![49]

Jene himmlische Gestalten
Sie fragen nicht nach Mann and Weib,
Und keine kleider, keine Falten
Umgeben den verklarten Leib.[50]

The child who sang this was a prophetic form, expressive of the longing for a state of perfect freedom, pure love. She could not remain here, but was transplanted to another air. And it may be that the air of this earth will never be so tempered that such can bear it long. But, while they stay, they must bear testimony to the truth they are constituted to demand.

That an era approaches which shall approximate nearer to such a temper than any has yet done, there are many tokens, indeed so many, that only a few of the most prominent can here be enumerated.

The reigns of Elizabeth of England and Isabella of Castile foreboded this era.[51] They expressed the beginning of the new state, while they forwarded its progress. These were strong characters and in harmony with the wants of their time. One showed that this strength did not unfit a woman

---

[48] Schiller, *Gedichte. Die Worte des Glaubens*, Str. 2.

[49] Olympus, a mountaintop on which the Greek gods and goddesses dwelt; Emanuel Swedenborg (1688-1722), Swedish mystic and scientist.

[50] "In that celestial form
 You do not ask about man and wife,
 And in no dress, no folds,
 Do you surround that transfigured body."
Unidentified.

[51] Queen Isabella I (1451-1504), united Castille and Aragon by her marriage to Ferdinand of Aragon, making Spain a single political unit.

for the duties of a wife and a mother, the other that it could enable her to live and die alone, a wide energetic life, a courageous death. Elizabeth is certainly no pleasing example. In rising above the weakness, she did not lay aside the weaknesses ascribed to her sex; but her strength must be respected now, as it was in her own time.

Elizabeth and Mary Stuart seem types, moulded by the spirit of the time, and placed upon an elevated platform to show to the coming ages, woman such as the conduct and wishes of man in general is likely to make her, lovely even to allurement, quick in apprehension and weak in judgment, with grace and dignity of sentiment, but no principle; credulous and indiscreet, yet artful; capable of sudden greatness or of crime, but not of a steadfast wisdom, or self-restraining virtue; and woman half-emancipated and jealous of her freedom, such as she has figured before and since in many a combative attitude, mannish, not equally manly, strong and prudent more than great or wise; able to control vanity, and the wish to rule through coquetry and passion, but not to resign these dear deceits, from the very foundation, as unworthy a being capable of truth and nobleness. Elizabeth, taught by adversity, put on her virtues as armor, more than produced them in a natural order from her soul. The time and her position called on her to act the wise sovereign, and she was proud that she could do so, but her tastes and inclinations would have led her to act the weak woman. She was without magnanimity of any kind.

We may accept as an omen for ourselves, that it was Isabella who furnished Columbus with the means of coming hither. This land must pay back its debt to woman, without whose aid it would not have been brought into alliance with the civilized world.

A graceful and meaning figure is that introduced to us by Mr. Prescott, in the Conquest of Mexico, in the Indian girl Marina, who accompanied Cortes, and was his interpreter in all the various difficulties of his career. She stood at his side, on the walls of the besieged palace, to plead with her enraged countrymen. By her name he was known in New Spain, and, after the conquest, her gentle intercession was often of avail to the conquered. The poem of the Future may be read in some features of the story of "Malinche."[52]

The influence of Elizabeth on literature was real, though, by sympathy with its finer productions, she was no more entitled to give name to an era than Queen Anne.[53] It was simply that the fact of having a female sovereign on the throne affected the course of a writer's thoughts. In this sense, the presence of a woman on the throne always makes its mark. Life is lived before the eyes of men, by which their imaginations are stimulated as to the possibilities of woman. "We will die for our King, Maria Theresa," cry the wild warriors, clashing their swords, and the sounds vibrate through the poems of that generation. The range of female character in Spenser alone might content us for one period. Britomart and Belphœbe have as much room on the canvass as Florimel; and where this is the case, the haughtiest amazon will not murmur that Una should be felt to be the fairest type.[54]

Unlike as was the English Queen to a fairy queen, we may yet conceive that it was the image of *a* queen before the poet's mind, that called up this splendid court of women. Shakspeare's range is also great; but he has left out the heroic characters, such as the Macaria of Greece, the Britomart of Spenser.[55] Ford and Massinger have, in this respect, soared to a higher flight of feeling than he.[56] It was the holy and heroic woman they most loved, and if they could not paint an

---

[52] William Hickling Prescott (1796-1859), American historian whose *History of the Conquest of Mexico* was published in 1843; Hernando Cortes (1485-1547), conqueror of Mexico for Spain; Malinche, Indian slave girl acting as Cortes' guide and mistress, baptised "Marina" by him.

[53] Anne Boleyn (*c.* 1507-1536), second wife of Henry VIII, beheaded by him. The length of her reign has made her known as "Anne of the Thousand Days."

[54] Edmund Spenser (*c.* 1552-1579), English poet whose *Faerie Queen* (1590-1596) portrays Britomart as a female knight personifying chastity, Belphoebe as representative of Queen Elizabeth as a young woman, Florimel as a good chaste lady symbolizing the charm of womanhood, and Una as the personification of truth.

[55] Macaria, in Euripides, *The Children of Hercules*, sacrifices herself to save her brothers and sisters.

[56] John Ford (1586-*c.*1639) and Philip Massinger (1583-1640), English dramatists.

Imogen, a Desdemona, a Rosalind, yet, in those of a stronger mould, they showed a higher ideal, though with so much less poetic power to embody it, than we see in Portia or Isabella. The simple truth of Cordelia, indeed, is of this sort.[57] The beauty of Cordelia is neither male nor female; it is the beauty of virtue.

The ideal of love and marriage rose high in the mind of all the Christian nations who were capable of grave and deep feeling. We may take as examples of its English aspect, the lines,

> "I could not love thee, dear, so much,
> Loved I not honor more."[58]

Or the address of the Commonwealth's man to his wife, as she looked out from the Tower window to see him for the last time, on his way to the scaffold. He stood up in the cart, waved his hat, and cried, "To Heaven, my love, to Heaven, and leave you in the storm?"

Such was the love of faith and honor, a love which stopped, like Colonel Hutchinson's, "on this side idolatry," because it was religious.[59] The meeting of two such souls Donne describes as giving birth to an "abler soul."[60]

Lord Herbert wrote to his love,

> "Were not our souls immortal made,
> Our equal loves can make them such."[61]

In the "Broken Heart" of Ford, Penthea, a character which engages my admiration even more deeply than the famous one of Calanthe, is made to present to the mind the most beautiful picture of what these relations should be in their

---

[57] Characters in Shakespeare's plays: Imogen, daughter of the title character in *Cymbeline*; Desdemona, murdered by her husband in a fit of misdirected jealousy in *Othello*; Rosalind, loves Orlando in *As You Like It* (1623); and Cordelia, Lear's youngest daughter and the only one to aid her father in *King Lear* (1608).

[58] Richard Lovelace (1618-1658), "To Lucasta, Going to the Wars."

[59] Thomas Hutchinson (1711-1780), American official who supported Parliamentary supremacy over the colonies.

[60] John Donne (1573?-1631), English metaphysical poet, quoted from "The Exstacie."

[61] Edward Herbert (1583-1648), English philosophical poet, quoted from "An Ode upon a Question moved, Whether Love should continue forever?"

purity. Her life cannot sustain the violation of what she so clearly felt.[62]

Shakspeare, too, saw that, in true love as in fire, the utmost ardor is coincident with the utmost purity. It is a true lover that exclaims in the agony of Othello,

"If thou art false, O then Heaven mocks itself."[63]

The son, framed like Hamlet, to appreciate truth in all the beauty of relations, sinks into deep melancholy, when he finds his natural expectations disappointed. He has no mother. She to whom he gave the name, disgraces from his heart's shrine all the sex.

"Frailty, thy name is woman."

It is because a Hamlet could find cause to say so, that I have put the line, whose stigma has never been removed, at the head of my work. But, as a lover, surely a Hamlet would not have so far mistook, as to have finished with such a conviction. He would have felt the faith of Othello, and that faith could not, in his more dispassionate mind, have been disturbed by calumny.

In Spain, this thought is arrayed in a sublimity, which belongs to the sombre and passionate genius of the nation. Calderon's Justina resists all the temptation of the Demon, and raises her lover, with her, above the sweet lures of mere temporal happiness.[64] Their marriage is vowed at the stake; their souls are liberated together by the martyr flame into "a purer state of sensation and existence."

In Italy, the great poets wove into their lives an ideal love which answered to the highest wants. It included those of the intellect and the affections, for it was a love of spirit for spirit. It was not ascetic, or superhuman, but, interpreting all things, gave their proper beauty to details of the common life, the common day; the poet spoke of his love, not as a flower to place in his bosom, or hold carelessly in his hand,

---

[62] In Ford's play *The Broken Heart* (1633), Calanthe dies of a broken heart after hearing of the deaths of her father, brother, and friend; Panthea dies driven mad by a forced, unhappy marriage.

[63] *Othello*, III, iii, 1. 278.

[64] Pedro Calderón de la Barca (1600-1681), Spanish poet and dramatist. Justina appears in his religious play, *El Magico Prodigioso* (1637).

but as a light towards which he must find wings to fly, or "a stair to heaven." He delighted to speak of her, not only as the bride of his heart, but the mother of his soul; for he saw that, in cases where the right direction had been taken, the greater delicacy of her frame, and stillness of her life, left her more open to spiritual influx than man is. So he did not look upon her as betwixt him and earth, to serve his temporal needs, but, rather, betwixt him and heaven, to purify his affections and lead him to wisdom through love. He sought, in her, not so much the Eve, as the Madonna.

In these minds the thought, which gleams through all the legends of chivalry, shines in broad intellectual effulgence, not to be misinterpreted, and their thought is reverenced by the world, though it lies so far from the practice of the world as yet, so far, that it seems as though a gulf of death yawned between.

Even with such men, the practice was, often, widely different from the mental faith. I say mental, for if the heart were thoroughly alive with it, the practice could not be dissonant. Lord Herbert's was a marriage of convention, made for him at fifteen; he was not discontented with it, but looked only to the advantages it brought of perpetuating his family on the basis of a great fortune. He paid, in act, what he considered a dutiful attention to the bond; his thoughts travelled elsewhere; and while forming a high ideal of the companionship of minds in marriage, he seems never to have doubted that its realization must be postponed to some other state of being. Dante, almost immediately after the death of Beatrice, married a lady chosen for him by his friends,[65] and Boccaccio, in describing the miseries that attended, in this case,

"The form of an union where union is none,"

speaks as if these were inevitable to the connection, and the scholar and poet, especially, could expect nothing but misery and obstruction in a domestic partnership with woman.

Centuries have passed since, but civilized Europe is still

---

[65] Dante Aligheri (1265-1321), great Italian poet, held Beatrice Portinari as his courtly ideal and source of poetic inspiration. Following her death in 1290, he married Gemma Donati, to whom he had been betrothed as a boy.

in a transition state about marriage; not only in practice, but in thought. It is idle to speak with contempt of the nations where polygamy is an institution, or seraglios[66] a custom, when practices far more debasing haunt, well nigh fill, every city and every town. And so far as union of one with one is believed to be the only pure form of marriage, a great majority of societies and individuals are still doubtful whether the earthly bond must be a meeting of souls, or only supposes a contract of convenience and utility. Were woman established in the rights of an immortal being, this could not be. She would not, in some countries, be given away by her father, with scarcely more respect for her feelings than is shown by the Indian chief, who sells his daughter for a horse, and beats her if she runs away from her new home. Nor, in societies where her choice is left free, would she be perverted, by the current of opinion that seizes her, into the belief that she must marry, if it be only to find a protector, and a home of her own.

Neither would man, if he thought the connection of permanent importance, form it so lightly. He would not deem it a trifle, that he was to enter into the closest relations with another soul, which, if not eternal in themselves, must eternally affect his growth.

Neither, did he believe woman capable of friendship,* would he, by rash haste, lose the chance of finding a friend in the person who might, probably, live half a century by his side. Did love, to his mind, stretch forth into infinity, he would not miss his chance of its revelations, that he might, the sooner, rest from his weariness by a bright fireside, and secure a sweet and graceful attendant "devoted to him alone." Were he a step higher, he would not carelessly enter into a relation where he might not be able to do the duty of a friend, as well as a protector from external ill, to the other party, and have a being in his power pining for sympathy, intelligence and aid, that he could not give.

What deep communion, what real intercourse is implied by the sharing the joys and cares of parentage, when any degree

[66] "seraglios." Muslim harems.
* See Appendix D, Spinoza's view. [Fuller's note.] Appendix D is printed on pp. 216-23.

of equality is admitted between the parties! It is true that, in a majority of instances, the man looks upon his wife as an adopted child, and places her to the other children in the relation of nurse or governess, rather than of parent. Her influence with them is sure, but she misses the education which should enlighten that influence, by being thus treated. It is the order of nature that children should complete the education, moral and mental, of parents, by making them think what is needed for the best culture of human beings, and conquer all faults and impulses that interfere with their giving this to these dear objects, who represent the world to them. Father and mother should assist one another to learn what is required for this sublime priesthood of nature. But, for this, a religious recognition of equality is required.

Where this thought of equality begins to diffuse itself, it is shown in four ways.

The household partnership. In our country, the woman looks for a "smart but kind" husband; the man for a "capable, sweet-tempered" wife.

The man furnishes the house; the woman regulates it. Their relation is one of mutual esteem, mutual dependence. Their talk is of business, their affection shows itself by practical kindness. They know that life goes more smoothly and cheerfully to each for the other's aid; they are grateful and content. The wife praises her husband as a "good provider;" the husband, in return, compliments her as a "capital housekeeper." This relation is good, as far as it goes.

Next comes a closer tie, which takes the two forms, either of mutual idolatry, or of intellectual companionship. The first, we suppose, is to no one a pleasing subject of contemplation. The parties weaken and narrow one another; they lock the gate against all the glories of the universe, that they may live in a cell together. To themselves they seem the only wise, to all others steeped in infatuation; the gods smile as they look forward to the crisis of cure; to men, the woman seems an unlovely syren; to women, the man an effeminate boy.

The other form, of intellectual companionship, has become more and more frequent. Men engaged in public life, literary men, and artists, have often found in their wives companions and confidants in thought no less than in feeling. And as the intellectual development of woman has spread wider and risen higher, they have, not unfrequently, shared the same employment. As in the case of Roland and his wife, who were friends in the household and in the nation's councils, read, regulated home affairs, or prepared public documents together, indifferently.[67]

It is very pleasant, in letters begun by Roland, and finished by his wife, to see the harmony of mind, and the difference of nature; one thought, but various ways of treating it.

This is one of the best instances of a marriage of friendship. It was only friendship, whose basis was esteem; probably neither party knew love, except by name.

Roland was a good man, worthy to esteem, and be esteemed; his wife as deserving of admiration, as able to do without it. Madame Roland is the fairest specimen we have yet of her class, as clear to discern her aim, as valiant to pursue it, as Spenser's Britomart; austerely set apart from all that did not belong to her, whether as woman or as mind. She is an antetype of a class to which the coming time will afford a field, the Spartan matron, brought by the culture of the age of Books to intellectual consciousness and expansion.

Self-sufficingness, strength, and clear-sightedness were, in her, combined with a power of deep and calm affection. She, too, would have given a son or husband the device for his shield, "Return with it or upon it;" and this, not because she loved little, but much. The page of her life is one of unsullied dignity.

Her appeal to posterity is one against the injustice of those who committed such crimes in the name of Liberty. She makes it in behalf of herself and her husband. I would put beside it, on the shelf, a little volume, containing a similar appeal from the verdict of contemporaries to that of mankind, made by Godwin in behalf of his wife, the celebrated, the, by most men, detested, Mary Wolstonecraft.[68] In his view, it was

[67] Jean Marie Roland (1734-1793) committed suicide when he learned of his wife's execution during the French Revolution. Her last words are said to be "O Liberty, what crimes are committed in thy name!"

[68] William Godwin (1756-1836), English political philosopher, married the woman's rights advocate Mary Wolstonecraft (1759-1797) in 1797. Her most famous work is *Vindication of the Rights of Women* (1792).

an appeal from the injustice of those who did such wrong in the name of virtue.

Were this little book interesting for no other cause, it would be so for the generous affection evinced under the peculiar circumstances. This man had courage to love and honor this woman in the face of the world's sentence, and of all that was repulsive in her own past history. He believed he saw of what soul she was, and that the impulses she had struggled to act out were noble, though the opinions to which they had led might not be thoroughly weighed. He loved her, and he defended her for the meaning and tendency of her inner life. It was a good fact.

Mary Wolstonecraft, like Madame Dudevant, (commonly known as George Sand,) in our day, was a woman whose existence better proved the need of some new interpretation of woman's rights, than any thing she wrote.[69] Such beings as these, rich in genius, of most tender sympathies, capable of high virtue and a chastened harmony, ought not to find themselves, by birth, in a place so narrow, that, in breaking bonds, they become outlaws. Were there as much room in the world for such, as in Spenser's poem for Britomart, they would not run their heads so wildly against the walls, but prize their shelter rather. They find their way, at last, to light and air, but the world will not take off the brand it has set upon them. The champion of the Rights of Woman found, in Godwin, one who would plead that cause like a brother. He who delineated with such purity of traits the form of woman in the Marguerite, of whom the weak St. Leon could never learn to be worthy, a pearl indeed whose price was above rubies, was not false in life to the faith by which he had hallowed his romance.[70] He acted as he wrote, like a brother. This form of appeal rarely fails to touch the basest man. "Are you acting towards other women in the way you would have men act towards your sister?" George Sand smokes, wears male attire, wishes to be addressed as "Mon frère;"—perhaps, if she found those who were as brothers, indeed, she would not

[69] Baroness Dudevant (1804-1876), French novelist and playwright writing as George Sand, also known for her independent private life, which included affairs with the poet Alfred de Musset and Frédéric Chopin.

[70] Marguerite, heroine of Godwin's novel St. Leon (1799).

care whether she were brother or sister.*

* Since writing the above, I have read with great satisfaction, the following sonnets addressed to George Sand by a woman who has precisely the qualities that the author of Simon and Indiana lacks. It is such a woman, so unblemished in character, so high in aim, and pure in soul, that should address this other, as noble in nature, but clouded by error, and struggling with circumstances. It is such women that will do justice. They are not afraid to look for virtue and reply to aspiration, among those who have *not* "dwelt in decencies forever." It is a source of pride and happiness to read this address from the heart of Elizabeth Barrett.

TO GEORGE SAND.

A DESIRE.

Thou large-brained woman and large-hearted man,
   Self-called George Sand! whose soul, amid the lions
   Of thy tumultuous senses moans defiance,
And answers roar for roar, as spirits can:
I would some mild miraculous thunder ran
   Above the applauded circus, in appliance
   Of thine own nobler nature's strength and science,
   Drawing two pinions, white as wings of swan,
From the strong shoulders, to amaze the place
   With holier light! that thou to woman's claim,
And man's might join, beside, the angel's grace
   Of a pure genius sanctified from blame;
Till child and maiden pressed to thine embrace,
   To kiss upon thy lips a stainless fame.

TO THE SAME.

A RECOGNITION.

True genius, but true woman! dost deny
   Thy woman's nature with a manly scorn,
And break away the gauds and armlets worn
   By weaker women in captivity?
Ah, vain denial! that revolted cry
   Is sobbed in by a woman's voice forlorn:—
Thy woman's hair, my sister, all unshorn,
   Floats back dishevelled strength in agony,
Disproving thy man's name, and while before
   The world thou burnest a poet-fire,
We see thy woman-heart beat evermore
   Through the large flame. Beat purer, heart, and higher,
Till God unsex thee on the spirit-shore;
   To which alone unsexing, purely aspire.

This last sonnet seems to have been written after seeing the pic-

We rejoice to see that she, who expresses such a painful contempt for men in most of her works, as shows she must have known great wrong from them, depicting in "La Roche Mauprat," a man raised by the workings of love, from the depths of savage sensualism, to a moral and intellectual life.[71] It was love for a pure object, for a steadfast woman, one of those who, the Italian said, could make the stair to heaven.

This author, beginning like the many in assault upon bad institutions, and external ills, yet deepening the experience through comparative freedom, sees at last, that the only efficient remedy must come from individual character. These bad institutions, indeed, it may always be replied, prevent individuals from forming good character, therefore we must remove them. Agreed, yet keep steadily the higher aim in view. Could you clear away all the bad forms of society, it is vain, unless the individual begin to be ready for better. There must be a parallel movement in these two branches of life. And all the rules left by Moses availed less to further the best life than the living example of one Messiah.

Still, still the mind of the age struggles confusedly with these problems, better discerning as yet the ill it can no longer bear, than the good by which it may supersede it. But women, like Sand, will speak now and cannot be silenced; their characters and their eloquence alike foretell an era when such as they shall easier learn to lead true lives. But though such forebode, not such shall be the parents of it.* Those who would reform the world must show that they do not speak in the heat of wild impulse; their lives must be unstained by passionate error; they must be severe lawgivers to themselves. They must be religious students of the divine

---

ture of Sand, which represents her in a man's dress, but with long loose hair, and an eye whose mournful fire is impressive even in the caricatures. [Fuller's note.]

Sand published her novels *Simon* and *Indiana* in, respectively, 1836 and 1832. Elizabeth Barrett (1806-1861), English poet who married her fellow poet Robert Browning in 1846, quoted from her *Poems* (1844).

For an example of the type of picture of Sand which Fuller mentions, see Frances Winwar, *The Life and the Heart: George Sand and Her Times* (New York: Harpers, 1945), facing p. 220.

[71] Sand's *Mauprat*, a novel of an idealized love, was published in 1837.

* Appendix, E. [Fuller's note.] Appendix E is printed on pp. 223-224.

purpose with regard to man, if they would not confound the fancies of a day with the requisitions of eternal good. Their liberty must be the liberty of law and knowledge. But, as to the transgressions against custom which have caused such outcry against those of noble intention, it may be observed, that the resolve of Eloisa to be only the mistress of Abelard, was that of one who saw in practice around her, the contract of marriage made the seal of degradation. Shelley feared not to be fettered, unless so to be was to be false. Wherever abuses are seen, the timid will suffer; the bold will protest. But society has a right to outlaw them till she has revised her law; and this she must be taught to do, by one who speaks with authority, not in anger or haste.

If Godwin's choice of the calumniated authoress of the "Rights of Woman," for his honored wife, be a sign of a new era, no less so is an article to which I have alluded some pages back, published five or six years ago in one of the English Reviews, where the writer, in doing full justice to Eloisa, shows his bitter regret that she lives not now to love him, who might have known better how to prize her love than did the egotistical Abelard.

These marriages, these characters, with all their imperfections, express an onward tendency. They speak of aspiration of soul, of energy of mind, seeking clearness and freedom. Of a like promise are the tracts lately published by Goodwyn Barmby, (the European Pariah, as he calls himself,) and his wife Catharine.[72] Whatever we may think of their measures, we see in them wedlock; the two minds are wed by the only contract that can permanently avail, of a common faith and a common purpose.

We might mention instances, nearer home, of minds, partners in work and in life, sharing together, on equal terms, public and private interests, and which wear not, on any side, the aspect of offence shown by those last-named: persons who steer straight onward, yet, in our comparatively free life, have not been obliged to run their heads against any wall. But the principles which guide them might, under petrified and oppressive institutions, have made them warlike,

[72] John Goodwyn Barmby (1820-1881), Christian socialist. Pariahs are outcasts.

paradoxical, and in some sense, Pariahs. The phenomena are different, the law is the same, in all these cases. Men and women have been obliged to build up their house anew from the very foundation. If they found stone ready in the quarry, they took it peaceably, other wise they alarmed the country by pulling down old towers to get materials.

These are all instances of marriage as intellectual companionship. The parties meet mind to mind, and a mutual trust is produced, which can buckler them against a million. They work together for a common purpose, and, in all these instances, with the same implement, the pen. The pen and the writing-desk furnish forth as naturally the retirement of woman as of man.

A pleasing expression, in this kind, is afforded by the union in the names of the Howitts. William and Mary Howitt we heard named together for years, supposing them to be brother and sister; the equality of labors and reputation, even so, was auspicious; more so, now we find them man and wife. In his late work on Germany, Howitt mentions his wife, with pride, as one among the constellation of distinguished English-women, and in a graceful simple manner.[73]

Our pleasure, indeed, in this picture, is marred by the vulgar apparition which has of late displaced the image, which we had from her writings cherished of a pure and gentle Quaker poetess. The surprise was painful as that of the little sentimentalist in the tale of "L'Amie Inconnue" when she found her correspondent, the poetess, the "adored Araminta," scolding her servants in Welsh, and eating toasted cheese and garlic. Still, we cannot forget what we have thought of the partnership in literature and affection between the Howitts, the congenial pursuits and productions, the pedestrian tours where the married pair showed that marriage, on a wide enough basis, does not destroy the "inexhaustible" entertainment which lovers found in one another's company.

In naming these instances, I do not mean to imply that community of employment is essential to union of husband and wife, more than to the union of friends. Harmony exists

[73] William (1792-1879) and Mary (1799-1888) Howitt, English authors. His *The Rural and Domestic Life of Germany* was published in 1842.

in difference, no less than in likeness, If only the same key-note govern both parts. Woman the poem, man the poet! Woman the heart, man the head! Such divisions are only important when they are never to be transcended. If nature is never bound down, nor the voice of inspiration stifled, that is enough. We are pleased that women should write and speak, if they feel the need of it, from having something to tell; but silence for ages would be no misfortune, if that silence be from divine command, and not from man's tradition.

While Goetz Von Berlichingen rides to battle, his wife is busy in the kitchen; but difference of occupation does not prevent that community of inward life, that perfect esteem, with which he says—

"Whom God loves, to him gives he such a wife."[74]

Manzoni thus dedicates his "Adelchi."

"To his beloved and venerated wife, Enrichetta Luigia Blondel, who, with conjugal affection and maternal wisdom, has preserved a virgin mind, the author dedicates this "Adelchi," grieving that he could not, by a more splendid and more durable monument, honor the dear name, and the memory of so many virtues."

The relation could not be fairer, or more equal, if she, too, had written poems. Yet the position of the parties might have been the reverse as well; the woman might have sung the deeds, given voice to the life of the man, and beauty would have been the result, as we see, in pictures of Arcadia, the nymph singing to the shepherds, or the shepherd, with his pipe, alluring the nymphs;[75] either makes a good picture. The sounding lyre requires, not muscular strength, but energy of soul to animate the hand which would control it. Nature seems to delight in varying the arrangements, as if to show that she will be fettered by no rule, and we must admit the same varieties that she admits.

The fourth and highest grade of marriage union, is the religious, which may be expressed as pilgrimage towards a

---

[74] Götz von Berlichingen (c.1480-1562), German feudal knight. Fuller quotes from Goethe's play named after him published in 1773.

[75] Arcadia, isolated mountain area in ancient Greece known for its simplicity.

common shrine. This includes the others; home sympathies
and household wisdom, for these pilgrims must know how to
assist each other along the dusty way; intellectual communion, for how sad it would be on such a journey to have a
companion to whom you could not communicate thoughts
and aspirations as they sprang to life; who would have no
feeling for the prospects that open, more and more glorious
as we advance; who would never see the flowers that may be
gathered by the most industrious traveller. It must include all
these. Such a fellow-pilgrim Count Zinzendorf seems to have
found in his Countess, of whom he thus writes:

"Twenty-five years' experience has shown me that just the
help-mate whom I have, is the only one that could suit my
vocation. Who else could have so carried through my family
affairs? Who lived so spotlessly before the world? Who so
wisely aided me in my rejection of a dry morality? Who so
clearly set aside the Pharisaism which, as years passed,
threatened to creep in among us? Who so deeply discerned
as to the spirits of delusion, which sought to bewilder us?
Who would have governed my whole economy so wisely,
richly, and hospitably, when circumstances commanded?
Who have taken indifferently the part of servant or mistress,
without, on the one side, affecting an especial spirituality; on
the other, being sullied by any wordly pride? Who, in a community where all ranks are eager to be on a level, would,
from wise and real causes, have known how to maintain inward and outward distinctions? Who, without a murmur,
have seen her husband encounter such dangers by land and
sea? Who undertaken with him, and *sustained* such astonishing pilgrimages? Who, amid such difficulties, always held up
her head and supported me? Who found such vast sums of
money, and acquitted them on her own credit? And, finally,
who, of all human beings, could so well understand and interpret to others my inner and outer being as this one, of such
nobleness in her way of thinking, such great intellectual
capacity, and free from the theological perplexities that
enveloped me!"[76]

Let any one peruse, with all their power, the lineaments of
this portrait, and see if the husband had not reason, with this

[76] Nicholaus Ludwig Graf von Zinzendorf (1700-1760), German prelate.

air of solemn rapture and conviction, to challenge comparison? We are reminded of the majestic cadence of the line
whose feet step in the just proportions of Humanity,

"Daughter of God and Man, accomplished Eve!"[77]

An observer* adds this testimony:

"We may, in many marriages, regard it as the best arrangement, if the man has so much advantage over his wife,
that she can, without much thought of her own, be, by him,
led and directed as by a father. But it was not so with the
Count and his consort. She was not made to be a copy; she
was an original; and, while she loved and honored him, she
thought for herself, on all subjects, with so much intelligence, that he could and did look on her as sister and friend
also."

Compare with this refined specimen of a religiously
civilized life, the following imperfect sketch of a North
American Indian, and we shall see that the same causes will
always produce the same results. The Flying Pigeon (Ratchewaine) was the wife of a barbarous chief, who had six
others, but she was his only true wife, because the only one
of a strong and pure character, and, having this, inspired a
veneration, as like as the mind of the man permitted, to that
inspired by the Countess Zinzendorf. She died when her son
was only four years old, yet left on his mind a feeling of
reverent love worthy the thought of Christian chivalry.
Grown to manhood, he shed tears on seeing her portrait.

THE FLYING PIGEON

"Ratchewaine was chaste, mild, gentle in her disposition,
kind, generous, and devoted to her husband. A harsh word
was never known to proceed from her mouth; nor was she
ever known to be in a passion. Mahaskah used to say of her,
after her death, that her hand was shut, when those, who did
not want, came into her presence; but when the really poor
came in, it was like a strainer full of holes, letting all she held

---

[77] Milton, *Paradise Lost*, Book 4, l. 660.
* Spangenberg. [Fuller's note.] August Gottlieb Spangenberg (1704-
1792), German secretary who fell under Zinzendorf's religious guidance.

in it pass through. In the exercise of generous feeling she was uniform. It was not indebted for its exercise to whim, or caprice, or partiality. No matter of what nation the applicant for her bounty was, or whether at war or peace with her nation; if he were hungry, she fed him; if naked, she clothed him; and if houseless, she gave him shelter. The continued exercise of this generous feeling kept her poor. And she has been known to give away her last blanket—all the honey that was in the lodge, the last bladder of bear's oil, and the last piece of dried meat.

"She was scrupulously exact in the observance of all the religious rites which her faith imposed upon her. Her conscience is represented to have been extremely tender. She often feared that her acts were displeasing to the Great Spirit, when she would blacken her face, and retire to some lone place, and fast and pray."

To these traits should be added, but for want of room, anecdotes which show the quick decision and vivacity of her mind. Her face was in harmony with this combination. Her brow is as ideal and the eyes and lids as devout and modest as the Italian pictures of the Madonna, while the lower part of the face has the simplicity and childish strength of the Indian race. Her picture presents the finest specimen of Indian beauty we have ever seen.

Such a woman is the sister and friend of all beings, as the worthy man is their brother and helper.

With like pleasure we survey the pairs wedded on the eve of missionary effort. They, indeed, are fellow pilgrims on a well-made road, and whether or no they accomplish all they hope for the sad Hindoo, or the nearer savage, we feel that, in the burning waste, their love is like to be a healing dew, in the forlorn jungle, a tent of solace to one another. They meet, as children of one Father, to read together one book of instruction.

We must insert in this connection the most beautiful picture presented by ancient literature of wedded love under this noble form.

It is from the romance in which Xenophon, the chivalrous Greek, presents his ideal of what human nature should be.[78]

[78] The following pages are quoted from Xenophon's *Cyropædia*.

The generals of Cyrus had taken captive a princess, a woman of unequalled beauty, and hastened to present her to the prince as the part of the spoil he would think most worthy of his acceptance.

Cyrus visits the lady, and is filled with immediate admiration by the modesty and majesty with which she receives him. He finds her name is Panthea, and that she is the wife of Abradatus, a young king whom she entirely loves. He protects her as a sister, in his camp, till he can restore her to her husband.

After the first transports of joy at this re-union, the heart of Panthea is bent on showing her love and gratitude to her magnanimous and delicate protector. And as she has nothing so precious to give as the aid of Abradatus, that is what she most wishes to offer. Her husband is of one soul with her in this, as in all things.

The description of her grief and self-destruction, after the death which ensued upon this devotion, I have seen quoted, but never that of their parting when she sends him forth to battle. I shall copy both. If they have been read by any of my readers, they may be so again with profit in this connexion, for never were the heroism of a true woman, and the purity of love, in a true marriage, painted in colors more delicate or more lively.

"The chariot of Abradatus, that had four perches and eight horses, was completely adorned for him; and when he was going to put on his linen corslet, which was a sort of armor used by those of his country, Panthea brought him a golden helmet, and arm-pieces, broad bracelets for his wrists, a purple habit that reached down to his feet, and hung in folds at the bottom, and a crest dyed of a violet color. These things she had made unknown to her husband, and by taking the measure of his armor. He wondered when he saw them, and inquired thus of Panthea: "And have you made me these arms, woman, by destroying your own ornaments?" "No, by Jove," said Panthea, "not what is the most valuable of them; for it is you, if you appear to others to be what I think you, that will be my greatest ornament." And, saying that, she put on him the armor, and, though she endeavored to conceal it, the tears poured down her cheeks. When Abradatus, who was before a man of fine appearance, was set out in those arms, he appeared the most beautiful and noble of all, especially, being likewise so by nature. Then, taking the reins from the driver, he was just preparing to mount the chariot, when Panthea, after she had desired all that were there to retire, thus said:

'O Abradatus! if ever there was a woman who had a greater regard to her husband than to her own soul, I believe you know that I am such an one; what need I therefore speak of things in particular? for I reckon that my actions have convinced you more than any words I can now use. And yet, though I stand thus affected towards you, as you know I do, I swear by this friendship of mine and yours, that I certainly would rather choose to be put under ground jointly with you, approving yourself a brave man, than to live with you in disgrace and shame; so much do I think you and myself worthy of the noblest things. Then I think that we both lie under great obligations to Cyrus, that, when I was a captive, and chosen out for himself, he thought fit to treat me neither as a slave, nor, indeed, as a woman of mean account, but he took and kept me for you, as if I were his brother's wife. Besides, when Araspes, who was my guard, went away from him, I promised him, that, if he would allow me to send for you, you would come to him, and approve yourself a much better and more faithful friend than Araspes.'

"Thus she spoke; and Abradatus being struck with admiration at her discourse, laying his hand gently on her head, and lifting up his eyes to heaven, made this prayer: 'Do thou, O greatest Jove! grant me to appear a husband worthy of Panthea, and a friend worthy of Cyrus, who has done us so much honor!'

"Having said this, he mounted the chariot by the door of the driver's seat; and, after he had got up, when the driver shut the door, Panthea, who had now no other way to salute him, kissed the seat of the chariot. The chariot then moved, and she, unknown to him, followed, till Abradatus turning about, and seeing her, said: 'Take courage, Panthea! Fare you happily and well, and now go your ways.' On this her women and servants carried her to her conveyance, and, laying her down, concealed her by throwing the covering of a tent over her. The people, though Abradatus and his chariot made a noble spectacle, were not able to look at him till Panthea was gone."

After the battle—

"Cyrus calling to some of his servants, 'Tell me,' said he, 'has any one seen Abradatus? for I admire that he now does not appear.' One replied, 'My sovereign, it is because he is not living, but died in the battle as he broke in with his chariot on the Egyptians. All the rest, except his particular companions, they say, turned off when they saw the Egyptians' compact body. His wife is now said to have taken up his dead body, to have placed it in the carriage that she herself was conveyed in, and to have brought it hither to some place on the river Pactolus, and her servants are digging a grave on a certain elevation. They say that his wife, after setting him out with all the ornaments she has, is sitting on the ground with his head on her knees.' Cyrus, hearing this, gave himself a blow on the thigh, mounted his horse at a leap, and taking with him a thousand horse, rode away to this scene of affliction; but gave orders to Gadatas and Gobryas to take with them all the rich ornaments proper for a friend and an excellent man deceased, and to follow after him; and whoever had herds of cattle with him, he ordered them to take both oxen, and horses, and sheep in good number, and to bring them away to the place where, by inquiry, they should find him to be, that he might sacrifice these to Abradatus.

"As soon as he saw the woman sitting on the ground, and the dead body there lying, he shed tears at the afflicting sight, and said: 'Alas! thou brave and faithful soul, hast thou left us, and art thou gone?' At the same time he took him by the right hand, and the hand of the deceased came away, for it had been cut off, with a sword, by the Egyptians. He, at the sight of this, became yet much more concerned than before. The woman shrieked out in a lamentable manner, and, taking the hand from Cyrus, kissed it, fitted it to its proper place again, as well as she could, and said, 'The rest, Cyrus, is in the same condition, but what need you see it? And I know that I was not one of the least concerned in these his sufferings, and, perhaps, you were not less so, for I, fool that I was! frequently exhorted him to behave in such a manner as to appear a friend to you, worthy of notice; and I know he never thought of what he himself should suffer, but of what he should do to please you. He is dead, therefore,' said she, 'without reproach, and I, who urged him on, sit here alive.'

Cyrus, shedding tears for some time in silence, then spoke—'He has died, woman, the noblest death; for he has died victorious! do you adorn him with these things that I furnish you with.' (Gobryas and Gadatas were then come up and had brought rich ornaments in great abundance with them.) 'Then,' said he, 'be assured that he shall not want respect and honor in all other things: but, over and above, multitudes shall concur in raising him a monument that shall be worthy of us, and all the sacrifices shall be made him that are proper to be made in honor of a brave man. You shall not be left destitute, but, for the sake of your modesty and every other virtue, I will pay you all other honors, as well as place those about you who will conduct you wherever you please. Do you but make it known to me where it is that you desire to be conveyed to.' And Panthea replied, 'Be confident, Cyrus,' said she, 'I will not conceal from you to whom it is that I desire to go.'

"He, having said this, went away with great pity for her that she should have lost such a husband, and for the man that he should have left such a wife behind him, never to see her more. Panthea then gave orders for her servants to retire, 'Till such time,' said she, 'as I shall have lamented my husband, as I please.' Her nurse she bid to stay, and gave orders that, when she was dead, she would wrap her and her husband up in one mantle together. The nurse, after having repeatedly begged her not to do this, and meeting with no success, but observing her to grow angry, sat herself down, breaking out into tears. She, being before-hand provided with a sword, killed herself, and, laying her head down on her husband's breast, she died. The nurse set up a lamentable cry, and covered them both as Panthea had directed.

"Cyrus, as soon as he was informed of what the woman had done, being struck with it, went to help her if he could. The servants, three in number, seeing what had been done, drew their swords and killed themselves, as they stood at the place where she had ordered them. And the monument is now said to have been raised by continuing the mount on to the servants; and on a pillar above, they say, the names of the man and woman were written in Syriac letters.

"Below were three pillars, and they were inscribed thus, "Of the servants." Cyrus, when he came to this melancholy scene, was struck with admiration of the woman, and, having lamented over her, went away. He took care, as was proper, that all the funeral rites should be paid them in the noblest manner, and the monument, they say, was raised up to a very great size."

These be the ancients, who, so many assert had no idea of the dignity of woman, or of marriage. Such love Xenophon could paint as subsisting between those who after death "would see one another never more." Thousands of years have passed since, and with the reception of the cross, the nations assume the belief that those who part thus, may meet again and forever, if spirutually fitted to one another, as Abradatus and Panthea were, and yet do we see such marriages among them? If at all, how often?

I must quote two more short passages from Xenophon, for he is a writer who pleases me well.

Cyrus receiving the Armenians whom he had conquered.

"Tigranes," said he, "at what rate would you purchase the regaining of your wife?" Now Tigranes happened to be *but lately married*, and had a very great love for his wife," (that clause perhaps sounds *modern*.)

"Cyrus," said he, "I would ransom her at the expense of my life."

"Take then your own to yourself," said he. * * *

When they came home, one talked of Cyrus' wisdom, another of his patience and resolution, another of his mildness. One spoke of his beauty and the smallness of his person, and, on that, Tigranes asked his wife, "And do you, Armenian dame, think Cyrus handsome?" "Truly," said she, "I did not look at him." "At whom, then, did you look?" said Tigranes. "At him who said that, to save me from servitude, he would ransom me at the expense of his own life."

From the Banquet.—

Socrates, who observed her with pleasure, said, "This young girl has confirmed me in the opinion I have had, for a long time, that the female sex are nothing inferior to ours, excepting only in strength of body, or, perhaps, in steadiness of judgment."

In the Economics, the manner in which the husband gives counsel to his young wife, presents the model of politeness and refinement. Xenophon is thoroughly the gentleman, gentle in breeding and in soul. All the men he describes are so, while the shades of manner are distinctly marked. There is the serene dignity of Socrates, with gleams of playfulness thrown across its cool religious shades, the princely mildness of Cyrus, and the more domestic elegance of the husband in the Economics.

There is no way that men sin more against refinement, as well as discretion, than in their conduct towards their wives. Let them look at the men of Xenophon. Such would know how to give counsel, for they would know how to receive it. They would feel that the most intimate relations claimed most, not least, of refined courtesy. They would not suppose that confidence justified carelessness, nor the reality of affection want of delicacy in the expression of it.

Such men would be too wise to hide their affairs from the wife and then expect her to act as if she knew them. They would know that if she is expected to face calamity with courage, she must be instructed and trusted in prosperity, or, if they had failed in wise confidence such as the husband shows in the Economics, they would be ashamed of anger or querulous surprise at the results that naturally follow.

Such men would not be exposed to the bad influence of bad wives, for all wives, bad or good, loved or unloved, inevitably influence their husbands, from the power their position not merely gives, but necessitates, of coloring evidence and infusing feelings in hours when the patient, shall I call him? is off his guard. Those who understand the wife's mind, and think it worth while to respect her springs of action, know better where they are. But to the bad or thoughtless man who lives carelessly and irreverently so near another mind, the wrong he does daily back upon himself recoils. A Cyrus, an Abradatus knows where he stands.

But to return to the thread of my subject.

Another sign of the times is furnished by the triumphs of female authorship. These have been great and constantly increasing. Women have taken possession of so many provinces for which men had pronounced them unfit, that though these still declare there are some inaccessible to them, it is difficult to say just *where* they must stop.

The shining names of famous women have cast light upon

the path of the sex, and many obstructions have been removed. When a Montague could learn better than her
brother, and use her lore afterward to such purpose, as an
observer, it seemed amiss to hinder woman from preparing
themselves to see, or from seeing all they could, when prepared. Since Somerville has achieved so much, will any
young girl be prevented from seeking a knowledge of the
physical sciences, if she wishes it?[79] De Stael's name was
not so clear of offence; she could not forget the woman in the
thought; while she was instructing you as a mind, she wished
to be admired as a woman; sentimental tears often dimmed
the eagle glance.[80] Her intellect too, with all its splendor,
trained in a drawing-room, fed on flattery, was tainted and
flawed; yet its beams make the obscurest school-house in
New-England warmer and lighter to the little rugged girls,
who are gathered together on its wooden bench. They may
never through life hear her name, but she is not the less their
benefactress.

The influence has been such, that the aim certainly is,
now, in arranging school instruction for girls, to give them as
fair a field as boys. As yet, indeed, these arrangements are
made with little judgment or reflection; just as the tutors of
Lady Jane Grey,[81] and other distinguished women of her
time, taught them Latin and Greek, because they knew nothing else themselves, so now the improvement in the education of girls is to be made by giving them young men as
teachers, who only teach what has been taught themselves at
college, while methods and topics need revision for these
new subjects, which could better be made by those who had
experienced the same wants. Women are, often, at the head
of these institutions, but they have, as yet, seldom been
thinking women, capable to organize a new whole for the
wants of the time, and choose persons to officiate in the departments. And when some portion of instruction is got of a

[79] Mary Somerville (1780-1872), Scottish mathematician and science
writer.
[80] Mme. De Staël (1766-1817), French writer whose novel *Corinne* (1807)
was much-read in America. Fuller herself was often referred to as "the
American Corinne."
[81] Lady Jane Grey (*c.* 1537-1554), English noblewoman who was profi-
cient in six languages at age fifteen.

good sort from the school, the far greater proportion which is infused from the general atmosphere of society contradicts its purport. Yet books and a little elementary instruction are not furnished, in vain. Women are better aware how great and rich the universe is, not so easily blinded by narrowness or partial views of a home circle. "Her mother did so before her," is no longer a sufficient excuse. Indeed, it was never received as an excuse to mitigate the severity of censure, but was adduced as a reason, rather, why there should be no effort made for reformation.

Whether much or little has been done or will be done, whether women will add to the talent of narration, the power of systematizing, whether they will carve marble, as well as draw and paint, is not important. But that it should be acknowledged that they have intellect which needs developing, that they should not be considered complete, if beings of affection and habit alone, is important.

Yet even this acknowledgement, rather conquered by woman than proffered by man, has been sullied by the usual selfishness. So much is said of women being better educated, that they may become better companions and mothers *for men*. They should be fit for such companionship, and we have mentioned, with satisfaction, instances where it has been established. Earth knows no fairer, holier relation than that of a mother. It is one which, rightly understood, must both promote and require the highest attainments. But a being of infinite scope must not be treated with an exclusive view to any one relation. Give the soul free course, let the organization, both of body and mind, be freely developed, and the being will be fit for any and every relation to which it may be called. The intellect, no more than the sense of hearing, is to be cultivated merely that she may be a more valuable companion to man, but because the Power who gave a power, by its mere existence, signifies that it must be brought out towards perfection.

In this regard of self-dependence, and a greater simplicity and fulness of being, we must hail as a preliminary the increase of the class contemptuously designated as old maids.

We cannot wonder at the aversion with which old bachelors and old maids have been regarded. Marriage is the natural means of forming a sphere, of taking root on the earth; it requires more strength to do this without such an opening; very many have failed, and their imperfections have been in every one's way. They have been more partial, more harsh, more officious and impertinent than those compelled by severer friction to render themselves endurable. Those, who have a more full experience of the instincts, have a distrust, as to whether they can be thoroughly human and humane, such as is hinted in the saying, "Old maids' and bachelors' children are well cared for," which derides at once their ignorance and their presumption.

Yet the business of society has become so complex, that it could now scarcely be carried on without the presence of these despised auxiliaries; and detachments from the army of aunts and uncles are wanted to stop gaps in every hedge. They rove about, mental and moral Ishmaelites, pitching their tents amid the fixed and ornamented homes of men.[82]

In a striking variety of forms, genius of late, both at home and abroad, has paid its tribute to the character of the Aunt, and the Uncle, recognizing in these personages the spiritual parents, who had supplied defects in the treatment of the busy or careless actual parents.

They also gain a wider, if not so deep experience. Those who are not intimately and permanently linked with others, are thrown upon themselves, and, if they do not there find peace and incessant life, there is none to flatter them that they are not very poor and very mean.

A position which so constantly admonishes, may be of inestimable benefit. The person may gain, undistracted by other relationships, a closer communion with the one. Such a use is made of it by saints and sybils. Or she may be one of the lay sisters of charity, a Canoness, bound by an inward vow! Or the useful drudge of all men, the Martha, much sought, little prized![83] Or the intellectual interpreter of the varied life she sees; the Urania of a half-formed world's twilight.[84]

Or she may combine all these. Not "needing to care that

---

[82] Ishmael, son of Hagar, was cast out with his mother from Abraham's tents; hence, a name associated with outcasts or misfits. See also note 146, p. 202.

[83] Martha, patron saint of housewives.

[84] Urania, Greek muse of Astronomy.

she may please a husband," a frail and limited being, her thoughts may turn to the centre, and she may, by steadfast contemplation entering into the secret of truth and love, use it for the use of all men, instead of a chosen few, and interpret through it all the forms of life. It is possible, perhaps, to be at once a priestly servant, and a loving muse.

Saints and geniuses have often chosen a lonely position in the faith that if, undisturbed by the pressure of near ties, they would give themselves up to the inspiring spirit, it would enable them to understand and reproduce life better than actual experience could.

How many old maids take this high stand, we cannot say: it is an unhappy fact, that too many who have come before the eye are gossips rather, and not always good-natured gossips. But if these abuse, and none make the best of their vocation, yet it has not failed to produce some good results. It has been seen by others, if not by themselves, that beings, likely to be left alone, need to be fortified and furnished within themselves, and education and thought have tended more and more to regard these beings as related to absolute Being, as well as to other men. It has been seen that, as the breaking of no bond ought to destroy a man, so ought the missing of none to hinder him from growing. And thus a circumstance of the time, which springs rather from its luxury than its purity, has helped to place women on the true platform.

Perhaps the next generation, looking deeper into this matter, will find that contempt is put upon old maids, or old women at all, merely because they do not use the elixir which would keep them always young. Under its influence a gem brightens yearly which is only seen to more advantage through the fissures Time makes in the casket.* No one thinks of Michael Angelo's Persican Sibyl, or St. Theresa, or Tasso's Leonora, or the Greek Electra, as an old maid, more than of Michael Angelo or Canova as old bachelors, though all had reached the period in life's course appointed to take that degree.[85]

---

* Appendix, F. [Fuller's note.] Appendix F is printed on p. 224.
[85] Michelangelo Buonorati (1475-1564), Italian sculptor, painter, and architect; for Saint Teresa, see note 41, p. 116; Tasso's love for Leonora, daughter of Alfonso II, led to his imprisonment; see note 28, p. 108; Elec-

See a common woman at forty; scarcely has she the remains of beauty, of any soft poetic grace which gave her attraction as woman, which kindled the hearts of those who looked on her to sparkling thoughts, or diffused round her a roseate air of gentle love. See her, who was, indeed, a lovely girl, in the coarse full-blown dahlia flower of what is commonly called matron-beauty, fat, fair, and forty, showily dressed, and with manners as broad and full as her frill or satin cloak. People observe, "how well she is preserved;" "she is a fine woman still," they say. This woman, whether as a duchess in diamonds, or one of our city dames in mosaics, charms the poet's heart no more, and would look much out of place kneeling before the Madonna. She "does well the honors of her house," "leads society," is, in short, always spoken and thought of upholstery-wise.

Or see that care-worn face, from which every soft line is blotted, those faded eyes from which lonely tears have driven the flashes of fancy, the mild white beam of a tender enthusiasm. This woman is not so ornamental to a tea party; yet she would please better, in picture. Yet surely she, no more than the other, looks as a human being should at the end of forty years. Forty years! have they bound those brows with no garland? shed in the lamp no drop of ambrosial oil?

Not so looked the Iphigenia in Aulis.[86] Her forty years had seen her in anguish, in sacrifice, in utter loneliness. But those pains were borne for her father and her country; the sacrifice she had made pure for herself and those around her. Wandering alone at night in the vestal solitude of her imprisoning grove, she has looked up through its "living summits" to the stars, which shed down into her aspect their own lofty melody. At forty she would not misbecome the marble.

Not so looks the Persica.[87] She is withered, she is faded; the drapery that enfolds her has, in its dignity an angularity, too, that tells of age, of sorrow, of a stern composure to the

tra, daughter of Agamemnon and Clytemnestra; Antonio Canova (1757-1822), Italian sculptor.

[86] When Agamemnon's fleet sailing against Troy was becalmed at Aulis, he planned to sacrifice his daughter Iphigenia, but the goddess Diana carried her away and a substitute was killed instead.

[87] Persican or Persian Sibyl, painted by Michelangelo on the ceiling of the Sistine Chapel, was the oldest of the Sibyls.

must. But her eye, that torch of the soul, is untamed, and in
the intensity of her reading, we see a soul invincibly young
in faith and hope. Her age is her charm, for it is the night of
the Past that gives this beacon fire leave to shine. Wither
more and more, black Chrysalid![88] thou dost but give the
winged beauty time to mature its splendors.

Not so looked Vittoria Colonna, after her life of a great
hope, and of true conjugal fidelity.[89] She had been, not
merely a bride, but a wife, and each hour had helped to
plume the noble bird. A coronet of pearls will not shame her
brow; it is white and ample, a worthy altar for love and
thought.

Even among the North American Indians, a race of men as
completely engaged in mere instinctive life as almost any in
the world, and where each chief, keeping many wives as
useful servants, of course looks with no kind eye on celibacy
in woman, it was excused in the following instance mentioned by Mrs. Jameson.[90] A woman dreamt in youth that she
was betrothed to the Sun. She built her a wigwam apart,
filled it with emblems of her alliance, and means of an independent life. There she passed her days, sustained by her
own exertions, and true to her supposed engagement.

In any tribe, we believe, a woman, who lived as if she was
betrothed to the Sun, would be tolerated, and the rays which
made her youth blossom sweetly, would crown her with a
halo in age.

There is, on this subject, a nobler view than heretofore, if
not the noblest, and improvement here must coincide with
that in the view taken of marriage.

We must have units before we can have union, says one of
the ripe thinkers of the times.

If larger intellectual resources begin to be deemed needful
to woman, still more is a spiritual dignity in her, or even the
mere assumption of it, looked upon with respect. Joanna
Southcott and Mother Anne Lee are sure of a band of

---

[88] Chrysalid, technically the chrysalis or dormant, metamorphic stage of
insect life; in mythology, any undeveloped object, the soul veiled in flesh.
[89] Vittoria Colonna (1490-1547), Italian poet and friend of Michelangelo,
who addressed several sonnets to her.
[90] Anna Brownell Jameson (1794-1860), British author; see also pp. 173
and note 121 below.

disciples;[91] Ecstatica, Dolorosa, of enraptured believers who will visit them in their lowly huts, and wait for days to revere them in their trances. The foreign noble traverses land and sea to hear a few words from the lips of the lowly peasant girl, whom he believes especially visited by the Most High. Very beautiful, in this way, was the influence of the invalid of St. Petersburg, as described by De Maistre.[92]

Mysticism, which may be defined as the brooding soul of the world, cannot fail of its oracular promise as to woman. "The mothers"—"The mother of all things," are expressions of thought which lead the mind towards this side of universal growth. Whenever a mystical whisper was heard, from Behmen down to St. Simon, sprang up the thought, that, if it be true, as the legend says, that humanity withers through a fault committed by and a curse laid upon woman, through her pure child, or influence, shall the new Adam, the redemption, arise.[93] Innocence is to be replaced by virtue, dependence by a willing submission, in the heart of the Virgin Mother of the new race.

The spiritual tendency is towards the elevation of woman, but the intellectual by itself is not so. Plato sometimes seems penetrated by that high idea of love, which considers man and woman as the two-fold expression of one thought. This the angel of Swedenborg, the angel of the coming age, cannot surpass, but only explain more fully. But then again Plato, the man of intellect, treats woman in the Republic as property, and, in the Timæus, says that man, if he misuse the privileges of one life, shall be degraded into the form of woman, and then, if he do not redeem himself, into that of a bird. This, as I said above, expresses most happily how antipoetical is this state of mind. For the poet, contemplating the world of things, selects various birds as the symbols of his most gracious and ethereal thoughts, just as he calls upon his genius, as muse, rather than as God. But the intellect, cold, is

[91] Joanna Southcott (1750-1814), English religious fanatic whose sect, built around her supposed prophetic gifts, numbered 100,000 at its peak; Mother Ann Lee (1736-1784), English mystic and founder of the Shakers.
[92] Xavier de Maistre (1763-1852), Christian philosopher.
[93] Jacob Behmen (or Böhme, 1575-1624), German mystic with pantheistic leanings; Claude Henri de Rouvroy, Comte de Saint-Simon (1760-1825), French social philosopher.

ever more masculine than feminine; warmed by emotion, it rushes towards mother earth, and puts on the forms of beauty.

The electrical, the magnetic element in woman has not been fairly brought out at any period. Every thing might be expected from it; she has far more of it than man. This is commonly expressed by saying that her intuitions are more rapid and more correct. You will often see men of high intellect absolutely stupid in regard to the atmospheric changes, the fine invisible links which connect the forms of life around them, while common women, if pure and modest, so that a vulgar self do not overshadow the mental eye, will seize and delineate these with unerring discrimination.

Women who combine this organization with creative genius, are very commonly unhappy at present. They see too much to act in conformity with those around them, and their quick impulses seem folly to those who do not discern the motives. This is an usual effect of the apparition of genius, whether in man or woman, but is more frequent with regard to the latter, because a harmony, an obvious order and self-restraining decorum, is most expected from her.

Then women of genius, even more than men, are likely to be enslaved by an impassioned sensibility. The world repels them more rudely, and they are of weaker bodily frame.

Those, who seem overladen with electricity, frighten those around them. "When she merely enters the room, I am what the French call *hérissé*," said a man of petty feelings and worldly character of such a woman, whose depth of eye and powerful motion announced the conductor of the mysterious fluid.

Wo to such a woman who finds herself linked to such a man in bonds too close. It is the cruellest of errors. He will detest her with all the bitterness of wounded self-love. He will take the whole prejudice of manhood upon himself, and to the utmost of his power imprison and torture her by its imperious rigors.

Yet, allow room enough, and the electric fluid will be found to invigorate and embellish, not destroy life. Such women are the great actresses, the songsters. Such traits we read in a late searching, though too French analysis of the character of Mademoiselle Rachel, by a modern La

Rochefoucauld.[94] The Greeks thus represent the muses; they have not the golden serenity of Apollo; they are *over*-flowed with thought; there is something tragic in their air. Such are the Sibyls of Guercino, the eye is over-full of expression, dilated and lustrous; it seems to have drawn the whole being into it.

Sickness is the frequent result of this over-charged existence. To this region, however misunderstood, or interpreted with presumptuous carelessness, belong the phenomena of magnetism, or mesmerism, as it is now often called, where the trance of the Ecstatica purports to be produced by the agency of one human being on another, instead of, as in her case, direct from the spirit.

The worldling has his sneer at this as at the services of religion. "The churches can always be filled with women." "Show me a man in one of your magnetic states, and I will believe."

Women are, indeed, the easy victims both of priestcraft and self-delusion, but this would not be, if the intellect was developed in proportion to the other powers. They would, then, have a regulator, and be more in equipoise, yet must retain the same nervous susceptibility, while their physical structure is such as it is.

It is with just that hope, that we welcome every thing that tends to strengthen the fibre and develope the nature on more sides. When the intellect and affections are in harmony; when intellectual consciousness is calm and deep; inspiration will not be confounded with fancy.

> Then, "she who advances
> With rapturous, lyrical glances,
> Singing the song of the earth, singing
> Its hymn to the Gods,"[95]

will not be pitied, as a madwoman, nor shrunk from as unnatural.

The Greeks, who saw every thing in forms, which we are trying to ascertain as law, and classify as cause, embodied all

---

[94] Mdll. Rachel (1820-1858), French tragedienne; François, Duc de la Rochefoucauld (1613-1680), French writer of maxims.
[95] Unidentified.

this in the form of Cassandra.[96] Cassandra was only unfortunate in receiving her gift too soon. The remarks, however, that the world still makes in such cases, are well expressed by the Greek dramatist.

In the Trojan Dames, there are fine touches of nature with regard to Cassandra. Hecuba shows that mixture of shame and reverence that prosaic kindred always do towards the inspired child, the poet, the elected sufferer for the race.[97]

When the herald announces that Cassandra is chosen to be the mistress of Agamemnon, Hecuba answers, with indignation, betraying the pride and faith she involuntarily felt in this daughter.

Hec.   'The maiden of Phoebus, to whom the golden haired
          Gave as a privilege a virgin life!
Tal.   Love of the inspired maiden hath pierced him.
Hec.   Then cast away, my child, the sacred keys, and from thy
          person
          The consecrated garlands which thou wearest.'

Yet, when a moment after, Cassandra appears, singing, wildly, her inspired song, Hecuba calls her, "My *frantic* child."

Yet how graceful she is in her tragic *raptus*, the chorus shows.

Chor.   'How sweetly at thy house's ills thou smil'st,
             Chanting what, haply, thou wilt not show true.'

If Hecuba dares not trust her highest instinct about her daughter, still less can the vulgar mind of the herald Talthybius, a man not without feeling, but with no princely, no poetic blood, abide the wild prophetic mood which insults all his prejudices.

Tal.   'The venerable, and that accounted wise,
          Is nothing better than that of no repute,
          For the greatest king of all the Greeks,
          The dear son of Atreus, is possessed with the love
          Of this madwoman. I, indeed, am poor,
          Yet, I would not receive her to my bed.'[98]

[96] Cassandra; see note 39, p. 114.
[97] Hecuba, legendary queen of Troy, enslaved by Ulysses after the fall of her city.
[98] Euripides, *The Daughters of Troy*.

The royal Agamemnon could see the beauty of Cassandra, HE was not afraid of her prophetic gifts.

The best topic for a chapter on this subject in the present day, would be the history of the Seeress of Prevorst, the best observed subject of magnetism in our present times, and who, like her ancestresses of Delphos, was roused to ecstacy or phrenzy by the touch of the laurel.[99]

I observe in her case, and in one known to me here, that, what might have been a gradual and gentle disclosure of remarkable powers, was broken and jarred into disease by an unsuitable marriage. Both these persons were unfortunate in not understanding what was involved in this relation, but acted ignorantly as their friends desired. They thought that this was the inevitable destiny of woman. But when engaged in the false position, it was impossible for them to endure its dissonances, as those of less delicate perceptions can, and the fine flow of life was checked and sullied. They grew sick, but, even so, learnt and disclosed more than those in health are wont to do.

In such cases, worldlings sneer, but reverent men learn wondrous news, either from the person observed, or by thoughts caused in themselves by the observation. Fenelon learns from Guyon, Kerner, from his Seeress, what we fain would know.[100] But to appreciate such disclosures one must be a child, and here the phrase, "women and children" may, perhaps, be interpreted aright, that only little children shall enter into the kingdom of heaven.

All these motions of the time, tides that betoken a waxing moon, overflow upon our land. The world, at large, is readier to let woman learn and manifest the capacities of her nature than it ever was before, and here is a less encumbered field and freer air than any where else. And it ought to be so; we ought to pay for Isabella's jewels.

The names of nations are feminine—religion, virtue, and

[99] Frederica Hauffe, central figure in a study of spiritualism, *The Seeress of Prevorst* (1829) by Justinus Kerner (1786-1862), German poet and physician. Fuller describes her case at length in *Summer on the Lakes*, pp. 133-164. The oracle at Delphos was the most famous of antiquity.

[100] François Fénelon (1651-1751). French prelate and author; Jeanne Guyon (1648-1717), French mystic and a founder of quietism, a sect holding that there is a mystical connection between man and God.

victory are feminine. To those who have a superstition, as to outward reigns, it is not without significance that the name of the queen of our mother-land should at this crisis be Victoria—Victoria the First. Perhaps to us it may be given to disclose the era thus outwardly presaged.

Another Isabella too at this time ascends the throne. Might she open a new world to her sex! But, probably, these poor little women are, least of any, educated to serve as examples or inspirers for the rest. The Spanish queen is younger; we know of her that she sprained her foot the other day, dancing in her private apartments; of Victoria, that she reads aloud, in a distinct voice and agreeable manner, her addresses to parliament on certain solemn days, and, yearly, that she presents to the nation some new prop of royalty. These ladies have, very likely, been trained more completely to the puppet life than any other. The queens, who have been queens indeed, were trained by adverse circumstances to know the world around them and their own powers.

It is moving, while amusing, to read of the Scottish peasant measuring the print left by the queen's foot as she walks, and priding himself on its beauty. It is so natural to wish to find what is fair and precious in high places, so astonishing to find the Bourbon a glutton, or the Guelph a dullard or gossip.[101]

In our own country, women are, in many respects, better situated than men. Good books are allowed, with more time to read them. They are not so early forced into the bustle of life, nor so weighed down by demands for outward success. The perpetual changes, incident to our society, make the blood circulate freely through the body politic, and, if not favorable at present to the grace and bloom of life, they are so to activity, resource, and would be to reflection, but for a low materialist tendency, from which the women are generally exempt in themselves, though its existence, among the men, has a tendency to repress their impulses and make them doubt their instincts, thus, often, paralyzing their action during the best years.

But they have time to think, and no traditions chain them, and few conventionalities compared with what must be met

---

[101] Bourbon, French royal family; Guelph, papal and popular party of the Italian middle ages.

in other nations. There is no reason why they should not discover that the secrets of nature are open, the revelations of the spirit waiting for whoever will seek them. When the mind is once awakened to this consciousness, it will not be restrained by the habits of the past, but fly to seek the seeds of a heavenly future.

Their employments are more favorable to meditation than those of men.

Woman is not addressed religiously here, more than elsewhere. She is told she should be worthy to be the mother of a Washington, or the companion of some good man. But in many, many instances, she has already learnt that all bribes have the same flaw; that truth and good are to be sought solely for their own sakes. And, already, an ideal sweetness floats over many forms, shines in many eyes.

Already deep questions are put by young girls on the great theme: What shall I do to enter upon the eternal life?

Men are very courteous to them. They praise them often, check them seldom. There is chivalry in the feeling towards "the ladies," which gives them the best seats in the stage-coach, frequent admission, not only to lectures of all sorts, but to courts of justice, halls of legislature, reform conventions. The newspaper editor "would be better pleased that the Lady's Book should be filled up exclusively by ladies. It would then, indeed, be a true gem, worthy to be presented by young men to the mistresses of their affections." Can gallantry go further?

In this country is venerated, wherever seen, the character which Goethe spoke of an Ideal, which he saw actualized in his friend and patroness, the Grand Duchess Amelia. "The excellent woman is she, who, if the husband dies, can be a father to the children." And this, if read aright, tells a great deal.

Women who speak in public, if they have a moral power, such as has been felt from Angelina Grimke and Abby Kelley;[102] that is, if they speak for conscience' sake, to serve a cause which they hold sacred, invariably subdue the prejudices of their hearers, and excite an interest proportionate to

---

[102] Angelina Grimké (1805-1879) and Abby Kelley (1811-1887), American anti-slavery and woman's rights advocates.

the aversion with which it had been the purpose to regard them.

A passage in a private letter so happily illustrates this, that it must be inserted here.

Abby Kelley in the Town-House of ——.

"The scene was not unheroic—to see that woman, true to humanity and her own nature, a centre of rude eyes and tongues, even gentlemen feeling licensed to make part of a species of mob around a female out of her sphere. As she took her seat in the desk amid the great noise, and in the throng, full, like a wave, of something to ensue, I saw her humanity in a gentleness and unpretension, tenderly open to the sphere around her, and, had she not been supported by the power of the will of genuineness and principle, she would have failed. It led her to prayer, which, in woman especially, is childlike; sensibility and will going to the side of God and looking up to him; and humanity was poured out in aspiration.

"She acted like a gentle hero, with her mild decision and womanly calmness. All heroism is mild and quiet and gentle, for it is life and possession, and combativeness and firmness show a want of actualness. She is as earnest, fresh, and simple as when she first entered the crusade. I think she did much good, more than the men in her place could do, for woman feels more as being and reproducing, this brings the subject more into home relations. Men speak through, and mostly from intellect, and this addresses itself in others, which creates and is combative."

Not easily shall we find elsewhere, or before this time, any written observations on the same subject, so delicate and profound.

The late Dr. Channing, whose enlarged and tender and religious nature, shared every onward impulse of his time, though his thoughts followed his wishes with a deliberative caution, which belonged to his habits and temperament, was greatly interested in these expectations for women. His own treatment of them was absolutely and thoroughly religious. He regarded them as souls, each of which had a destiny of its own, incalculable to other minds, and whose leading it must follow, guided by the light of a private conscience. He had

sentiment, delicacy, kindness, taste; but they were all pervaded and ruled by this one thought, that all beings had
souls, and must vindicate their own inheritance. Thus all
beings were treated by him with an equal, and sweet, though
solemn, courtesy. The young and unknown, the woman and
the child, all felt themselves regarded with an infinite expectation, from which there was no reaction to vulgar prejudice.
He demanded of all he met, to use his favorite phrase, "great
truths."

His memory, every way dear and reverend, is, by many,
especially cherished for this intercourse of unbroken respect.

At one time, when the progress of Harriet Martineau
through this country, Angelina Grimke's appearance in public, and the visit of Mrs. Jameson had turned his thoughts to
this subject, he expressed high hopes as to what the coming
era would bring to woman.[103] He had been much pleased
with the dignified courage of Mrs. Jameson in taking up the
defence of her sex, in a way from which women usually
shrink, because, if they express themselves on such subjects
with sufficient force and clearness to do any good, they are
exposed to assaults whose vulgarity makes them painful. In
intercourse with such a woman, he had shared her indignation at the base injustice, in many respects, and in many
regions, done to the sex; and been led to think of it far more
than ever before. He seemed to think that he might some
time write upon the subject. That his aid is withdrawn from
the cause is a subject of great regret, for, on this question as
on others, he would have known how to sum up the evidence
and take, in the noblest spirit, middle ground. He always
furnished a platform on which opposing parties could stand,
and look at one another under the influence of his mildness
and enlightened candor.

Two younger thinkers, men both, have uttered noble
prophecies, auspicious for woman. Kinmont, all whose
thoughts tended towards the establishment of the reign of
love and peace, thought that the inevitable means of this

---

[103] Harriet Martineau (1802-1876), English traveller and author familiar
to New England through her *Society in America* (1837) and *Retrospect of
Western Travel* (1838).

would be an increased predominance given to the idea of woman.[104] Had he lived longer, to see the growth of the peace party, the reforms in life and medical practice which seek to substitute water for wine and drugs, pulse for animal food, he would have been confirmed in his view of the way in which the desired changes are to be effected.

In this connection, I must mention Shelley, who, like all men of genius, shared the feminine development, and, unlike many, knew it. His life was one of the first pulse-beats in the present reform-growth. He, too, abhorred blood and heat, and, by his system and his song, tended to reinstate a plant-like gentleness in the development of energy. In harmony with this, his ideas of marriage were lofty, and, of course, no less so of woman, her nature, and destiny.

For woman, if, by a sympathy as to outward condition she is led to aid the enfranchisement of the slave, must be no less so, by inward tendency, to favor measures which promise to bring the world more thoroughly and deeply into harmony with her nature. When the lamb takes place of the lion as the emblem of nations, both women and men will be as children of one spirit, perpetual learners of the word and doers thereof, not hearers only.

A writer in the New-York Pathfinder, in two articles headed "Femality," has uttered a still more pregnant word than any we have named.[105] He views woman truly from the soul, and not from society, and the depth and leading of his thoughts are proportionably remarkable. He views the feminine nature as a harmonizer of the vehement elements, and this has often been hinted elsewhere; but what he expresses most forcibly is the lyrical, the inspiring, and inspired apprehensiveness of her being.

This view being identical with what I have before attempted to indicate, as to her superior susceptibility to magnetic or electric influence, I will now try to express myself more fully.

There are two aspects of woman's nature, represented by the ancients as Muse and Minerva. It is the former to which the writer in the Pathfinder looks. It is the latter which

[104] Alexander Kinmont; see note 5, p. 78.
[105] V., "Femality," *Pathfinder*, 18 March 1843, pp. 35-36, 51-52.

Wordsworth has in mind, when he says—

> "With a placid brow,
> Which woman ne'er should forfeit, keep thy vow."[106]

The especial genius of woman I believe to be electrical in movement, intuitive in function, spiritual in tendency. She excels not so easily in classification, or re-creation, as in an instinctive seizure of causes, and a simple breathing out of what she receives that has the singleness of life, rather than the selecting and energizing of art.

More native is it to her to be the living model of the artist than to set apart from herself any one form in objective reality; more native to inspire and receive the poem, than to create it. In so far as soul is in her completely developed, all soul is the same; but as far as it is modified in her as woman, it flows, it breathes, it sings, rather than deposits soil, or finishes work, and that which is especially feminine flushes, in blossom, the face of earth, and pervades, like air and water, all this seeming solid globe, daily renewing and purifying its life. Such may be the especially feminine element, spoken of as Femality. But it is no more the order of nature that it should be incarnated pure in any form, than that the masculine energy should exist unmingled with it in any form.

Male and female represent the two sides of the great radical dualism. But, in fact, they are perpetually passing into one another. Fluid hardens to solid, solid rushes to fluid. There is no wholly masculine man, no purely feminine woman.

History jeers at the attempts of physiologists to bind great original laws by the forms which flow from them. They make a rule; they say from observation, what can and cannot be. In vain! Nature provides exceptions to every rule. She sends women to battle, and sets Hercules spinning; she enables women to bear immense burdens, cold, and frost; she enables the man, who feels maternal love, to nourish his infant like a mother. Of late she plays still gayer pranks. Not only she deprives organizations, but organs, of a necessary end. She enables people to read with the top of the head, and see

---

[106] Wordsworth, "Liberty."

with the pit of the stomach. Presently she will make a female Newton, and a male Syren.

Man partakes of the feminine in the Apollo, woman of the masculine as Minerva.

What I mean by the Muse is the unimpeded clearness of the intuitive powers which a perfectly truthful adherence to every admonition of the higher instincts would bring to a finely organized human being. It may appear as prophecy or as poesy. It enabled Cassandra to foresee the results of actions passing round her; the Seeress to behold the true character of the person through the mask of his customary life. (Sometimes she saw a feminine form behind the man, sometimes the reverse.) It enabled the daughter of Linnæus to see the soul of the flower exhaling from the flower.* It gave a man, but a poet man, the power of which he thus speaks: "Often in my contemplation of nature, radiant intimations, and as it were sheaves of light appear before me as to the facts of cosmogony in which my mind has, perhaps, taken especial part." He wisely adds, "but it is necessary with earnestness to verify the knowledge we gain by these flashes of light." And none should forget this. Sight must be verified by life before it can deserve the honors of piety and genius. Yet sight comes first, and of this sight of the world of causes, this approximation to the region of primitive motions, women I hold to be especially capable. Even without equal freedom with the other sex, they have already shown themselves so, and should these faculties have free play, I believe they will open new, deeper and purer sources of joyous inspiration than have as yet refreshed the earth.

Let us be wise and not impede the soul. Let her work as she will. Let us have one creative energy, one incessant revelation. Let it take what form it will, and let us not bind it by the past to man or woman, black or white. Jove sprang from Rhea, Pallas from Jove.[107] So let it be.

---

* The daughter of Linnaeus states, that while looking steadfastly at the red lily, she saw its spirit hovering above it, as a red flame. It is true, this, like many fair spirit-stories, may be explained away as an optical illusion, but its poetic beauty and meaning would, even then, make it valuable, as an illustration of the spiritual fact. [Fuller's note.] Carolin Linnaeus (1707-1778), Swedish scientist and biologist.

[107] Jove, Roman supreme diety (Zeus in Greek mythology); Rhea, great

If it has been the tendency of these remarks to call woman rather to the Minerva side,—if I, unlike the more generous writer, have spoken from society no less than the soul,—let it be pardoned! It is love that has caused this, love for many incarcerated souls, that might be freed, could the idea of religious self-dependence be established in them, could the weakening habit of dependence on others be broken up.

Proclus teaches that every life has, in its sphere, a totality or wholeness of the animating powers of the other spheres; having only, as its own characteristic, a predominance of some one power. Thus Jupiter comprises, within himself, the other twelve powers, which stand thus: The first triad is *demiurgic or fabricative*, i.e., Jupiter, Neptune, Vulcan; the second, *defensive*, Vesta, Minerva, Mars; the third, *vivific*, Ceres, Juno, Diana; and the fourth, Mercury, Venus, Apollo, *elevating and harmonic*. In the sphere of Jupiter, energy is predominant—with Venus, beauty; but each comprehends and apprehends all the others.

When the same community of life and consciousness of mind begins among men, humanity will have, positively and finally, subjugated its brute elements and Titanic childhood; criticism will have perished; arbitrary limits and ignorant censure be impossible; all will have entered upon the liberty of law, and the harmony of common growth.

Then Apollo will sing to his lyre what Vulcan forges on the anvil, and the Muse weave anew the tapestries of Minerva.

It is, therefore, only in the present crisis that the preference is given to Minerva. The power of continence must establish the legitimacy of freedom, the power of self-poise the perfection of motion.

Every relation, every gradation of nature is incalculably precious, but only to the soul which is poised upon itself, and to whom no loss, no change, can bring dull discord, for it is in harmony with the central soul.

If any individual live too much in relations, so that he becomes a stranger to the resources of his own nature, he falls, after a while, into a distraction, or imbecility, from which he can only be cured by a time of isolation, which

mother goddess of Greek mythology; Pallas Athena, Roman goddess who sprang fully created from Jove's forehead.

gives the renovating fountains time to rise up. With a society it is the same. Many minds, deprived of the traditionary or instinctive means of passing a cheerful existence, must find help in self-impulse, or perish. It is therefore that, while any elevation, in the view of union, is to be hailed with joy, we shall not decline celibacy as the great fact of the time. It is one from which no vow, no arrangement, can at present save a thinking mind. For now the rowers are pausing on their oars; they wait a change before they can pull together. All tends to illustrate the thought of a wise cotemporary. Union is only possible to those who are units. To be fit for relations in time, souls, whether of man or woman, must be able to do without them in the spirit.

It is therefore that I would have woman lay aside all thought, such as she habitually cherishes, of being taught and led by men. I would have her, like the Indian girl, dedicate herself to the Sun, the Sun of Truth, and go no where if his beams did not make clear the path. I would have her free from compromise, from complaisance, from helplessness, because I would have her good enough and strong enough to love one and all beings, from the fulness, not the poverty of being.

Men, as at present instructed, will not help this work, because they also are under the slavery of habit. I have seen with delight their poetic impulses. A sister is the fairest ideal, and how nobly Wordsworth, and even Byron, have written of a sister.[108]

There is no sweeter sight than to see a father with his little daughter. Very vulgar men become refined to the eye when leading a little girl by the hand. At that moment the right relation between the sexes seems established, and you feel as if the man would aid in the noblest purpose, if you ask him in behalf of his little daughter. Once two fine figures stood before me, thus. The father of very intellectual aspect, his falcon eye softened by affection as he looked down on his fair child, she the image of himself, only more graceful and brilliant in expression. I was reminded of Southey's Kehama;[109]

---

[108] See Wordsworth's "To My Sister" and Byron's "Epistle to Augusta."
[109] Robert Southey (1774-1843), British poet and essayist, quoted from *The Curse of Kehama* (1810).

when lo, the dream was rudely broken. They were talking of education, and he said,

"I shall not have Maria brought too forward. If she knows too much, she will never find a husband; superior women hardly ever can."

"Surely," said his wife, with a blush, "you wish Maria to be as good and wise as she can, whether it will help her to marriage or not."

"No," he persisted, "I want her to have a sphere and a home, and some one to protect her when I am gone."

It was a trifling incident, but made a deep impression. I felt that the holiest relations fail to instruct the unprepared and perverted mind. If this man, indeed, could have looked at it on the other side, he was the last that would have been willing to have been taken himself for the home and protection he could give, but would have been much more likely to repeat the tale of Alcibiades with his phials.[110]

But men do *not* look at both sides, and women must leave off asking them and being influenced by them, but retire within themselves, and explore the groundwork of life till they find their peculiar secret. Then, when they come forth again, renovated and baptized, they will know how to turn all dross to gold, and will be rich and free though they live in a hut, tranquil, if in a crowd. Then their sweet singing shall not be from passionate impulse, but the lyrical over–flow of a devine rapture, and a new music shall be evolved from this many-chorded world.

Grant her, then, for a while, the armor and the javelin. Let her put from her the press of other minds and meditate in virgin loneliness. The same idea shall re-appear in due time as Muse, or Ceres, the all-kindly patient Earth-Spirit.

Among the throng of symptoms which denote the present tendency to a crisis in the life of woman, which resembles the change from girlhood with its beautiful instincts, but unharmonized thoughts, its blind pupilage and restless seeking, to self-possessed, wise, and graceful womanhood, I have attempted to select a few.

---

[110] Alcibiades (*c.*450-404 B.C.), Greek general and political opportunist who stole the gold and silver cups of Anytus.

One of prominent interest is the unison of three male minds, upon the subject, which, for width of culture, power of self-concentration and dignity of aim, take rank as the prophets of the coming age, while their histories and labors are rooted in the past.

Swedenborg came, he tells us, to interpret the past revelation and unfold a new. He announces the new church that is to prepare the way for the New Jerusalem, a city built of precious stones, hardened and purified by secret processes in the veins of earth through the ages.

Swedenborg approximated to that harmony between the scientific and poetic lives of mind, which we hope from the perfected man. The links that bind together the realms of nature, the mysteries that accompany her births and growths, were unusually plain to him. He seems a man to whom insight was given at a period when the mental frame was sufficiently matured to retain and express its gifts.

His views of woman are, in the main, satisfactory. In some details, we may object to them as, in all his system, there are still remains of what is arbitrary and seemingly groundless; fancies that show the marks of old habits, and a nature as yet not thoroughly leavened with the spiritual leaven. At least so it seems to me now. I speak reverently, for I find such reason to venerate Swedenborg, from an imperfect knowledge of his mind, that I feel one more perfect might explain to me much that does not now secure my sympathy.

His idea of woman is sufficiently large and noble to interpose no obstacle to her progress. His idea of marriage is consequently sufficient. Man and woman share an angelic ministry, the union is from one to one, permanent and pure.

As the New Church extends its ranks, the needs of woman must be more considered.

Quakerism also establishes woman on a sufficient equality with man. But though the original thought of Quakerism is pure, its scope is too narrow, and its influence, having established a certain amount of good and made clear some truth, must, by degrees, be merged in one of wider range.* The

---

* In worship at stated periods, in daily expression, whether by word or deed, the Quakers have placed woman on the same platform with man. Can any one assert that they have reason to repent this? [Fuller's note.]
The Quakers or Society of Friends, English religious body organized by

mind of Swedenborg appeals to the various nature of man and allows room for æsthetic culture and the free expression of energy.

As apostle of the new order, of the social fabric that is to rise from love, and supersede the old that was based on strife, Charles Fourier comes next, expressing, in an outward order, many facts of which Swedenborg saw the secret springs.[111] The mind of Fourier, though grand and clear, was, in some respects, superficial. He was a stranger to the highest experiences. His eye was fixed on the outward more than the inward needs of man. Yet he, too, was a seer of the divine order, in its musical expression, if not in its poetic soul. He has filled one department of instruction for the new era, and the harmony in action, and freedom for individual growth he hopes shall exist; and if the methods he proposes should not prove the true ones, yet his fair propositions shall give many hints, and make room for the inspiration needed for such.

He, too, places woman on an entire equality with man, and wishes to give to one as to the other that independence which must result from intellectual and practical development.

Those who will consult him for no other reason, might do so to see how the energies of woman may be made available in the pecuniary way. The object of Fourier was to give her the needed means of self help, that she might dignify and unfold her life for her own happiness, and that of society. The many, now, who see their daughters liable to destitution, or vice to escape from it, may be interested to examine the means, if they have not yet soul enough to appreciate the ends he proposes.

On the opposite side of the advancing army, leads the great apostle of individual culture, Goethe. Swedenborg makes organization and union the necessary results of solitary thought. Fourier, whose nature was, above all, constructive, looked to them too exclusively. Better institutions, he

George Fox (1624-1691), believed that each individual had direct access to God through his or her "inner light."

[111] Charles Fourier (1772-1837), French socialist whose writings greatly influenced George Ripley at the Brook Farm community at West Roxbury, Massachusetts, and who was championed in America by Horace Greeley in the pages of his *New-York Tribune*.

thought, will make better men. Goethe expressed, in every way, the other side. If one man could present better forms, the rest could not use them till ripe for them.

Fourier says, As the institutions, so the men! All follies are excusable and natural under bad institutions.

Goethe thinks, As the man, so the institutions! There is no excuse for ignorance and folly. A man can grow in any place, if he will.

Ay! but Goethe, bad institutions are prison walls and impure air that make him stupid, so that he does not will.

And thou, Fourier, do not expect to change mankind at once, or even "in three generations" by arrangement of groups and series, or flourish of trumpets for attractive industry. If these attempts are made by unready men, they will fail.

Yet we prize the theory of Fourier no less than the profound suggestion of Goethe. Both are educating the age to a clearer consciousness of what man needs, what man can be, and better life must ensue.

Goethe, proceeding on his own track, elevating the human being in the most imperfect states of society, by continual efforts at self-culture, takes as good care of women as of men. His mother, the bold, gay Frau Aja, with such playful freedom of nature; the wise and gentle maiden, known in his youth, over whose sickly solitude "the Holy Ghost brooded as a dove;" his sister, the intellectual woman *par excellence:* the Duchess Amelia; Lili, who combined the character of the woman of the world with the lyrical sweetness of the shepherdess, on whose chaste and noble breast flowers and gems were equally at home;[112] all these had supplied abundant suggestions to his mind, as to the wants and the possible excellencies of woman. And, from his poetic soul, grew up forms new and more admirable than life has yet produced, for whom his clear eye marked out paths in the future.

In Faust, we see the redeeming power, which, at present, upholds woman, while waiting for a better day, in Margaret.[113] The lovely little girl, pure in instinct, ignorant in

[112] Lili Schöneman, engaged to Goethe briefly in 1775.

[113] Margaret (or Gretchen), innocent young maiden personifying fearless womanly love who acts as a foil to the Devil in Goethe's *Faust* (1808).

mind, is misled and profaned by man abusing her confidence.* To the Mater *Dolorosa* she appeals for aid.[114] It is given to the soul, if not against outward sorrow; and the maiden, enlightened by her sufferings, refusing to receive temporal salvation by the aid of an evil power, obtains the eternal in its stead.

In the second part, the intellectual man, after all his manifold strivings, owes to the interposition of her whom he had betrayed *his* salvation. She intercedes, this time herself a glorified spirit, with the Mater *Gloriosa*.[115]

Leonora, too, is woman, as we see her now, pure, thoughtful, refined by much acquaintance with grief.[116]

Iphigenia he speaks of in his journals as his "daughter," and she is the daughter† whom a man will wish, even if he has chosen his wife from very mean motives. She is the virgin, steadfast soul, to whom falsehood is more dreadful than any other death.

But it is to Wilhelm Meister's Apprenticeship and Wandering Years that I would especially refer, as these volumes contain the sum of the Sage's observations during a long life, as to what man should do, under present circumstances, to obtain mastery over outward, through an initiation into inward life, and severe discipline of faculty.[117]

* As Faust says, her only fault was a "Kindly delusion,"—"ein guter wahn." [Fuller's note.]

[114] Mater *Dolorosa*, Mary, Mother of Sorrows.

[115] Mater *Gloriosa*, Mary, Full of Glory.

[116] Leonora, loved by the title character in Goethe's *Torquato Tasso*; see also note 28, p. 108.

† Goethe was as false to his ideas in practice, as Lord Herbert. And his punishment was the just and usual one of connections formed beneath the standard of right, from the impulses of the baser self. Iphigenia was the worthy daughter of his mind, but the son, the child of his degrading connection in actual life, corresponded with that connection. This son, on whom Goethe vainly lavished so much thought and care, was like his mother, and like Goethe's attachment for his mother. "This young man," says a late well informed writer, (M. Henri Blaze,) "Wieland, with good reason, was called the son of the servant, *der Sohn der Magd*. He inherited from his father only his name and his *physique*." [Fuller's note.]

Goethe's wife was socially and intellectual beneath him; Henri Blaze (1813-1888), French literary critic.

[117] Goethe's *Wilhelm Meister's Apprenticeship* (1795-1796) was made popular in America by Thomas Carlyle's translation in 1824.

As Wilhelm advances in the upward path he becomes acquainted with better forms of woman by knowing how to seek, and how to prize them when found. For the weak and immature man will, often, admire a superior woman, but he will not be able to abide by a feeling, which is too severe a tax on his habitual existence. But, with Wilhelm, the gradation is natural and expresses ascent in the scale of being. At first he finds charm in Mariana and Philina, very common forms of feminine character, not without redeeming traits, no less than charms, but without wisdom or purity. Soon he is attended by Mignon, the finest expression ever yet given to what I have called the lyrical element in woman. She is a child, but too full-grown for this man; he loves, but cannot follow her; yet is the association not without an enduring influence. Poesy has been domesticated in his life, and, though he strives to bind down her heavenward impulse, as art or apothegm, these are only the tents, beneath which he may sojourn for a while, but which may be easily struck, and carried on limitless wanderings.

Advancing into the region of thought, he encounters a wise philanthropy in Natalia, (instructed, let us observe, by an *uncle*,) practical judgment and the outward economy of life in Theresa, pure devotion in the Fair Saint.

Farther and last he comes to the house of Macaria, the soul of a star, *i.e.* a pure and perfected intelligence embodied in feminine form, and the centre of a world whose members revolve harmoniously round her. She instructs him in the archives of a rich human history, and introduces him to the contemplation of the heavens.

From the hours passed by the side of Mariana to these with Macaria, is a wide distance for human feet to traverse. Nor has Wilhelm travelled so far, seen and suffered so much in vain. He now begins to study how he may aid the next generation; he sees objects in harmonious arrangement, and from his observations deduces precepts by which to guide his course as a teacher and a master, "help-full, comfort-full."

In all these expressions of woman, the aim of Goethe is satisfactory to me. He aims at a pure self-subsistence, and free development of any powers with which they may be gifted by nature as much for them as for men. They are units, addressed as souls. Accordingly the meeting between man and woman, as represented by him, is equal and noble, and, if he does not depict marriage, he makes it possible.

In the Macaria, bound with the heavenly bodies in fixed revolutions, the centre of all relations, herself unrelated, he expresses the Minerva side of feminine nature. It was not by chance that Goethe gave her this name. Macaria, the daughter of Hercules, who offered herself as a victim for the good of her country, was canonized by the Greeks, and worshipped as the Goddess of true Felicity. Goethe has embodied this Felicity as the Serenity that arises from Wisdom, a Wisdom, such as the Jewish wise man venerated, alike instructed in the designs of heaven, and the methods necessary to carry them into effect upon earth.

Mignon is the electrical, inspired, lyrical nature. And wherever it appears we echo in our aspirations that of the child,

> "So let me seem until I be:—
> Take not the *white robe* away."
>
> *   *   *   *   *
>
> "Though I lived without care and toil,
> Yet felt I sharp pain enough,
> Make me again forever young."[118]

All these women, though we see them in relations, we can think of as unrelated. They all are very individual, yet seem, nowhere, restrained. They satisfy for the present, yet arouse an infinite expectation.

The economist Theresa, the benevolent Natalia, the fair Saint, have chosen a path, but their thoughts are not narrowed to it. The functions of life to them are not ends, but suggestions.

Thus, to them, all things are important, because none is necessary. Their different characters have fair play, and each is beautiful in its minute indications, for nothing is enforced or conventional, but every thing, however slight, grows from the essential life of the being.

Mignon and Theresa wear male attire when they like, and it is graceful for them to do so, while Macaria is confined to

---

[118] *Wilhelm Meister's Apprenticeship*, Book VIII, Chapter 2.

her arm-chair behind the green curtain, and the Fair Saint could not bear a speck of dust on her robe.

All things are in their places in this little world, because all is natural and free, just as "there is room for everything out of doors." Yet all is rounded in by natural harmony, which will always arise where Truth and Love are sought in the light of Freedom.

Goethe's book bodes an era of freedom like its own of "extraordinary generous seeking," and new revelations. New individualities shall be developed in the actual world, which shall advance upon it as gently as the figures come out upon his canvass.[119]

I have indicated on this point the coincidence between his hopes and those of Fourier, though his are directed by an infinitely higher and deeper knowledge of human nature. But, for our present purpose, it is sufficient to show how surely these different paths have conducted to the same end two earnest thinkers. In some other place I wish to point out similar coincidences between Goethe's model school and the plans of Fourier, which may cast light upon the page of prophecy.

Many women have observed that the time drew nigh for a better care of the sex, and have thrown out hints that may be useful. Among these may be mentioned—

Miss Edgeworth, who, although restrained by the habits of her age and country, and belonging more to the eighteenth than the nineteenth century, has done excellently as far as she goes.[120] She had a horror of sentimentalism, and the love of notoriety, and saw how likely women, in the early stages of culture, were to aim at these. Therefore she bent her efforts to recommending domestic life. But the methods she recommends are such as will fit a character for any position to which it may be called. She taught a contempt of falsehood, no less in its most graceful, than in its meanest apparitions; the cultivation of a clear, independent judgment, and

---

[119] The text of "The Great Lawsuit" contains only four more paragraphs after this point; the remainder of *Woman in the Nineteenth Century* is original material except the four final paragraphs from "The Great Lawsuit," incorporated at 206.16–37 below.

[120] Maria Edgeworth (1767-1849), English writer best known for her Gothic novels.

adherence to its dictates; habits of various and liberal study and employment, and a capacity for friendship. Her standard of character is the same for both sexes. Truth, honor, enlightened benevolence, and aspiration after knowledge. Of poetry, she knows nothing, and her religion consists in honor and loyalty to obligations once assumed, in short, in "the great idea of duty which holds us upright." Her whole tendency is practical.

Mrs. Jameson is a sentimentalist, and, therefore, suits us ill in some respects, but she is full of talent, has a just and refined perception of the beautiful, and a genuine courage when she finds it necessary. She does not appear to have thought out, thoroughly, the subject on which we are engaged, and her opinions, expressed as opinions, are sometimes inconsistent with one another. But from the refined perception of character, admirable suggestions are given in her "Women of Shakspeare," and "Loves of the Poets."[121]

But that for which I most respect her is the decision with which she speaks on a subject which refined women are usually afraid to approach, for fear of the insult and scurril jest they may encounter; but on which she neither can nor will restrain the indignation of a full heart. I refer to the degradation of a large portion of women into the sold and polluted slaves of men, and the daring with which the legislator and man of the world lifts his head beneath the heavens, and says "this must be; it cannot be helped; it is a necessary accompaniment of *civilization*."

So speaks the *citizen*. Man born of woman, the father of daughters, declares that he will and must buy the comforts and commercial advantages of his London, Vienna, Paris, New-York, by conniving at the moral death, the damnation, so far as the action of society can insure it, of thousands of women for each splendid metropolis.

O men! I speak not to you. It is true that your wickedness (for you must not deny that, at least, nine thousand out of the

---

[121] Fuller refers to Mrs. Jameson's *Women of Shakespeare* (also titled *The Heroines of Shakespeare*), first published as *Characteristics of Women* in 1832, and *Loves of the Poets* (1829). Fuller reviewed *The Heroines of Shakespeare* in the 30 June 1846 *New-York Daily Tribune* and Mrs. Jameson's *Memoirs and Letters* in the paper's 24 July 1846 number.

ten fall through the vanity you have systematically flattered, or the promises you have treacherously broken;) yes, it is true that your wickedness is its own punishment. Your forms degraded and your eyes clouded by secret sin; natural harmony broken and fineness of perception destroyed in your mental and bodily organization; God and love shut out from your hearts by the foul visitants you have permitted there; incapable of pure marriage; incapable of pure parentage; incapable of worship; oh wretched men, your sin is its own punishment! You have lost the world in losing yourselves. Who ruins another has admitted the worm to the root of his own tree, and the fuller ye fill the cup of evil, the deeper must be your own bitter draught. But I speak not to you—you need to teach and warn one another. And more than one voice rises in earnestness. And all that *women* say to the heart that has once chosen the evil path, is considered prudery, or ignorance, or perhaps, a feebleness of nature which exempts from similar temptations.

But to you, women, American women, a few words may not be addressed in vain. One here and there may listen.

You know how it was in the Oriental clime. One man, if wealth permitted, had several wives and many hand-maidens. The chastity and equality of genuine marriage, with "the thousand decencies that flow," from its communion, the precious virtues that gradually may be matured, within its enclosure, were unknown.

But this man did not wrong according to his light. What he did, he might publish to God and Man; it was not a wicked secret that hid in vile lurking-places and dens, like the banquets of beasts of prey. Those women were not lost, not polluted in their own eyes, nor those of others. If they were not in a state of knowledge and virtue, they were at least in one of comparative innocence.

You know how it was with the natives of this continent. A chief had many wives whom he maintained and who did his household work; those women were but servants, still they enjoyed the respect of others and their own. They lived together in peace. They knew that a sin against what was in their nation esteemed virtue, would be as strictly punished in man as in woman.

Now pass to the countries where marriage is between one

and one. I will not speak of the Pagan nations, but come to those which own the Christian rule. We all know what that enjoins; there is a standard to appeal to.

See now, not the mass of the people, for we all know that it is a proverb and a bitter jest to speak of the "down-trodden million." We know that, down to our own time, a principle never had so fair a chance to pervade the mass of the people, but that we must solicit its illustration from select examples.

Take the Paladin, take the Poet.[122] Did *they* believe purity more impossible to man than to woman? Did they wish woman to believe that man was less amenable to higher motives, that pure aspirations would not guard him against bad passions, that honorable employments and temperate habits would not keep him free from slavery to the body. O no! Love was to them a part of heaven, and they could not even wish to receive its happiness, unless assured of being worthy of it. Its highest happiness to them was, that it made them wish to be worthy. They courted probation. They wished not the title of knight, till the banner had been upheld in the heats of battle, amid the rout of cowards.

I ask of you, young girls—I do not mean *you*, whose heart is that of an old coxcomb, though your locks have not yet lost their sunny tinge. Not of you whose whole character is tainted with vanity, inherited or taught, who have early learnt the love of coquettish excitement, and whose eyes rove restlessly in search of a "conquest" or a "beau." You who are ashamed *not* to be seen by others the mark of the most contemptuous flattery or injurious desire. To such I do not speak. But to thee, maiden, who, if not so fair, art yet of that unpolluted nature which Milton saw when he dreamed of Comus and the Paradise.[123] Thou, child of an unprofaned wedlock, brought up amid the teachings of the woods and fields, kept fancy-free by useful employment and a free flight into the heaven of thought, loving to please only those whom thou wouldst not be ashamed to love; I ask of thee, whose cheek has not forgotten its blush nor thy heart its lark-like hopes, if he whom thou mayst hope the Father will send

---

[122] Paladin, one of twelve legendary champions in attendance upon the great emperor Charlemagne (742-814).
[123] Milton's play *Comus* (1634) is set in a dream-like atmosphere.

thee, as the companion of life's toils and joys, is not to thy
thought pure? Is not manliness to thy thought purity, *not*
lawlessness? Can his lips speak falsely? Can he do, in secret,
what he could not avow to the mother that bore him? O say,
dost thou not look for a heart free, open as thine own, all
whose thoughts may be avowed, incapable of wronging the
innocent, or still farther degrading the fallen. A man, in short,
in whom brute nature is entirely subject to the impulses of
his better self.

Yes! it was thus that thou didst hope, for I have many,
many times seen the image of a future life, of a destined
spouse, painted on the tablets of a virgin heart.

It might be that she was not true to these hopes. She was
taken into what is called "the world," froth and scum as it
mostly is on the social caldron. There, she saw fair woman
carried in the waltz close to the heart of a being who appeared to her a Satyr.[124] Being warned by a male friend that
he was in fact of that class, and not fit for such familiar nearness to a chaste being, the advised replied that "women
should know nothing about such things." She saw one fairer
given in wedlock to a man of the same class. "Papa and
mamma said that 'all men were faulty, at some time in their
lives; they had a great many temptations. Frederick would be
so happy at home; he would not want to do wrong.'" She
turned to the married women; they, oh tenfold horror!
laughed at her supposing "men were like women." Sometimes, I say, she was not true and either sadly accommodated
herself to "woman's lot," or acquired a taste for satyr-society,
like some of the Nymphs, and all the Bacchanals of old. But
to these who could not and would not accept a mess of pot-
tage, or a Circe cup, in lieu of their birthright, and to these
others who have yet their choice to make, I say, Courage! I
have some words of cheer for you. A man, himself of unbroken purity, reported to me the words of a foreign artist,
that "the world would never be better till men subjected
themselves to the same laws they had imposed on women;"
that artist, he added, was true to the thought. The same was
true of Canova, the same of Beethoven. "Like each other

---

[124] Satyr, a classical lascivious woodland diety, half man and half goat,
and a name which has come to be associated with lecherous behavior.

demi-god, they kept themselves free from stain," and Michael Angelo, looking over here from the loneliness of his century, might meet some eyes that need not shun his glance.

In private life, I am assured by men who are not so sustained and occupied by the worship of pure beauty, that a similar consecration is possible, is practiced. That many men feel that no temptation can be too strong for the will of man, if he invokes the aid of the Spirit instead of seeking extenuation from the brute alliances of his nature. In short, what the child fancies is really true, though almost the whole world declares it a lie. Man is a child of God; and if he seek His guidance to keep the heart with diligence, it will be so given that all the issues of life may be pure. Life will then be a temple.

> The temple round
> Spread green the pleasant ground;
>   The fair colonnade
> Be of pure marble pillars made;
> Strong to sustain the roof,
>   Time and tempest proof,
> Yet, amidst which, the lightest breeze
>   Can play as it please;
>   The audience hall
>   Be free to all
>   Who revere
> The Power worshipped here,
>   Sole guide of youth
>   Unswerving Truth:
>   In the inmost shrine
>   Stands the image divine,
>   Only seen
> By those whose deeds have worthy been—
>   Priestlike clean.
> Those, who initiated are,
>   Declare,
>   As the hours
> Usher in varying hopes and powers;
>   It changes its face,
>   It changes its age,
>   Now a young beaming Grace,
>   Now Nestorian Sage:
>   But, to the pure in heart,

This shape of primal art
In age is fair,
In youth seems wise,
Beyond compare,
Above surprise;
What it teaches native seems
Its new lore our ancient dreams;
Incense rises from the ground,
Music flows around;
Firm rest the feet below, clear gaze the eyes above,
When Truth to point the way through Life assumes the wand of Love;
But, if she cast aside the robe of green,
Winter's silver sheen,
White, pure as light,
Makes gentle shroud as worthy weed as bridal robe had been.*

We are now in a transition state, and but few steps have yet been taken. From polygamy, Europe passed to the marriage *de convenance*. This was scarcely an improvement. An attempt was then made to substitute genuine marriage, (the mutual choice of souls inducing a permanent union,) as yet baffled on every side by the haste, the ignorance, or the impurity of man.

Where man assumes a high principle to which he is not yet ripened; it will happen, for a long time, that the few will be nobler than before; the many worse. Thus now. In the country of Sidney and Milton, the metropolis is a den of wickedness, and a stye of sensuality; in the country of Lady Russell,[125] the custom of English Peeresses, of selling their daughters to the highest bidder, is made the theme and jest of fashionable novels by unthinking children who would

---

* (As described by the historian.)

The temple of Juno is like what the character of woman should be.
Columns! graceful decorums, attractive yet sheltering.
Porch! noble inviting aspect of the life.
Kaos! receives the worshippers. See here the statue of the Divinity.
Ophistodomos! Sanctuary where the most precious possessions were kept safe from the hand of the spoiler and the eye of the world.
[Fuller's note.]

The poem above is by Fuller.
[125] Lady Russell, in *Persuasion* (1818) by Jane Austen (1775-1817), attempts to force a loveless union.

stare at the idea of sending them to a Turkish slave dealer, though the circumstances of the bargain are there less degrading, as the will and thoughts of the person sold are not so degraded by it, and it is not done in defiance of an acknowledged law of right in the land and the age.

I must here add that I do not believe there ever was put upon record more depravation of man, and more despicable frivolity of thought and aim in woman, than in the novels which purport to give the picture of English fashionable life, which are read with such favor in our drawing rooms, and give the tone to the manners of some circles. Compared with the hard-hearted cold folly there described, crime is hopeful, for it, at least, shows some power remaining in the mental constitution.

To return: Attention has been awakened among men to the stains of celibacy, and the profanations of marriage. They begin to write about it and lecture about it. It is the tendency now to endeavor to help the erring by showing them the physical law. This is wise and excellent; but forget not the better half. Cold bathing and exercise will not suffice to keep a life pure, without an inward baptism and noble and exhilarating employment for the thoughts and the passions. Early marriages are desirable, but if, (and the world is now so out of joint that there are a hundred thousand chances to one against it,) a man does not early, or at all, find the person to whom he can be united in the marriage of souls, will you give him in the marriage *de convenance*,[126] or if not married, can you find no way for him to lead a virtuous and happy life? Think of it well, ye who think yourselves better than pagans, for many of *them* knew this sure way.*

[126] Marriage *de convenance*, marriage of convenience, one dictated by expediency rather than love.

* The Persian sacred books, the Desatir, describe the great and holy prince Ky Khosrou, as being "an angel, and the son of an angel," one to whom the Supreme says, "Thou art not absent from before me for one twinkling of an eye. I am never out of thy heart. And I am contained in nothing but in thy heart, and in a heart like thy heart. And I am nearer unto thee than thou art to thyself." This Prince had in his Golden Seraglio three ladies of surpassing beauty, and all four, in this royal monastery, passed their lives, and left the world, as virgins.

The Persian people had no scepticism when the history of such a mind was narrated. They were Catholics. [Fuller's note.]

To you, women of America, it is more especially my business to address myself on this subject, and my advice may be classed under three heads:

Clear your souls from the taint of vanity.

Do not rejoice in conquests, either that your power to allure may be seen by other women, or for the pleasure of rousing passionate feelings that gratify your love of excitement.

It must happen, no doubt, that frank and generous women will excite love they do not reciprocate, but, in nine cases out of ten, the woman has, half consciously, done much to excite. In this case she shall not be held guiltless, either as to the unhappiness or injury to the lover. Pure love, inspired by a worthy object, must ennoble and bless, whether mutual or not; but that which is excited by coquettish attraction of any grade of refinement, must cause bitterness and doubt, as to the reality of human goodness, so soon as the flush of passion is over. And that you may avoid all taste for these false pleasures

"Steep the soul
In one pure love, and it will last thee long."[127]

The love of truth, the love of excellence, which, whether you clothe them in the person of a special object or not, will have power to save you from following Duessa, and lead you in the green glades where Una's feet have trod.[128]

It was on this one subject that a venerable champion of good, the last representative of the spirit which sanctified the revolution and gave our country such a sunlight of hope in the eyes of the nations, the same who lately in Boston offered anew to the young men the pledge taken by the young men of his day, offered, also, his counsel, on being addressed by the principal of a girl's school, thus:

REPLY OF MR. ADAMS

Mr. Adams was so deeply affected by the address of Miss Foster, as to be for some time inaudible. When heard, he

[127] Unidentified.
[128] Duessa, in Spenser's *Faerie Queen*, typifies the treachery and falsehood of the Roman church.

spoke as follows:

"This is the first instance in which a lady has thus addressed me personally; and I trust that all the ladies present will be able sufficiently to enter into my feelings to know, that I am more affected by this honor, than by any other I could have received.

"You have been pleased, Madam, to allude to the character of my father, and the history of my family, and their services to the country. It is indeed true, that from the existence of the Republic as an independent nation, my father and myself have been in the public service of the country, almost without interruption. I came into the world, as a person having personal responsibilities, with the Declaration of Independence, which constituted us a nation. I was a child at that time, and had then perhaps the greatest of blessings that can be bestowed on man—a mother who was anxious and capable to form her children to what they ought to be. From that mother I derived whatever instruction—religious especially, and moral—has pervaded a long life; I will not say perfectly, and as it ought to be; but I will say, because it is justice only to the memory of her whom I revere, that if, in the course of my life, there has been any imperfection, or deviation from what she taught me, the fault is mine, and not hers.

"With such a mother, and such other relations with the sex, of sister, wife, and daughter, it has been the perpetual instruction of my life to love and revere the female sex. And in order to carry that sentiment of love and reverence to its highest degree of perfection, I know of nothing that exists in human society better adapted to produce that result, than institutions of the character that I have now the honor to address.

"I have been taught, as I have said, through the course of my life, to love and to revere the female sex; but I have been taught, also—and that lesson has perhaps impressed itself on my mind even more strongly, it may be, than the other—I have been taught not to flatter them. It is not unusual in the intercourse of man with the other sex—and especially for young men—to think, that the way to win the hearts of ladies is by flattery.—To love and to revere the sex, is what I think the duty of man; but *not to flatter them*; and this I would say to the young ladies here; and if they, and others present, will

allow me, with all the authority which nearly four score years
may have with those who have not yet attained one score—I
would say to them what I have no doubt they say to themselves, and are taught here, not to take the flattery of men as
proof of perfection.

"I am now, however, I fear, assuming too much of a character that does not exactly belong to me. I therefore conclude,
by assuring you, Madam, that your reception of me has affected me, as you perceive, more than I can express in words;
and that I shall offer my best prayers, till my latest hour, to
the Creator of us all, that this institution especially, and all
others of a similar kind, designed to form the female mind to
wisdom and virtue, may prosper to the end of time."

It will be interesting to add here the character of Mr.
Adams's mother, as drawn by her husband, the first John
Adams, in a family letter* written just before his death.

"I have reserved for the last the life of Lady Russell.[129]
This I have not yet read, because I read it more than forty
years ago. On this hangs a tale which you ought to know and
communicate it to your children. I bought the life and letters
of Lady Russell, in the year 1775, and sent it to your grand-
mother, with an express intent and desire, that she should
consider it a mirror in which to contemplate herself; for, at
that time, I thought it extremely probable, from the daring
and dangerous career I was determined to run, that she
would one day find herself in the situation of Lady Russell,
her husband without a head. This lady was more beautiful
than Lady Russell, had a brighter genius, more information, a
more refined taste, and, at least, her equal in the virtues of
the heart; equal fortitude and firmness of character, equal
resignation to the will of Heaven, equal in all the virtues and
graces of the christian life. Like Lady Russell, she never, by
word or look, discouraged me from running all hazards for
the salvation of my country's liberties; she was willing to
share with me, and that her children should share with us

* Journal and Correspondence of Miss Adams, vol. i, p. 246. [Fuller's
note.] This edition was published in New York by Wiley & Putnam in
1841; Adams' letter is dated 12 July 1820.

[129] The letters of Lady Rachel Russell (1636-1723) were first published in
1773.

both, in all the dangerous consequences we had to hazard."

Will a woman who loves flattery or an aimless excitement, who wastes the flower of her mind on transitory sentiments, ever be loved with a love like that, when fifty years trial have entitled to the privileges of "the golden marriage?"

Such was the love of the iron-handed warrior for her, not his hand-maid, but his help-meet:

"Whom God loves, to him gives he such a wife."

I find the whole of what I want in this relation, in the two epithets by which Milton makes Adam address *his* wife.

In the intercourse of every day he begins:

> "Daughter of God and man, *accomplished* Eve."*

In a moment of stronger feeling,

> "Daughter of God and man, IMMORTAL Eve."[130]

What majesty in the cadence of the line; what dignity, what reverence in the attitude, both of giver and receiver!

The woman who permits, in her life, the alloy of vanity; the woman who lives upon flattery, coarse or fine, shall never be thus addressed. She is *not* immortal as far as her will is concerned, and every woman who does so creates miasma, whose spread is indefinite. The hand, which casts into the waters of life a stone of offence, knows not how far the circles thus caused, may spread their agitations.

A little while since, I was at one of the most fashionable places of public resort. I saw there many women, dressed without regard to the season or the demands of the place, in apery, or, as it looked, in mockery of European fashions. I saw their eyes restlessly courting attention. I saw the way in which it was paid, the style of devotion, almost an open sneer, which it pleased those ladies to receive from men whose expression marked their own low position in the moral and intellectual world. Those women went to their pillows with their heads full of folly, their hearts of jealousy, or gratified vanity: those men, with the low opinion they already entertained of woman confirmed. These were Ameri-

---

* See Appendix, H. [Fuller's note.] Appendix H is printed on pp. 238-39.
[130] *Paradise Lost*, Book IV, 1. 660, and Book IX, 1. 291.

can *ladies*; i.e., they were of that class who have wealth and
leisure to make full use of the day, and confer benefits on
others. They were of that class whom the possession of external advantages makes of pernicious example to many, if
these advantages be misused.

Soon after, I met a circle of women, stamped by society as
among the most degraded of their sex. "How," it was asked
of them, "did you come here?" for, by the society that I saw
in the former place, they were shut up in a prison. The
causes were not difficult to trace: love of dress, love of flattery, love of excitement. They had not dresses like the other
ladies, so they stole them; they could not pay for flattery by
distinctions, and the dower of a worldly marriage, so they
paid by the profanation of their persons. In excitement, more
and more madly sought from day to day, they drowned the
voice of conscience.

Now I ask you, my sisters, if the women at the fashionable
house be not answerable for those women being in the
prison?

As to position in the world of souls, we may suppose the
women of the prison stood fairest, both because they had
misused less light, and because loneliness and sorrow had
brought some of them to feel the need of better life, nearer
truth and good. This was no merit in them, being an effect of
circumstance, but it was hopeful. But you, my friends, (and
some of you I have already met,) consecrate yourselves without waiting for reproof, in free love and unbroken energy, to
win and to diffuse a better life. Offer beauty, talents, riches,
on the altar; thus shall ye keep spotless your own hearts, and
be visibly or invisibly the angels to others.

I would urge upon those women who have not yet considered this subject, to do so. Do not forget the unfortunates
who dare not cross your guarded way. If it do not suit you to
act with those who have organized measures of reform, then
hold not yourself excused from acting in private. Seek out
these degraded women, give them tender sympathy, counsel,
employment. Take the place of mothers, such as might have
saved them originally.

If you can do little for those already under the ban of the
world, and the best considered efforts have often failed, from
a want of strength in those unhappy ones to bear up against

the sting of shame and the prejudices of the world, which makes them seek oblivion again in their old excitements, you will at least leave a sense of love and justice in their hearts that will prevent their becoming utterly imbittered and corrupt. And you may learn the means of prevention for those yet uninjured. There will be found in a diffusion of mental culture, simple tastes, best taught by your example, a genuine self-respect, and above all, what the influence of man tends to hide from woman, the love and fear of a divine, in preference to a human tribunal.

But suppose you save many who would have lost their bodily innocence (for as to mental, the loss of that is incalculably more general,) through mere vanity and folly; there still remain many, the prey and spoil of the brute passions of man. For the stories frequent in our newspapers outshame antiquity, and vie with the horrors of war.

As to this, it must be considered that, as the vanity and proneness to seduction of the imprisoned women represented a general degradation in their sex; so do these acts a still more general and worse in the male. Where so many are weak it is natural there should be many lost, where legislators admit that ten thousand prostitutes are a fair proportion to one city, and husbands tell their wives that it is folly to expect chastity from men, it is inevitable that there should be many monsters of vice.

I must in this place mention, with respect and gratitude, the conduct of Mrs. Child in the case of Amelia Norman.[131] The action and speech of this lady was of straight-forward nobleness, undeterred by custom or cavil from duty towards an injured sister. She showed the case and the arguments the counsel against the prisoner had the assurance to use in their true light to the public. She put the case on the only ground of religion and equity. She was successful in arresting the attention of many who had before shrugged their shoulders, and let sin pass as necessarily a part of the company of men. They begin to ask whether virtue is not possible, perhaps

---

[131] Lydia Maria Child (1802-1880), American author and abolitonist. Amelia Norman had been acquitted of the charge of stabbing her seducer on the steps of the Astor House in New York. Child championed her case in print and later helped her to start a new life.

necessary, to man as well as to woman. They begin to fear that the perdition of a woman must involve that of a man. This is a crisis. The results of this case will be important.

In this connection I must mention Eugene Sue, the French novelist, several of whose works have been lately transplanted among us, as having the true spirit of reform as to women.[132] Like every other French writer, he is still tainted with the transmissions of the old regime. Still falsehood may be permitted for the sake of advancing truth, evil as the way to good. Even George Sand, who would trample on every graceful decorum, and every human law for the sake of a sincere life, does not see that she violates it by making her heroines able to tell falsehoods in a good cause. These French writers need ever to be confronted by the clear perception of the English and German mind, that the only good man, consequently the only good reformer, is he

"Who bases good on good alone, and owes
To virtue every triumph that he knows."[133]

Still, Sue has the heart of a reformer, and especially towards women, he sees what they need, and what causes are injuring them. From the histories of Fleur de Marie and La Louve, from the lovely and independent character of Rigolette, from the distortion given to Matilda's mind, by the present views of marriage, and from the truly noble and immortal character of the "hump-backed Sempstress" in the "Wandering Jew," may be gathered much that shall elucidate doubt and direct inquiry on this subject.[134] In reform, as in philosophy, the French are the interpreters to the civilized world. Their own attainments are not great, but they make clear the past, and break down barriers to the future.

Observe that the good man of Sue is pure as Sir Charles Grandison.[135]

---

[132] Eugène Sue (1804-1857), French author best known in America for his *Mysteries of Paris* (1842-1843) and *The Wandering Jew* (1844-1845).

[133] Unidentified.

[134] Fleur-de-Marie, central character in *Mysteries of Paris* who goes from a criminal life to a convent by the book's end; Rigolette, in *Mysteries of Paris*, a kind-hearted and hard-working young woman.

[135] Fuller refers to *A History of Sir Charles Grandison* (1754), a novel by Samuel Richardson (1689-1761).

Apropos to Sir Charles, women are accustomed to be told
by men that the reform is to come *from them*. "You," say the
men, "must frown upon vice, you must decline the attentions
of the corrupt, you must not submit to the will of your husband when it seems to you unworthy, but give the laws in
marriage, and redeem it from its present sensual and mental
pollutions."

This seems to us hard. Men have, indeed, been, for more
than a hundred years, rating women for countenancing vice.
But at the same time, they have carefully hid from them its
nature, so that the preference often shown by women for bad
men, arises rather from a confused idea that they are bold
and adventurous, acquainted with regions which women are
forbidden to explore, and the curiosity that ensues, than a
corrupt heart in the woman. As to marriage it has been incul-
cated on women for centuries, that men have not only
stronger passions than they, but of a sort that it would be
shameful for them to share or even understand. That, therefore, they must "confide in their husbands," i.e., submit im-
plicitly to their will. That the least appearance of coldness or
withdrawal, from whatever cause, in the wife is wicked, because liable to turn her husband's thoughts to illicit indulgence; for a man is so constituted that he must indulge his
passions or die!

Accordingly a great part of women look upon men as a kind
of wild beasts, but "suppose they are all alike;" the unmar-
ried are assured by the married that, "if they knew men as
they do," i.e., by being married to them, "they would not
expect continence or self-government from them."

I might accumulate illustrations on this theme, drawn from
acquaintance with the histories of women, which would startle and grieve all thinking men, but I forbear. Let Sir Charles
Grandison preach to his own sex, or if none there be, who
feels himself able to speak with authority from a life unspot-
ted in will or deed, let those who are convinced of the practicability and need of a pure life, as the foreign artist was,
advise the others, and warn them by their own example, if
need be.

The following passage from a female writer on female affairs, expresses a prevalent way of thinking on this subject.

"It may be that a young woman, exempt from all motives of

vanity, determines to take for a husband a man who does not inspire her with a very decided inclination. Imperious circumstances, the evident interest of her family, or the danger of a suffering celibacy, may explain such a resolution. If, however, she were to endeavor to surmount a personal repugnance, we should look upon this as *injudicious*. Such a rebellion of nature marks the limit that the influence of parents, or the self-sacrifice of the young girl, should never pass. *We shall be told that this repugnance is an affair of the imagination*; it may be so; but imagination is a power which it is temerity to brave; and its antipathy is more difficult to conquer than its preference."*

Among ourselves, the exhibition of such a repugnance from a woman who had been given in marriage "by advice of friends," was treated by an eminent physician as sufficient proof of insanity. If he had said sufficient cause for it, he would have been nearer right.

It has been suggested by men who were pained by seeing bad men admitted, freely, to the society of modest women, thereby encouraged to vice by impunity, and corrupting the atmosphere of homes; that there should be a senate of the matrons in each city and town, who should decide what candidates were fit for admission to their houses and the society of their daughters.†

Such a plan might have excellent results, but it argues a moral dignity and decision, which does not yet exist, and needs to be induced by knowledge and reflection. It has been the tone to keep women ignorant on these subjects, or when they were not, to command that they should seem so. "It is indelicate," says the father or husband, "to inquire into the private character of such an one. It is sufficient that I do not think him unfit to visit you." And so, this man, who would not tolerate these pages in his house, "unfit for family reading," because they speak plainly, introduces there a man whose shame is written on his brow, as well as the open secret of the whole town, and, presently, if *respectable* still,

---

* Madame Necker de Saussure. [Fuller's note.] Suzanne Necker (1739-1794), French writer and mother of Mme. de Staël.

† See Goethe's Tasso. "A synod of good women should decide,"—if the golden age is to be restored. [Fuller's note.]

and rich enough, gives him his daughter to wife. The mother affects ignorance, "supposing he is no worse than most men." The daughter *is* ignorant; something in the mind of the new spouse seems strange to her, but she supposes it is "woman's lot" not to be perfectly happy in her affections; she has always heard, "men could not understand women," so she weeps alone, or takes to dress and the duties of the house. The husband, of course, makes no avowal, and dreams of no redemption.

"In the heart of every young woman," says the female writer, above quoted, addressing herself to the husband, "depend upon it, there is a fund of exalted ideas; she conceals, represses, without succeeding in smothering them. *So long as these ideas in your wife are directed to* YOU, *they are, no doubt, innocent,* but take care that they be not accompanied with *too much* pain. In other respects, also, spare her delicacy. Let all the antecedent parts of your life, if there are such, which would give her pain, be concealed from her; *her happiness and her respect for you would suffer from this misplaced confidence.* Allow her to retain that flower of purity, *which should distinguish her in your eyes from every other woman.*" We should think so, truly, under this canon. Such a man must esteem purity an exotic that could only be preserved by the greatest care. Of the degree of mental intimacy possible, in such a marriage, let every one judge for himself!

On this subject, let every woman, who has once begun to think, examine herself, see whether she does not suppose virtue possible and necessary to man, and whether she would not desire for her son a virtue which aimed at a fitness for a divine life, and involved, if not asceticism, that degree of power over the lower self, which shall "not exterminate the passions, but keep them chained at the feet of reason." The passions, like fire, are a bad master; but confine them to the hearth and the altar, and they give life to the social economy, and make each sacrifice meet for heaven.

When many women have thought upon this subject, some will be fit for the Senate, and one such Senate in operation would affect the morals of the civilized world.

At present I look to the young. As preparatory to the Senate, I should like to see a society of novices, such as the world has never yet seen, bound by no oath, wearing no badge. In place of an oath they should have a religious faith in the capacity of man for virtue; instead of a badge, should wear in the heart a firm resolve not to stop short of the destiny promised him as a son of God. Their service should be action and conservatism, not of old habits, but of a better nature, enlightened by hopes that daily grow brighter.

If sin was to remain in the world, it should not be by their connivance at its stay, or one moment's concession to its claims.

They should succor the oppressed, and pay to the upright the reverence due in hero-worship by seeking to emulate them. They would not denounce the willingly bad, but they could not be with them, for the two classes could not breathe the same atmosphere.

They would heed no detention from the time-serving, the worldly and the timid.

They could love no pleasures that were not innocent and capable of good fruit.

I saw, in a foreign paper, the title now given to a party abroad, "Los Exaltados."[136] Such would be the title now given these children by the world: Los Exaltados, Las Exaltadas; but the world would not sneer always, for from them would issue a virtue by which it would, at last, be exalted too.

I have in my eye a youth and a maiden whom I look to as the nucleus of such a class. They are both in early youth, both as yet uncontaminated, both aspiring, without rashness, both thoughtful, both capable of deep affection, both of strong nature and sweet feelings, both capable of large mental development. They reside in different regions of earth, but their place in the soul is the same. To them I look, as, perhaps, the harbingers and leaders of a new era, for never yet have I known minds so truly virgin, without narrowness or ignorance.

When men call upon women to redeem them, they mean such maidens. But such are not easily formed under the present influences of society. As there are more such young men

---

[136] Los Exaltados, liberal Spanish political party.

to help give a different tone, there will be more such maidens.

The English novelist, D'Israeli, has, in his novel of the "Young Duke," made a man of the most depraved stock be redeemed by a woman who despises him when he has only the brilliant mask of fortune and beauty to cover the poverty of his heart and brain, but knows how to encourage him when he enters on a better course.[137] But this woman was educated by a father who valued character in women.

Still there will come now and then, one who will, as I hope of my young Exaltada, be example and instruction to the rest. It was not the opinion of woman current among Jewish men that formed the character of the mother of Jesus.

Since the sliding and backsliding men of the world, no less than the mystics declare that, as through woman man was lost, so through woman must man be redeemed, the time must be at hand. When she knows herself indeed as "accomplished," still more as "immortal Eve," this may be.

As an immortal, she may also know and inspire immortal love, a happiness not to be dreamed of under the circumstances advised in the last quotation. Where love is based on concealment, it must, of course, disappear when the soul enters the scene of clear vision!

And, without this hope, how worthless every plan, every bond, every power!

"The giants," said the Scandinavian Saga, "had induced Loke, (the spirit that hovers between good and ill,) to steal for them Iduna, (Goddess of Immortality,) and her apples of pure gold. He lured her out, by promising to show, on a marvellous tree he had discovered, apples beautiful as her own, if she would only take them with her for a comparison. Thus, having lured her beyond the heavenly domain, she was seized and carried away captive by the powers of misrule.

As now the gods could not find their friend Iduna, they were confused with grief; indeed they began visibly to grow old and gray. Discords arose, and love grew cold. Indeed,

---

[137] Benjamin Disraeli (1804-1881) published his autobiographical novel *The Young Duke* in 1831.

Odur, spouse of the goddess of love and beauty, wandered away and returned no more. At last, however, the gods, discovering the treachery of Loke, obliged him to win back Iduna from the prison in which she sat mourning. He changed himself into a falcon, and brought her back as a swallow, fiercely pursued by the Giant King, in the form of an eagle. So she strives to return among us, light and small as a swallow. We must welcome her form as the speck on the sky that assures the glad blue of Summer. Yet one swallow does not make a summer. Let us solicit them in flights and flocks!

Returning from the future to the present, let us see what forms Iduna takes, as she moves along the declivity of centuries to the valley where the lily flower may concentrate all its fragrance.

It would seem as if this time were not very near to one fresh from books, such as I have of late been—no: *not* reading, but sighing over. A crowd of books having been sent me since my friends knew me to be engaged in this way, on Woman's "Sphere," Woman's "Mission," and Woman's "Destiny," I believe that almost all that is extant of formal precept has come under my eye. Among these I read with refreshment, a little one called "The Whole Duty of Woman," "indited by a noble lady at the request of a noble lord," and which has this much of nobleness, that the view it takes is a religious one.[138] It aims to fit woman for heaven, the main bent of most of the others is to fit her to please, or, at least, not to disturb a husband.

Among these I select as a favorable specimen, the book I have already quoted, "The Study* of the Life of Woman, by Madame Necker de Saussure, of Geneva, translated from the French." This book was published at Philadelphia, and has been read with much favor here. Madame Necker is the

[138] *The Whole Duty of a Woman. By a Lady.* (1753), by William Kenrick (1725?-1779), was first published in America in 1783.

* This title seems to be incorrectly translated from the French. I have not seen the original. [Fuller's note.] *L' éducation progressive; or, Étude du cours de la vie, par Mme Necker de Saussure* was published in Paris between 1828 and 1832. Fuller may be thinking of an English edition (1839-1843), reprinted, possibly in Philadelphia, in three volumes, the last being titled *Observations on the Life of a Woman.*

cousin of Madame de Stael, and has taken from her works the motto prefixed to this.

"Cette vie n'a quelque prix que si elle sert a' l'education morale de notre cœur."[139]

Mde. Necker is, by nature, capable of entire consistency in the application of this motto, and, therefore, the qualifications she makes, in the instructions given to her own sex, show forcibly the weight which still paralyzes and distorts the energies of that sex.

The book is rich in passages marked by feeling and good suggestions, but taken in the whole the impression it leaves is this:

Woman is, and *shall remain* inferior to man and subject to his will, and, in endeavoring to aid her, we must anxiously avoid any thing that can be misconstrued into expression of the contrary opinion, else the men will be alarmed, and combine to defeat our efforts.

The present is a good time for these efforts, for men are less occupied about women than formerly. Let us, then, seize upon the occasion, and do what we can to make our lot tolerable. But we must sedulously avoid encroaching on the territory of man. If we study natural history, our observations may be made useful, by some male naturalist; if we draw well, we may make our services acceptable to the artists. But our names must not be known, and, to bring these labors to any result, we must take some man for our head, and be his hands.

The lot of woman is sad. She is constituted to expect and need a happiness that cannot exist on earth. She must stifle such aspirations within her secret heart, and fit herself, as well as she can, for a life of resignations and consolations.

She will be very lonely while living with her husband. She must not expect to open her heart to him fully, or that, after marriage, he will be capable of the refined service of love. The man is not born for the woman, only the woman for the man. "Men cannot understand the hearts of women." The life of woman must be outwardly a well-intentioned, cheerful dissimulation of her real life.

---

[139] "This life only has any value if it serves toward the moral education of our heart."

Naturally, the feelings of the mother, at the birth of a female child, resemble those of the Paraguay woman, described by Southey as lamenting in such heart-breaking tones that her mother did not kill her the hour she was born. "Her mother, who knew what the life of a woman must be;"—or those women seen at the north by Sir A. Mackenzie, who performed this pious duty towards female infants whenever they had an opportunity.[140]

"After the first delight, the young mother experiences feelings a little different, according as the birth of a son or a daughter has been announced.

"Is it a son? A sort of glory swells at this thought the heart of the mother; she seems to feel that she is entitled to gratitude. She has given a citizen, a defender to her country. To her husband an heir of his name, to herself a protector. And yet the contrast of all these fine titles with this being, so humble, soon strikes her. At the aspect of this frail treasure, opposite feelings agitate her heart; she seems to recognize in him *a nature superior to her own*, but subjected to a low condition, and she honors a future greatness in the object of extreme compassion. Somewhat of that respect and adoration for a feeble child, of which some fine pictures offer the expression in the features of the happy Mary, seem reproduced with the young mother who has given birth to a son.

"Is it a daughter? There is usually a slight degree of regret; so deeply rooted is the idea of the superiority of man in happiness and dignity, and yet, as she looks upon this child, she is more and more *softened* towards it—a deep sympathy —a sentiment of identity with this delicate being takes possession of her; an extreme pity for so much weakness, a more pressing need of prayer stirs her heart. Whatever sorrows she may have felt, she dreads for her daughter; but she will guide her to become much wiser, much better than herself. And then the gayety, the frivolity of the young woman have their turn. This little creature is a flower to cultivate, a doll to decorate."

Similar sadness at the birth of a daughter I have heard mothers express not unfrequently.

[140] Sir Alexander Mackenzie (1755?-1820), Scottish explorer of North America.

As to this living so entirely for men, I should think when it was proposed to women they would feel, at least, some spark of the old spirit of races allied to our own. If he is to be my bridegroom *and lord*, cries Brunhilda,* he must first be able to pass through fire and water. I will serve at the banquet, says the Valkyrie, but only him who, in the trial of deadly combat, has shown himself a hero.

If women are to be bond-maids, let it be to men superior to women in fortitude, in aspiration, in moral power, in refined sense of beauty! You who give yourselves "to be supported," or because "one must love something," are they who make the lot of the sex such that mothers are sad when daughters are born.

It marks the state of feeling on this subject that it was mentioned, as a bitter censure on a woman who had influence over those younger than herself. "She makes those girls want to see heroes?"

"And will that hurt them?"

"Certainly; how *can* you ask? They will find none, and so they will never be married."

"*Get* married" is the usual phrase, and the one that correctly indicates the thought, but the speakers, on this occasion, were persons too outwardly refined to use it. They were ashamed of the word, but not of the thing. Madame Necker, however, sees good possible in celibacy.

Indeed, I know not how the subject could be better illustrated, than by separating the wheat from the chaff in Madame Necker's book; place them in two heaps and then summon the reader to choose; giving him first a near-sighted glass to examine the two; it might be a christian, an astronomical, or an artistic glass, any kind of good glass to obviate acquired defects in the eye. I would lay any wager on the result.

But time permits not here a prolonged analysis. I have given the clues for fault-finding.

As a specimen of the good take the following passage, on

* See the Nibelungen Lays. [Fuller's note.] Brünnehilde, legendary queen of Iceland in *Nibelungenlied*, killed Siegfried out of revenge for a trick he had played on her.

the phenomena of what I have spoken of, as the lyrical or electric element in woman.

"Women have been seen to show themselves poets in the most pathetic pantomimic scenes, where all the passions were depicted full of beauty; and these poets used a language unknown to themselves, and the performance once over, their inspiration was a forgotten dream. Without doubt there is an interior development to beings so gifted, but their sole mode of communication with us is their talent. They are, in all besides, the inhabitants of another planet."

Similar observations have been made by those who have seen the women at Irish wakes, or the funeral ceremonies of modern Greece or Brittany, at times when excitement gave the impulse to genius; but, apparently, without a thought that these rare powers belonged to no other planet, but were a high development of the growth of this, and might by wise and reverent treatment, be made to inform and embellish the scenes of every day. But, when woman has her fair chance, they will do so, and the poem of the hour will vie with that of the ages. I come now with satisfaction to my own country, and to a writer, a female writer, whom I have selected as the clearest, wisest, and kindliest, who has as yet, used pen here on these subjects. This is Miss Sedgwick.[141]

Miss Sedgwick, though she inclines to the private path, and wishes that, by the cultivation of character, might should vindicate right, sets limits nowhere, and her objects and inducements are pure. They are the free and careful cultivation of the powers that have been given, with an aim at moral and intellectual perfection. Her speech is moderate and sane, but never palsied by fear or sceptical caution.

Herself a fine example of the independent and beneficent existence that intellect and character can give to woman, no less than man, if she know how to seek and prize it; also that the intellect need not absorb or weaken, but rather will refine and invigorate the affections, the teachings of her practical good sense come with great force, and cannot fail to avail much. Every way her writings please me both as to the

---

[141] Catharine Maria Sedgwick (1789-1867), American novelist.

means and the ends. I am pleased at the stress she lays on observance of the physical laws, because the true reason is given. Only in a strong and clean body can the soul do its message fitly.

She shows the meaning of the respect paid to personal neatness both in the indispensable form of cleanliness, and of that love of order and arrangement, that must issue from a true harmony of feeling.

The praises of cold water seem to me an excellent sign in the age. They denote a tendency to the true life. We are now to have, as a remedy for ills, not orvietan, or opium, or any quack medicine, but plenty of air and water, with due attention to warmth and freedom in dress, and simplicity of diet.

Every day we observe signs that the natural feelings on these subjects are about to be reinstated, and the body to claim care as the abode and organ of the soul, not as the tool of servile labor, or the object of voluptuous indulgence.

A poor woman who had passed through the lowest grades of ignominy, seemed to think she had never been wholly lost, "for," said she, "I would always have good underclothes;" and, indeed, who could doubt that this denoted the remains of private self-respect in the mind?

A woman of excellent sense said, "it might seem childish, but to her one of the most favorable signs of the times, was that the ladies had been persuaded to give up corsets."

Yes! let us give up all artificial means of distortion. Let life be healthy, pure, all of a piece. Miss Sedgwick, in teaching that domestics must have the means of bathing as much as their mistresses, and time, too, to bathe, has symbolized one of the most important of human rights.

Another interesting sign of the time is the influence exercised by two women, Miss Martineau and Miss Barrett, from their sick rooms. The lamp of life which, if it had been fed only by the affections, depended on precarious human relations, would scarce have been able to maintain a feeble glare in the lonely prison, now shines far and wide over the nations, cheering fellow sufferers and hallowing the joy of the healthful.

These persons need not health or youth, or the charms of personal presence, to make their thoughts available. A few more such, and old woman* shall not be the synonyme for imbecility, nor old maid a term of contempt, nor woman be spoken of as a reed shaken in the wind.

It is time, indeed, that men and women both should cease to grow old in any other way than as the tree does, full of grace and honor. The hair of the artist turns white, but his eye shines clearer than ever, and we feel that age brings him maturity, not decay. So would it be with all were the springs of immortal refreshment but unsealed within the soul, then like these women they would see, from the lonely chamber window, the glories of the universe; or, shut in darkness, be visited by angels.

I now touch on my own place and day, and, as I write, events are occurring that threaten the fair fabric approached by so long an avenue. Week before last the Gentile was requested to aid the Jew to return to Palestine, for the Millennium, the reign of the Son of Mary, was near. Just now, at high and solemn mass, thanks were returned to the Virgin for having delivered O'Connell from unjust imprisonment, in requital of his having consecrated to her the league formed in behalf of Liberty on Tara's Hill.[142] But, last week brought news which threatens that a cause identical with the enfranchisement of Jews, Irish, women, ay, and of Americans in general, too, is in danger, for the choice of the people threatens to rivet the chains of slavery and the leprosy of sin permanently on this nation, through the annexation of Texas!

Ah! if this should take place, who will dare again to feel the throb of heavenly hope, as to the destiny of this country? The noble thought that gave unity to all our knowledge, harmony to all our designs;—the thought that the progress of history had brought on the era, the tissue of prophecies pointed out the spot, where humanity was, at last, to have a fair chance to know itself, and all men be born free and equal for the eagle's flight, flutters as if about to leave the breast,

---

* An apposite passage is quoted in Appendix F. [Fuller's note.] Appendix F is printed on p. 224.

[142] Daniel O'Connell (1775-1847), Irish nationalist whose actions on behalf of the Catholic Association culminated in a meeting in 1843 at Tara's Hill to urge repeal of the Act of Union between Great Britain and Ireland, after which he was jailed.

which, deprived of it, will have no more a nation, no more a home on earth.

Women of my country!—Exaltadas! if such there be,—Women of English, old English nobleness, who understand the courage of Boadicea, the sacrifice of Godiva, the power of Queen Emma to tread the red hot iron unharmed.[143] Women who share the nature of Mrs. Hutchinson, Lady Russell, and the mothers of our own revolution: have you nothing to do with this?[144] You see the men, how they are willing to sell shamelessly, the happiness of countless generations of fellow-creatures, the honor of their country, and their immortal souls, for a money market and political power. Do you not feel within you that which can reprove them, which can check, which can convince them? You would not speak in vain; whether each in her own home, or banded in unison.

Tell these men that you will not accept the glittering baubles, spacious dwellings, and plentiful service, they mean to offer you through these means. Tell them that the heart of women demands nobleness and honor in man, and that, if they have not purity, have not mercy, they are no longer fathers, lovers, husbands, sons of yours.

This cause is your own, for as I have before said, there is a reason why the foes of African slavery seek more freedom for women; but put it not upon that ground, but on the ground of right.

If you have a power, it is a moral power. The films of interest are not so close around you as around the men. If you will but think, you cannot fail to wish to save the country from this disgrace. Let not slip the occasion, but do something to lift off the curse incurred by Eve.

You have heard the women engaged in the abolition movement accused of boldness, because they lifted the voice in public, and lifted the latch of the stranger. But were these

[143] Boadicea (d. 62 A.D.), Celtic queen who led an unsuccessful revolt against the Romans; Lady Godiva (c. 1100) rode nude on horseback through Coventry as a condition for her husband to lift the burdensome taxes he had levied on his subjects; Emma (d. 1052), queen of England who, according to legend, underwent the ordeal of hot iron to prove herself innocent of a charge of unchastity.

[144] Anne Hutchinson (1591-1643), English colonist in America whose religious beliefs caused her to be expelled from Massachusetts.

acts, whether performed judiciously or no, *so* bold as to dare before God and man to partake the fruits of such offence as this?

You hear much of the modesty of your sex. Preserve it by filling the mind with noble desires that shall ward off the corruptions of vanity and idleness. A profligate woman, who left her accustomed haunts and took service in a New-York boarding-house, said "she had never heard talk so vile at the Five Points, as from the ladies at the boarding-house."[145] And why? Because they were idle; because, having nothing worthy to engage them, they dwelt, with unnatural curiosity, on the ill they dared not go to see.

It will not so much injure your modesty to have your name, by the unthinking, coupled with idle blame, as to have upon your soul the weight of not trying to save a whole race of women from the scorn that is put upon *their* modesty.

Think of this well! I entreat, I conjure you, before it is too late. It is my belief that something effectual might be done by women, if they would only consider the subject, and enter upon it in the true spirit, a spirit gentle, but firm, and which feared the offence of none, save One who is of purer eyes than to behold iniquity.

And now I have designated in outline, if not in fulness, the stream which is ever flowing from the heights of my thought.

In the earlier tract, I was told, I did not make my meaning sufficiently clear. In this I have consequently tried to illustrate it in various ways, and may have been guilty of much repetition. Yet, as I am anxious to leave no room for doubt, I shall venture to retrace, once more, the scope of my design in points, as was done in old-fashioned sermons.

Man is a being of two-fold relations, to nature beneath, and intelligences above him. The earth is his school, if not his birth-place: God his object: life and thought, his means of interpreting nature, and aspiring to God.

Only a fraction of this purpose is accomplished in the life of any one man. Its entire accomplishment is to be hoped only from the sum of the lives of men, or man considered as a whole.

As this whole has one soul and one body, any injury or

---

[145] Five Points, area in New York City known for its vice and crime.

obstruction to a part, or to the meanest member, affects the whole. Man can never be perfectly happy or virtuous, till all men are so.

To address man wisely, you must not forget that his life is partly animal, subject to the same laws with nature.

But you cannot address him wisely unless you consider him still more as soul, and appreciate the conditions and destiny of soul.

The growth of man is two-fold, masculine and feminine.

As far as these two methods can be distinguished they are so as

Energy and Harmony.

Power and Beauty.

Intellect and Love.

Or by some such rude classification, for we have not language primitive and pure enough to express such ideas with precision.

These two sides are supposed to be expressed in man and woman, that is, as the more and less, for the faculties have not been given pure to either, but only in preponderance. There are also exceptions in great number, such as men of far more beauty than power, and the reverse. But as a general rule, it seems to have been the intention to give a preponderance on the one side, that is called masculine, and on the other, one that is called feminine.

There cannot be a doubt that, if these two developments were in perfect harmony, they would correspond to and fulfil one another, like hemispheres, or the tenor and bass in music.

But there is no perfect harmony in human nature; and the two parts answer one another only now and then, or, if there be a persistent consonance, it can only be traced, at long intervals, instead of discoursing an obvious melody.

What is the cause of this?

Man, in the order of time, was developed first; as energy comes before harmony; power before beauty.

Woman was therefore under his care as an elder. He might have been her guardian and teacher.

But as human nature goes not straight forward, but by excessive action and then reaction in an undulated course, he misunderstood and abused his advantages, and became her temporal master instead of her spiritual sire.

On himself came the punishment. He educated woman more as a servant than a daughter, and found himself a king without a queen.

The children of this unequal union showed unequal natures, and, more and more, men seemed sons of the handmaid, rather than princes.

At last there were so many Ishmaelites that the rest grew frightened and indignant. They laid the blame on Hagar, and drove her forth into the wilderness.[146]

But there were none the fewer Ishmaelites for that.

At last men became a little wiser, and saw that the infant Moses was, in every case, saved by the pure instincts of woman's breast. For, as too much adversity is better for the moral nature than too much prosperity, woman, in this respect, dwindled less than man, though in other respects, still a child in leading strings.

So man did her more and more justice, and grew more and more kind.

But yet, his habits and his will corrupted by the past, he did not clearly see that woman was half himself, that her interests were identical with his, and that, by the law of their common being, he could never reach his true proportions while she remained in any wise shorn of hers.

And so it has gone on to our day; both ideas developing, but more slowly than they would under a clearer recognition of truth and justice, which would have permitted the sexes their due influence on one another, and mutual improvement from more dignified relations.

Wherever there was pure love, the natural influences were, for the time, restored.

Wherever the poet or artist gave free course to his genius, he saw the truth, and expressed it in worthy forms, for these men especially share and need the feminine principle. The divine birds need to be brooded into life and song by mothers.

Wherever religion (I mean the thirst for truth and good, not the love of sect and dogma,) had its course, the original de-

---

[146] Hagar, concubine of Abraham who bore him a son, Ishmael, when his wife Sarah proved barren. But after the birth of Sarah's son Isaac, the now-haughty Hagar was banished from Abraham's tents.

sign was apprehended in its simplicity, and the dove pre-saged sweetly from Dodona's oak.[147]

I have aimed to show that no age was left entirely without a witness of the equality of the sexes in function, duty and hope.

Also that, when there was unwillingness or ignorance, which prevented this being acted upon, women had not the less power for their want of light and noble freedom. But it was power which hurt alike them and those against whom they made use of the arms of the servile; cunning, blandishment, and unreasonable emotion.

That now the time has come when a clearer vision and better action are possible. When man and woman may regard one another as brother and sister, the pillars of one porch, the priests of one worship.

I have believed and intimated that this hope would receive an ampler fruition, than ever before, in our own land.

And it will do so if this land carry out the principles from which sprang our national life.

I believe that, at present, women are the best helpers of one another.

Let them think; let them act; till they know what they need.

We only ask of men to remove arbitrary barriers. Some would like to do more. But I believe it needs for woman to show herself in her native dignity, to teach them how to aid her; their minds are so encumbered by tradition.

When Lord Edward Fitzgerald travelled with the Indians, his manly heart obliged him at once, to take the packs from the squaws and carry them.[148] But we do not read that the red men followed his example, though they are ready enough to carry the pack of the white woman, because she seems to them a superior being.

Let woman appear in the mild majesty of Ceres, and rudest churls will be willing to learn from her.

You ask, what use will she make of liberty, when she has so long been sustained and restrained?

[147] The oak grove in Dodona, in ancient Greece, housed an oracle dedicated to Zeus.

[148] Lord Edward Fitzgerald (1763-1798), Irish politician who travelled down the Mississippi River.

I answer; in the first place, this will not be suddenly given. I read yesterday a debate of this year on the subject of enlarging women's rights over property. It was a leaf from the class-book that is preparing for the needed instruction. The men learned visibly as they spoke. The champions of woman saw the fallacy of arguments, on the opposite side, and were startled by their own convictions. With their wives at home, and the readers of the paper, it was the same. And so the stream flows on; thought urging action, and action leading to the evolution of still better thought.

But, were this freedom to come suddenly, I have no fear of the consequences. Individuals might commit excesses, but there is not only in the sex a reverence for decorums and limits inherited and enhanced from generation to generation, which many years of other life could not efface, but a native love, in woman as woman, of proportion, of "the simple art of not too much," a Greek moderation, which would create immediately a restraining party, the natural legislators and instructors of the rest, and would gradually establish such rules as are needed to guard, without impeding, life.

The Graces would lead the choral dance, and teach the rest to regulate their steps to the measure of beauty.

But if you ask me what offices they may fill; I reply—any. I do not care what case you put; let them be sea-captains, if you will. I do not doubt there are women well fitted for such an office, and, if so, I should be glad to see them in it, as to welcome the maid of Saragossa, or the maid of Missolonghi, or the Suliote heroine, or Emily Plater.[149]

I think women need, especially at this juncture, a much greater range of occupation than they have, to rouse their latent powers. A party of travellers lately visited a lonely hut on a mountain. There they found an old woman that told them she and her husband had lived there forty years. "Why," they said, "did you choose so barren a spot?" She "did not know; *it was the man's notion.*"

---

[149] Saragossa, city in northern Spain and capital of the kingdom of Aragon; Missolonghi, town in Greece at which Byron died (1824) during the struggle for Greek independence from Turkey; Suliotes, people of Greece defeated by the Turks in 1822 but who nevertheless played an important role in the Greek war of liberation.

And, during forty years, she had been content to act, without knowing why, upon "the man's notion." I would not have it so.

In families that I know, some little girls like to saw wood, others to use carpenters' tools. Where these tastes are indulged, cheerfulness and good humor are promoted. Where they are forbidden, because "such things are not proper for girls," they grow sullen and mischievous.

Fourier had observed these wants of women, as no one can fail to do who watches the desires of little girls, or knows the ennui that haunts grown women, except where they make to themselves a serene little world by art of some kind. He, therefore, in proposing a great variety of employments, in manufactures or the care of plants and animals, allows for one third of woman, as likely to have a taste for masculine pursuits, one third of men for feminine.

Who does not observe the immediate glow and serenity that is diffused over the life of women, before restless or fretful, by engaging in gardening, building, or the lowest department of art. Here is something that is not routine, something that draws forth life toward the infinite.

I have no doubt, however, that a large proportion of women would give themselves to the same employments as now, because there are circumstances that must lead them. Mothers will delight to make the nest soft and warm. Nature would take care of that; no need to clip the wings of any bird that wants to soar and sing, or finds in itself the strength of pinion for a migratory flight unusual to its kind. The difference would be that *all* need not be constrained to employments, for which *some* are unfit.

I have urged upon the sex self-subsistence in its two forms of self-reliance and self-impulse, because I believe them to be the needed means of the present juncture.

I have urged on woman independence of man, not that I do not think the sexes mutually needed by one another, but because in woman this fact has led to an excessive devotion, which has cooled love, degraded marriage, and prevented either sex from being what it should be to itself or the other.

I wish woman to live, *first* for God's sake. Then she will not make an imperfect man her god, and thus sink to idolatry. Then she will not take what is not fit for her from a sense of weakness and poverty. Then, if she finds what she needs in man embodied, she will know how to love, and be worthy of being loved.

By being more a soul, she will not be less woman, for nature is perfected through spirit.

Now there is no woman, only an overgrown child.

That her hand may be given with dignity, she must be able to stand alone. I wish to see men and women capable of such relations as are depicted by Landor in his Pericles and Aspasia, where grace is the natural garb of strength, and the affections are calm, because deep. The softness is that of a firm tissue, as when

> "The gods approve
> The depth, but not the tumult of the soul,
> A fervent, not ungovernable love."[150]

A profound thinker has said, "no married woman can represent the female world, for she belongs to her husband. The idea of woman must be represented by a virgin."

But that is the very fault of marriage, and of the present relation between the sexes, that the woman does belong to the man, instead of forming a whole with him. Were it otherwise, there would be no such limitation to the thought.

Woman, self-centred, would never be absorbed by any relation; it would be only an experience to her as to man. It is a vulgar error that love, *a* love to woman is her whole existence; she also is born for Truth and Love in their universal energy. Would she but assume her inheritance, Mary would not be the only virgin mother. Not Manzoni alone would celebrate in his wife the virgin mind with the maternal wisdom and conjugal affections. The soul is ever young, ever virgin.

And will not she soon appear? The woman who shall vindicate their birthright for all women; who shall teach them what to claim, and how to use what they obtain? Shall not her name be for her era Victoria, for her country and life Virginia?[151] Yet predictions are rash; she herself must teach us to give her the fitting name.

---

[150] Wordsworth, "Laodamia."

[151] Victoria and Virginia, names signifying, respectively, "victorious" and "flourishing" or "virgin."

An idea not unknown to ancient times has of late been revived, that, in the metamorphoses of life, the soul assumes the form, first of man, then of woman, and takes the chances, and reaps the benefits of either lot. Why then, say some, lay such emphasis on the rights or needs of woman? What she wins not, as woman, will come to her as man.

That makes no difference. It is not woman, but the law of right, the law of growth, that speaks in us, and demands the perfection of each being in its kind, apple as apple, woman as woman. Without adopting your theory I know that I, a daughter, live through the life of man; but what concerns me now is, that my life be a beautiful, powerful, in a word, a complete life in its kind. Had I but one more moment to live, I must wish the same.

Suppose, at the end of your cycle, your great world-year, all will be completed, whether I exert myself or not (and the supposition is *false*,) but suppose it true, am I to be indifferent about it? Not so! I must beat my own pulse true in the heart of the world; for *that* is virtue, excellence, health.

Thou, Lord of Day! didst leave us to-night so calmly glorious, not dismayed that cold winter is coming, not postponing thy beneficence to the fruitful summer! Thou didst smile on thy day's work when it was done, and adorn thy down-going as thy up-rising, for thou art loyal, and it is thy nature to give life, if thou canst, and shine at all events!

I stand in the sunny noon of life. Objects no longer glitter in the dews of morning, neither are yet softened by the shadows of evening. Every spot is seen, every chasm revealed. Climbing the dusty hill, some fair effigies that once stood for symbols of human destiny have been broken; those I still have with me, show defects in this broad light. Yet enough is left, even by experience, to point distinctly to the glories of that destiny; faint, but not to be mistaken streaks of the future day. I can say with the bard,

"Though many have suffered shipwreck, still beat noble hearts."[152]

Always the soul says to us all: Cherish your best hopes as a faith, and abide by them in action. Such shall be the effectual fervent means to their fulfilment,

---

[152] Unidentified.

For the Power to whom we bow
Has given its pledge that, if not now,
They of pure and stedfast mind,
By faith exalted, truth refined,
Shall hear all music loud and clear,
Whose first notes they ventured here.
Then fear not thou to wind the horn,
Though elf and gnome thy courage scorn;
Ask for the Castle's King and Queen;
Though rabble rout may rush between,
Beat thee senseless to the ground,
In the dark beset thee round;
Persist to ask and it will come,
Seek not for rest in humbler home;
So shalt thou see what few have seen,
The palace home of King and Queen.[153]

15th November, 1844.

[153] The poem is by Fuller.

Appendix

A.

Apparition of the goddess Isis to her votary, from Apuleius.[154]

"Scarcely had I closed my eyes, when behold (I saw in a dream) a divine form emerging from the middle of the sea, and raising a countenance venerable, even to the gods themselves. Afterwards, the whole of the most splendid image seemed to stand before me, having gradually shaken off the sea. I will endeavor to explain to you its admirable form, if the poverty of human language will but afford me the power of an appropriate narration; or if the divinity itself, of the most luminous form, will supply me with a liberal abundance of fluent diction. In the first place, then, her most copious and long hairs, being gradually intorted, and promiscuously scattered on her divine neck, were softly defluous. A multiform crown, consisting of various flowers, bound the sublime summit of her head. And in the middle of the crown, just on her forehead, there was a smooth orb resembling a mirror, or rather a white refulgent light, which indicated that she was the moon. Vipers rising up after the manner of furrows, environed the crown on the right hand and on the left, and Cerealian ears of corn were also extended from above. Her garment was of many colors, and woven from the finest flax, and was at one time lucid with a white splendor, at another yellow from the flower of crocus, and at another flaming with a rosy redness. But that which most excessively dazzled my sight, was a very black robe, fulgid with a dark splendor, and which, spreading round and passing under her right side, and ascending to her left shoulder, there rose pro-

---

[154] Apuleius (b. *c.*123 A.D.), Roman author, quoted from *Metamorphoses* (*The Golden Ass*), Book XI.

tuberant, like the centre of a shield, the dependent part of her robe falling in many folds, and having small knots of fringe, gracefully flowing in its extremities. Glittering stars were dispersed through the embroidered border of the robe, and through the whole of its surface, and the full moon, shining in the middle of the stars, breathed forth flaming fires. A crown, wholly consisting of flowers and fruits of every kind, adhered with indivisible connexion to the border of the conspicuous robe, in all its undulating motions.

"What she carried in her hands also consisted of things of a very different nature. Her right hand bore a brazen rattle, through the narrow lamina of which, bent like a belt, certain rods passing, produced a sharp triple sound through the vibrating motion of her arm. An oblong vessel, in the shape of a boat, depended from her left hand, on the handle of which, in that part which was conspicuous, an asp raised its erect head and largely swelling neck. And shoes, woven from the leaves of the victorious palm tree, covered her immortal feet. Such, and so great a goddess, breathing the fragrant odour of the shores of Arabia the happy, deigned thus to address me."

The foreign English of the translator, Thomas Taylor, gives the description the air of being, itself, a part of the Mysteries.[155] But its majestic beauty requires no formal initiation to be enjoyed.

B.

I give this, in the original, as it does not bear translation. Those who read Italian will judge whether it is not a perfect description of a perfect woman.

LODI E PREGHIERE A MARIA.

Vergine bella che di sol vestita,
Coronata di stelle, al sommo Sole
   Piacesti si, che'n te sua luce ascose;
Amor mi spinge a dir di te parole:
   Ma non so 'ncominciar senza tu' aita,
E di Colui che amando in te si pose.
   Invoco lei che ben sempre rispose,
Chi la chiamò con fede.

---

[155] Thomas Taylor (1758-1835), English classical scholar and Platonist.

Vergine, s'a mercede
Miseria extrema dell' smane cose
  Giammai ti volse, al mio prego t'inchina:
Soccorri alla mia guerra;
  Bench' i' sia terra, e tu del ciel Regina.

Vergine saggia, e del bel numero una
Delle beate vergini prudenti;
  Anzi la prima, e con più chiara lampa;
O saldo scudo dell' afflitte gente
  Contra colpi di Morte e di Fortuna,
Sotto' l qual si trionfa, non pur scampa:
  O refrigerio alcieco ardor ch' avvampa
Qui fra mortali sciocchi,
  Vergine, que' begli occhi
Che vider tristi la spietata stampa
  Ne' dolci membri del tuo caro figlio,
Volgi al mio dubbio stato;
  Che sconsigliato a te vien per consiglio.

Vergine pura, d'ogni parte intera,
Del tuo parto gentil figliuola e madre;
  Che allumi questa vita, e l'altra adorni;
Per te il tuo Figlio e quel del sommo Padre,
  O finestra del ciel lucente altera,
Venne a salvarne in su gli estremi giorni,
  E fra tutt' i terreni altri soggiorni
Sola tu fusti eletta,
  Vergine benedetta;
Che 'l pianto d' Eva in allegrezza torni';
  Fammi; che puoi; della sua grazia degno,
Senza fine o beata,
  Già coronata nel superno regno.

Vergine santa d'ogni grazia piena;
Che per vera e altissima umiltate
  Salisti al ciel, onde miei preghi ascolti;
Tu partoristi il fonte di pietate,
  E di giustizia il Sol, che rasserena
Il secol pien d'errori oscuri e folti:
  Tre dolci e cari nomi ha' in te raccolti,
Madre, Figliuola, e Sposa;
  Vergine gloriosa,
Donna del Re che nostri lacci ha sciolti,
  E fatto 'l mondo libero e felice;
Nelle cui sante piaghe
  Prego ch'appaghe il cor, vera beatrice.

Vergine sola al mondo senza esempio,
Che 'l ciel di tue bellezze innamorasti,
     Cui nè prima fu simil, nè seconda;
Santi pensieri, atti pietosi e casti
     Al vero Dio sacrato, e vivo tempio
Fecero in tua virginita feconda.
     Per te può la mia vita esser gioconda,
S' a' tuoi preghi, o MARIA
     Vergine dolce, e pia,
Ove 'l fallo abbondò, la grazia abbonda.
     Con le ginocchia della mente inchine
Prego che sia mia scorta;
     E la mia torta via drizzi a buon fine.

Vergine chiara, e stabile in eterno,
Di questo tempestoso mare stella;
     D'ogni fedel nocchier fidata guida;
Pon mente in che terribile procella
     I mi ritrovo sol senza governo,
Ed ho gia' da vicin l'ultime strida:
     Ma pur' in te l'anima mia si fida;
Peccatrice; i' nol nego,
     Vergine: ma te prego
Che 'l tuo nemico del mia mal non rida:
     Ricorditi che fece il peccar nostro
Prender Dio, per scamparne,
     Umana carne al tuo virginal christro.

Vergine, quante lagrime ho già sparte,
Quante lusinghe, e quanti preghi indarno,
     Pur per mia pena, e per mio grave danno!
Da poi ch' i nacqui in su la riva d' Arno;
     Cercando or questa ed or quell altra parte,
Non è stata mia vita altro ch' affanno.
     Mortal bellezza, atti, e parole m' hanno
Tutta ingombrata l' alma.
     Vergine sacra, ed alma,
Non tardar; ch' i' non forse all' ultim 'ann,
     I di miei piu correnti che saetta,
Fra miserie e peccati
     Sonsen andati, e sol Morte n'aspetta.

Vergine, tale è terra, e posto ha in doglia
Lo mio cor; che vivendo in pianto il tenne;
     E di mille miei mali un non sapea;
E per saperlo, pur quel che n'avvenne,

Fora avvenuto: ch' ogni altra sua voglia
Era a me morte, ed a lei fama rea
Or tu, donna del ciel, tu nostra Dea,
Se dir lice, e conviensi;
Vergine d'alti sensi,
Tu vedi il tutto; e quel che non potea
Far altri, è nulla a e la tua gran virtute;
Pon fine al mio dolore;
Ch'a te onore ed a me fia salute.

Vergine, in cui ho tutta mia speranza
Che possi e vogli al gran bisogno aitarme;
Non mi lasciare in su l'estremo passo.
Non guardar me, ma chi degnò crearme;
No'l mio valor, ma l'alta sua sembianza;
Che in me ti mova a curar d'uorm si basso.
Medusa, e l'error mio io han fatto un sasso
D'umor vano stillante;
Vergine, tu di sante
Lagrime, e pie adempi 'l mio cor lasso;
Ch' almen l'ultimo pianto sia divoto,
Senza terrestro limo;
Come fu'l primo non d'insania voto.

Vergine umana, e nemica d'orgoglio,
Del comune principio amor t'induca;
Miserere d' un cor contrito umile;
Che se poca mortal terra caduca
Amar con si mirabil fede soglio;
Che devro far di te cosa gentile?
Se dal mio stato assai misero, e vile
Per le tue man resurgo,
Vergine; è' sacro, e purgo
Al tuo nome e pens ieri e'ngegno, e stile;
La lingua, e'l cor, le lagrime, e i sospiri,
Scorgimi al miglior guado;
E prendi in grado i cangiati desiri.

Il di s'appressa, e non pote esser lunge;
Si corre il tempo, e vola,
Vergine uuica, e sola;
F'l cor' or conscienza, or morte punge.
Raccommandami al tuo Figliuol, verace
Uomo, e verace Dio;
Ch accolga I mio spirto ultimo in pace.

As the Scandinavian represented Frigga the Earth, or World mother, knowing all things, yet never herself revealing them, though ready to be called to counsel by the gods. It represents her in action, decked with jewels and gorgeously attended. But, says the Mythos, when she ascended the throne of Odin, her consort (Haaven) she left with mortals, her friend, the Goddess of Sympathy, to protect them in her absence.

Since, Sympathy goes about to do good. Especially she devotes herself to the most valiant and the most oppressed. She consoled the Gods in some degree even for the death of their darling Baldur. Among the heavenly powers she has no consort.

C.

"THE WEDDING OF THE LADY THERESA."

FROM LOCKHART'S SPANISH BALLADS.[156]

" 'Twas when the fifth Alphonso in Leon held his sway,
    King Abdalla of Toledo an embassy did send;
He asked his sister for a wife, and in an evil day
    Alphonso sent her, for he feared Abdalla to offend;
He feared to move his anger, for many times before
He had received in danger much succor from the Moor.

Sad heart had fair Theresa, when she their paction knew;
    With streaming tears she heard them tell she 'mong the
        Moors must go;
That she, a Christian damsel, a Christian firm and true,
    Must wed a Moorish husband, it well might cause her wo;
But all her tears and all her prayers they are of small avail;
    At length she for her fate prepares, a victim sad and pale.

The king hath sent his sister to fair Toledo town,
    Where then the Moor Abdalla his royal state did keep;
When she drew near, the Moslem from his golden throne
        came down,
    And courteously received her, and bade her cease to
        weep;
With loving words he pressed her to come his bower within;
With kisses he caressed her, but still she feared the sin.

[156] John Gibson Lockhart (1794-1854), Scottish author, published his *Ancient Spanish Ballads* in 1823.

"Sir King, Sir King, I pray thee,"—'twas thus Theresa spake,
  "I pray thee, have compassion, and do to me no wrong;
For sleep with thee I may not, unless the vows I break,
  Whereby I to the holy church of Christ my Lord belong;
For thou hast sworn to serve Mahoun, and if this thing
    should be,
The curse of God it must bring down upon thy realm
    and thee.

"The angel of Christ Jesu, to whom my heavenly Lord
  Hath given my soul in keeping, is ever by my side;
If thou dost me dishonor, he will unsheath his sword,
  And smite thy body fiercely, at the crying of thy bride;
Invisible he standeth; his sword like fiery flame,
Will penetrate thy bosom, the hour that sees my shame."

The Moslem heard her with a smile; the earnest words
    she said,
  He took for bashful maiden's wile, and drew her to his
    bower:
In vain Theresa prayed and strove,—she pressed Abdalla's
    bed,
  Perforce received his kiss of love, and lost her maiden
    flower.
A woful woman there she lay, a loving lord beside,
And earnestly to God did pray, her succor to provide.

The angel of Christ Jesu her sore complaint did hear,
  And plucked his heavenly weapon from out his sheath
    unseen,
He waved the brand in his right hand, and to the King came
    near,
  And drew the point o'er limb and joint, beside the
    weeping Queen:
A mortal weakness from the stroke upon the King did fall;
He could not stand when daylight broke, but on his knees
    must crawl.

Abdalla shuddered inly, when he this sickness felt,
  And called upon his barons, his pillow to come nigh;
"Rise up," he said "my liegemen," as round his bed they
    knelt,
  "And take this Christian lady, else certainly I die;
Let gold be in your girdles, and precious stones beside,
  And swiftly ride to Leon, and render up my bride."

When they were come to Leon, Theresa would not go

Into her brother's dwelling, where her maiden years were
  spent;
But o'er her downcast visage a white veil she did throw,
  And to the ancient nunnery of Las Huelgas went.
There, long, from worldly eyes retired, a holy life she led;
There she, an aged saint, expired; there sleeps she with the
  dead."

D.

The following extract from Spinoza is worthy of attention,
as expressing the view which a man of the largest intellectual
scope may take of woman, if that part of his life to which her
influence appeals, has been left unawakened.

He was a man of the largest intellect, of unsurpassed reasoning powers, yet he makes a statement false to history, for
we well know how often men and women have ruled together without difficulty, and one in which very few men
even at the present day, I mean men who are thinkers, like
him, would acquiesce.

I have put in contrast with it three expressions of the latest
literature.

1st. From the poems of W. E. Channing, a poem called
"Reverence," equally remarkable for the deep wisdom of
its thought and the beauty of its utterance, and containing
as fine a description of one class of women as exists in
literature.[157]

In contrast with this picture of woman, the happy Goddess
of Beauty, the wife, the friend, "the summer queen," I add
one by the author of "Festus," of a woman of the muse, the
sybil kind, which seems painted from living experience.[158]

And thirdly, I subjoin Eugene Sue's description of a
wicked, but able woman of the practical sort, and appeal to
all readers whether a species that admits of three such varieties is so easily to be classed away, or kept within prescribed limits, as Spinoza, and those who think like him,
believe.

[157] William Ellery Channing (1818-1901), Transcendentalist poet and
Fuller's brother-in-law. "Reverence" is quoted from his *Poems* (1843).
[158] Philip James Bailey (1816-1902) first published his version of the Faust
story, *Festus*, in 1839.

SPINOZA. TRACTATUS POLITICI, DE DEMOCRATIA,

CAPUT XI.

"Perhaps some one will here ask, whether the supremacy of man over woman is attributable to nature or custom? For if it be human institutions alone to which this fact is owing, there is no reason why we should exclude women from a share in government. Experience, however, most plainly teaches that it is woman's weakness which places her under the authority of man. Since it has nowhere happened that men and women ruled together; but wherever men and women are found the world over, there we see the men ruling and the women ruled, and in this order of things men and women live together in peace and harmony. The Amazons, it is true, are reputed formerly to have held the reins of government, but they drove men from their dominions; the male of their offspring they invariably destroyed, permitting their daughters alone to live. Now if women were by nature upon an equality with men, if they equalled men in fortitude, in genius (qualities which give to men might, and consequently, right) it surely would be the case, that among the numerous and diverse nations of the earth, some would be found where both sexes ruled conjointly, and others where the men were ruled by the women, and so educated as to be mentally inferior: since this state of things no where exists, it is perfectly fair to infer that the rights of women are not equal to those of men; but that women must be subordinate, and therefore cannot have an equal, far less a superior place in the government. If, too, we consider the passions of men —how the love men feel towards women is seldom any thing but lust and impulse, and much less a reverence for qualities of soul than an admiration of physical beauty, observing, too, how men are afflicted when their sweethearts favor other wooers, and other things of the same character,—we shall see at a glance that it would be, in the highest degree, detrimental to peace and harmony, for men and women to possess an equal share in government."

"REVERENCE."

"As an ancestral heritage revere
All learning, and all thought. The painter's fame

Is thine, whate'er thy lot, who honorest grace.
And need enough in this low time, when they,
Who seek to captivate the fleeting notes
Of heaven's sweet beauty, must despair almost,
So heavy and obdurate show the hearts
Of their companions. Honor kindly then
Those who bear up in their so generous arms
The beautiful ideas of matchless forms;
For were these not portrayed, our human fate,—
Which is to be all high, majestical,
To grow to goodness with each coming age,
Till virtue leap and sing for joy to see
So noble, virtuous men,—would brief decay;
And the green, festering slime, oblivious, haunt
About our common fate. Oh honor them!

But what to all true eyes has chiefest charm,
And what to every breast where beats a heart
Framed to one beautiful emotion,—to
One sweet and natural feeling, lends a grace
To all the tedious walks of common life,
This is fair woman,—woman, whose applause
Each poet sings—woman the beautiful.
Not that her fairest brow, or gentlest form
Charm us to tears; not that the smoothest cheek,
Where ever rosy tints have made their home,
So rivet us on her; but that she is
The subtle, delicate grace,—the inward grace,
For words too excellent; the noble, true,
The majesty of earth; the summer queen;
In whose conceptions nothing but what's great
Has any right. And, O! her love for him,
Who does but his small part in honoring her;
Discharging a sweet office, sweeter none,
Mother and child, friend, counsel and repose;—
Nought matches with her, nought has leave with her
To highest human praise. Farewell to him
Who reverences not with an excess
Of faith the beauteous sex; all barren he
Shall live a living death of mockery.

Ah! had but words the power, what could we say
Of woman! We, rude men, of violent phrase,
Harsh action, even in repose inwardly harsh;
Whose lives walk blustering on high stilts, removed
From all the purely gracious influence

Of mother earth. To single from the host
Of angel forms one only, and to her
Devote our deepest heart and deepest mind
Seems almost contradiction. Unto her
We owe our greatest blessings, hours of cheer,
Gay smiles, and sudden tears, and more than these
A sure perpetual love. Regard her as
She walks along the vast still earth; and see!
Before her flies a laughing troop of joys,
And by her side treads old experience,
With never-failing voice admonitory;
The gentle, though infallible, kind advice,
The watchful care, the fine regardfulness,
Whatever mates with what we hope to find,
All consummate in her—the summer queen.

To call past ages better than what now
Man is enacting on life's crowded stage,
Cannot improve our worth; and for the world
Blue is the sky as ever, and the stars
Kindle their crystal flames at soft-fallen eve
With the same purest lustre that the east
Worshipped. The river gently flows through fields
Where the broad-leaved corn spreads out, and loads
Its ear as when the Indian tilled the soil.
The dark green pine,—green in the winter's cold,
Still whispers meaning emblems, as of old;
The cricket chirps, and the sweet, eager birds
In the sad woods crowd their thick melodies;
But yet, to common eyes, life's poetry
Something has faded, and the cause of this
May be that man, no longer at the shrine
Of woman, kneeling with true reverence,
In spite of field, wood, river, stars and sea
Goes most disconsolate. A babble now,
A huge and wind-swelled babble, fills the place
Of that great adoration which of old
Man had for woman. In these days no more
Is love the pith and marrow of man's fate.

Thou who in early years feelest awake
To finest impulses from nature's breath,
And in thy walk hearest such sounds of truth
As on the common ear strike without heed,
Beware of men around thee. Men are foul,
With avarice, ambition and deceit;

The worst of all, ambition. This is life
Spent in a feverish chase for selfish ends,
Which has no virtue to redeem its toil
But one long, stagnant hope to raise the self.
The miser's life to this seems sweet and fair;
Better to pile the glittering coin, than seek
To overtop our brothers and our loves.
Merit in this? Where lies it, though thy name
Ring over distant lands, meeting the wind
Even on the extremest verge of the wide world.
Merit in this? Better be hurled abroad
On the vast whirling tide, than in thyself
Concentred, feed upon thy own applause.
Thee shall the good man yield no reverence;
But, while the idle, dissolute crowd are loud
In voice to send thee flattery, shall rejoice
That he has scaped thy fatal doom, and known
How humble faith in the good soul of things
Provides amplest enjoyment. O my brother,
If the Past's counsel any honor claim
From thee, go read the history of those
Who a like path have trod, and see a fate
Wretched with fears, changing like leaves at noon,
When the new wind sings in the white birch wood.
Learn from the simple child the rule of life,
And from the movements of the unconscious tribes
Of animal nature, those that bend the wing
Or cleave the azure tide, content to be,
What the great frame provides,—freedom and grace.
Thee, simple child, do the swift winds obey,
And the white waterfalls with their bold leaps
Follow thy movements. Tenderly the light
Thee watches, girding with a zone of radiance,
And all the swinging herbs love thy soft steps."

DESCRIPTION OF ANGELA, FROM "FESTUS."

"I loved her for that she was beautiful,
And that to me she seemed to be all nature
And all varieties of things in one;
Would set at night in clouds of tears, and rise
All light and laughter in the morning; fear
No petty customs nor appearances,
But think what others only dreamed about;
And say what others did but think; and do

What others would but say; and glory in
What others dared but do; it was these which won me;
And that she never schooled within her breast
One thought or feeling, but gave holiday
To all; and that she told me all her woes
And wrongs and ills; and so she made them mine
In the communion of love, and we
Grew like each other, for we loved each other;
She, mild and generous as the sun in spring;
And I, like earth, all budding out with love.

   *   *   *

The beautiful are never desolate:
For some one alway loves them; God or man;
If man abandons, God Himself takes them:
And thus it was. She whom I once loved died,
The lightning loathes its cloud; the soul its clay.
Can I forget that hand I took in mine,
Pale as pale violets; that eye, where mind
And matter met alike divine?—ah, no!
May God that moment judge me when I do!
Oh! she was fair; her nature once all spring
And deadly beauty, like a maiden sword,
Startlingly beautiful. I see her now!
Wherever thou art thy soul is in my mind;
Thy shadow hourly lengthens o'er my brain
And peoples all its pictures with thyself;
Gone, not forgotten; passed, not lost; thou wilt shine
In heaven like a bright spot in the sun!
She said she wished to die, and so she died,
For, cloudlike, she poured out her love, which was
Her life, to freshen this parched heart. It was thus;
I said we were to part, but she said nothing;
There was no discord; it was music ceased,
Life's thrilling, bursting, bounding joy. She sate,
Like a house-god, her hands fixed on her knee,
And her dark hair lay loose and long behind her,
Through which her wild bright eye flashed like a flint;
She spake not, moved not, but she looked the more,
As if her eye were action, speech, and feeling.
I felt it all, and came and knelt beside her,
The electric touch solved both our souls together;
Then came the feeling which unmakes, undoes;
Which tears the sealike soul up by the roots,
And lashes it in scorn against the skies.

   *   *   *

It is the saddest and the sorest sight,
One's own love weeping. But why call on God?
But that the feeling of the boundless bounds
All feeling; as the welkin does the world;
It is this which ones us with the whole and God.
Then first we wept; then closed and clung together;
And my heart shook this building of my breast
Like a live engine booming up and down;
She fell upon me like a snow-wreath thawing.
Never were bliss and beauty, love and wo,
Ravelled and twined together into madness,
As in that one wild hour to which all else
The past, is but a picture. That alone
Is real, and forever there in front.

        *   *   *

      *   *   * After that I left her,
And only saw her once again alive."

"Mother Saint Perpetua, the superior of the convent, was a tall woman, of about forty years, dressed in dark gray serge, with a long rosary hanging at her girdle; a white mob cap, with a long black veil, surrounded her thin wan face with its narrow hooded border. A great number of deep transverse wrinkles plowed her brow, which resembled yellowish ivory in color and substance. Her keen and prominent nose was curved like the hooked beak of a bird of prey; her black eye was piercing and sagacious; her face was at once intelligent, firm, and cold.

"For comprehending and managing the material interests of the society, Mother Saint Perpetua could have vied with the shrewdest and most wily lawyer. When women are possessed of what is called *business talent*, and when they apply thereto the sharpness of perception, the indefatigable perseverance, the prudent dissimulation, and above all, the correctness and rapidity of judgment at first sight, which are peculiar to them, they arrive at prodigious results.

"To Mother Saint Perpetua, a woman of a strong and solid head, the vast monied business of the society was but child's play. None better than she understood how to buy depreciated properties, to raise them to their original value, and sell them to advantage; the average purchase of rents, the fluctuations of exchange, and the current prices of shares in all the leading speculations, were perfectly familiar to her. Never had she directed her agents to make a single false speculation, when it had been the question how to invest funds, with which good souls were constantly endowing the society of Saint Mary. She had established in the house a degree of order, of discipline, and, above all, of economy, that were indeed remarkable; the constant aim of all her exertions being, not to enrich herself, but the community over which she presided; for the spirit of association, when it is directed to an object of *collective selfishness*, gives to corporations all the faults and vices of individuals."

E.

The following is an extract from a letter addressed to me by one of the monks of the 19th century. A part I have omitted, because it does not express my own view, unless such qualifications which I could not make, except by full discussion of the subject.

"Woman in the 19th century should be a pure, chaste, holy being.

This state of being in woman is no more attained by the expansion of her intellectual capacity, than by the augmentation of her physical force.

Neither is it attained by the increase or refinement of her love for man, or for any object whatever, or for all objects collectively; but

This state of being is attained by the reference of all her powers and all her actions to the source of Universal Love, whose constant requisition is a pure, chaste and holy life.

So long as woman looks to man (or to society) for that which she needs, she will remain in an indigent state, for he himself is indigent of it, and as much needs it as she does.

So long as this indigence continues, all unions or relations constructed between man and woman are constructed in indigence, and can produce only indigent results or unhappy consequences.

The unions now constructing, as well as those in which the parties constructing them were generated, being based on self-delight, or lust, can lead to no more happiness in the 20th, than is found in the 19th century.

It is not amended institutions, it is not improved education, it is not another selection of individuals for union, that can meliorate the sad result, but the *basis* of the union must be changed.

If in the natural order Woman and Man would adhere strictly to physiological or natural laws, in physical chastity, a most beautiful amendment of the human race, and human condition, would in a few generations adorn the world.

Still, it belongs to Woman in the spiritual order, to devote herself wholly to her eternal husband, and become the Free Bride of the One who alone can elevate her to her true position, and reconstruct her a pure, chaste, and holy being."

F.

I have mislaid an extract from "The Memoirs of an American Lady" which I wished to use on this subject, but its import is, briefly, this:[159]

Observing of how little consequence the Indian women are in youth, and how much in age, because in that trying life, good counsel and sagacity are more prized than charms, Mrs. Grant expresses a wish that Reformers would take a hint from observation of this circumstance.

In another place she says: "The misfortune of our sex is, that young women are not regarded as the material from which old women must be made."

I quote from memory, but believe the weight of the remark is retained.

G.

EURIPIDES. SOPHOCLES.

As many allusions are made in the foregoing pages to characters of women drawn by the Greek dramatists, which may not be familiar to the majority of readers, I have borrowed from the papers of Miranda, some notes upon them.[160] I trust the girlish tone of apostrophizing rapture may be excused. Miranda was very young at the time of writing, com-

---

[159] Anne Grant (1755-1838), Scottish author whose *Memoirs of an American Lady* was published in 1808.

[160] Miranda, Fuller's name for herself; see also note 19, p. 101.

pared with her present mental age. *Now*, she would express
the same feelings, but in a worthier garb—if she expressed
them at all.

"Iphigenia! Antigone! you were worthy to live! *We* are fallen on evil times, my sisters! our feelings have been
checked; our thoughts questioned; our forms dwarfed and
defaced by a bad nurture. Yet hearts, like yours, are in our
breasts, living, if unawakened; and our minds are capable of
the same resolves. You, we understand at once, those who
stare upon us pertly in the street, we cannot—could never
understand.

You knew heroes, maidens, and your fathers were kings of
men. You believed in your country, and the gods of your
country. A great occasion was given to each, whereby to test
her character.

You did not love on earth; for the poets wished to show us
the force of woman's nature, virgin and unbiassed. You were
women; not wives, or lovers, or mothers. Those are great
names, but we are glad to see *you* in untouched flower.

Were brothers so dear, then, Antigone? We have no
brothers. We see no men into whose lives we dare look
steadfastly, or to whose destinies we look forward confidently. We care not for their urns; what inscription could we
put upon them? They live for petty successes; or to win daily
the bread of the day. No spark of kingly fire flashes from their
eyes.

None! are there *none?*

It is a base speech to say it. Yes! there are some such; we
have sometimes caught their glances. But rarely have they
been rocked in the same cradle as we, and they do not look
upon us much; for the time is not yet come.

Thou art so grand and simple! we need not follow thee;
thou dost not need our love.

But, sweetest Iphigenia; who knew *thee*, as to me thou art
known. I was not born in vain, if only for the heavenly tears I
have shed with thee. She will be grateful for them. I have
understood her wholly; as a friend should, better than she
understood herself.

With what artless art the narrative rises to the crisis. The
conflicts in Agamemnon's mind, and the imputations of
Menelaus give us, at once, the full image of him, strong in

will and pride, weak in virtue, weak in the noble powers of the mind that depend on imagination.[161] He suffers, yet it requires the presence of his daughter to make him feel the full horror of what he is to do.

"Ah me! that breast, those cheeks, those golden tresses!"

It is her beauty, not her misery, that makes the pathos. This is noble. And then, too, the injustice of the gods, that she, this creature of unblemished loveliness, must perish for the sake of a worthless woman. Even Menelaus feels it, the moment he recovers from his wrath.

> "What hath she to do,
> The virgin daughter, with my Helena!
>   *   *   Its former reasonings now
> My soul foregoes.   *   *   *   *
>   For it is not just
> That thou shouldst groan, but my affairs go pleasantly,
> That those of thy house should die, and mine see the light."

Indeed the overwhelmed aspect of the king of men might well move him.

> Men. "Brother, give me to take thy right hand,
> Aga.   I give it, for the victory is thine, and I am wretched.
>   I am, indeed, ashamed to drop the tear,
>   And not to drop the tear I am ashamed."

How beautifully is Iphigenia introduced; beaming more and more softly on us with every touch of description. After Clytemnestra has given Orestes (then an infant,) out of the chariot, she says:

> "Ye females, in your arms,
> Receive her, for she is of tender age.
> Sit here by my feet, my child,
> By thy mother, Iphigenia, and show
> These strangers how I am blessed in thee,
> And here address thee to thy father.
> Iphi. Oh mother, should I run, wouldst thou be angry?
> And embrace my father breast to breast?"

With the same sweet timid trust she prefers the request to

---

[161] The following lines are quoted from *Iphigenia at Aulis.*

himself, and as he holds her in his arms, he seems as noble as Guido's Archangel; as if he never could sink below the trust of such a being!

The Achilles, in the first scene, is fine. A true Greek hero; not too good; all flushed with the pride of youth; but capable of god-like impulses. At first, he thinks only of his own wounded pride, (when he finds Iphigenia has been decoyed to Aulis under the pretext of becoming his wife;) but the grief of the queen soon makes him superior to his arrogant chafings. How well he says:—

> "Far as a young man may, I will repress
> So great a wrong."

By seeing him here, we understand why he, not Hector, was the hero of the Iliad. The beautiful moral nature of Hector was early developed by close domestic ties, and the cause of his country. Except in a purer simplicity of speech and manner, he might be a modern and a christian. But Achilles is cast in the largest and most vigorous mould of the earlier day: his nature is one of the richest capabilities, and therefore less quickly unfolds its meaning. The impression it makes at the early period is only of power and pride; running as fleetly with his armor on, as with it off; but sparks of pure lustre are struck, at moments, from the mass of ore. Of this sort is his refusal to see the beautiful virgin he has promised to protect. None of the Grecians must have the right to doubt his motives. How wise and prudent, too, the advice he gives as to the queen's conduct! He will not show himself, unless needed. His pride is the farthest possible remote from vanity. His thoughts are as free as any in our own time.

> "The prophet? what is he? a man
> Who speaks 'mong many falsehoods, but few truths,
> Whene'er chance leads him to speak true; when false,
> The prophet is no more."

Had Agamemnon possessed like clearness of sight, the virgin would not have perished, but also, Greece would have had no religion and no national existence.

When, in the interview with Agamemnon, the Queen begins her speech, in the true matrimonial style, dignified though her gesture be, and true all she says, we feel that truth, thus sauced with taunts, will not touch his heart, nor turn him from his purpose. But when Iphigenia begins her exquisite speech, as with the breathings of a lute,

> "Had I, my father, the persuasive voice
> Of Orpheus, &c.
>
> Compel me not
> What is beneath to view. I was the first
> To call thee father; me thou first didst call
> Thy child: I was the first that on thy knees
> Fondly caressed thee, and from thee received
> The fond caress: this was thy speech to me:—
> 'Shall I, my child, e'er see thee in some house
> Of splendor, happy in thy husband, live
> And flourish, as becomes my dignity?'
> My speech to thee was, leaning 'gainst thy cheek,
> (Which with my hand I now caress:) 'And what
> Shall I then do for thee? shall I receive
> My father when grown old, and in my house
> Cheer him with each fond office, to repay
> The careful nurture which he gave my youth?'
> These words are in my memory deep impressed,
> Thou hast forgot them and will kill thy child."

Then she adjures him by all the sacred ties, and dwells pathetically on the circumstance which had struck even Menelaus.

> "If Paris be enamored of his bride,
> His Helen, what concerns it me? and how
> Comes he to my destruction?
>
> Look upon me;
> Give me a smile, give me a kiss, my father;
> That if my words persuade thee not, in death
> I may have this memorial of thy love."

Never have the names of father and daughter been uttered with a holier tenderness than by Euripides, as in this most lovely passage, or in the "Supplicants," after the voluntary death of Evadne;[162] Iphis says

> "What shall this wretch now do? Should I return
> To my own house?—sad desolation there

---

[162] Evadne threw herself on the funeral pyre of her husband, Capanaeus, after he was slain in battle.

I shall behold, to sink my soul with grief.
Or go I to the house of Capaneus?
That was delightful to me, when I found
My daughter there; but she is there no more:
Oft would she kiss my cheek, with fond caress
Oft soothe me. To a father, waxing old,
Nothing is dearer than a daughter! sons
Have spirits of higher pitch, but less inclined
To sweet endearing fondness. Lead me then,
Instantly lead me to my house, consign
My wretched age to darkness, there to pine
And waste away.
                    Old age,
Struggling with many griefs, O how I hate thee!"

But to return to Iphigenia,—how infinitely melting is her
appeal to Orestes, whom she holds in her robe.

"My brother, small assistance canst thou give
Thy friends; yet for thy sister with thy tears
Implore thy father that she may not die:
Even infants have a sense of ills; and see,
My father! silent though he be, he sues
To thee: be gentle to me; on my life
Have pity: thy two children by this beard
Entreat thee, thy dear children: one is yet
An infant, one to riper years arrived."

The mention of Orestes, then an infant, all through, though
slight, is of a domestic charm that prepares the mind to feel
the tragedy of his after lot. When the Queen says

"Dost thou sleep,
My son? The rolling chariot hath subdued thee;
Wake to thy sister's marriage happily."

We understand the horror of the doom which makes this
cherished child a parricide. And so when Iphigenia takes
leave of him after her fate is by herself accepted.

Iphi. "To manhood train Orestes,
Cly. Embrace him, for thou ne'er shalt see him more.
Iphi. (*To Orestes.*) Far as thou couldst, thou didst assist thy
    friends."

We know not how to blame the guilt of the maddened wife
and mother. In her last meeting with Agamemnon, as in her

previous expostulations and anguish, we see that a straw may
turn the balance, and make her his deadliest foe. Just then,
came the suit of Ægisthus, then, when every feeling was up-
rooted or lacerated in her heart.

Iphigenia's moving address has no further effect than to
make her father turn at bay and brave this terrible crisis. He
goes out, firm in resolve; and she and her mother abandon
themselves to a natural grief.

Hitherto nothing has been seen in Iphigenia, except the
young girl, weak, delicate, full of feeling and beautiful as a
sunbeam on the full green tree. But, in the next scene, the
first impulse of that passion which makes and unmakes us,
though unconfessed even to herself, though hopeless and un-
returned, raises her at once into the heroic woman, worthy of
the goddess who demands her.

Achilles appears to defend her, whom all others clamor-
ously seek to deliver to the murderous knife. She sees him,
and fired with thoughts, unknown before, devotes herself at
once for the country which has given birth to such a man.

> "To be too fond of life
> Becomes not me; nor for myself alone,
> But to all Greece, a blessing didst thou bear me.
> Shall thousands, when their country's injured, lift
> Their shields; shall thousands grasp the oar, and dare,
> Advancing bravely 'gainst the foe, to die
> For Greece? And shall my life, my single life,
> Obstruct all this? Would this be just? What word
> Can we reply? Nay more, it is not right
> That he with all the Grecians should contest
> In fight, should die, *and for a woman*. No:
> More than a thousand women is one man
> Worthy to see the light of day.
>   *   *   *   for Greece I give my life.
> Slay me; demolish Troy; for these shall be
> Long time my monuments, my children these,
> My nuptials and my glory."

This sentiment marks woman, when she loves enough to
feel what a creature of glory and beauty a true *man* would be,
as much in our own time as that of Euripides. Cooper makes
the weak Hetty say to her beautiful sister:

"Of course, I don't compare you with Harry. A handsome

man is always far handsomer than any woman."[163] True, it was the sentiment of the age, but it was the first time Iphigenia had felt it. In Agamemnon she saw *her father*, to him she could prefer her claim. In Achilles she saw *a man*, the crown of creation, enough to fill the world with his presence, were all other beings blotted from its spaces.*

The reply of Achilles is as noble. Here is his bride, he feels it now, and all his vain vauntings are hushed.

> "Daughter of Agamemnon, highly blessed
> Some god would make me, if I might attain
> Thy nuptials. Greece in thee I happy deem,
> And thee in Greece.   *   *
>   *   *   *   in thy thought
> Revolve this well; death is a dreadful thing."

How sweet is her reply, and then the tender modesty with which she addresses him here and elsewhere as "*stranger*."

> "Reflecting not on any, thus I speak:
> Enough of wars and slaughters from the charms
> Of Helen rise; but die not thou for me,
> O Stranger, nor distain thy sword with blood,
> But let me save my country if I may."
>
> *Achilles.* "O glorious spirit! nought have I 'gainst this
> To urge, since such thy will, for what thou sayst
> Is generous. Why should not the truth be spoken?"

But feeling that human weakness may conquer yet, he goes to wait at the altar, resolved to keep his promise of protection thoroughly.

In the next beautiful scene she shows that a few tears might overwhelm her in his absence. She raises her mother beyond weeping them, yet her soft purity she cannot impart.

---

[163] In *The Deerslayer* (1841) by James Fenimore Cooper (1789-1851), Hetty Hutter has a pure love for Hurry Harry March.

* Men do not often reciprocate this pure love.

> "Her prentice han' she tried on man,
> And then she made the lasses o',"

Is a fancy, not a feeling, in their more frequently passionate and strong, than noble or tender natures. [Fuller's note.] Quoted from Robert Burns' (1759-1796) "Green Grow the Rashes."

Iphi. "My father, and thy husband do not hate:
Cly. For thy dear sake fierce contests must he bear.
Iphi. For Greece reluctant me to death he yields;
Cly. Basely, with guile unworthy Atreus' son."

This is truth incapable of an answer and Iphigenia attempts none.

She begins the hymn which is to sustain her,

> "Lead me; mine the glorious fate,
> To o'erturn the Phrygian state."

After the sublime flow of lyric heroism, she suddenly sinks back into the tenderer feeling of her dreadful fate.

> "O my country, where these eyes
> Opened on Pelasgic skies!
> O ye virgins, once my pride,
> In Mycenæ who abide!
>   CHORUS.
> Why of Perseus name the town,
> Which Cyclopean ramparts crown?
>   IPHIGENIA.
> Me you rear'd a beam of light,
> Freely now I sink in night."

Freely; as the messenger afterwards recounts it.

                *   *   *

> "Imperial Agamemnon, when he saw
> His daughter, as a victim to the grave,
> Advancing, groan'd, and bursting into tears,
> Turned from the sight his head, before his eyes,
> Holding his robe. The virgin near him stood,
> And thus addressed him: 'Father, I to thee
> Am present; for my country, and for all
> The land of Greece, I freely give myself
> A victim: to the altar let them lead me,
> Since such the oracle. If aught on me
> Depends, be happy, and obtain the prize
> Of glorious conquest, and revisit safe
> Your country. Of the Grecians, for this cause,
> Let no one touch me; with intrepid spirit
> Silent will I present my neck.' She spoke.
> And all that heard revered the noble soul
> And virtue of the virgin."

How quickly had the fair bud bloomed up into its perfection. Had she lived a thousand years, she could not have
surpassed this. Goethe's Iphigenia, the mature woman, with
its myriad delicate traits, never surpasses, scarcely equals
what we know of her in Euripides.

Can I appreciate this work in a translation? I think so,
impossible as it may seem to one who can enjoy the thousand
melodies, and words in exactly the right place and cadence of
the original. They say you can see the Apollo Belvidere in a
plaster cast,[164] and I cannot doubt it, so great the benefit
conferred on my mind, by a transcript thus imperfect. And so
with these translations from the Greek. I can divine the original through this veil, as I can see the movements of a spirited horse by those of his coarse grasscloth muffler. Beside,
every translator who feels his subject is inspired, and the
divine Aura informs even his stammering lips.

Iphigenia is more like one of the women Shakspeare loved
than the others; she is a tender virgin, ennobled and
strengthened by sentiment more than intellect, what they
call a woman *par excellence*.

Macaria is more like one of Massinger's women. She advances boldly, though with the decorum of her sex and nation:

Macaria.   "Impute not boldness to me that I come
              Before you, strangers; this my first request
              I urge; for silence and a chaste reserve
              Is woman's genuine praise, and to remain
              Quiet within the house. But I come forth,
              Hearing thy lamentations, Iolaus:
              Though charged with no commission, yet perhaps,
              I may be useful."   *   *

Her speech when she offers herself as the victim, is
reasonable, as one might speak to-day. She counts the cost all
through. Iphigenia is too timid and delicate to dwell upon
the loss of earthly bliss, and the due experience of life, even

---

[164] Apollo Belvedere, famous Roman statue copied from the Greek, first
discovered in 1485 and placed in the Vatican.

as much as Jeptha's daughter did,[165] but Macaria is explicit,
as well befits the daughter of Hercules.

> "Should *these* die, myself
> Preserved, of prosperous future could I form
> One cheerful hope?
> A poor forsaken virgin who would deign
> To take in marriage? Who would wish for sons
> From one so wretched? Better then to die,
> Than bear such undeserved miseries:
> One less illustrious this might more beseem.
>
>   *   *   *
>
> I have a soul that unreluctantly
> Presents itself, and I proclaim aloud
> That for my brothers and myself I die.
> I am not fond of life, but think I gain
> An honorable prize to die with glory."

Still nobler when Iolaus proposes rather that she shall
draw lots with her sisters.

> "*By lot* I will not die, for to such death
> No thanks are due, or glory—name it not.
> If you accept me, if my offered life
> Be grateful to you, willingly I give it
> For these, but by constraint I will not die."

Very fine are her parting advice and injunctions to them
all:

> "Farewell! revered old man, farewell! and teach
> These youths in all things to be wise, like thee,
> Naught will avail them more."

Macaria has the clear Minerva eye: Antigone's is deeper,
and more capable of emotion, but calm. Iphigenia's, glisten-
ing, gleaming with angel truth, or dewy as a hidden violet.

I am sorry that Tennyson, who spoke with such fitness of
all the others in his "Dream of fair women," has not of
Iphigenia.[166] Of her alone he has not made a fit picture, but

---

[165] Jeptha had vowed that if victorious in battle he would sacrifice whatever he first saw when he returned home. His daughter was the first to greet
him and thus fulfill the vow.

[166] Alfred Lord Tennyson (1809-1892), English poet, published "A Dream
of Fair Woman" in the 1832 edition of his *Poems*.

only of the circumstances of the sacrifice. He can never have taken to heart this work of Euripides, yet he was so worthy to feel it. Of Jeptha's daughter, he has spoken as he would of Iphigenia, both in her beautiful song, and when

> "I heard Him, for He spake, and grief became
> A solemn scorn of ills.

> It comforts me in this one thought to dwell
> That I subdued me to my father's will;
> Because the kiss he gave me, ere I fell,
> Sweetens the spirit still.

> Moreover it is written, that my race
> Hewed Ammon, hip and thigh from Arroer
> Or Arnon unto Minneth. Here her face
> Glow'd as I look'd on her.

> She locked her lips; she left me where I stood;
> "Glory to God," she sang, and past afar,
> Thridding the sombre boskage of the woods,
> Toward the morning-star."

In the "Trojan dames" there are fine touches of nature with regard to Cassandra. Hecuba shows that mixture of shame and reverence, that prose kindred always do, towards the inspired child, the poet, the elected sufferer for the race.

When the herald announces that she is chosen to be the mistress of Agamemnon, Hecuba answers indignant, and betraying the involuntary pride and faith she felt in this daughter.

> "The virgin of Apollo, whom the God,
> Radiant with golden locks, allowed to live
> In her pure vow of maiden chastity?
> *Tal.*   With love the raptured virgin smote his heart.
> *Hec.*   Cast from thee, O my daughter, cast away
> Thy sacred wand, rend off the honored wreaths,
> The splendid ornaments that grace thy brows."

Yet the moment Cassandra appears, singing wildly her inspired song, Hecuba calls her

> "My *frantic* child."

Yet how graceful she is in her tragic phrenzy, the chorus shows—

> "How sweetly at thy house's ills thou smil'st,
> Chanting what haply thou wilt not show true?"

But if Hecuba dares not trust her highest instinct about her daughter, still less can the vulgar mind of the herald (a man not without tenderness of heart, but with no princely, no poetic blood,) abide the wild prophetic mood which insults his prejudices both as to country and decorums of the sex. Yet Agamemnon, though not a noble man, is of large mould and could admire this strange beauty which excited distaste in common minds.

> Tal. "What commands respect, and is held high
> As wise, is nothing better than the mean
> Of no repute: for this most potent king
> Of all the Grecians, the much honored son
> Of Atreus, is enamored with his prize,
> This frantic raver. I am a poor man,
> Yet would I not receive her to my bed."

Cassandra answers with a careless disdain,

> "This is a busy slave."

With all the lofty decorum of manners among the ancients, how free was their intercourse, man to man, how full the mutual understanding between prince and "busy slave!" Not here in adversity only, but in the pomp of power, it was so. Kings were approached with ceremonious obeisance, but not hedged round with etiquette, they could see and know their fellows.

The Andromache here is just as lovely as that of the Iliad.[167]

To her child whom they are about to murder, the same that was frightened at the "glittering plume."

> "Dost thou weep,
> My son? Hast thou a sense of thy ill fate?
> Why dost thou clasp me with thy hands, why hold
> My robes, and shelter thee beneath my wings,
> Like a young bird? No more my Hector comes,

[167] Andromache, Greek mythological symbol of the true wife and mother.

Returning from the tomb; he grasps no more
His glittering spear, bringing protection to thee."
*   *   *
*   *   "O soft embrace,
And to thy mother dear. O fragrant breath!
In vain I swathed thy infant limbs, in vain
I gave thee nurture at this breast, and toiled,
Wasted with care. *If ever*, now embrace,
Now clasp thy mother; throw thine arms around
My neck and join thy cheek, thy lips to mine."

As I look up I meet the eyes of Beatrice Cenci.[168] Beautiful
one, these woes, even, were less than thine, yet thou seemest
to understand them all. Thy clear melancholy gaze says, they,
at least, had known moments of bliss, and the tender relations of nature had not been broken and polluted from the
very first. Yes! the gradations of wo are all but infinite: only
good can be infinite.

Certainly the Greeks knew more of real home intercourse,
and more of woman than the Americans. It is in vain to tell
me of outward observances. The poets, the sculptors always
tell the truth. In proportion as a nation is refined, women
must have an ascendancy, it is the law of nature.

Beatrice! thou wert not "fond of life," either, more than
those princesses. Thou wert able to cut it down in the full
flower of beauty, as an offering to *the best* known to thee.
Thou wert not so happy as to die for thy country or thy breth-
ren, but thou wert worthy of such an occasion.

In the days of chivalry woman was habitually viewed more
as an ideal, but I do not know that she inspired a deeper and
more home-felt reverence than Iphigenia in the breast of
Achilles, or Macaria in that of her old guardian, Iolaus."[169]

We may, with satisfaction, add to these notes the words to
which Haydn has adapted his magnificent music in "The
Creation."

"In native worth and honor clad, with beauty, courage,

---

[168] Beatrice Cenci (1577-1599), beheaded after joining her family in
murdering her overbearing and violent father.
[169] Iolaus protects the dead Hercules' children from harm in Euripides'
The Children of Hercules.

strength adorned, erect to heaven, and tall, he stands, a
Man!—the lord and king of all! The large and arched front
sublime of wisdom deep declares the seat, and in his eyes
with brightness shines the soul, the breath and image of his
God. With fondness leans upon his breast the partner for him
formed, a woman fair, and graceful spouse. Her softly smiling
virgin looks, of flowery spring the mirror, bespeak him love,
and joy and bliss."

Whoever has heard this music must have a mental standard
as to what man and woman should be. Such was marriage in
Eden, when "erect to heaven *he* stood," but since, like other
institutions, this must be not only reformed, but revived, may
be offered as a picture of something intermediate,—the seed
of the future growth,—

H.

THE SACRED MARRIAGE.[170]

And has another's life as large a scope?
It may give due fulfilment to thy hope,
And every portal to the unknown may ope.

If, near this other life, thy inmost feeling
Trembles with fateful prescience of revealing
The future Deity, time is still concealing.

If thou feel thy whole force drawn more and more
To launch that other bark on seas without a shore;
And no still secret must be kept in store;

If meannesses that dim each temporal deed,
The dull decay that mars the fleshly weed,
And flower of love that seems to fall and leave no
    seed—

Hide never the full presence from thy sight
Of mutual aims and tasks, ideals bright,
Which feed their roots to-day on all this seeming blight.

Twin stars that mutual circle in the heaven,
Two parts for spiritual concord given,
Twin Sabbaths that inlock the Sacred Seven;[171]

[170] The poem is by Fuller.
[171] Sacred Seven, the Maharshis or highest saints of the Hindu religion.

Still looking to the centre for the cause,
Mutual light giving to draw out the powers,
And learning all the other groups by cognizance of one
    another's laws:

The parent love the wedded love includes,
The one permits the two their mutual moods,
The two each other know mid myriad multitudes;

With child-like intellect discerning love,
And mutual action energizing love,
In myriad forms affiliating love.

A world whose seasons bloom from pole to pole,
A force which knows both starting-point and goal,
A Home in Heaven,—the Union in the Soul.

Emerson's Essays*

At the distance of three years this volume follows the first series of Essays, which have already made to themselves a circle of readers, attentive, thoughtful, more and more intelligent, and this circle is a large one if we consider the circumstances of this country, and of England, also, at this time.

In England it would seem there are a larger number of persons waiting for an invitation to calm thought and sincere intercourse than among ourselves. Copies of Mr. Emerson's first published little volume called "Nature," have there been sold by thousands in a short time, while one edition has needed seven years to get circulated here. Several of his Orations and Essays from "The Dial" have also been republished there, and met with a reverent and earnest response.[1]

We suppose that while in England the want of such a voice is as great as here, a larger number are at leisure to recognize that want; a far larger number have set foot in the speculative region and have ears refined to appreciate these melodious accents.

Our people, heated by a partisan spirit, necessarily occupied in these first stages by bringing out the material resources of the land, not generally prepared by early training

---

* Ralph Waldo Emerson. *Essays: Second Series*. Boston: James Munroe, 1844. In *New-York Daily Tribune*, 7 December 1844, p. 1. Fuller had written Emerson on 17 December after receiving the book and gave this opinion: "In expression it seems far more adequate than the former volume [*Essays: First Series*, 1841], has more glow, more fusion. Two or three cavils I should make at present, but will not, till I have examined further if they be correct" (Emerson, *Letters*, III, 269).

[1] Besides editions of Emerson's *Essays*, English publishers had printed through 1844: *Man the Reformer* in 1842; *Nature: An Essay. And Orations* in 1843; and *Nature; an Essay. And Lectures on the Times, Orations, Lectures, and Addresses, Man Thinking*, and *The Young American* in 1844.

for the enjoyment of books that require attention and reflection, are still more injured by a large majority of writers and speakers, who lend all their efforts to flatter corrupt tastes and mental indolence, instead of feeling it their prerogative and their duty to admonish the community of the danger and arouse it to nobler energy. The aim of the writer or lecturer is not to say the best he knows in as few and well-chosen words as he can, making it his first aim to do justice to the subject. Rather he seeks to beat out a thought as thin as possible, and to consider what the audience will be most willing to receive.

The result of such a course is inevitable. Literature and Art must become daily more degraded; Philosophy cannot exist. A man who feels within his mind some spark of genius, or a capacity for the exercises of talent, should consider himself as endowed with a sacred commission. He is the natural priest, the shepherd of the people. He must raise his mind as high as he can toward the heaven of truth, and try to draw up with him those less gifted by nature with ethereal lightness. If he does not so, but rather employs his powers to flatter them in their poverty, and to hinder aspiration by useless words, and a mere seeming of activity, his sin is great, he is false to God, and false to man.

Much of this sin indeed is done ignorantly. The idea that literature calls men to the genuine hierarchy is almost forgotten. One, who finds himself able, uses his pen, as he might a trowel, solely to procure himself bread, without having reflected on the position in which he thereby places himself.

Apart from the troop of mercenaries, there is one, still larger, of those who use their powers merely for local and temporary ends, aiming at no excellence other than may conduce to these. Among these, rank persons of honor and the best intentions, but they neglect the lasting for the transient, as a man neglects to furnish his mind that he may provide the better for the house in which his body is to dwell for a few years.

When these sins and errors are prevalent, and threaten to become more so, how can we sufficiently prize and honor a mind which is quite pure from such? When, as in the present case, we find a man whose only aim is the discernment and interpretation of the spiritual laws by which we live and move and have our being, all whose objects are permanent, and whose every word stands for a fact.

If only as a representative of the claims of individual culture in a nation which tends to lay such stress on artificial organization and external results, Mr. Emerson would be invaluable here. History will inscribe his name as a father of the country, for he is one who pleads her cause against herself.

If New-England may be regarded as a chief mental focus to the New World, and many symptoms seem to give her this place, as to other centres the characteristics of heart and lungs to the body politic; if we may believe, as the writer does believe, that what is to be acted out in the country at large is, most frequently, first indicated there, as all the phenomena of the nervous system in the fantasies of the brain, we may hail as an auspicious omen the influence Mr. Emerson has there obtained, which is deep-rooted, increasing, and, over the younger portion of the community, far greater than that of any other person.

His books are received there with a more ready intelligence than elsewhere, partly because his range of personal experience and illustration applies to that region, partly because he has prepared the way for his books to be read by his great powers as a speaker.

The audience that waited for years upon the lectures, a part of which is incorporated into these volumes of Essays, was never large, but it was select, and it was constant. Among the hearers were some, who though, attracted by the beauty of character and manner, they were willing to hear the speaker through, always went away discontented. They were accustomed to an artificial method, whose scaffolding could easily be retraced, and desired an obvious sequence of logical inferences. They insisted there was nothing in what they had heard, because they could not give a clear account of its course and purport. They did not see that Pindar's odes might be very well arranged for their own purpose, and yet not bear translating into the methods of Mr. Locke.

Others were content to be benefitted by a good influence without a strict analysis of its means. "My wife says it is about the elevation of human nature, and so it seems to me;" was a fit reply to some of the critics. Many were satisfied to find themselves excited to congenial thought and nobler life, without an exact catalogue of the thoughts of the speaker.

Those who believed no truth could exist, unless encased by the burrs of opinion, went away utterly baffled. Sometimes they thought he was on their side, then presently would come something on the other. He really seemed to believe there were two sides to every subject, and even to intimate higher ground from which each might be seen to have an infinite number of sides or bearings, an impertinence not to be endured! The partisan heard but once and returned no more.

But some there were, simple souls, whose life had been, perhaps, without clear light, yet still a search after truth for its own sake, who were able to receive what followed on the suggestion of a subject in a natural manner, as a stream of thought. These recognized, beneath the veil of words, the still small voice of conscience, the vestal fires of lone religious hours, and the mild teachings of the summer woods.

The charm of the elocution, too, was great. His general manner was that of the reader, occasionally rising into direct address or invocation in passages where tenderness or majesty demanded more energy. At such times both eye and voice called on a remote future to give a worthy reply. A future which shall manifest more largely the universal soul as it was then manifest to this soul. The tone of the voice was a grave body tone, full and sweet rather than sonorous, yet flexible and haunted by many modulations, as even instruments of wood and brass seem to become after they have been long played on with skill and taste; how much more so the human voice! In the more expressive passages it uttered notes of silvery clearness, winning, yet still more commanding. The words uttered in those tones, floated awhile above us, then took root in the memory like winged seed.

In the union of an even rustic plainness with lyric inspirations, religious dignity with philosophic calmness, keen sagacity in details with boldness of view, we saw what brought to mind the early poets and legislators of Greece —men who taught their fellows to plow and avoid moral evil, sing hymns to the gods and watch the metamorphoses of nature. Here in civic Boston was such a man—one who could see man in his original grandeur and his original childishness, rooted in simple nature, raising to the heavens the brow and eyes of a poet.

And these lectures seemed not so much lectures as grave didactic poems, theogonies, perhaps, adorned by odes when some Power was in question whom the poet had best learned to serve, and with eclogues wisely portraying in familiar tongue the duties of man to man and "harmless animals."

Such was the attitude in which the speaker appeared to that portion of the audience who have remained permanently attached to him.—They value his words as the signets of reality; receive his influence as a help and incentive to a nobler discipline than the age, in its general aspect, appears to require; and do not fear to anticipate the verdict of posterity in claiming for him the honors of greatness, and, in some respects, of a Master.

In New-England he thus formed for himself a class of readers, who rejoice to study in his books what they already know by heart. For, though the thought has become familiar, its beautiful garb is always fresh and bright in hue.

A similar circle of like-minded the books must and do form for themselves, though with a movement less directly powerful, as more distant from its source.

The Essays have also been obnoxious to many charges. To that of obscurity, or want of perfect articulation. Of 'Euphuism,' as an excess of fancy in proportion to imagination, and an inclination, at times, to subtlety at the expense of strength, has been styled. The human heart complains of inadequacy, either in the nature or experience of the writer, to represent its full vocation and its deeper needs. Sometimes it speaks of this want as "under-development" or a want of expansion which may yet be remedied; sometimes doubts whether "in this mansion there be either hall or portal to receive the loftier of the Passions." Sometimes the soul is deified at the expense of nature, then again nature at that of man, and we are not quite sure that we can make a true harmony by balance of the statements.—This writer has never written one good work, if such a work be one where the whole commands more attention than the parts. If such an one be produced only where, after an accumulation of materials, fire enough be applied to fuse the whole into one new substance. This second series is superior in this respect to the former, yet in no one essay is the main stress so obvious as to produce on the mind the harmonious effect of a noble river or a tree in full leaf. Single passages and sentences engage our attention too much in proportion. These essays, it has been justly said, tire like a string of mosaics or a house built of medals. We miss what we expect in the work of the great poet, or the great philosopher, the liberal air of all the zones: the glow, uniform yet various in tint, which is given to a body by free circulation of the heart's blood from the hour of birth. Here is, undoubtedly, the man of ideas, but we want the ideal man also; want the heart and genius of human life to interpret it, and here our satisfaction is not so perfect. We doubt this friend raised himself too early to the perpendicular and did not lie along the ground long enough to hear the secret whispers of our parent life. We could wish he might be thrown by conflicts on the lap of mother earth, to see if he would not rise again with added powers.

All this we may say, but it cannot excuse us from benefitting by the great gifts that have been given, and assigning them their due place.

Some painters paint on a red ground. And this color may be supposed to represent the ground work most immediately congenial to most men, as it is the color of blood and represents human vitality. The figures traced upon it are instinct with life in its fulness and depth.

But other painters paint on a gold ground. And a very different, but no less natural, because also a celestial beauty, is given to their works who choose for their foundation the color of the sunbeam, which nature has preferred for her most precious product, and that which will best bear the test of purification, gold.

If another simile may be allowed, another no less apt is at hand. Wine is the most brilliant and intense expression of the powers of earth.—It is her potable fire, her answer to the sun. It exhilarates, it inspires, but then it is liable to fever and intoxicate too the careless partaker.

Mead was the chosen drink of the Northern gods. And this essence of the honey of the mountain bee was not thought unworthy to revive the souls of the valiant who had left their bodies on the fields of strife below.

Nectar should combine the virtues of the ruby wine, the golden mead, without their defects or dangers.

Two high claims our writer can vindicate on the attention

of his contemporaries. One from his sincerity. You have his thought just as it found place in the life of his own soul. Thus, however near or relatively distant its approximation to absolute truth, its action on you cannot fail to be healthful. It is a part of the free air.

He belongs to that band of whom there may be found a few in every age, and who now in known human history may be counted by hundreds, who worship the one God only, the God of Truth. They worship, not saints, nor creeds, nor churches, nor reliques, nor idols in any form. The mind is kept open to truth, and life only valued as a tendency toward it. This must be illustrated by acts and words of love, purity and intelligence. Such are the salt of the earth; let the minutest crystal of that salt be willingly by us held in solution.

The other is through that part of his life, which, if sometimes obstructed or chilled by the critical intellect, is yet the prevalent and the main source of his power. It is that by which he imprisons his hearer only to free him again as a "liberating God" (to use his own words). But indeed let us use them altogether, for none other, ancient or modern, can more worthily express how, making present to us the courses and destinies of nature, he invests himself with her serenity and animates us with her joy.

"Poetry was all written before time was, and whenever we are so finely organized that we can penetrate into that region where the air is music, we hear those primal warblings, and attempt to write them down, but we lose ever and anon a word, or a verse, and substitute something of our own, and thus miswrite the poem. The men of more delicate ear write down these cadences more faithfully, and these transcripts, though imperfect, become the songs of the nations."

"As the eyes of Lyncæus were said to see through the earth, so the poet turns the world to glass, and shows us all things in their right series and procession. For, through that better perception, he stands one step nearer to things, and sees the flowing or metamorphosis; perceives that thought is multiform; that within the form of every creature is a force impelling it to ascend into a higher form; and following with his eyes the life, uses the forms which express that life, and so the speech flows with the flowing of nature."

Thus have we in a brief and unworthy manner indicated some views of these books. The only true criticism of these, or any good books, may be gained by making them the companions of our lives. Does every accession of knowledge or a juster sense of beauty makes us prize them more? Then they are good, indeed, and more immortal than mortal. Let that test be applied to these; essays which will lead to great and complete poems—somewhere.

Thanksgiving*

Canst thou give thanks for aught that has been given
Except by making earth more worthy heaven?
Just stewardship the master hoped from thee;
Harvests from Time to bless Eternity.

THANKSGIVING is peculiarly the festival day of New-England. Elsewhere, other celebrations rival its attractions, but in that region where the Puritans first returned thanks that some among them had been sustained by a great hope and earnest resolve amid the perils of the ocean, wild beasts and famine, the old spirit which hallowed the day still lingers, and forbids that it should be entirely devoted to play and plum-pudding.

And yet, as there is always this tendency; as the twelfth-night cake is baked by many a hostess who would be puzzled if you asked her, "Twelfth night after or before what?" and the Christmas cake by many who know no other Christmas service, so it requires very serious assertion and proof from the minister to convince his parishioners that the turky and plum-pudding, which are presently to occupy his place in their attention, should not be the chief objects of the day.

And, in other regions, where the occasion is observed, it is still more as one for a meeting of families and friends to the enjoyment of a good dinner, than for any higher purpose.

This, indeed, is one which we want not to depreciate. If this manner of keeping the day be likely to persuade the juniors of the party that the celebrated Jack Horner is the prime model for brave boys, and that grand parents are chiefly to be respected as the givers of grand feasts, yet a meeting in the spirit of kindness, however dull and blind, is

* In *New-York Daily Tribune*, 12 December 1844, p. 2.

not wholly without use in healing differences and promoting good intentions. The instinct of family love, intended by Heaven to make those of one blood the various and harmonious organs of one mind, is never wholly without good influence. Family love, I say, for family pride is never without bad influence, and it too often takes the place of its mild and healthy sister.

Yet where society is at all simple, it is cheering to see the family circle thus assembled, if only because its patriarchal form is in itself so excellent. The presence of the children animates the old people, while the respect and attention they demand refines the gaiety of the young. Yes, it is cheering to see, in some large room, the elders talking near the bright fire, while the cousins of all ages are amusing themselves in knots. Here is almost all the good, and very little of the ill, that can be found in society, got together merely for amusement.

Yet how much nobler, more exhilarating and purer would be the atmosphere of that circle if the design of its pious founders were remembered by those who partake this festival! If they dared not attend the public jubilee till private retrospect of the past year had been taken in the spirit of the old rhyme, which we all bear in mind if not in heart—

> "What hast thou done that's worth the doing,
> And what pursued that's worth pursuing?
> What sought thou knew'st that thou shouldst shun,
> What done thou shouldst have left undone?"

and a crusade been vowed into the wild places of the bosom, which should take for its device, "Lord, cleanse thou me from secret faults"—"Keep back thy servant also from presumptuous sins"—would not that circle be happy as if music, from invisible agents, floated through it—if each member of it considered every other member as a bequest from heaven—if he supposed that the appointed nearness in blood or lot was a sign to him that he must exercise his gifts of every kind as given peculiarly in their behalf—that if richer in temper, in talents, in knowledge, or in worldly goods, here was the innermost circle of his poor—that he must clothe these naked, whether in body or mind, soothing the perverse, casting light into the narrow chamber, or, most welcome task

of all! extending a hand at the right moment to one uncertain
of his way. It is this spirit that makes the old man to be
revered as a Nestor, rather than put aside like a worn-out
garment. It is such a spirit that sometimes has given to the
young child a ministry as of a parent in the house.

But, if charity begin at home, it must not end there; and
while purifying the innermost circle, let us not forget that it
depends upon the great circle, and that again on it; that no
home can be healthful in which are not cherished seeds of
good for the world at large. Thy child, thy brother are given
to thee only as an example of what is due from thee to all
men. It is true that, if you, in anger, call your brother fool, no
deeds of so-called philanthropy shall have you from the
punishment; for your philanthropy must be from the love of
excitement, not the love of man, or of goodness. But then you
must visit the Gentiles also, and take time for knowing what
aid the woman of Samaria may need.[1]

A noble Catholic writer, in the true sense as well as by
name a Catholic, describes a tailor as giving a dinner on an
occasion which had brought honor to his house, which,
though humble, was not a poor house. In his glee, the tailor
was boasting a little of the favors and blessings of his lot,
when suddenly a thought stung him. He stopped, and cutting
away half the fowl that lay before him, sent it in a dish with
the best knives, bread, and napkin, and a brotherly message
that was better still, to a widow near, who must, he knew, be
sitting in sadness and poverty among her children. His little
daughter was the messenger. If parents followed up the indulgences heaped upon their children at Thanksgiving dinners with similar messages, there would not be danger that
children should think enjoyment of sensual pleasures the
only occasion that demands Thanksgiving.

And suppose while the children were absent on their errands of justice, as they could not fail to think them, if they
compared the hovels they must visit with their own comfortable homes, their elders, touched by a sense of right, should
be led from discussion of the rivalries of trade or fashion to
whether they could not impart of all that was theirs, not
merely one poor dinner once a year, but all their mental and

[1] Jesus' conversation with the woman of Samaria is in John 4:1-26.

material wealth for the benefit of all men. If they do not sell it *all* at once, as the rich young man was bid to do as a test of his sincerity, they may find some way in which it could be invested so as to show enough obedience to the Law and the Prophets to love our neighbor as ourselves.

And he who once gives himself to such thoughts will find it is not merely moral gain for which he shall return thanks another year with the return of this day. In the present complex state of human affairs, you cannot be kind unless you are wise. Thoughts of amaranthine bloom will spring up in the fields plowed to give food to suffering men. It would, indeed, seem to be a simple matter at first glance. "Lovest thou me?"—"Feed my lambs." But now we have not only to find pasture, but to detect the lambs under the disguise of wolves, and restore them by a spell, like that the Shepherd used, to their natural form and whiteness.

And for this present day appointed for Thanksgiving, we may say that if we know of so many wrongs, woes, and errors in the world yet unredressed; if in this nation recent decisions have shown a want of moral discrimination on important subjects, that make us pause and doubt whether we can join in the formal congratulations that we are still bodily alive, unassailed by the ruder modes of warfare, and enriched with the fatness of the land; yet on the other side, we know of causes not so loudly proclaimed why we should give thanks. Abundantly and humbly we must render them for the movement, now sensible in the heart of the civilized world, although it has not pervaded the entire frame. For that movement of contrition and love which forbids men of earnest thought to eat, drink, or be merry, while other men are steeped in ignorance, corruption and wo; which calls the King from his throne of gold, and the Poet from his throne of Mind to lie with the beggar in the kennel, or raise him from it; which says to the Poet, "You must reform rather than create a world," and to him of the golden crown, "You cannot long remain a King unless you are also a Man."

Wherever this impulse of social or political reform darts up its rill through the crusts of selfishness, scoff and dread arise and hang like a heavy mist above it. But the voice of the rill penetrates far enough for those who have ears to hear. And, sometimes, it is the case that 'those who came to scoff remain to pray.' In two articles of reviews, one foreign and one domestic, which have come under our eye within the last fortnight, the writers who began by jeering at the visionaries, seemed as they wrote to be touched by a sense that without a high and pure faith none can have the only true vision of the intention of God as to the Destiny of Man.

We recognized as a happy omen that there is cause for thanksgiving and that our people may be better than they seem, the meeting last week to organize an Association for the benefit of Prisoners. We shall not, then, be wholly Pharisees. We shall not ask the blessing of this day in the mood of "Lord, I thank thee that I, and my son, and my brother, are not as other men are,—not as these publicans imprisoned there," while the still, small voice cannot make us hear its evidence that, but for instruction, example, and the "preventing God," every sin that can be named might riot in our hearts. The prisoner, too, may become a man. Neither his open nor our secret faults, must utterly dismay us. We will treat him as if he had a soul. We will not dare to hunt him into a beast of prey, or trample him into a serpent. We will give him some crumbs from the table which grace from above and parent love below have spread for us, and, perhaps, he will recover from these ghastly ulcers that deform him now.

We were much pleased with the spirit of the meeting. It was simple, business-like, in a serious, affectionate temper. The speakers did not make phrases or compliments; did not slur over the truth. The audience showed a ready vibration to the touch of just and tender feeling. The time was evidently ripe for this movement. We doubt not that many now darkened souls will give thanks for the ray of light that will have been let in by this time next year. It is but a grain of mustard seed, but the promised tree will grow swiftly if tended in a pure spirit; and the influence of good measures in any one place will be immediate in this province, as has been the case with every attempt in behalf of the insane.

While reading a notice of a successful attempt to have musical performances carried through in concert by the insane at Rouen, we were forcibly reminded of a similar performance we heard a few weeks ago at Sing Sing. There the female describes the last thoughts of a spirit about to be enfranchised from the body; each stanza of which ends with the words, "All is well;" and they sang it—those suffering, degraded children of society—with as gentle and resigned an expression as if they were sure of going to sleep in the arms of a pure mother. The good spirit that dwelt in the music made them its own. And shall not the good spirit of religious sympathy make them its own also, and more permanently? We shall see. Should the morally insane, by wise and gentle cure, be won back to health, as the wretched bedlamites have been, will not the angels themselves give thanks? And will any man dare take the risk of opposing plans that afford even a chance of such a result?

Apart, then, from good that is public and many-voiced, do not each of us know, in private experience, much to be thankful for? Not only the innocent and daily pleasures that we have prized according to our wisdom; of the sun and starry skies, the fields of green, or snow scarcely less beautiful, the loaf eaten with an appetite, the glow of labor, the gentle signs of common affection. But have not some, have not many of us cause to be thankful for enfranchisement from error or infatuation; a growth in knowledge of outward things, and instruction within the soul from a higher source. Have we not acquired a sense of more refined enjoyments; clear convictions; sometimes a serenity in which, as in the first days of June, all things grow, and the blossom gives place to fruit? Have we not been weaned from what was unfit for us, or unworthy our care? and have not those ties been drawn more close, and are not those objects seen more distinctly, which shall for ever be worthy the purest desires of our souls? Have we learned to do any thing, the humblest, in the service and by the spirit of the power which meaneth all things well? If so we may give thanks, and, perhaps, venture to offer our solicitations in behalf of those as yet less favored by circumstances. When even a few shall dare do so with the whole heart—for only a pure heart can "avail much" in such prayers—the ALL shall soon be well.

Christmas*

Our Festivals come rather too near together, since we have so few of them; Thanksgiving, Christmas, New Year's day —and then none again till July. We know not but these four, with the addition of "a day set apart for fasting and prayer," might answer the purposes of rest and edification, as well as a calendar full of saints' days, if they were observed in a better spirit.—But Thanksgiving is devoted to good dinners; Christmas and New Years' days to making presents and compliments; Fast-day to playing at cricket and other games, and the Fourth of July to boasting of the past, rather than to plans how to deserve its benefits and secure its fruits.

We value means of marking time by appointed days, because man, on one side of his nature so ardent and aspiring, is on the other so slippery and indolent a being, that he needs incessant admonitions to redeem the time. Time flows on steadily, whether he regards it or not, yet unless *he keep time* there is no music in that flow.—The sands drop with inevitable speed, yet each waits long enough to receive, if it be ready, the intellectual touch that should turn it to a sand of gold.

Time, says the Grecian fable, is the parent of Power; Power is the father of Genius and Wisdom; Time then is grandfather of the noblest of the human family, and we must respect the aged sire whom we see on the frontispiece of the almanacs and believe his sythe was meant to mow down harvests ripened for an immortal use.

Yet the best provision made by the mind of society, at large, for these admonitions, soon loses its efficacy and requires that individual earnestness, individual piety should

* In *New–York Weekly Tribune*, 21 December 1844, p. 1.

continually reinform the most beautiful form. The world has never seen arrangements which might more naturally offer good suggestions than those of the Church of Rome. The founders of that Church stood very near a history radiant at every page with divine light. All their rites and ceremonial days illustrate facts of an universal interest. But the life with which piety, first, and, afterward, the genius of great artists invested these symbols waned at last, except to a thoughtful few. Reverence was forgotten in the multitude of genuflexions; the rosary became a string of beads, rather than a series of religious meditations, and "the glorious company of saints and martyrs" were not regarded as much the teachers of heavenly truth, as intercessors to obtain for their votaries the temporal gifts they craved.

Yet we regret that some of those symbols had not been more reverenced by Protestants, as the possible occasion of good thoughts. And among others we regret that the day set apart to commemorate the birth of Jesus should have been stripped, even by those who observe it, of many impressive and touching accessories.

If ever there was an occasion on which the arts could become all but omnipotent in the service of a holy thought, it is this of the birth of the child Jesus. In the palmy days of the Catholic religion, they may be said to have wrought miracles in its behalf, and, in our colder time, when we rather reflect that light from a different point of view, than transport ourselves into it; who that has an eye and ear faithful to the soul is not conscious of inexhaustible benefits from some of the works by which sublime geniuses have expressed their ideas in the adorations of the Magi and the Shepherds, in the Virgin with the infant Jesus, or that work which expresses what Christendom at large has not even begun to realize, that work which makes us conscious, as we listen, why the soul of man was thought worthy and able to upbear a cross of such dreadful weight—the Messiah of Handel.

Christmas would seem to be the day peculiarly sacred to children, and something of this feeling there shows itself among us, though rather from German influence, than of native growth. The evergreen tree is often reared for the children on Christmas evening, and its branches cluster with little tokens that may, at least, give them a sense that the world is rich, and that there are some in it who care to bless them. It is a charming sight to see their glittering eyes, and well worth much trouble in preparing the Christmas tree.

Yet, on this occasion as on all others, we could wish to see pleasure offered them in a form less selfish than it is. When shall we read of banquets prepared for the halt, the lame and the blind, on the day that is said to have brought *their* friend into the world? When will the children be taught to ask all the cold and ragged little ones, whom they have seen during the day wistfully gazing at the displays in the shop windows, to share the joys of Christmas eve?

We borrow the Christmas tree from Germany. Might we but borrow with it that feeling which pervades all their stories about the influence of the Christ child, and has, I doubt not—for the spirit of literature is always, though refined, the essence of popular life—pervaded the conduct of children there.

We will mention two of these as happily expressive of different sides of the desirable character. One is a legend of the Saint Hermann Joseph. The legend runs that this saint, when a little boy, passed daily by a niche where was an image of the Virgin and Child, and delighted there to pay his devotions. His heart was so drawn toward the holy child, that, one day, having received what seemed to him a gift truly precious—to wit, a beautiful red and yellow apple—he ventured to offer it, with his prayer. To his unspeakable delight, the child put forth its hand and took the apple. After that day, never was a gift bestowed upon the little Hermann that was not carried to the same place. He needed nothing for himself; but dedicated all his childish goods to the altar.

After a while, he is in grief. His father, who was a poor man, finds it necessary to take him from school and bind him to a trade. He communicates his woes to his friends of the niche, and the Virgin comforts him, like a mother, and bestows on him money by means of which he rises (not to ride in a gilt coach like Lord Mayor Whittington,)[1] but to be a learned and tender shepherd of men.

---

[1] Richard Whittington (d. 1423), Lord Mayor of London, noted for his liberality, was in legend supposed to have risen to Mayor with the aid of his cat.

Another still more touching story is that of the holy Rupert. Rupert was the only child of a princely house, and had something to give beside apples. But his generosity and human love were such that, as a child, he could never see poor children suffering without despoiling himself of all he had with him in their behalf. His mother was, at first, displeased at this, but when he replied, "they are thy children too," her reproofs yielded to tears.

One time, when he had given away his coat to a poor child, he got wearied and belated on his homeward way. He lay down awhile and fell asleep. Then he dreamed that he was on a river-shore, and saw a mild and noble old man bathing many children. After he had plunged them into the water, he would place them on a beautiful island, where they looked white and glorious as little angels. Rupert was seized with strong desire to join them, and begged the old man to bathe him, also, in the stream. But he was answered, "It is not yet time." Just then a rainbow spanned the island, and in its arch was enthroned the child Jesus, dressed in a coat that Rupert knew to be his own. And the Child said to the others, "See this coat; it is one my brother Rupert has just sent to me. He has given us many gifts from his love: shall we not ask him to join us here?" And they shouted a musical "yes;" and the child started from his dream. But he had lain too long on the damp bank of the river without his coat. A cold and fever soon sent him to join the band of his brothers in their home.

These are legends, superstitions, will you say? But, in casting aside the shell, have we retained the kernel? The image of the child Jesus is not seen in the open street; does his heart find other means to express itself there? Protestantism did not mean, we suppose, to deaden the spirit in excluding the form?

The thought of a Jesus, as a child, has great weight with children who have learned to think of him at all. In thinking of him, they form an image all that the morning of a pure and fervent life should be and bring. In former days I knew a boy artist, whose genius, at that time, showed high promise. He was not more than fourteen years old, a slight, pale boy, with a beaming eye. The hopes and sympathy of friends, gained by his talent, had furnished him with a studio and orders for some pictures. He had picked up from the streets a boy still younger and poorer than himself to take care of the room and prepare his colors, and the two boys were as content in their relation as Michael Angelo with his Urbino.[2] If you went there you found exposed to view many pretty pictures, "A Girl with a Dove," "The Guitar Player," and such subjects as are commonly supposed to interest at his age. But, hid in a corner, and never shown, unless to the beggar page, or some most confidential friend, was the real object of his love and pride, the slowly growing work of secret hours. The subject of this picture was Christ teaching the Doctors. And in those Doctors he had expressed all he had already observed of the pedantry and shallow conceit of those in whom mature years have not unfolded the soul. And in the child all he felt that early youth should be and seek, though, alas! his own feet failed him on the difficult road. This one record of the youth Jesus had, at least, been much to his mind.

In earlier days, the little saints thought they best imitated the Immanuel by giving apples and coats;[3] but we know not why, in our age, that esteems itself so enlightened, they should not become also the givers of spiritual gifts. We see in them, continually, impulses that only require a good direction to effect infinite good. See the little girls at work for foreign missions: that is not useless. They devote the time to a purpose that is not selfish; the horizon of their thoughts is extended. But they are perfectly capable of becoming home missionaries as well.—The principle of stewardship would make them so.

I have seen a little girl of thirteen, who had much service, too, to do, for a hard-working mother, in the midst of a circle of poor children whom she gathered daily to a morning school. She took them from the door-steps and the ditch; she washed their hands and faces; she taught them to read and to sew; and she told them little stories that had delighted her own infancy. In her face, though in feature and complexion plain, was something, already, of a Madonna sweetness, and it had no way eclipsed the gayety of childhood.

I have seen a boy scarce older, brought up for some time

---

[2] Urbino, Michelangelo's servant for over twenty years.

[3] Immanuel ("God is with us"), name given to a child whose birth Isaiah predicted.

with the sons of laborers, who so soon as he found himself possessed of superior advantages, thought not of surpassing others, but of excelling and then imparting, and he was able to do it. If the other boys had less leisure and could pay for less instruction, they did not suffer for it. He could not be happy unless they also could enjoy Milton and pass from nature to natural philosophy. He performed, though in a childish way, and in no Grecian garb, the part of Apollo amid the herdsmen of Admetus.[4]

The cause of Education would be indefinitely furthered, if, in addition to formal means, there were but this principle awakened in the hearts of the young, that what they have they must bestow. All are not natural instructors, but a large proportion are; and those who do possess such a talent are the best possible teachers to those a little younger than themselves. They have more patience with the difficulties they have lately left behind, and enjoy their power of assisting more than those farther removed in age and knowledge do.

Then the intercourse may be far more congenial and profitable than where the teacher receives for hire all sorts of pupils as they are sent him by their guardians. Here he need only choose those who have a predisposition for what he is best able to teach. And, as I would have the so-called higher instruction as much diffused in this way as the lower, there would be a chance of awakening all the power that now lies latent.

If a girl for instance, who has only a passable talent for music, but who, from the advantage of social position, has been able to gain thorough instruction, felt it her duty to teach whomsoever she knew that had such a talent, without money to cultivate it, the good is obvious.

Those who are learning receive an immediate benefit by an effort to rearrange and interpret what they learn, so the use of this justice would be twofold.

Some efforts are made here and there; nay, sometimes there are those who can say they have returned usury for every gift of fate. And, would others make the same experi-

---

[4] The story of how Apollo saved Admetus from an early death is given in Euripides' *Alcestis*.

ments, they might find Utopia not so far off as the children of this world, wise in securing their own selfish ease, would persuade us it must always be.

We have hinted what sort of Christmas box we would wish for the children. It should be one full as that of the Child Christ must be, of the pieces of silver that were lost and are found. But Christmas with its peculiar associations has deep interest for men, and women too no less. It has so in their mutual relations. At the time thus celebrated a pure woman saw in her child what the Son of Man should be as a child of God. She anticipated for him a life of glory to God, peace and good will to man. In every young mother's heart, who has any purity of heart, the same feelings arise. But most of these mothers let them go without obeying their instructions. If they did not, we should see other children, other men than now throng our streets. The boy could not invariably disappoint the mother, the man the wife, who steadily demanded of him such a career.

And man looks upon woman, in this relation, always as he should. Does he see in her a holy mother, worthy to guard the infancy of an immortal soul? Then she assumes in his eyes those traits which the Romish Church loved to revere in Mary. Frivolity, base appetite, contempt are exorcised; and man and woman appear again in unprofaned connexion, as brother and sister, the children and the servants of the one Divine Love, and pilgrims to a common aim.

Were all this right in the private sphere, the public would soon right itself also, and the nations of Christendom might join in a celebration, such as "Kings and Prophets waited for" and so many martyrs died achieve, of Christ-Mass.

New Year's Day*

It was a beautiful custom among some of the Indian tribes, once a year, to extinguish all the fires, and, by a day of fasting and profound devotion, to propitiate the Great Spirit for the coming year. They then produced sparks by friction, and lit up afresh the altar and the hearth with the new fire.

And this was considered as the most precious and sacred gift from one person to another, binding them in bonds of inviolate friendship for that year, certainly; with a hope that the same might endure through life. From the young to the old it was a token of the highest respect; from the old to the young, of a great expectation.

To us might it be granted to solemnize the new year by the mental renovation of which this ceremony was the eloquent symbol! Might we extinguish, if only for a day, those fires where an uninformed religious ardor has led to human sacrifices; which have warmed the household, but, also, prepared pernicious, more than wholesome, viands for their use.

The Indian produced the new spark by friction. It would be a still more beautiful emblem, and expressive of the more extended powers of civilized men, if we should draw the spark from the centre of our system and the source of light by means of the burning glass.

Where, then, is to be found the new knowledge, the new thought, the new hope, that shall begin a new year in a spirit not discordant with 'the acceptable year of the Lord?' Surely, there must be such existing, if latent—some sparks of new fire, pure from ashes and from smoke, worthy to be offered as a new-year's gift? Let us look at the signs of the

* In *New-York Weekly Tribune,* 28 December 1844, p. 1.

times, to see in what spot this fire shall be sought—on what fuel it may be fed. The ancients poured out libations of the choicest juices of Earth, to express their gratitude to the Power that had enabled them to be sustained from her bosom. They enfranchised slaves, to show that devotion to the Gods induced a sympathy with men.

Let us look about us to see with what rites, what acts of devotion, this modern Christian nation greets the approach of the New Year; by what signs she denotes the clear morning of a better day, such as may be expected when the eagle has entered into convenant with the dove!

This last week brings tidings that a portion of the inhabitants of Illinois, the rich and blooming region on which every gift of nature has been lavished to encourage the industry and brighten the hopes of man, not only refuses a libation to the Power that has so blessed their fields, but declares that the dew is theirs, and the sunlight is theirs, that they live from and for themselves, acknowledging no obligation and no duty to God or to man.

One man has freed a slave,—but a great part of the nation is now busy in contriving measures that may best rivet the fetters on those now chained, and forge them strongest for millions yet unborn.

Selfishness and tyranny no longer wear the mask; they walk haughtily abroad, affronting with their hard-hearted boasts and brazen resolves the patience of the sweet heavens. National Honor is trodden under foot for a National bribe, and neither sex nor age defends the redresser of injuries from the rage of the injurer.

Yet, amid these reports which come flying on the paper wings of every day, the scornful laugh of the gnomes, who begin to believe they can buy all souls with their gold, was checked a moment when the aged knight of the better cause answered the challenge—truly in keeping with the 'chivalry' of the time,—"You are in the wrong, and I will kick you," by holding the hands of the chevalier till those around secured him. We think the man of old must have held him with his eye, as physicians of moral power can insane patients;—great as are his exploits for his age, he cannot have much bodily strength, unless by miracle.

The treatment of Mr. Adams and Mr. Hoar seems to show

that we are not fitted to emulate the savages in preparation
for the new fire.[1] The Indians knew how to reverence the old
and the wise.

Among the manifestos of the day it is impossible not to
respect that of the Mexican Minister for the manly indignation with which he has uttered truths, however deep our
mortification at hearing them.[2] It has been observed for the
last fifty years that the tone of diplomatic correspondence
was much improved as to simplicity and directness. Once,
diplomacy was another name for intrigue, and a paper of this
sort was expected to be a mesh of artful phrases, through
which the true meaning might be detected, but never actually grasped. Now here is one where an occasion being afforded by the unutterable folly of the corresponding party, a
Minister speaks the truth as it lies in his mind, directly and
plainly, as man speaks to man. His statement will command
the sympathy of the civilized world.

As to the State papers that have followed, they are of a
nature to make the Austrian despot sneer, as he counts in his
oratory the woolen stockings he has got knit by imprisoning
all the free geniuses in his dominions. He, at least, only appeals to the legitimacy of blood; these dare appeal to legitimacy, as seen from a moral point of view. History will class
them with the brags of sharpers, who bully their victims
about their honor, while they stretch forth their hands for the
gold they have won with loaded dice.—"Do you dare to say
the dice are loaded? Prove it; *and* I will shoot you for injuring my honor."

The Mexican makes his gloss on the page of American
Honor. The girl in the Kentucky prison on that of her Freedom. The delegate of Massachusetts on that of her Union. Ye

[1] Samuel Hoar (1778-1856) was sent to Charleston, South Carolina, in
1844 by the state of Massachusetts to prepare a test case on behalf of some
imprisoned Massachusetts free Negro seamen. He was declared an emis-
sary of a foreign government and expelled from the city. John Quincy
Adams represented his hometown of Quincy, Massachusetts, in the House
of Representatives from 1831 until his death; see also note 17, p. 96
above.

[2] The border dispute between the United States and Mexico climaxed
with the annexation of Texas in March 1845 and the arrival of an American
force under Zachary Taylor on the disputed land that summer.

stars! whose image she has placed upon her banner, answer us! Are not your Unions of a different sort? Do they not work to other results?

Yet we cannot lightly be discouraged or alarmed as to the destiny of our Country. The whole history of its discovery and early progress indicates too clearly the purposes of Heaven with regard to it. Could we relinquish the thought that it was destined for the scene of a new and illustrious act in the great drama, the Past would be inexplicable, no less than the Future without hope.

Last week, which brought us so many unpleasant notices of home affairs, brought also an account of the magnificent telescope lately perfected by the Earl of Rosse. With means of observation, now almost divine, we perceive that some of the brightest stars, of which Sirius is one, have dark companions, whose presence is, by earthly spectators, only to be detected from the inequalities they cause in the motions of their radiant companions.

It was a new and most imposing illustration how, in carrying out the Divine scheme, of which we have as yet only spelt out the few first few lines, the dark is made to wait upon and, in the full result, harmonize with, the bright. The sense of such pervasive analogies should enlarge patience and animate hope.

Yet, if offences must come, wo be to those by whom they come, and that of men, who sin against a heritage like ours, is as that of the backsliders among the Chosen People of the elder day. We too have been chosen, and plain indications been given, by a wonderful conjunction of auspicious influences, that the ark of human hopes has been placed for the present in our charge. Wo be to those who betray this trust! On their heads are to be heaped the curses of unnumbered ages!

Can he sleep, who in this past year has wickedly or lightly committed acts calculated to injure the few or many—who has poisoned the ears and the hearts he might have rightly informed—who has steeped in tears the cup of thousands —who has put back, as far as in him lay, the accomplishment of general good and happiness for the sake of his selfish aggrandizement or selfish luxury—who has sold to a party what is meant for mankind? If such sleep, dreadful shall be the waking.

Deliver us from evil. In public or in private it is easy to
give pain—hard to give pure pleasure; easy to do evil—hard
to do good. God does His good in the whole, despite of bad
men; but only from a very pure mind will He permit original
good to proceed in the day. Happy those who can feel that
during the past year, they have, to the best of their knowledge, refrained from evil. Happy those who determine to
proceed in this by the light of Conscience. It is but a spark;
yet from that spark may be drawn fire-light enough for worlds
and systems of worlds, and that light is ever new.

And with this thought rises again the memory of the fair
lines that light has brought to view in the histories of some
men. If the nation tends to wrong, there are yet present the
ten just men. The hands and lips of this great form may be
impure, but pure blood flows yet within her veins—the blood
of the noble bands who first sought these shores from the
British isles and France for conscience sake. Too many have
come since for bread alone. We cannot blame—we must not
reject them, but let us teach them, in giving them bread, to
prize that salt, too, without which all on earth must lose its
savor. Yes! let us teach them, not rail at their inevitable ignorance and unenlightened action, but teach them and their
children as our own; if we do so, their children and ours may
yet act as one body obedient to one soul, and if we should act
rightly now, that soul a pure soul.

And ye, sable bands, forced hither against your will, kept
down here now by a force hateful to Nature, a will alien from
God; it does sometimes seem as if the Avenging Angel wore
your hue and would place in your hands the sword to punish
the cruel injustice of our fathers, the selfish perversity of the
sons. Yet, are there no means of atonement? Must the innocent suffer with the guilty? Teach us, oh All-Wise! the clue
out of this labyrinth, and if we faithfully encounter its darkness and dread, and emerge into clear light, wilt Thou not
bid us 'go and sin no more?'

Meanwhile, let us proceed as we can, *picking our steps*
along the slippery road. If we keep the right direction, what
matters it that we must pass through so much mud? The
promise is sure:

Angels shall free the feet from stain, to their own hue of snow,
If, undismayed, we reach the hills where the true olives grow.

The olive-groves, which we must seek in cold and damp,
Alone can yield us oil for a perpetual lamp.
Then sound again the golden horn with promise ever new;
The princely deer will ne'er be caught by those that slack pursue;
Let the 'White Doe' of angel hopes be always be kept in view.

Yes! sound again the horn—of Hope the golden horn!
Answer it, flutes and pipes, from valleys still and lorn;
Warders, from your high towers, with trumps of silver scorn,
And harps in maidens' bowers, with strings from deep hearts torn,
All answer to the horn—of Hope the golden horn!

There is still hope, there is still an America, while private lives are ruled by the Puritan, by the Huguenot conscientiousness, and while there are some who can repudiate, not their debts, but the supposition that they will not strive to pay their debts to their age, and to Heaven who gave them a share in its great promise.

Children's Books *

There is no branch of literature that better deserves cultivation, and none that so little obtains it from worthy hands as
this of Children's books. It requires a peculiar development
of the genius and sympathies, rare among the men of facti-
tious life, who are not men enough to revive, with force and
beauty, the thoughts and scenes of childhood.

It is all idle to talk baby-talk, with malice prepense, and to
give shallow accounts of deep things, thinking thereby to
interest the child.—He does not like to be too much puzzled,
but it is simplicity he wants and not silliness. We fancy, their
angels, who are always waiting in the courts of our Father,
smile, somewhat sadly, at the ignorance of those who would
feed them on milk and water too long, and think it would be
quite as well to give them a stone.

There is too much among us of the French way of palming
off false accounts of things on children *to do them good*, and
showing nature to them in a magic lantern, "purified for the
use of childhood," and telling stories of good little girls, and
sweet little girls, or brave little boys; oh! all *so* good! or *so*
bad! and, above all, so *little*, and every thing about them so
little!—Children, accustomed to move in full-sized apartments, and converse with full-grown men and women, do not
need so much of this baby-house style in their literature.
They like, or would like, if they could get them, better things
much better. They like the "Arabian Nights," and "Pilgrim's
Progress," and "Bunyan's Emblems," and Shakspeare, and
the "Iliad" and "Odyssey;" at least, they used to like them;
and, if they do not now, it is because their taste has been

* *The Child's Friend: Designed for Families and Sunday Schools*, edited
by Eliza L. Follen, had begun publication in 1843. In *New-York Daily
Tribune*, 5 February 1845, p. 1; title supplied.

injured by so many sugar-plums. The books that were written
in the childhood of nations suit an uncorrupt childhood now.
They are simple, picturesque, robust. Their moral is not
forced, nor is the truth veiled with a well-meant, but sure-to-
fail, hypocrisy. Sometimes they are not moral at all, only free
plays of the fancy and intellect. There, also, the child needs,
just as the infant needs to stretch its limbs, and grasp at
objects it cannot hold. We have become so fond of the moral
that we forget the nature in which it must find its root; so
fond of instruction, that we forget development.

Where ballads, legends, and fairy-tales *are* moral, the morality is heart-*felt*; if instructive, it is from the healthy common sense of mankind, and not for the convenience of nur-
sery rule nor the "peace of schools and families."

O that winter! freezing, snow-laden winter, which slowly
ushered in our eighth birth-day.—There, in the lonely farm-
house, the day's work done, and the bright wood fire a' in a
low, we were permitted to slide back the panel of the cup-
board in the wall; most fascinating object still in our eyes,
with which no stateliest alcoved library can vie; and there
saw, neatly ranged on its two shelves, *not*, praised be our
natal star! Peter Parley nor "A history of the good little boy
that never took anything that did not belong to him;" but
—the "Spectator," "Telemadan," "Goldsmith's Animated Nature" and the "Iliad."[1]

Forms of gods and heroes more distinctly seen and with
eyes of nearer love then than now!—Our true Uncle, Sir
Roger de Coverley,[2] and ye, fair realms of Nature's history
whose pictures we tormented all grown persons to illustrate
with more knowledge—still more, how we bless the chance
that gave to us your great realities which life has daily helped
us—helps us still, to interpret, instead of thin and baseless
fictions that would, all this time, have hampered us although
only with cobwebs.

Children need some childish talk, some childish play,

[1] "Telemadan," unidentified; Oliver Goldsmith (1730?-1774) published
his *An History of the Earth and Animated Nature*, which he considered
hackwork, in the year of his death.
[2] Sir Roger de Coverley, a gentlemanly character used by Joseph Addison
(1672-1719) and Sir Richard Steele (1672-1729) in their *Spectator* papers
(1711-1712, 1714).

some childish books. But they also need, and need more, difficulties to overcome, and a sense of the vast mysteries which the progress of their intelligence shall aid them to unravel. This sense is naturally their delight, as it is their religion, and it must not be dulled by premature explanations, nor subterfuges of any kind. There has been too much of this lately.

Miss Edgeworth is an excellent writer for children.[3] She is a child herself as she writes, armed anew by her own genius. It is not by imitating but by reproducing childhood that the writer becomes its companion. Then, indeed, we have something especially good, for

> "Like wine, well-kept and long;
> Heady; nor harsh; nor strong;
> With each succeeding year is quaffed
> A richer, purer, mellower draught."

Miss Edgeworth's grown people live naturally with the children; they do not talk to them continually about angels, or flowers, or blue riband, but about the things that interest themselves.—They do not force them forward nor keep them back. The relations are simple and honorable; all ages in the family seem at home under one roof and sheltered by one care.

"The Juvenile Miscellany," formerly published by Mrs. Child, was much and deservedly esteemed by children.[4] It was a healthy, cheerful, natural and entertaining companion to them.

"The Child's Friend" is edited by Mrs. Follen, a lady admired and loved by a large circle of personal friends, best known to the public at large by a memoir of her husband worthy in its time of the beauty of its subject.[5] No task could have been more difficult; few have been fulfilled with such delicacy.—We think this periodical for children is, in some

---

[3] Maria Edgeworth (see note 120, p. 172 above) was also known for her tales for young people.

[4] *The Juvenile Miscellany*, a Boston children's magazine published between 1826 and 1834 and edited for a time by Fuller's friend, Lydia Maria Child.

[5] Eliza Lee Follen (1787-1860) published a memoir of her husband Charles (1796-1840) and edited his memoirs during 1841-1842.

degree, obnoxious to the censure of too monotonously tender a manner, and too constant attention to the moral inference. We should prefer a larger proportion of the facts of natural or human history, and that they should speak for themselves. There are many good things in the work, and it is calculated to lead the child into the region of worthy resolve and liberal views. Among the contributions from other hands, we would notice a translation of Goethe's excellent tale of "Ferdinand" and a story called "The Little Expecter," which, if it betray too great a degree of intellectual consciousness for the free flow of fairy poesy, has refined fancy and judgment, with a simplicity and strength in manner rarely seen in modern fantasies of this kind.

Etherology*

Man is always trying to get charts and directions for the super-sensual element in which he finds himself involuntarily moving. Sometimes, indeed, for long periods, a life of continual activity in supplying bodily wants or warding off bodily dangers will make him inattentive to the circumstances of this other life. Then, in an interval of leisure, he will start to find himself pervaded by the power of this more subtle and searching energy, and will turn his thoughts, with new force, to scrutinize its nature and its promises.

At such times a corps is formed of workmen, furnished with various implements for the work. Some collect facts from which they hope to build up a theory; others propose theories by whose light they hope to detect valuable facts; a large number are engaged in circulating reports of these labors; a larger in attempting to prove them invalid and absurd. These last are of some use by shaking the canker-worms from the trees; all are of use in elucidating truth.

Such a course of study has the civilized world been engaged in for some years back with regard to what is called Animal Magnetism. We say the civilized world, because, though a large portion of the learned and intellectual, to say nothing of the thoughtless and the prejudiced, view such researches as folly, yet we believe that those prescient souls,

* J. Stanley Grimes. *Etherology; Or The Philosophy of Mesmerism and Phrenology; Including a New Philosophy of Sleep and of Consciousness, with a Review of the Pretensions of Neurology and Phreno-Magnetism.* New York: Saxton & Miles, 1845. In *New-York Daily Tribune,* 17 February 1845, p. 1; title supplied. Mesmerism was hypnosis; phrenology, a way of reading a person's character through the configuration of his skull. An example of Fuller's interest in the occult, a "psychometric" reading of her character, is given in Evelyn Winslow Orr, "Two Margaret Fuller Manuscripts," *New England Quarterly,* XI (December 1938), 794-802.

those minds more deeply alive, which are the heart of this and the parents of the next era, all, more or less, consciously or unconsciously, share the belief in such an agent as is understood by the largest definition of Animal Magnetism; that is, a means by which influence and thought may be communicated from one being to another, independent of the usual organs, and with a completeness and precision rarely attained through these.

For ourselves, since we became conscious at all of our connexion with the two forms of being called the spiritual and material, we have perceived the existence of such an agent, and should have no doubts on the subject, if we had never heard one human voice in correspondent testimony with our perceptions. The existence of such an agent we know, have tested some of its phenomena, but of its law and its analysis find ourselves nearly as ignorant as in earliest childhood. And we must confess that the best writers we have read seem to us about equally ignorant. We derive pleasure and profit in very unequal degrees from their statements, in proportion to their candor, clearness of perception, severity of judgment, and largeness of view. If they possess these elements of wisdom, their statements are valuable as affording materials for the true theory, but theories proposed by them affect us, as yet, only as partially sustained hypotheses. Too many among them are stained by faults which must prevent their coming to any valuable results, sanguine haste, jealous vanity, a lack of that profound devotion which alone can win Truth from her cold well, careless classification, abrupt generalizations. We see, as yet, no writer great enough for the patient investigation, in a spirit liberal yet severely true, which the subject demands. We see no man of Shakspearean, Newtonian incapability of deceiving himself or others.

However, no such man is needed, and we believe that it is pure democracy to rejoice that, in this department as in others, it is no longer some one great genius that concentrates within himself the vital energy of his time. It is many working together who do the work. The waters spring up in every direction, as little rills, each of which does its work. We see a movement corresponding with this in the region of exact science, and we have no doubt that in the course of fifty

years a new circulation will be comprehended as clearly as
the circulation of the blood is now.

In metaphysics, in phrenology, in animal magnetism, in
electricity, in chemistry, the tendency is the same, even
when conclusions seem most dissonant. The mind presses
nearer home to the seat of consciousness the more intimate
law and rule of life, and old limits become fluid beneath the
fire of thought. We are learning much, and it will be a grand
music, that shall be played on this organ of many pipes.

With regard to Mr. Grimes's book, in the first place, we do
not possess sufficient knowledge of the subject to criticise it
thoroughly; and secondly, if we did, it could not be done in
narrow limits.—To us his classification is unsatisfactory, his
theory inadequate, his point of view uncongenial. We disap-
prove of the spirit in which he himself criticises other disciples in this science who have, we believe, made some good
observations, with many failures, though, like himself, they
do not hold themselves lowly as disciples enough to suit
us.—For we do not believe there is any man, *yet*, who is
entitled to give himself the air of having taken a degree on
this subject. We do not want the tone of qualification or
mincing apology. We want no mock modesty, but its reality,
which is the almost sure attendant on greatness. What a lesson it would be for this country if a body of men could be at
work together in that harmony which would not fail to ensue
on a *disinterested* love of discovering truth, and with that
patience and exactness in experiment without which no
machine was ever invented worthy a patent. The most superficial, go-ahead, hit-or-miss American knows that no machine
was ever perfected without this patience and exactness; and
let no one hope to achieve victories in the realm of mind at a
cheaper rate than in that of matter!

In speaking thus of Mr. Grimes's book, we can still cordially recommend it to the perusal of our readers. Its statements are full and sincere. The writer has abilities which
only need to be used with more thoroughness and a higher
aim to guide him to valuable attainments. It appears from
notices affixed to his book that he has commanded an unusual share of attention, in a field where he has many com-
petitors, and we think his book would win for him the same.
It will bestow on those who do not find in it positive instruc-

tion, information and suggestion enough to requite a careful
perusal. The best criticism on this as on other such works is
to associate it as a manual with our own inquiries.

It will be the best justice to Mr. Grimes after what we have
said of our impression as to the tone of his work to publish
the following extracts from his own preface:

"When the doctrines of Phreno-Magnetism and Neurology
were announced, and were making converts by thousands, and
multitudes of new organs were daily discovered by these
means, so that my private science was threatened with an over-
whelming inundation, I was forced to take up this subject in
earnest. About every friend I met asked my opinion of the new
doctrines and new organs, and seemed surprized at my skepticism. This has led me to the determination of publishing this
volume, that I may thus at once justify myself, and vindicate
what seem to me the true principles of Phrenology. If I am
mistaken in any of the propositions which I have assumed,
there will be enough to correct me, and I shall acknowledge the
correction with gratitude.   *   *   *   *

"There has[1] [have?] been so many new doctrines advanced
within a short time, both on the subject of Phrenology and
Mesmerism, that I must necessarily assume the office of a critic
in speaking of the performances of others. I am aware that I
shall be liable to the charge of arrogance; but, at the present
time, scarcely any two Phrenologians nor Mesmerologists can
be found who agree; any one, therefore, who treats upon both
these subjects at once, with the design of producing an harmonious system, must seem to assume that he is wiser than all
others, and capable of filling the chair of the grand-master of the
fraternity. No modesty of expression nor respectfulness of style
can shield him from this imputation. Under these circumstances
I have deemed it best to 'speak right straight on' regardless of
the apparent egotism, and to 'utter my thoughts with entire independence of everything but truth and justice.'"

Mr. Grimes's work opens with an introduction which he
calls "Synopsis of Etherology," and whoever reads that will
be likely to find his interest so far awakened as to give fair
attention to the book.

In this connection we will relate a passage from personal

[1] Thus in the original.

experience to us powerfully expressive of the nature of this
higher agent in the intercourse of minds:

Some years ago the writer went, unexpectedly, into a
house where a blind girl, thought at that time to have attained an extraordinary degree of clairvoyance, lay in a trance
of somnambulism.—The writer was not invited there, nor
known to the party, but accompanied a gentleman who was.

The Somnambulist was in a very happy state. On her lips
was the satisfied smile, and her features expressed the gentle
elevation incident to the state. The writer had never seen any
one in it, and had formed no image or opinion on the subject.
She was agreeably impressed by the Somnambulist, but on
listening to the details of her observations on a distant place,
thought she had really no vision, but was merely led or impressed by the mind of the person who held her hand.

After awhile, the writer was beckoned forward, and her
hand given to the blind girl. The latter instantly dropped it
with an expression of pain, and complained that she should
have been brought in contact with a person so sick and suffering at that moment under violent nervous headache. This
really was the case, but no one present could have been
aware of it.

After a while, the Somnambulist seemed penitent and
troubled. She asked again for the hand she had rejected, and,
while holding it, attempted to magnetize the sufferer. She
seemed touched by profound pity, spoke most intelligently of
the disorder of health and its causes, and gave advice, which,
if followed at that time, the writer has every reason to believe
would have remedied the ill.

Not only no other person present, but the person advised
also, had no adequate idea then of the extent to which health
was affected, nor saw fully till some time after the justice of
what was said by the Somnambulist. There is every reason to
believe that neither she, nor the persons who had the care of
her, knew even the name of the person whom she so affec-
tionately wished to help.

Several years after, the writer in visiting an asylum for the
blind saw this girl seated there.—She was no longer a somnambulist, though, from a nervous disease, very susceptible
to magnetic influences. I went to her among the crowd of

strangers and shook hands with her as several others had done. I then asked, "Do you not know me?" She answered "No." "Do you not remember ever to have met me?" She tried to recollect, but still said "No." I then addressed a few remarks to her about her situation there, but she seemed preoccupied, and, while I turned to speak with some one else, wrote with a pencil these words which she gave me at parting:

> "The ills that Heaven decrees
> The brave with courage bear."

Others may explain this as they will, to me it was a token that the same affinity that had acted before, gave the same knowledge; for the writer was at the time ill in the same way as before. It also seemed to indicate that the somnambulic trance was only a form of the higher development, the sensibility to more subtle influences, in the terms of Mr. Grimes, a susceptibility to Etherium. The blind girl perhaps never knew who the writer was, but saw my true state more clearly than any other person did, and I have kept those penciled lines written in the stiff round character proper to the blind, as a talisman of "Credenciveness", as the book before me styles it, credulity as the world at large does, and, to my own mind, as one of the clues granted during this earthly life to the mysteries of future states of being and more rapid and complete modes of intercourse between mind and mind.

St. Valentine's Day—Bloomingdale Asylum for the Insane*

This merry season of light jokes and lighter love-tokens in which Cupid presents the feathered end of the dart, as if he meant to tickle before he wounded the captive, has always had a great charm for me. When but a child, I saw Allston's picture of the "Lady reading a Valentine," and the mild womanliness of the picture, so remote from passion no less than vanity, so capable of tenderness, so chastely timid in its self-possession, has given a color to the gayest thoughts connected with the day.[1] From the ruff of Allston's Lady, whose clear starch is made to express all rosebud thoughts of girlish retirement, the soft unfledged hopes which never yet were tempted from the nest, to Sam Weller's Valentine is indeed a broad step,[2] but one which we can take without material change of mood.

But of all the thoughts and pictures associated with the day, none can surpass in interest those furnished by the way in which we celebrated it last week.

The Bloomingdale Asylum for the Insane is conducted on the most wise and liberal plan known at the present day. Its superintendent, Dr. Earle, has had ample opportunity to observe the best modes of managing this class of diseases both here and in Europe, and he is one able, by refined sympathies and intellectual discernment, to apply the best that is known and to discover more.

Under his care the beautifully situated establishment at

---

* In *New-York Daily Tribune*, 22 February 1845, p. 1.
[1] Washington Allston's "The Valentine" was painted during 1809-1811.
[2] Sam Weller, the servant of Mr. Pickwick in Charles Dickens' *Pickwick Papers* (1836-1837).

Bloomingdale loses every sign of the hospital and the prison, not long since thought to be inseparable from such a place. It is a house of refuge where those too deeply wounded or disturbed in body or spirit to keep up that semblance or degree of sanity which the conduct of affairs in the world at large demands may be soothed by gentle care, intelligent sympathy, and a judicious attention to their physical welfare, into health, or, at least, into tranquility.

Dr. Earle, in addition to modes of turning the attention from causes of morbid irritation, and promoting brighter and juster thoughts, which he uses in common with other institutions, has this winter delivered a course of lectures to the patients. We were present at one of these some weeks since. The subjects touched upon were, often, of a nature to demand as close attention as an audience of regular students (not college students, but real students) can be induced to give. The large assembly present were almost uniformly silent, to appearance interested, and showed a power of decorum and self-government often wanting among those who esteem themselves in healthful mastery of their morals and manners. We saw, with great statisfaction, generous thoughts and solid pursuits offered as well as light amusements for the choice of the sick in mind. For it is our experience that such sickness arises as often from want of concentration as any other cause. One of the noblest youths that ever trod this soil was want to say "he was never tired, if he could only see far enough." He is now gone where his view may be less bounded, but we, who stay behind, may take the hint that mania, no less than the commonest forms of prejudice, bespeaks a mind which does not see far enough to connect partial impressions. No doubt in many cases, dissipation of thought, after attention is once distorted into some morbid direction, may be the first method of cure, but we are glad to see others provided for those who are ready for them.

St. Valentine's Eve had been appointed for one of the dancing-parties at the Institution, and a few friends from "the world's people" invited to be present.

At an early hour the company assembled in the well-lighted hall, still gracefully wreathed with its Christmas evergreens; the music struck up and the company entered.

And these are the people who, half a century ago, would

have been chained in solitary cells, screaming out their anguish till silenced by threats or blows, lost, forsaken, hopeless, a blight to earth, a libel upon heaven.

Now they are many of them happy, all interested. Even
those who are troublesome and subject to violent excitement
in every-day scenes, show here that the power of self-control
is not lost, only lessened. Give them an impulse strong
enough, favorable circumstances, and they will begin to use
it again. They regulate their steps to music; they restrain
their impatient impulses from respect to themselves and to
others. The power which shall yet shape order from all disorder and turn ashes to beauty, as violets spring up from
green graves, hath them also in its keeping.

The party were well-dressed, with care and taste. The
dancing was better than usual, because there was less of affectation and ennui. The party was more entertaining, because native traits came out more clear from the disguises of
vanity and tact.

There was the blue-stocking lady, a mature belle and bel-
esprit. Her condescending graces, her rounded compliments,
her girlish, yet "highly intellectual" vivacity, expressed no
less in her headdress than in her manner, were just that touch
above the common with which the illustrator of Dickens has
thought fit to highten the charms of Mrs. Leo Hunter.[3]

There was the traveled Englishman, *au fait* to every thing
beneath the moon and beyond. With his clipped and glib
phrases, his bundle of conventionalities carried so neatly
under his arm, and his "My dear sir," in the perfection of
cockney dignity, what better could the most select dinner
party furnish us in the way of distinguished strangerhood?

There was the hoydenish young girl, and the decorous
elegant lady smoothing down "the wild little thing." There
was the sarcastic observer on the folly of the rest; in that, the
greatest fool of all, unbeloved and unannealed. In contrast to
this were characters altogether lovely, full of all sweet affections, whose bells, if jangled out of tune, still retained their
true tone.

One of the best things on the evening was a dance impro-

---

[3] Mrs. Leo Hunter, a lady of literary aspirations and author of "Ode to an
Expiring Frog," appears in *Pickwick Papers*.

vised by two elderly women. They asked the privilege of the
floor, and, a suitable measure being played, performed this
dance in a style lively, characteristic, yet moderate enough. It
was true dancing, like peasant dancing.

An old man sang comic songs in the style of various nations
and characters, with a dramatic expression that would have
commanded applause "on any stage."

And all was done decently, and in order; each biding his
time. Slight symptoms of impatience here and there were
easily soothed by the approach of this, truly a "good physician," the touch of whose hand seemed to possess a talis-
manic power to soothe. We doubt not that all went to their
beds exhilarated, free from irritation, and more attuned to
concord than before. Good bishop Valentine? thy feast was
well kept, and not without the usual jokes and flings at old
bachelors, the exchange of sugar-plums, mottos and repar-
tees.

This is the second festival I have kept with those whom
society has placed, not outside her pale, indeed, but outside
the hearing of her benison. Christmas I passed in a prison![4]
There too, I saw marks of the miraculous power of Love,
when guided by a pure faith in the goodness of its source,
and intelligence as to the design of the creative intelligence.
I saw enough of its power, impeded as it was by the ignorance of those who, eighteen hundred years after the coming
of Christ, still believe more in fear and force. I saw enough, I
say, of this power to convince me, if I needed conviction, that
it is indeed omnipotent, as he said it was.

A companion, of that delicate nature by which a scar is felt
as a wound, was saddened by the sense how very little our
partialities, undue emotions, and manias need to be exaggerated to entitle us to rank among madmen. I cannot view it so.
Rather let the sense that, with all our faults and follies, there
is still a sound spot, a presentiment of eventual health in the
inmost nature, embolden us to hope—to *know* it is the same
with all. A great thinker has spoken of the Greek, for highest
praise as "a self-renovating character." But we are all Greeks,
if we will but think so. For the mentally or morally insane,

---

[4] Fuller spent Christmas Day 1844 in a woman's prison in New York; see
p. 24 above.

there is no irreparable ill if the principle of life can but be aroused. And it can never be finally benumbed, except by our own will.

One of the famous pictures at Munich is of a mad house. The painter has represented the moral obliquities of society exaggerated into madness; that is to say, self-indulgence has, in each instance, destroyed the power to forbear the ill or to discern the good. A celebrated writer has added a little book, to be used while looking at the picture, and drawn inferences of universal interest.

Such would we draw; such as this! Let no one dare to call another mad who is not himself willing to rank in the same class for every perversion and fault of judgment. Let no one dare aid in punishing another as criminal who is not willing to suffer the penalty due to his own offences.

Yet, while owning that we are all mad, all criminal, let us not despair, but rather believe that the Ruler of all never could permit such wide-spread ill but to good ends. It is permitted to give us a field to redeem it—

> ————"to transmute, bereave
> Of an ill influence and a good receive."

It flows inevitably from the emancipation of our wills, the development of individuality in us. These aims accomplished, all shall yet be well; and it is ours to learn *how* that good time may be hastened.

We know no sign of the times more encouraging than the increasing nobleness and wisdom of view as to the government of asylums for the insane and of prisons. Whatever is learnt as to these forms of society is learnt for all. There is nothing that can be said of such government that must not be said, also, of the government of families, schools, and States. But we have much to say on this subject, and shall revert to it again, and often, though, perhaps, not with so pleasing a theme as this of St. Valentine's Eve.

Cheap Postage Bill*

While the merchants are looking with anxiety for a change so important to their interests, and the people at large, including those few who write no letters, are demanding it as a matter of justice, we look on it with interest in a literary regard. Will twice as many, or ten times as many letters be written, when correspondence is a less expensive pleasure than at present? Here then is another tax on the intellects of our devoted people; already they, almost all, write for the press; now, beside, they are to carry on this immense correspondence. The empire which our people seem determined to grasp, from sea to sea, is to be pierced with canals and railroads, till there is scarcely a green nook or shady lane left for the retirement of lovers and poets: newspapers are to flutter into the lowliest huts with every breeze; lectures on all the arts and sciences are to be given hourly for a penny an entrance; the infinite divisibility of sects is to be proved by the infinitely active acuteness of disputants; the Magnetic Telegraph is to bind pole with pole in lively intercourse of gossip and repartee; the collision of character from every region will demand a mercurial temperature to melt the various elements into one mass; in short, a life as intense, a communication more rapid, than pervaded the little State of Attica in its day of glory, is to be established throughout this vast country.[1] How all that is necessary is to be learned and done, even in the most superficial way, we do not yet see. Not only there is a limit set to human strength and activity, but from the pressure of care and excitement which has already began

* In *New-York Daily Tribune*, 24 February 1845, p. 2. In 1845 unnaturally high postal rates—it often cost more to mail a letter than to ship a barrel of flour—were drastically reduced.

[1] Attica, a division of ancient Greece whose chief city was Athens.

to deteriorate the race from generation to generation here, it arrives unusually quick with us.

And now, in addition to all the other demands upon our energies, comes this inducement to write many and long letters. Yet there is one good thing about it: this private literature is likely to be more sincere, more characterisitc, than that which is designed for the public. When books are to be placarded in letters two inches long, so that the most ardent runner cannot help reading their titles, if no more, letters where there is more of family sacredness, genuine affinity and untarnished sentiment may be a useful countercheck. And yet we fear that these, too, will become mere gazettes and circulars. We know a distinguished person, all whose letters have that air. If at any crisis a particularly pointed expression occur to him, *all* his friends may be sure to find it in the letters addressed to each. That is like the gentleman who sent three similar Valentines to three ladies on the same day. "How happy would I be with either!" Ah grant, bright genius of America, that, in becoming universal, we lose not the fine flavor of individuality!—that, in our rapid passage over the outlines of so many objects, we be not quite estranged from their secret soul, quite uninformed by their vital energy!

The Excellence of Goodness*

This discourse derives interest, not so much from intrinsic claims, as from the circumstances under which it was delivered, and the position occupied by the preacher in New England.

We cannot wonder at the hopes entertained by the ancient Catholic church, of seeing its dominion renewed and strengthened on earth, when we see the almost universal dereliction among Protestants from the great principle of Protestantism;—respect for the right of private judgment and the decision of conscience in the individual. From Luther downward, each sect claiming to be Protestant, has claimed no less to utter its anathema against those who differed from it, with the authority of a Golden Bull, nor were Lutherans distinguished for tolerating any new evidences of the spirit of Luther. In our own country this has been manifested in the most marked manner. The Puritans came hither to vindicate for themselves the rights of conscience, but learnt from their experience of suffering no lesson that enabled them to respect those rights in others and, as yet, in this country, after so many years of political tolerance, there exists very little notion, far less practice, of spiritual tolerance. Men cannot be content, even in cases where they see the practice bear excellent fruit, to leave the doctrine between the man and his God. Each little coterie has its private pope, distinguished, indeed, from the old by the impossibility of obtaining from him indulgences (at least for heresy;) and an infidelity in the power of Truth, and the wisdom of the Ruler of the Universe

* Theodore Parker, *The Excellence of Goodness. A Sermon Preached at the Church of the Disciples, in Boston, on Sunday, January 26, 1845.* Boston: Benjamin H. Greene, 1845. In *New-York Daily Tribune*, 26 February 1845, p. 1; title supplied.

is betrayed, which darkens the intellect and checks the good impulses of natural sympathy.

The Unitarians of New-England saw these errors, in looking over the history of opinion, and promised themselves and others that they would refrain from such. They arrogated to themselves the title of LIBERAL CHRISTIANS, and they did not fail to be steadily admonished, by the dread, the scorn, or unthinking blame, heaped by other sects upon them, of the desirableness of reviving in Christendom the spirit of him who feared not to call the Gentile to his flock, and had no difficulty in worshiping upon the mountains outside Jewry. "By their *fruits*," said he, "ye shall know them."

There have not been wanting some among them who were true to this desire, and could be called liberal Christians, not only in reference to those who did not go so far, but to those who went a little farther than themselves. The late Dr. Channing, the greatest man who has yet arisen among them, was truly a liberal Christian. He had confidence in the vital energy of Truth, and was not afraid to trust others with the same privileges he had vindicated for himself, even if they made use of them in a different manner. He had preached much of "the dignity of human nature," and he showed by his tolerance of its varied manifestations and modes of growth, that he deeply believed what he preached.

How often must we mourn his departure! for there seems to be no mind which, by its union of decision and mildness with an appreciation of its own principles, could so well fulfil the office of a Peace-maker. For that office consists not in hushing up truth, or stifling individual feeling, but in allowing distinctly the claims of all, and casting a light *from above* upon their nature and their significance. He is much wanted now to cast this light upon the course taken by the Unitarian clergy in the case of Mr. Parker.

Mr. Parker was a highly esteemed member of the Christian Unitarian body till, some four years since, he uttered himself with freedom on a few points, in a way distasteful to the majority. Part of the offence consisted in views expressed by him as to the nature of inspiration, and the facts of Bible history, in which he really differs from the majority; part in attacks upon abuses which he saw, or thought he saw, in the church to which he belonged, such as may be inferred from the heads of "The Pharisees," "Idolatry," &c.

Then arose a good deal of outcry which was well, for it called on Mr. Parker to explain himself, and give the multitude of hearers an opportunity to consider his arguments, and judge whether they coincided with his censures. He delivered many lectures to full and eager audiences, and, no doubt, where there existed in that community a tendency congenial with his, has been a principal agent in its development. At the same time, a very strong and wide dissent was manifested.

A tacit persecution followed on the part of the clergy, in which they were sustained by a part of the community. It was almost impossible for Mr. Parker to obtain an exchange with any pulpit. As to this, we think that a clergyman has a right to avoid uncongenial coöperation in this way, just as he has to decline uncongenial books, or uncongenial visitors, but we think also that it is unwise to exercise this right. 1st; because we all need uncongenial statements, and the view of the other side, to prevent the mind from becoming petrified and narrowed. Free air is needed, even if it do sometimes come harshly, sometimes sultry. 2d; It is the sure way to give the proscribed party influence. So it was in this case. The flock ran out of the fold to seek the wolf. Mr. Parker was invited to lecture every where, and the *meeting-house* was deserted for the lecture-room.

There seemed reason too to think that the clergy were not only repelled by the opinions of Mr. Parker, but nettled by his assaults, and extremely afraid of the scandal; that they had not confidence enough in those principles which had been the animating soul of their body to be raised above dread of the comment passed by other sects upon this latitudinarian conduct among them. "It will do great hurt," they cried, and, in so doing, echoed the tones of bigotry about themselves and deserted their banner.

Still it was not so bad while each one, for himself merely, abstained from exchanging with Mr. Parker and cast private blame on the few who did, as they might have censured any other act in which they, as men, did not sympathize. Their censure was personal more than clerical. But there has lately been an attempt to put down bodily any willingness to make these exchanges, which deserves severe censure, and will receive it from the page of history.

Two clergymen, the Rev. Mr. Sargent and the Rev. Mr. Clarke,[1] of the Church of the Disciples, have this winter chosen to exchange with the excommunicated preacher, not, as they explicitly declare, from sympathy with his doctrines, but with the wise and generous perception that, in so doing, they upheld the principles of liberal Christianity, allowing to each man the right of private interpretation as to the great truths he professes to acknowledge, and the right to be heard, if he can find persons disposed to listen. For these acts they have been visited, the one by the associate clergy, the other by certain self-elected deacons of his church, with a sort and degree of reproof entirely false to the basis Unitarian Christianity assumed in its early stages. Much has been spoken and published on this subject and much in a spirit of narrowness, and short-sighted self-conceit, mortifying to those who look upon Massachusetts as a candle set upon a hill. Remarks have been published such as could not have been expected at this stage of mental development in the civilized world. The effect, of course, of all the opposition has been to strengthen Mr. Parker. Hundreds go to hear him to one that went before.

The Rev. Mr. Clarke, of the Church of the Disciples, has, in the public prints upon this occasion, in a truly manly and enlightened manner, exhibited the true grounds and modes of tolerance.

The discourse before us is the one preached upon the occasion of his exchange with Mr. Parker.—There is nothing very marked in it; except a large and healthy manner of treatment; the writer did not take the occasion to bring forward his peculiar views.

Mr. Parker is a man of vigorous abilities and extensive information. He writes in a forcible and full, but not diffuse,

[1] The Boston Association of ministers had forbidden its members to exchange with the reform minister Theodore Parker (1810-1860) because they believed his views to be heretical. In November 1844 the Rev. John Turner Sargent, a member of the Association, allowed Parker to preach in his church and was forced to resign his position as a result. In January 1845, the Rev. James Freeman Clarke of the Church of the Disciples, even though he disagreed with Parker's views, also allowed Parker to preach but, because he was an independent minister, no action could be taken. *The Excellence of Goodness* was Parker's discourse upon the latter occasion.

style. His great attraction for his hearers is his perfect frankness. He is willing to lay his mind completely open, without circumlocution or complaisance, and possesses the power of doing this adequately. What God sees, man may see and make what use of it he can.—He is no orator, but has a full and manly style of speaking commensurate with his matter. We do not find in Mr. Parker a depth of spiritual discernment, nor the poetic faculty. He is, as a mind, more broad than high or deep. Persons of far inferior mental development can see clearly fallacies in his estimate of facts in religious history. He is too combative for our taste; he loves to assail the false, or what he esteems to be such, as well as to declare truths. But his large ken and mental integrity entitle him to be heard. We doubt not that any agitation caused by him in the atmosphere will show, in its results, the purifying power of electricity. And we regret that, in the nineteenth century, "liberal Christians" should not be liberal enough cheerfully to allow an honorable mind free course, and fearlessly leave the result to God and His unfailing Agent, Time.

American Facts*

Such is the title of a volume just issued from the press:—a grand title, which suggests the epic poet or the philosopher. The purpose, however, of the work is modest. It is merely a compilation, from which those who have lived at some distance from the great highway may get answers to their questions, as to events and circumstances which have escaped them. It is one of those books which will be valued in the back-woods.

It would be a great book, indeed, and one that would require the eye and heart of a great man,—great as a judge, great as a seer, and great as a prophet—that could select for us and present in harmonious outline the true American facts. To select the right point of view supposes command of the field.

Such a man must be attentive, a quiet observer of the slighter signs of growth. But he must not be one to dwell superstitiously on details, nor one to hasten to conclusions. He must have the eye of the eagle, the courage of the lion, the patience of the worm, and faith such as is the prerogative of Man alone, and of Man on the highest step of his culture.

We doubt not the destiny of our Country, that she is destined to accomplish great things for Human Nature and be the mother of a nobler race, perhaps, than the world has yet known. But she has been so false to the scheme made out at her nativity that it is now hard to say which way that destiny points. We can hardly point out the true American facts,

* George Palmer Putnam. *American Facts. Notes and Statistics Relative to the Government, Resources, Engagements, Manufactures, Commerce, Religion, Education, Literature, Fine Arts, Manners and Customs of the United States of America.* London: Wiley & Putnam, 1845. In *New-York Daily Tribune*, 19 May 1845, p. 1.

without some idea of the true character of America. Only one thing seems clear, that the energy here at work is very great, though the men employed in carrying out its purposes may have generally no more individual ambition to understand those purposes or cherish noble ones of their own, than the coral insect through whose restless working new continents are upheaved from Ocean's breast.

Such a man passing in a boat from one extremity of the Mississippi to another, and observing every object on the shore as he passed, would yet learn nothing of universal or general value, because he has no principles, even in hope, by which to classify them. American facts! Why! what has been done that marks individuality? Among men there is Franklin! he is a fact, and an American fact. Niagara is another, in a different style. The way that newspapers and other periodicals are managed is American. A go-ahead, fearless adroitness is American; so is *not*, exclusively, the want of strict honor. But we look about in vain for traits as characteristic of what may be individually the character of the Nation, as we can find at a glance of Spain, England, France or Turkey. America is as yet but an European babe:—some new ways and motions she has, consequent on a new position, but that soul that may shape her mature life scarce begins to know itself yet. One thing is certain: we live in a large place, no less morally than physically; wo to him who lives meanly there and knows the exhibitions of selfishness and vanity as the only American facts.

Prevalent Idea that Politeness is too great a Luxury to be given to the Poor*

A few days ago, a lady, crossing in one of the ferry boats that ply from this city, saw a young boy, poorly dressed, sitting with an infant in his arms on one of the benches. She observed that the child looked sickly and coughed. This, as the day was raw, made her anxious in its behalf, and she went to the boy and asked whether he was alone there with the baby, and if he did not think the cold breeze dangerous for it. He replied that he was sent out with the child to take care of it, and that his father said the fresh air from the water would do it good.

While he made this simple answer, a number of persons had collected around to listen, and one of them, a well-dressed woman, addressed the boy in a string of such questions and remarks as these:

"What is your name? Where do you live? Are you telling us the truth? It's a shame to have that baby out in such weather; you'll be the death of it. (To the bystanders:) I would go and see his mother and tell her about it, if I was sure he had told us the truth about where he lived. How do you expect to get back? Here, (in the rudest voice,) somebody says you have not told the truth as to where you live."

The child, whose only offence consisted in taking care of the little one in public, and answering when he was spoken to, began to shed tears at the accusations thus grossly preferred against him. The bystanders stared at both; but among them all there was not one with sufficiently clear notions of

* In *New-York Daily Tribune*, 31 May 1845, p. 2.

propriety and moral energy to say to this impudent ques-
tioner, "Woman! do you suppose, because you wear a handsome shawl, and that boy a patched jacket, that you have any
right to speak to him at all, unless he wishes it, far less to
prefer against him those rude accusations. Your vulgarity is
unendurable; leave the place or alter your manner."

Many such instances have we seen of insolent rudeness or
more insolent affability founded on no apparent grounds, except an apparent difference in pecuniary position, for no one
can suppose in such cases the offending party has really enjoyed the benefit of refined education and society, but all
present let them pass as matters of course. It was sad to see
how the poor would endure—mortifying to see how the
purse-proud dared offend. An excellent man who was, in his
early years, a missionary to the poor, used to speak afterwards with great shame of the manner in which he had conducted himself towards them.—"When I recollect," said he,
"the freedom with which I entered their houses, inquired
into all their affairs, commented on their conduct and disputed their statements I wonder I was never horsewhipped
and feel that I ought to have been; it would have done me
good, for I needed as severe a lesson on the universal obligations of politeness in its only genuine form of respect for man
as man, and delicate sympathy with each in his peculiar position."

Charles Lamb, who was indeed worthy to be called a
human being from those refined sympathies, said, "You call
him a gentleman: does his washerwoman find him so?" We
may say, if she did so, she found him a *man*, neither treating
her with vulgar abruptness, nor giving himself airs of condescending liveliness, but treating her with that genuine respect which a feeling of equality inspires.

To doubt the veracity of another is an insult which in most
civilized communities must in the so-called higher classes be
atoned for by blood, but, in those same communities, the
same men will, with the utmost lightness, doubt the truth of
one who wears a ragged coat, and thus do all they can to
injure and degrade him by assailing his self-respect, and
breaking the feeling of personal honor—a wound to which
hurts a man as a wound to its bark does a tree.

Then how rudely are favors conferred, just as a bone is
thrown to a dog. A gentleman indeed will not do *that* without

accompanying signs of sympathy and regard. Just as this woman said, "If you have told the truth I will go and see your mother," are many acts performed on which the actors pride themselves as kind and charitable.

All men might learn from the French in these matters. That people, whatever be their faults, are really well-bred, and many acts might be quoted from their romantic annals, where gifts were given from rich to poor with a graceful courtesy, equally honorable and delightful to the giver and the receiver.

In Catholic countries there is more courtesy, for charity is there a duty, and must be done for God's sake; there is less room for a man to give himself the Pharisaical tone about it. A rich man is not so surprised to find himself in contact with a poor one; nor is the custom of kneeling on the open pavement, the silk robe close to the beggar's rags, without profit. The separation by pews, even on the day when all meet nearest, is as bad for the manners as the soul.

Blessed be he or she who has passed through this world, not only with an open purse and willingness to render the aid of mere outward benefits, but with an open eye and open heart, ready to cheer the downcast, and enlighten the dull by words of comfort and looks of love. The wayside charities are the most valuable both as to sustaining hope and diffusing knowledge, and none can render them who has not an expansive nature, a heart alive to affection, and some true notion, however imperfectly developed, of the nature of human brotherhood.

Such an one can never sauce the given meat with taunts, freeze the bread by a cold glance of doubt, or plunge the man who asked for his hand deeper back into the mud by any kind of rudeness.

In the little instance with which we begun, no help *was* asked, unless by the sight of the timid little boy's old jacket. But the license which this seemed to the well-clothed woman to give to rudeness was so characteristic of a deep fault now existing, that a volume of comments might follow and a host of anecdatos be drawn from almost any one's experience in exposition of it. These few words, perhaps, may awaken thought in those who have drawn tears from others' eyes through an ignorance brutal, but not hopelessly so, if they are willing to rise above it.

Frederick Douglass*

Frederick Douglass has been for some time a prominent member of the Abolition party. He is said to be an excellent speaker—can speak from a thorough personal experience —and has upon the audience, beside, the influence of a strong character and uncommon talents. In the book before us he has put into the story of his life the thoughts, the feelings and the adventures that have been so affecting through the living voice; nor are they less so from the printed page. He has had the courage to name the persons, times and places, thus exposing himself to obvious danger, and setting the seal on his deep convictions as to the religious need of speaking the whole truth. Considered merely as a narrative, we have never read one more simple, true, coherent, and warm with genuine feeling. It is an excellent piece of writing, and on that score to be prized as a specimen of the powers of the Black Race, which Prejudice persists in disputing. We prize highly all evidence of this kind, and it is becoming more abundant. The Cross of the Legion of Honor has just been conferred in France on Dumas and Soule, both celebrated in the paths of light literature.[1] Dumas, whose father was a General in the French Army, is a Mulatto; Soule, a Quadroon. He went from New-Orleans, where, though to the eye a white man, yet, as known to have African blood in his veins, he could never have enjoyed the privileges due to a human being. Leaving the Land of Free-

* Frederick Douglass. *Narrative of the Life of Frederick Douglass, an American Slave*. Boston: Anti-Slavery Society, 1845. In *New-York Daily Tribune*, 10 June 1845, p. 1; title supplied.
[1] Alexandre Dumas (1802-1870), son of a black woman and a white Marquis, became a famous general; Pierre Soulé (1801-1870), French-born American Lawyer.

dom, he found himself free to develope the powers that God had given.

Two wise and candid thinkers,—the Scotchman, Kinmont, prematurely lost to this country, of which he was so faithful and generous a student, and the late Dr. Channing,[2]—both thought that the African Race had in them a peculiar element, which, if it could be assimilated with those imported among us from Europe, would give to genius a development, and to the energies of character a balance and harmony beyond what has been seen heretofore in the history of the world. Such an element is indicated in their lowest estate by a talent for melody, a ready skill at imitation and adaptation, an almost indestructible elasticity of nature. It is to be remarked in the writings both of Soule and Dumas, full of faults, but glowing with plastic life and fertile in invention. The same torrid energy and saccharine fulness may be felt in the writings of this Douglass, though his life being one of action or resistance, was less favorable to *such* powers than one of a more joyous flow might have been.

The book is prefaced by two communications,—one from Garrison, and one from Wendell Phillips.[3] That from the former is in his usual over-emphatic style. His motives and his course have been noble and generous. We look upon him with high respect, but he has indulged in violent invective and denunciation till he has spoiled the temper of his mind. Like a man who has been in the habit of screaming himself hoarse to make the deaf hear, he can no longer pitch his voice on a key agreeable to common ears. Mr. Phillips's remarks are equally decided, without this exaggeration in the tone. Douglass himself seems very just and temperate. We feel that his view, even of those who have injured him most, may be relied upon. He knows how to allow for motives and influences. Upon the subject of Religion, he speaks with great force, and not more than our own sympathies can respond to. The inconsistencies of Slaveholding professors of

[2] Alexander Kinmont, see note 5, p. 78 above; the Rev. William Ellery Channing, a long-time opponent of slavery, published many pamphlets attacking the practice, the most famous being *Emancipation* (1840).

[3] William Lloyd Garrison (1805-1879), abolitionist editor of the *Liberator* and president of the American Anti-Slavery Society from 1843 to 1865; Wendell Phillips (1811-1884), abolitionist, orator, and reformer.

religion cry to Heaven. We are not disposed to detest, or
refuse communion with them. Their blindness is but one
form of that prevalent fallacy which substitutes a creed for a
faith, a ritual for a life. We have seen too much of this system
of atonement not to know that those who adopt it often began
with good intentions, and are, at any rate, in their mistakes
worthy of the deepest pity. But that is no reason why the
truth should not be uttered, trumpet-tongued, about the
thing. "Bring no more vain oblations"; sermons must daily be
preached anew on that text. Kings, five hundred years ago,
built Churches with the spoils of War; Clergymen to-day
command Slaves to obey a Gospel which they will not allow
them to read, and call themselves Christians amid the curses
of their fellow men.—The world ought to get on a little faster
than that, if there be really any principle of improvement in
it. The Kingdom of Heaven may not at the beginning have
dropped seed larger than a mustard-seed, but even from that
we had a right to expect a fuller growth than can be believed
to exist, when we read such a book as this of Douglass. Un-
speakably affecting is the fact that he never saw his mother at
all by day-light.

"I do not recollect of ever seeing my mother by the light of day.
She was with me in the night, She would lie down with me, and
get me to sleep, but long before I waked she was gone."

The following extract[4] presents a suitable answer to the
hacknied argument drawn by the defender of Slavery from
the songs of the Slave, and is also a good specimen of the
powers of observation and manly heart of the writer. We wish
that every one may read his book and see what a mind might
have been stifled in bondage,—what a man may be subjected
to the insults of spendthrift dandies, or the blows of mercenary brutes, in whom there is no whiteness except of the
skin, no humanity except in the outward form, and of whom
the Avenger will not fail yet to demand—"Where is thy
brother?"

[4] The long extract from Chapter Two of the *Narrative* which follows is
here omitted.

Fourth of July*

The bells ring; the cannon rouse the echoes along the river shore; the boys sally forth with shouts and little flags and crackers enough to frighten all the people they meet from sunrise to sunset. The orator is conning for the last time the speech in which he has vainly attempted to season with some new spice the yearly panegyric upon our country; its happiness and glory; the audience is putting on its best bib and tucker, and its blandest expression to listen.

And yet, no heart, we think, can beat to-day with one pulse of genuine, noble joy. Those who have obtained their selfish objects will not take especial pleasure in thinking of them to-day, while to unbiased minds must come sad thoughts of National Honor soiled in the eyes of other nations, of a great inheritance, risked, if not forfeited.

Much has been achieved in this country since the first Declaration of Independence. America is rich and strong; she has shown great talent and energy; vast prospects of aggrandizement open before her. But the noble sentiment which she expressed in her early youth is tarnished; she has shown that righteousness is not her chief desire, and her name is no longer a watchword for the highest hopes to the rest of the world. She knows this, but takes it very easily; she feels that she is growing richer and more powerful, and that seems to suffice her.

These facts are deeply saddening to those who can pronounce the words 'My Country' with pride and peace only so far as steadfast virtues, generous impulses find their home in that country. They cannot be satisfied with superficial benefits, with luxuries and the means of obtaining knowledge

* In *New-York Daily Tribune*, 4 July 1845, p. 2.

which are multiplied for them. They could rejoice in full
hands and a busy brain, if the soul were expanding and the
heart pure, but, the higher conditions being violated, what is
done cannot be done for good.

Such thoughts shadow patriot minds as the cannon-peal
bursts upon the ear. This year, which declares that the people at large consent to cherish and extend Slavery as one of
our "domestic institutions," takes from the patriot his home.
This year, which attests their insatiate love of wealth and
power, quenches the flame upon the altar.

Yet there remains that good part which cannot be taken
away. If nations go astray, the narrow path may always be
found and followed by the individual man. It is hard, hard
indeed, when politics and trade are mixed up with evils so
mighty that he scarcely dares touch them for fear of being
defiled. He finds his activity checked in great natural outlets
by the scruples of conscience. He cannot enjoy the free use
of his limbs, glowing upon a favorable tide; but struggling,
panting, must fix his eyes upon his aim and fight against the
current to reach it. It is not easy, it is very hard just now to
realize the blessings of Independence.

For what is Independence if it does not lead to Freedom?
—Freedom from fraud and meanness, from selfishness, from
public opinion so far as it does not consent with the still
small voice of one's better self?

Yet there is still a great and worthy part to play. This country presents great temptations to ill, but also great inducements to good. Her health and strength are so remarkable;
her youth so full of life that disease cannot yet have taken
deep hold of her. It has bewildered her brain, made her steps
totter, fevered, but not yet tainted, her blood. Things are still
in that state when ten just men may save the city. A few men
are wanted, able to think and act upon principles of an eternal value. The safety of the country must lie in a few such
men—men who have achieved the genuine independence,
independence of wrong, of violence, of falsehood.

We want individuals to whom all eyes may turn as an example of the practicability of virtue. We want shining examples. We want deeply rooted characters, who cannot be
moved by flattery, by fear, even by hope, for they work in
faith. The opportunity for such men is great, they will not be

burnt at the stake in their prime for bearing witness to the truth, yet they will be tested most severely in their adherence to it. There is nothing to hinder them from learning what is true and best, no physical tortures will be inflicted on them for expressing it. Let men feel that in private lives, more than in public measures must the salvation of the country lie. If that country has so widely veered from the course she prescribed to herself and that the hope of the world prescribed to her, it must be because she had not men ripened and confirmed for better things. They leaned too carelessly on one another; they had not deepened and purified the private lives from which the public must spring, as the verdure of the plain from the fountains of the hills.

What a vast influence is given by sincerity alone? The bier of General Jackson has just passed, upbearing a golden urn. The men who placed it there lament his departure and esteem the measures which have led this country to her present position wise and good. The other side esteem them unwise, unjust, and disastrous in their consequences. But both respect him thus far that his conduct was boldly sincere. The sage of Quincy![1] Men differ in their estimate of his abilities. None, probably, esteem his mind as one of the first magnitude. But both sides, all men, are influenced by the bold integrity of his character. Mr. Calhoun speaks straight out what he thinks.[2] So far as this straightforwardness goes, he confers the benefits of virtue. If a character be uncorrupted, whatever bias it takes, it thus far is good and does good. It may help others to a higher, wiser, larger independence than its own.

We know not where to look for an example of all or many of the virtues we would seek from the man who is to begin the new dynasty that is needed of Fathers of the Country. The Country needs to be born again; she is polluted with the lust of power, the lust of gain. She needs Fathers good enough to be God-fathers—men who will stand sponsors at the baptism with *all* they possess, with all the goodness they can cherish and all the wisdom they can win, to lead this child the way

---

[1] John Quincy Adams.

[2] John C. Calhoun (1782-1850), South Carolina Congressman who consistently represented Southern views, especially states' rights.

she should go, and never one step in another. Are there not
in schools and colleges the boys who will become such men?
Are there not those on the threshold of manhood who have
not yet chosen the broad way into which the multitude
rushes, led by the banner on which, strange to say, the royal
Eagle is blazoned, together with the word Epediency? Let
him decline that road, and take the narrow, thorny path
where Integrity leads, though with no prouder emblem than
the dove. He may there find the needed remedy which, like
the white root, the *Moly*, detected by the patient and resolved Odysseus, shall have power to restore the herd of
men, disguised by the enchantress to whom they had willingly yielded in the forms of brutes, to the stature and beauty
of men.[3]

[3] In the *Odyssey*, Ulysses is protected by the herb moly when Circe turns
his companions into swine.

Poe's *Tales**

Mr. Poe's tales need no aid of newspaper comment to give them popularity; they have secured it. We are glad to see them given to the public in this neat form, so that thousands more may be entertained by them without injury to their eye-sight.

No form of literary activity has so terribly degenerated among us as the tale. Now that every body who wants a new hat or bonnet takes this way to earn one from the magazines or annuals, we are inundated with the very flimsiest fabrics ever spun by mortal brain. Almost every person of feeling or fancy could supply a few agreeable and natural narratives, but when, instead of using their materials spontaneously, they set to work, with geography in hand, to find unexplored nooks of wild scenery in which to locate their Indians, or interesting farmers' daughters, or with some abridgement of history to hunt up monarchs or heroes yet unused to become the subjects of their crude coloring, the sale-work produced is a sad affair indeed and "gluts the market" to the sorrow both of buyers and lookers-on.

In such a state of things, the writings of Mr. Poe are a refreshment, for they are the fruit of genuine observations and experience, combined with an invention, which is not "making up," as children call *their* way of contriving stories, but a penetration into the causes of things which leads to original but credible results. His narrative proceeds with vigor, his colors are applied with discrimination, and where the effects are fantastic they are not unmeaningly so.

* Edgar A. Poe. *Tales.* New York: Wiley & Putnam, 1845. In *New-York Daily Tribune*, 11 July 1845, p. 1; title supplied.

The "Murders of the Rue Morgue" especially made a great impression upon those who did not know its author and were not familiar with his mode of treatment. Several of his stories make us wish he would enter the higher walk of the metaphysical novel, and, taking a mind of the self-possessed and deeply marked sort that suits him, give us a deeper and longer acquaintance with its life and the springs of its life than is possible in the compass of these tales.

As Mr. Poe is a professed critic, and of all the band the most unsparing to others, we are surprized to find some inaccuracies in the use of words, such as these "he had with him many books, but rarely *employed* them."—"His results have, in truth, the *whole air* of intuition."

The degree of skill shown in the management of revolting or terrible circumstances makes the pieces that have such subjects more interesting than the others. Even the failures are those of an intellect of strong fibre and well-chosen aim.

The Wrongs of American Women
and
The Duty of American Women*

The same day brought us a copy of Mr. Burdett's little book, in which the sufferings and difficulties that beset the large class of women who must earn their subsistence in a city like New-York are delineated with so much simplicity, feeling and exact adherence to the facts—and a printed circular containing proposals for immediate practical adoption of the plan more fully described in a book published some weeks since under the title "The Duty of American Women to their Country," which was ascribed alternately to Mrs. Stone and Miss Catherine Beecher, but of which we understand both those ladies decline the responsibility.[1] The two matters seemed linked with one another by natural piety. Full acquaintance with the wrong must call forth all manner of inventions for its redress.

The Circular, in showing the vast want that already exists of good means for instructing the children of this nation, especially in the West, states also the belief that among women, as being less immersed in other cares and toils, from the preparation it gives for their task as mothers, and from the

---

* Charles Burdett, Wrongs of American Women. First Series. The Elliott Family; or the Trials of New York Seamstresses. New York: E. Winchester, 1845; and [Catharine Beecher], The Duty of American Women to Their Country. New York: Harpers, 1845. In New-York Daily Tribune, 30 September 1845, p. 1; title supplied.

[1] Mrs. Lucy Stone (1818-1893), woman suffrage and anti-slavery reformer; Mrs. Catharine Beecher (1800-1878), educational reformer and Harriet Beecher Stowe's sister. Her name often appeared as "Catherine" in Fuller's time.

necessity in which a great proportion stand of earning a subsistence somehow, at least during the years which precede
marriage, if they *do* marry, must the number of teachers
wanted be found, which is estimated already at *sixty thousand*.

We cordially sympathize with these views.

Much has been written about Woman's keeping within her
sphere, which is defined as the domestic sphere. As a little
girl she is to learn the lighter family duties, while she ac-
quires that limited acquaintance with the realm of literature
and science that will enable her to superintend the instruction of children in their earliest years. It is not generally
proposed that she should be sufficiently instructed and developed to understand the pursuits or aims of her future husband; she is not to be a helpmeet to him, in the way of
companionship or counsel, except in the care of his house
and children. Her youth is to be passed partly in learning to
keep house and the use of the needle, partly in the social
circle where her manners may be formed, ornamental ac-
complishments perfected and displayed, and the husband
found who shall give her the domestic sphere for which exclusively she is to be prepared.

Were the destiny of Woman thus exactly marked out, did
she invariably retain the shelter of a parent's or a guardian's
roof till she married, did marriage give her a sure home and
protector, were she never liable to be made a widow, or, if
so, sure of finding immediate protection from a brother or
new husband, so that she might never be forced to stand
alone one moment, and were her mind given for this world
only, with no faculties capable of eternal growth and infinite
improvement, we would still demand for her a far wider and
more generous culture than is proposed by those who so
anxiously define her sphere. We would demand it that she
might not ignorantly or frivolously thwart the designs of her
husband, that she might be the respected friend of her sons
no less than her daughters, that she might give more refinement, elevation and attraction to the society which is needed
to give the characters of *men* polish and plasticity—no less so
than to save them from vicious and sensual habits. But the
most fastidious critic on the departure of Woman from her
sphere, can scarcely fail to see at present that a vast propor- ·

tion of the sex, if not the better half, do not, CANNOT, have this domestic sphere. Thousands and scores of thousands in this country no less than in Europe are obliged to maintain themselves alone. Far greater numbers divide with their husbands the care of earning a support for the family. In England, now, the progress of society has reached so admirable a pitch that the position of the sexes is frequently reversed, and the husband is obliged to stay at home and "mind the house and bairns"[2] while the wife goes forth to the employment she alone can secure.

We readily admit that the picture of this is most painful —that Nature made entirely an opposite distribution of functions between the sexes. We believe the natural order to be the best, and that, if it could be followed in an enlightened spirit, it would bring to Woman all she wants, no less for her immortal than her mortal destiny. We are not surprised that men, who do not look deeply or carefully at causes or tendencies, should be led by disgust at the hardened, hackneyed characters which the present state of things too often produces in women to such conclusions as they are. We, no more than they, delight in the picture of the poor woman digging in the mines in her husband's clothes. We, no more than they, delight to hear their voices shrilly raised in the market-place, whether of apples or celebrity. But we see that at present they must do as they do for bread. Hundreds and thousands must step out of that hallowed domestic sphere, with no choice but to work or steal, or belong to men, not as wives, but as the wretched slaves of sensuality.

And this transition state, with all its revolting features, indicates, we do believe, the approach of a nobler era than the world has yet known. We trust that by the stress and emergencies of the present and coming time, the minds of women will be formed to more reflection and higher purposes than heretofore—their intent powers developed, their characters strengthened and eventually beautified and harmonized. Should the state of society then be such that each may remain, as Nature seems to have intended, the tutelary genius of a home, while men manage the out-door business of life, both may be done with a wisdom, a mutual under-

---

[2] "home and children".

standing and respect unknown at present. Men will be no
less the gainers by this than women, finding in pure and
more religious marriages the joys of friendship and love
combined—in their mothers and daughters better instruction,
sweeter and nobler companionship, and in society at large an
excitement to their finer powers and feelings unknown at
present except in the region of the fine arts.

Blest be the generous, the wise among them who seek to
forward hopes like these, instead of struggling against the fiat
of Providence and the march of Fate to bind down rushing
Life to the standard of the Past. Such efforts are vain, but
those who make them are unhappy and unwise.

It is not, however, to such that we address ourselves, but to
those who seek to make the best of things as they are, while
they also strive to make them better. Such persons will have
seen enough of the state of things in London, Paris, New-
York, and manufacturing regions every where, to feel that
there is an imperative necessity for opening more avenues of
employment to women, and fitting them better to enter them,
rather than keeping them back. Women have invaded many
of the trades and some of the professions. Sewing, to the
present killing extent, they cannot long bear. Factories seem
likely to afford them permanent employment. In the culture
of fruit, flowers and vegetables, even in the sale of them, we
rejoice to see them engaged. In domestic service they will be
aided, but can never be supplanted, by machinery. As much
room as there is here for woman's mind and woman's labor
will always be filled. A few have usurped the martial province, but these must always be few; the nature of woman is
opposed to war. It is natural enough to see "Female Physicians," and we believe that the lace cap and work-bag are as
much at home here as the wig and gold-headed cane. In the
priesthood they have from all time shared more or less—in
many eras more than at the present. We believe there has
been no female lawyer, and probably will be none. The pen,
many of the fine arts they have made their own, and, in the
more refined countries of the world, as writers, as musicians,
as painters, as actors, women occupy as advantageous ground
as men. Writing and music may be esteemed professions for
them more than any other.

But there are two others where the demand must invariably be immense, and for which they are naturally better fitted than men, for which we should like to see them better prepared and better rewarded than they are. These are the professions of nurse to the sick and of teacher. The first of these professions we have warmly desired to see dignified. It is a noble one, now most unjustly regarded in the light of menial service. It is one which no menial, no servile nature can fitly occupy. We were rejoiced when an intelligent lady of Massachusetts made the refined heroine of a little romance select that calling. This lady (Mrs. George Lee) has looked on society with unusual largeness of spirit and healthiness of temper.[3] She is well acquainted with the world of conventions, but, sees beneath it the world of nature. She is a generous writer and unpretending, as the generous are wont to be. We do not recall the name of the tale, but the circumstance above mentioned marks its temper. We hope to see the time when the refined and cultivated will choose this profession and learn it, not only through experience under the direction of the doctor, but by acquainting themselves with the laws of matter and of mind, so that all they do shall be intelligently done, and afford them the means of developing intelligence as well as the nobler, tenderer feelings of humanity; for even the last part of the benefit they cannot receive if their work be done in a selfish or mercenary spirit.

The other profession is that of teacher, for which women are peculiarly adapted by their nature, superiority in tact, quickness of sympathy, gentleness, patience, and a clear and animated manner in narration or description. To form a good teacher should be added to this sincere modesty combined with firmness, liberal views with a power and will to liberalize them still further, a good method and habits of exact and thorough investigation. In the two last requisites women are generally deficient, but there are now many shining examples to prove that if they are immethodical and superficial as teachers it is because it is the custom so to teach them, and that when aware of these faults they can and will correct them.

The profession is of itself an excellent one for the improvement of the teacher during that interim between youth

---

[3] Mrs. Hannah F. Lee (1780-1865), a popular writer of the period.

and maturity when the mind needs testing, tempering, and to review and rearrange the knowledge it has acquired. The natural method of doing this for one's self is to attempt teaching others; those years also are the best of the practical teacher. The teacher should be near the pupil both in years and feelings—no oracle, but the elder brother or sister of the pupil. More experience and years form the lecturer and the director of studies, but injure the powers as to familiar teaching.

These are just the years of leisure in the lives even of those women who are to enter the domestic sphere, and this calling most of all compatible with a constant progress as to qualifications for that.

Viewing the matter thus it may well be seen that we should hail with joy the assurance that sixty thousand *female* teachers are wanted, and more likely to be, and that a plan is projected which looks wise, liberal and generous, to afford the means of those whose hearts answer to his high calling obeying their dictates.

The plan is to have Cincinnati for a central point, where teachers shall be for a short time received, examined and prepared for their duties. By mutual agreement and cooperation of the various sects funds are to be raised and teachers provided according to the wants and tendencies of the various locations now destitute. What is to be done for them centrally, is for suitable persons to examine into their various kinds of fitness, communicate some general views whose value has been tested, and counsel adapted to the difficulties and advantages of their new positions. The Central Committee are to have the charge of raising funds and finding teachers and places where teachers are wanted.

The passage of thoughts, teachers and funds will be from East to West, the course of sunlight upon this earth.

The plan is offered as the most extensive and pliant means of doing a good and preventing ill to this nation, by means of a national education, whose normal school shall have an invariable object in the search after truth and the diffusion of the means of knowledge, while its form shall be plastic according to the wants of the time. This normal school promises to have good effects, for it proposes worthy aims through simple means, and the motive for its formation and support seems to be disinterested philanthropy.

It promises to eschew the bitter spirit of sectarianism and proselytism, else we, for one party, could have nothing to do with it. Men, no doubt, have been oftentimes kept from absolute famine by the wheat with which such tares are mingled; but we believe the time is come when a purer and more generous food is to be offered to the people at large. We believe the aim of all education to be to rouse the mind to action, show it the means of discipline and of information; then leave it free, with God, Conscience, and the love of Truth for its guardians and teachers. Wo be to those who sacrifice these aims of universal and eternal value to the propagation of a set of opinions. But on this subject we can accept such doctrine as is offered by Rev. Calvin Stowe,[4] one of the committee, in the following passage:

"In judicious practice, I am persuaded there will seldom be any very great difficulty, especially if there be excited in the community anything like a whole-hearted honesty and enlightened sincerity in the cause of public instruction.

"It is all right for people to suit their own taste and convictions in respect to sect; and by fair means and at proper times to teach their children and those under their influence to prefer the denominations which they prefer; but farther than this no one has any right to go. It is all wrong to hazard the well being of the soul, to jeopardize great public interests for the sake of advancing the interests of a sect. People must learn to practise some self-denial, on Christian principles, in respect to their denominational preferences, as well as in respect to other things, before pure Religion can ever gain a complete victory over every form of human selfishness."

The persons who propose themselves to the examination and instruction of the teachers at Cincinnati, till the plan shall be sufficiently under weigh to provide regularly for the office, are Mrs. Stowe and Miss Catherine Beecher, ladies well known to fame, as possessing unusual qualifications for the task.[5]

As to finding abundance of teachers, who that reads this little book of Mr. Burdett's, or the account of the compensation of female labor in New-York, and the hopeless, comfort-

[4] The Rev. Calvin Stowe (1802-1866), then professor of Biblical literature at Cincinnati.

[5] Harriet Beecher Stowe (1811-1896), later author of *Uncle Tom's Cabin* (1852).

less, useless, pernicious lives those who have even the advantage of getting work must live with the sufferings and almost inevitable degradation to which those who cannot are exposed, but must long to snatch such as are capable of this better profession, and among the multitude there must be many who are or could be made so, from their present toils and make them free and the means of freedom and growth to others.

To many books on such subjects, among others to "Woman in the Nineteenth Century,"[6] the objection has been made that they exhibit ills without specifying any practical means for their remedy. The writer of the last named essay does indeed think that it contains one great rule which, if laid to heart, would prove a practical remedy for many ills, and of such daily and hourly efficacy in the conduct of life that any extensive observance of it for a single year would perceptibly raise the tone of thought, feeling and conduct throughout the civilized world. But to those who ask not only such a principle, but an external method for immediate use, we say, there is one proposed that looks noble and promising, the proposers offer themselves to the work with heart and hand, with time and purse: Go ye and do likewise.

Those who wish details as to this plan, will find them in the "Duty of American Women to their Country," published by Harper & Brothers, Cliff-st. The publishers may, probably, be able to furnish also the Circular to which we have referred. At a leisure day we shall offer some suggestions and remarks as to the methods and objects there proposed.

[6] Fuller's *Woman in the Nineteenth Century* had been published in early February 1845.

Poe's *The Raven and Other Poems* *

Mr. Poe throws down the gauntlet in his preface, by what he says of "the paltry compensations or more paltry commendations of mankind." Some champion might be expected to start up from the "somewhat sizeable" class embraced, or more properly speaking, boxed on the ear, by this defiance, who might try whether the sting of Criticism was as indifferent to this knight of the pen as he professes its honey to be.

Were there such a champion, gifted with acumen to dissect, and a swift glancing wit to enliven the operation, he could find no more legitimate subject, no fairer game than Mr. Poe, who has wielded the weapons of criticism, without relenting, whether with the dagger he rent and tore the garment in which some favored Joseph had pranked himself,[1] secure of honor in the sight of all men, or whether with uplifted tomahawk he rushed upon the newborn children of some hapless genius, who had fancied and persuaded his friends to fancy that they were beautiful and worthy a long and honored life.[2] A large band of these offended dignitaries and aggrieved parents must be on the watch for a volume of "Poems by Edgar A. Poe," ready to cut, rend and slash in turn, and hoping to see his own Raven left alone to prey upon the slaughter of which it is the herald.

* Edgar A. Poe. *The Raven and Other Poems*. New York: Wiley & Putnam, 1845. In *New-York Daily Tribune*, 26 November 1845, p. 1; title supplied.

[1] In the Bible, Joseph's coat of many colors set him off from his brothers and made them turn against him.

[2] Fuller may have had in mind Poe's review of the *Poems* of her brother-in-law, Ellery Channing, which began by complaining "Were we to quote specimens under the general head of 'utter and irredeemable nonsense,' we should quote nine tenths of the book." Indeed, wrote Poe, the main mistake of the poems was "that of their having been printed at all" (*Graham's Magazine*, XXIII [August 1843], 113-117).

Such joust and tournament we look to see and, indeed, have some stake in the matter so far as we have friends whose wrongs cry aloud for the avenger. Natheless we could not take part in the *melée*, except to join the crowd of lookers-on in the cry—Heaven speed the right!

Early we read that fable of Apollo who rewarded the critic, who had painfully winnowed the wheat, with the chaff for his pains.[3] We joined the gentle Affirmative School, and have confidence that if we indulge ourselves chiefly with the appreciation of good qualities, Time will take care of the faults.—For Time holds a strainer like that used in the diamond mines;—have but patience and the water and gravel will all pass through and only the precious stones be left. Yet we are not blind to the uses of severe criticism, and of just censure, especially in a time and place so degraded by venal and indiscriminate praise as the present. That unholy alliance, that shameless sham, whose motto is

> "Caw me
> And I'll caw thee."[4]

That system of mutual adulation and organized puff which was carried to such perfection in the time and may be seen drawn to the life in the correspondence of Miss Hannah More, is fully represented in our day and generation.[5] We see that it meets a counter-agency, from the league of Truthtellers, few, but each of them mighty as Fingal or any other hero of the sort.[6] Let such tell the whole truth, as well as nothing but the truth, but let their sternness be in the spirit of Love. Let them seek to understand the purpose and scope

[3] King Midas once judged Pan to be a better flute player than Apollo, who changed the king's ears to those of an ass, as an indication of his stupidity.

[4] In a review of Manzoni's *I Promessi Sposi* in the May 1835 *Southern Literary Messenger*, Poe himself wrote: " 'Ca me; Ca thee,' is the order of the day" (I, 521).

[5] Many of the letters between Hannah More (1745-1833), English philanthropist and prose writer, and her correspondents show the existence of an uncritical mutual admiration society; see William Roberts, *Memoirs of the Life and Correspondence of Mrs. Hannah More* (New York: Harpers, 1835).

[6] Fingal, hero of *The Poems of Ossian* (1762, 1763), a spurious Gaelic myth created by James Macpherson (1736-1796).

of an author, his capacity as well as his fulfilments, and how his faults are made to grow by the same sunshine that acts upon his virtues, for this is the case with talents no less than with character. The rich field requires frequent and careful weeding; frequent, lest the weeds exhaust the soil; careful, lest the flowers and grain be pulled up along with the weeds.

Well! but to return to Mr. Poe; we are not unwilling that cavil should do her worst on his book, because both by act and word he has challenged it, but as this is no office for us, we shall merely indicate, in our usual slight way, what, naturally and unsought, has struck ourselves in the reading of these verses.

It has often been our case to share the mistake of Gil Blas, with regard to the Archbishop.[7] We have taken people at their word, and while rejoicing that women could bear neglect without feeling mean pique, and that authors, rising above self-love, could show candor about their works and magnanimously meet both justice and injustice, we have been rudely awakened from our dream, and found that Chanticleer, who crowed so bravely, showed himself at last but a dunghill fowl. Yet Heaven grant we never become too worldly-wise thus to trust a generous word, and we surely are not so yet, for we believe Mr. Poe to be sincere when he says:

> "In defence of my own taste, it is incumbent upon me to say that I think nothing in this volume of much value to the public or very creditable to myself. Events not to be controlled have prevented me from making, at any time, any serious effort in what, under happier circumstances, would have been the field of my choice."

We believe Mr. Poe to be sincere in this declaration; if he is, we respect him; if otherwise, we do not. Such things should never be said unless in hearty earnest. If in earnest, they are honorable pledges; if not, a pitiful fence and foil of vanity. Earnest or not, the words are thus far true: the productions in this volume indicate a power to do something far better. With the exception of The Raven, which seems in-

---

[7] In Alain René Le Sage's (1668-1747) novel *Gil Blas of Santillane* (1715-1735), the hero is discharged by his employer, the archbishop, for truthfully pointing out the lack of quality in his sermons.

tended chiefly to show the writer's artistic skill, and is in its way a rare and finished specimen, they are all fragments— *fyttes* upon the lyre, almost all of which leave us something to desire or demand. This is not the case, however, with these lines:

TO ONE IN PARADISE.

Thou wast all that to me, love,
    For which my soul did pine—
A green isle in the sea, love,
    A fountain and a shrine,
All wreathed with fairy fruits and flowers,
    And all the flowers were mine.

Ah, dream too bright to last!
    Ah, starry Hope! that didst arise
But to be overcast!
    A voice from out the Future cries,
"On! on!"—but o'er the Past
    (Dim gulf!) my spirit hovering lies
Mute, motionless, aghast!

For, alas! alas! with me
    The light of Life is o'er!
No more—no more—no more—
    (Such language holds the solemn sea
    To the sands upon the shore)
Shall bloom the thunder-blasted tree,
    Or the stricken eagle soar!

And all my days are trances,
    And all my nightly dreams
And where thy dark eye glances,
    And where thy footstep gleams—
In what ethereal dances,
    By what eternal streams.

The poems breathe a passionate sadness, relieved sometimes by touches very lovely and tender:

    "Amid the earnest woes
      That crowd around my earthly path
    (Drear path, alas! where grows
      Not even one lonely rose.)" *

    *   *   *   *   *

"For her, the fair and debonair, that now so lowly lies,
The life upon her yellow hair, but not within her eyes—
The life still there, upon her hair—the death upon her
    eyes."

This kind of beauty is especially conspicuous, then rising into dignity, in the poem called "The Haunted Palace."

The imagination of this writer rarely expresses itself in pronounced forms, but rather in a sweep of images, thronging and distant like a procession of moonlight clouds on the horizon, but like them characteristic and harmonious one with another, according to their office.

The descriptive power is greatest when it takes a shape not unlike an incantation, as in the first part of "The Sleeper," where

"I stand beneath the mystic moon,
An opiate vapor, dewy, dim,
Exhales from out a golden rim,
And, softly dripping, drop by drop,
Upon the quiet mountain top,
Steals drowsily and musically
Into the Universal valley."

Why *universal?*—"resolve me that, Master Moth."

And farther on, "The lily *lolls* upon the wave."

This word lolls, often made use of in these poems, presents a vulgar image to our thought; we know not how it is to that of others.

The lines which follow about the open window are highly poetical. So is the "Bridal Ballad" in its power of suggesting a whole tribe and train of thoughts and pictures by few and simple touches.

The Poems written in youth, written, indeed, we understand, in childhood, before the author was ten years old, are a great psychological curiosity. Is it the delirium of a prematurely excited brain that causes such a rapture of words? What is to be gathered from seeing the future so fully anticipated in the germ? The passions are not unfrequently felt in their full shock, if not in their intensity, at eight or nine years old, but here they are reflected upon,

> "Sweet was their death—with them to die was rife
> With the last ecstacy of satiate life."[8]

The scenes from Politian are done with clear, sharp strokes; the power is rather metaphysical than dramatic. We must repeat what we have heretofore said, that we could wish to see Mr. Poe engaged in a metaphysical romance. He needs a sustained flight and a fair range to show what his powers really are. Let us have from him the analysis of the Passions, with their appropriate Fates; let us have his speculations clarified; let him intersperse dialogue or poem as the occasion prompts, and give us something really good and strong, firmly wrought, and fairly blazoned. Such would be better employment than detecting literary larcenies, not worth pointing out if they exist.[9] Such employment is quite unworthy of one who dares vie with the Angel.[10]

[8] "Al Aaraaf."

[9] Poe was fond of pointing out what he considered cases of plagiarism by other authors; see Sydney P. Moss, *Poe's Literary Battles* (Durham: Duke University Press, 1963).

[10] The complete text of "Israfel" which follows is here omitted.

Longfellow's *Poems**

Poetry is not a superhuman or supernatural gift. It is, on the contrary, the fullest and therefore most completely natural expression of what is human.—It is that of which the rudiments lie in every human breast, but developed to a more complete existence than the obstructions of daily life permit, clothed in an adequate form, domesticated in nature by the use of apt images, the perception of grand analogies, and set to the music of the spheres for the delight of all who have ears to hear. We have uttered these remarks, which may, to many of our readers, seem truisms, for the sake of showing that our definition of poetry is large enough to include all kinds of excellence. It includes not only the great bards, but the humblest minstrels. The great bards bring to light the more concealed treasures, gems which centuries have been employed in forming and which it is their office to reveal, polish and set for the royal purposes of man; the wandering minstrel with his lighter but beautiful office calls the attention of men to the meaning of the flowers, which also is hidden from the careless eye, though they have grown and bloomed in full sight of all who chose to look. All the poets are the priests of Nature, though the greatest are also the prophets of the manhood of man.—For, when fully grown, the life of man must be all poetry; each of his thoughts will be a key to the treasures of the universe; each of his acts a revelation of beauty, his language will be music, and his habitual presence will overflow with more energy and in-

* Henry Wadsworth Longfellow. *Poems*. Philadelphia: Carey & Hart, 1845. In *New-York Daily Tribune*, 10 December 1845, p. 1; title supplied. For Fuller's other comments on Longfellow and his response, see pp. 25–27 above.

spire with a nobler rapture than do the fullest strains of lyric
poetry now.

Meantime we need poets; men more awakened to the
wonders of life and gifted more or less with a power to express what they see, and to all who possess, in any degree,
those requisites we offer and we owe welcome and tribute,
whether the place of their song be in the Pantheon, from
which issue the grand decrees of immortal thought, or by the
fireside, where hearts need kindling and eyes need clarifying
by occasional drops of nectar in their tea.

But this—this alone we claim, and can welcome none who
cannot present this title to our hearing; that the vision be
genuine, the expression spontaneous. No imposition upon
our young fellow citizens of pinchback for gold! they must
have the true article, and pay the due intellectual price, or
they will wake from a life-long dream of folly to find themselves beggars.

And never was a time when satirists were more needed to
scourge from Parnassus the magpies who are devouring the
food scattered there for the singing birds. There will always
be a good deal of mock poetry in the market with the genuine; it grows up naturally as tares among the wheat, and,
while there is a fair proportion perserved, we abstain from
severe weeding lest the two come up together; but when the
tares have almost usurped the field, it is time to begin and
see if the field cannot be freed from them and made ready for
a new seed-time.

The rules of versification are now understood and used by
those who have never entered into that soul from which
metres grow as acorns from the oak, shapes as characteristic
of the parent tree, containing in like manner germs of limitless life for the future. And as to the substance of these jin-
gling rhymes, and dragging, stumbling rhythms, we might
tell of bombast, or still worse, an affected simplicity, sickly
sentiment, or borrowed dignity; but it is sufficient to com-
prise all in this one censure. The writers did not write because they felt obliged to relieve themselves of the swelling
thought within, but as an elegant exercise which may win
them rank and reputation above the crowd. Their lamp is not
lit by the sacred and inevitable lightning from above, but
carefully fed by their own will to be seen of men.

There are very few now rhyming in England, not obnoxious to this censure, still fewer in our America. For such no laurel blooms. May the friendly poppy soon crown them and grant us stillness to hear the silver tones of genuine music, for, if such there be, they are at present almost stifled by these fifes and gongs.

Yet there is a middle class, composed of men of little original poetic power, but of much poetic, taste and sensibility, whom we would not wish to have silenced. They do no harm but much good, (if only their minds are not confounded with those of a higher class,) by educating in others the faculties dominant in themselves. In this class we place the writer at present before us.

We must confess to a coolness toward Mr. Longfellow, in consequence of the exaggerated praises that have been bestowed upon him. When we see a person of moderate powers receive honors which should be reserved for the highest, we feel somewhat like assailing him and taking from him the crown which should be reserved for grander brows. And yet this is, perhaps, ungenerous. It may be that the management of publishers, the hyperbole of paid or undiscerning reviewers, or some accidental cause which gives a temporary interest to productions beyond what they would permanently command, have raised such an one to a place as much above his wishes as his claims, and which he would rejoice, with honorable modesty, to vacate at the approach of one worthier. We the more readily believe this of Mr. Longfellow, as one so sensible to the beauties of other writers and so largely indebted to them, *must* know his own comparative rank better than his readers have known it for him.

And yet so much adulation is dangerous. Mr. Longfellow, so lauded on all hands—now able to collect his poems which have circulated so widely in previous editions, and been paid for so handsomely by the handsomest annuals, in this beautiful volume, illustrated by one of the most distinguished of our younger artists—has found a flatterer in that very artist. The portrait which adorns this volume is not merely flattered or idealized, but there is an attempt at adorning it by expression thrown into the eyes with just that which the original does not possess, whether in face or mind. We have often seen faces whose usually coarse and heavy lineaments were harmonized at times into beauty by the light that rises from the soul into the eyes. The intention Nature had with regard to the face and its wearer, usually eclipsed beneath bad habits or a bad education, is then disclosed and we see what hopes Death has in store for that soul. But here the enthusiasm thrown into the eyes only makes the rest of the face look more weak, and the idea suggested is the anomalous one of a Dandy Pindar.

Such is not the case with Mr. Longfellow himself. He is never a Pindar, though he is sometimes a Dandy even in the clean and elegantly ornamented streets and trim gardens of his verse. But he is still more a man of cultivated taste, delicate though not deep feeling, and some, though not much, poetic force.

Mr. Longfellow has been accused of plagiarism.[1] We have been surprised that any one should have been anxious to fasten special charges of this kind upon him, when we had supposed it so obvious that the greater part of his mental stores were derived from the works of others. He has no style of his own growing out of his own experiences and observations of nature. Nature with him, whether human or external, is always seen through the windows of literature. There are in his poems sweet and tender passages descriptive of his personal feelings, but very few showing him as an observer, at first hand, of the passions within, or the landscape without.

This want of the free breath of nature, this perpetual borrowing of imagery, this excessive, because superficial, culture which he has derived from an acquaintance with the elegant literature of many nations and men out of proportion to the experience of life within himself, prevent Mr. Longfellow's verses from ever being a true refreshment to ourselves. He says in one of his most graceful verses:

> From the cool cisterns of the midnight air
>   My spirit drank repose;
> The fountain of perpetual peace flows there,
>   From those deep cisterns flows.[2]

[1] The background to Poe's accusation that Longfellow was guilty of plagiarism is discussed in Moss, *Poe's Literary Battles*.
[2] "Hymn to the Night."

Now this is just what we cannot get from Mr. Longfellow.
No solitude of the mind reveals to us the deep cisterns.

Let us take, for example of what we do not like, one of his
worst pieces, the Prelude to the Voices of the Night—

> Beneath some patriarchal tree
> I lay upon the ground;
> His hoary arms uplifted be,
> And all the broad leaves over me
> Clapped their little hands in glee
> With one continuous sound.

What an unpleasant mixture of images! Such never rose in
a man's mind, as he lay on the ground and looked up to the
tree above him. The true poetry for this stanza would be to
give us an image of what was in the writer's mind as he lay
there and looked up. But this idea of the leaves clapping
their little hands with glee is taken out of some book; or, at
any rate, is a book thought and not one that came in the
place, and jars entirely with what is said of the tree uplifting
its hoary arms. Then take this other stanza from a man whose
mind *should* have grown up in familiarity with the American
genius loci.

> Therefore at Pentecost, which brings
> The Spring clothed like a bride,
> When nestling buds unfold their wings,
> And bishop's caps have golden rings,
> Musing upon many things,
> I sought the woodlands wide.

Musing upon many things—ay! and upon many books too,
or we should have nothing of Pentecost or bishop's caps with
their golden rings. For ourselves, we have not the least idea
what bishop's caps are;—are they flowers?—or what? Truly,
the schoolmaster was abroad in the woodlands that day! As to
the conceit of the wings of the buds, it is a false image,
because one that cannot be carried out. Such will not be
found in the poems of poets; with such the imagination is all
compact, and their works are not dead mosaics, with substances inserted merely because pretty, but living growths,
homogenous and satisfactory throughout.

Such instances could be adduced every where throughout

the poems, depriving us of any clear pleasure from any one piece, and placing his poems beside such as these of Bryant in the same light as that of the prettiest *made* shell, beside those whose every line and hue tells a history of the action of winds and waves and the secrets of one class of organizations.[3]

But, do we, therefore esteem Mr. Longfellow a wilful or conscious plagiarist? By no means. It is his misfortune that other men's thoughts are so continually in his head as to overshadow his own. The order of fine development is for the mind the same as the body, to take in just so much food as will sustain it in its exercise and assimilate with its growth. If it is so assimilated—if it becomes a part of the skin, hair and eyes of the man, it is his own, no matter whether he pick it up in the wood, or borrow from the dish of a fellow man, or receive it in the form of manna direct from Heaven. "Do you ask the genius" said Goethe "to give an account of what he has taken from others. As well demand of the hero an account of the beeves and loaves which have nourished him to such martial stature."

But Mr. Longfellow presents us, not with a new product in which all the old varieties are melted into a fresh form, but rather with a tastefully arranged Museum, between whose glass cases are interspersed neatly potted rose trees, geraniums and hyacinths, grown by himself with aid of in-door heat. Still we must acquit him of being a willing or conscious plagiarist. Some objects in the collection are his own; as to the rest, he has the merit of appreciation, and a rearrangement, not always judicious, but the result of feeling on his part.

Such works as Mr. Longfellow's we consider injurious only if allowed to usurp the place of better things. The reason of his being overrated here, is because through his works breathes the air of other lands with whose products the public at large is but little acquainted. He will do his office, and a desirable one, of promoting a taste for the literature of these lands before his readers are aware of it. As a translator he shows the same qualities as in his own writings; what is

[3] William Cullen Bryant (1794-1878), New York poet and magazine editor.

forcible and compact he does not render adequately, grace and sentiment he appreciates and reproduces. Twenty years hence when he stands upon his own merits, he will rank as a writer of elegant, if not always accurate taste, of great imitative power, and occasional felicity in an original way, where his feelings are really stirred. He has touched no subject where he has not done somewhat that is pleasing, though also his poems are much marred by ambitious failings. As instances of his best manner we would mention "The Reaper and the Flowers," "Lines to the Planet Mars," "A Gleam of Sunshine," and "The Village Blacksmith." His two ballads are excellent imitations, yet in them is no spark of fire. In "Nuremberg" are charming passages. Indeed the whole poem is one of the happiest specimens of Mr. L.'s poetic feeling, taste and tact in making up a rosary of topics and images—Thinking it may be less known than most of the poems we will quote it. The engraving which accompanies it of the rich old architecture is a fine gloss on its contents.[4]

*   *   *   *   *

This image of the thought gathered like a flower from the crevice of the pavement, is truly natural and poetical.

Here is another image which came into the mind of the writer as he looked at the subject of his verse, and which pleases accordingly. It is from one of the new poems, addressed to Driving Cloud, "chief of the mighty Omahaws."

> Wrapt in thy scarlet blanket I see thee stalk through
>   the city's
> Narrow and populous streets, as once by the margin of
>   rivers
> Stalked those birds unknown, that have left us only
>   their foot-prints,
> What, in a few short years, will remain of thy race but
>   the foot-prints?[5]

Here is another very graceful and natural simile:

---

[4] Following this "Nuremberg" is printed; here it is omitted, with asterisks indicating the omission.
[5] "To the Driving Cloud."

> A feeling of sadness and longing,
>   That is not akin to pain,
> And resembles sorrow only
>   As the mist resembles rain.[6]

Another—

> I will forget her! All dear recollections,
> Pressed in my heart like flowers within a book,
> Shall be torn out and scattered to the winds.[7]

The Drama from which this is taken is an elegant exercise of the pen, after the fashion of the best models. Plan, figures, all are academical. It is a faint reflex of the actions and passions of men, tame in the conduct and lifeless in the characters, but not heavy, and containing good meditative passages.

And now farewell to the handsome book, with its Preciosos and Preciosas, its Vikings and knights, and cavaliers, its flowers of all climes, and wild flowers of none. We have not wished to depreciate those writings below their current value more than truth absolutely demands. We have not forgotten that, if a man cannot himself sit at the feet of the Muse, it is much if he prizes those who may; it makes him a teacher to the people. Neither have we forgotten that Mr. Longfellow has a genuine respect for his pen, never writes carelessly, nor when he does not wish to, nor for money alone. Nor are we intolerant to those who prize hot-house bouquets beyond all the free beauty of nature; that helps the gardener and has its uses. But still let us not forget —Excelsior!!

---

[6] "The Day is Done."
[7] *The Spanish Student*, Act III. Preciosa is the heroine of the drama.

Cassius M. Clay*

The meeting on Monday night at the Tabernacle was to us an occasion of deep and peculiar interest. It was deep, for the feelings there expressed and answered bore witness to the truth of our belief, that the sense of right is not dead, but only sleepeth in this nation. A man who is manly enough to appeal to it will be answered, in feeling, at least, if not in action, and while there is life there is hope. Those who so rapturously welcomed one who had sealed his faith by deeds of devotion, must yet acknowledge in their breasts the germs of like nobleness.

It was an occasion of peculiar interest, such as we have not had occasion to feel since, in childish years, we saw Lafayette welcomed by a grateful people.[1] Even childhood well understood that the gratitude then expressed was not so much for the aid which had been received as for the motives and feelings with which it was given. The nation rushed out as one man to thank Lafayette, that he had been able, amid the prejudices and indulgences of high rank in the old *regime* of society, to understand the great principles which were about to create a new form, and answer manlike with love, service, and contempt of selfish interests to the voice of Humanity, demanding its rights. Our freedom would have been achieved without Lafayette, but it was a happiness and a blessing to number the young French nobleman as the champion of American Independence, and to know that he had given the prime of his life to our cause, because it was the cause of justice. With similar feelings of joy, pride and

---

* In *New-York Daily Tribune*, 14 January 1846, p. 1. Cassius Clay (1810-1903), well-known anti-slavery advocate and speaker.
[1] Fuller had probably seen General Lafayette (1757-1834), who aided in the American Revolution, when he visited Cambridge in 1824.

hope we welcome Cassius M. Clay, a man who has, in like manner, freed himself from the prejudices of his position, disregarded selfish considerations, and quitting the easy path in which he might have walked to station in the sight of men, and such external distinctions as his State and Nation readily confer on men so born and bred, and with such abilities, chose rather an interest in their souls, and the honors history will not fail to award to the man who enrols his name and elevates his life for the cause of right and those universal principles, whose recognition can alone secure to man the destiny without which he cannot be happy, but which he is continually sacrificing for the impure worship of idols. Yea, in this country, more than in the old Palestine, do they give their children to the fire in honor of Moloch,[2] and sell the ark confided to them by the Most High for shekels of gold and of silver. Partly it was the sense of this position which Mr. Clay holds, as a man who esteems his own individual convictions of right more than local interests or partial, political schemes, that gave him such an enthusiastic welcome on Monday night from the very hearts of the audience, but still more that his honor is at this moment identified with the liberty of the press, which has been insulted and infringed in him. About this there can be in fact but one opinion. In vain Kentucky calls meetings, states reasons, gives names of her own to what has been done. The rest of the world knows very well what has been done, and will call it by but one name. Regardless of this ostrich mode of defence the world has laughed and scoffed at the act of a people, professing to be free and defenders of freedom, and the recording Angel has written down the deed as a lawless act of violence and tyranny, from which the man is happy who can call himself pure.

With the usual rhetoric of the wrong side, the apologists for this act of mob violence have wished to injure Mr. Clay by the epithets of "hot-headed," "visionary," "fanatical." But, if any have believed that such could apply to a man so clear-sighted as to his objects and the way of achieving them, the mistake must have been corrected on Monday night. Whoever saw Mr. Clay that night, saw in him a man of deep and

---

[2] Moloch, a form of the devil worshipped by the Canaanites.

strong nature, thoroughly in earnest, who had well considered his ground, and saw that though open, as the noble must be, to new views and convictions, yet his direction is taken, and the improvement to be made will not be to turn aside, but to expedite and widen his course in that direction —Mr. Clay is young, thank Heaven! young enough to promise a long career of great thoughts and honourable deeds. But still, to those who esteem youth an unpardonable fault, and one that renders incapable of counsel, we would say that he is at the age when a man is capable of great thoughts and great deeds, if ever. His is not a character that will ever grow old; it is not capable of a petty and short-sighted prudence, but can only be guided by a large wisdom which is more young than old, for it has within itself the springs of perpetual youth, and which being far-sighted and prophetical, joins ever with the Progress party without waiting till it be obviously in the ascendant.

Mr. Clay has eloquence, but only from the soul.—He does not possess the art of oratory, as an art.—Before he gets warmed he is too slow, and breaks his sentences too much. His transitions are not made with skill, nor is the structure of his speech as a whole, symmetrical; yet, throughout, his grasp is firm upon his subject, and all the words are laden with the electricity of a strong mind and generous nature. When he begins to glow, and his deep mellow eye fills with light, the speech melts and glows too, and he is able to impress upon the hearer the full effect of firm conviction, conceived with impassioned energy. His often rugged and harsh emphasis flashes and sparkles then, and we feel that there is in the furnace a stream of iron—iron!—fortress of the nations and victor of the seas, worth far more, in stress of storm than all the gold and gems of rhetoric.

The great principle that he who wrongs one wrongs all, and that no part can be wounded without endangering the whole, was the healthy root of Mr. Clay's speech. The report does not do justice to the turn of expression in some parts which were most characteristic. These, indeed, depended much on the tones and looks of the speaker. We should speak of them as full of a robust and homely sincerity, dignified by the heart of the gentleman, a heart too secure of its respect for the rights of others to need any of the usual interpositions.

His good-humored sarcasm on occasion of several vulgar interruptions was very pleasant, and easily at those times might be recognized in him the man of heroical nature, who can only show himself adequately in time of interruption and of obstacle. If that be all that is wanted, we shall surely see him wholly; there will be no lack of American occasions to call out the Greek fire—We want them all,—the Grecian men, who feel a god-like thirst for immortal glory, and to develop the peculiar powers with which the gods have gifted them. We want them all, the poet, the thinker, the hero. Whether our heroes need *swords*, is a more doubtful point, we think, than Mr. Clay believes. Neither do we believe in some of the means he proposes to further his aims. God uses all kinds of means, but men, his priests, must keep their hands pure. Nobody that needs a bribe shall be asked to further our schemes for emancipation. But there is room enough and time enough to think out these points till all is in harmony. For the good that has been done and the truth that has been spoken, for the love of such that has been seen in this great city struggling up through the love of money, we should to-day be thankful—and we are so.

The Rich Man—
An Ideal Sketch*

In my walks through this City, the sight of spacious and expensive dwelling houses now in process of building, has called up the following reverie.

All benevolent persons, whether deeply thinking on, or only deeply feeling, the woes, difficulties and dangers of our present social system, are agreed either that great improvements are needed, or a thorough reform.

Those who desire the latter, include the majority of thinkers. And we ourselves, both from personal observation and the testimony of others, are convinced that a radical reform is needed. Not a reform that rejects the instruction of the past, or asserts that God and man have made mistakes till now. We believe that all past developments have taken place under natural and necessary laws, and that the Paternal Spirit has at no period forgot his children, but granted to all ages and generations their chances of good to balance inevitable ills.—We prize the Past; we recognize it as our parent, our nurse and our teacher, and we know that for a time the new wine required the old bottles to prevent its being spilled upon the ground.

Still we feel that the time is come which not only permits, but demands, a wider statement, and a nobler action. The aspect of society presents mighty problems, which must be solved by the soul of Man "divinely intending" itself to the task, or all will become worse instead of better, and ere long the social fabric totter to decay.

Yet while the new measures are ripening and the new men educating, there is yet room on the old platform for some worthy action. It is possible for a man of piety, resolution and

* In *New-York Daily Tribune*, 6 February 1846, p. 1.

good sense, to lead a life which, if not expansive, generous, graceful, and pure from suspicion and contempt, is yet not entirely unworthy of his position as the child of God and ruler of a planet.

Let us take then some men just where they find themselves, in a mixed state of society where, in quantity, we are free to say the bad preponderates, though the good, from its superior energy in quality, may finally redeem and efface its plague-spots.

Our society is ostensibly under the rule of the precepts of Jesus. We will then suppose a youth sufficiently imbued with these to understand what is conveyed under the parables of the unjust steward and the prodigal son, as well as the denunciations of the opulent Jews. He understands that is needful to preserve purity and teachableness, since of those most like little children is the kingdom of Heaven's mercy for the sinner, since there is peculiar joy in Heaven at the salvation of such perpetual care for the unfortunate, since only to the just steward shall his possessions be pardoned. Imbued with such lore the young man joins the active—we will say, in choosing an instance, joins the commercial world.

His views of his profession are not those which make of the many a herd, not superior, except in the far reach of their selfish instincts, to the animals, mere calculating, money-making machines.

He sees in commerce a representation of most important interests, a grand school that may teach the heart and soul of the civilized world to a willing, thinking mind. He plays his part in the game, but not for himself alone; he sees the interests of all mankind engaged with his, and remembers them while he furthers his own. His intellectual discernment, no less than his moral, thus teaching the undesirableness of lying and stealing, he does not practice or connive at the falsities and meannesses so frequent among his fellows; he suffers many turns of the wheel of Fortune to pass unused, since he cannot avail himself of them and keep clean his hands. What he gains is by superior assiduity, still in combination and calculation, and quickness of sight. His gains are legitimate so far as the present state of things permits any gains to be.

Nor is this honorable man denied his due rank in the most

corrupt state of society. Here, happily, we draw from life, and speak of what we know.—Honesty is, indeed, the best policy, only it is so in the long run, and therefore a policy which a selfish man has not faith and patience to pursue. The influence of the honest man is in the end predominent, and the rogues who sneer because he will not shuffle the cards in *their* way, are forced to bow to it at last.

But, while thus conscientious and mentally progressive, he does not forget to live. The sharp and care-worn faces, the joyless lives that throng his busy street, do not make him forget his need of tender affections, of the practices of bounty and love. His family, his acquaintance, especially those who are struggling with the difficulties of life, are not obliged to wait till he has accumulated a certain sum. He is sunlight and dew to them now, day by day. No less do all in his employment prize and bless the just, the brotherly man. He dares not, would not climb to power upon their necks. He requites their toil handsomely always: if his success be unusual, they share the benefit.—Their comfort is cared for in all the arrangements for their work. He takes care, too, to be personally acquainted with those he employs, regarding them, not as mere tools of his purpose, but as human beings also; he keeps them in his eye, and if it be in his power to supply their need of consolation, instruction, or even pleasure, they find they have a friend.

"Nonsense!" exclaims our sharp-eyed, thin-lipped antagonist. "Such a man would never get rich, or even *get along*."

You are mistaken, Mr. Stock-jobber. Thus far many lines are drawn from real life, though for the second part which follows, we want, as yet, a worthy model.

We must imagine, then, our ideal merchant to have grown rich in some forty years of toil passed in the way we have indicated. His hair is touched with white, but his form is vigorous yet. Neither *gourmandise* nor the fever of gain have destroyed his complexion, quenched the light of his eye, or substituted sneers for smiles. He is an upright, strong, sagacious, generous looking man, and if his movements be abrupt and his language concise somewhat beyond the standard of beauty, he is still the gentleman mercantile, but a mercantile nobleman.

Our nation is not silly in striving for an aristocracy. Humanity longs for its upper classes. But the silliness consists in making them out of clothes, equipage, and a servile imitation of foreign manners, instead of the genuine elegance and distinction that can only be produced by genuine culture. Shame upon the stupidity which, when all circumstances leave us free for the introduction of a real aristocracy, such as the world never saw, bases its pretensions on, or makes its bow to, the footman behind the coach, instead of the person within it.

But our merchant shall be a real nobleman, whose noble manners spring from a noble mind, whose fashions from a sincere and intelligent love of the Beautiful.

We will also indulge the fancy of giving him a wife and children congenial with himself. Having lived in sympathy with him, they have acquired no taste for luxury; they do not think that the best use of wealth and power is in self indulgence, but, on the contrary, that it is more blessed to give than to receive.

He is now having one of these fine houses built, and, as in other things, proceeds on a few simple principles. It is substantial, for he wishes to give no countenance to the paper buildings that correspond with other worthless paper currency of a credit system. It is thoroughly finished and furnished, for he has a conscience about his house, as about the neatness of his person. All must be of a piece—harmony and a wise utility are consulted without regard to show. Still, as he is a rich man, we allow him reception rooms, lofty, large, adorned with good copies of ancient works of art, and fine specimens of modern.

N.B.—I admit, in this instance, the propriety of my nobleman, often choosing by advice of friends who may have had more leisure and opportunity to acquire a sure appreciation of merit in these walks. His character being simple, he will, no doubt, appreciate a great part of what is truly grand and beautiful. But, also, from imperfect culture, he might often reject what in the end he would have found most valuable to himself and others. For he has not done learning, but only acquired the privilege of helping to open a domestic school in which he will find himself a pupil as well as master. So he may well make use, in furnishing himself with the school apparatus, of the best counsel. The same applies to making his library a good one. Only there must be no sham; no pluming himself on possessions that represent his wealth, but the taste of others. Our nobleman is incapable of pretension, or the airs of connoisseurship; his object is to furnish a home with those testimonies of a higher life in man that may best aid to cultivate the same in himself and those assembled round him.

He shall also have a fine garden and green-houses. But the flowers shall not be used only to decorate his apartments or the hair of his daughters, but shall often bless, by their soft and exquisite eloquence, the poor invalid, or others whose sorrowful hearts find in their society a consolation and a hope which nothing else bestows. For flowers, the highest expression of the bounty of Nature, declare that for all men not merely labor or luxury but gentle, buoyant, ever energetic joy was intended, and bid us hope that we shall not forever be kept back from our inheritance.

All the persons who have aided in building up this domestic temple, from the artist who painted the ceilings to the poorest hodman, shall be well paid and cared for during its erection, for it is a necessary part of the happiness of our nobleman to feel that all concerned in creating his home are the happier for it.

We have said nothing about the architecture of the house, and yet this is only for want of room. We do consider it one grand duty of every person able to build a good house, also to aim at building a beautiful one. We do not want imitations of what was used in other ages, nations and climates, but what is simple, noble and in conformity with the wants of our own. Room enough, simplicity of design, and judicious adjustment of the parts to their uses and to the whole, are the first requisites, the ornaments are merely the finish on these. We hope to see a good style of civic architecture long before any material improvement in the country edifices, for reasons that would be tedious to enumerate here. Suffice it to say that we are far more anxious to see an American architecture, than an American literature, for we are here sure there is already something individual to express.

Well, suppose the house built and equipped with man and horse. You may be sure my nobleman gives his "hired help" good accommodations, both for their sleeping and waking hours,—baths, books, and some leisure to use them. Nay! I assure you, and this assurance also is drawn from life, that it is possible, even in our present social relations, for the man who does common justice in these respects to his fellows, and shows a friendly heart that thoroughly feels service no degradation, but an honor,

> "A man's a man for a' that."
> Honor in the king the wisdom of his service.
> Honor in the serf the fidelity of his service,

can have around him those who do their work in serenity of mind, neither deceiving nor envying those whom circumstances have enabled to command their service. As to the carriage that is used for the purpose of going to and fro in bad weather, or ill health, or haste, or for drives to enjoy the country. But my nobleman and his family are too well born and bred not to prefer using their own feet when possible. And their carriage is much appropriated to the use of poor invalids, even among the abhorred class of poor relations, so that they often have not room in it for themselves, much less for flaunting dames and lazy dandies.

We need hardly add that their attendants wear no liveries. They are aware that, in a society where none of the causes exist that justify this habit abroad, the practice would have no other result than to call up a sneer to the lips of the most complaisant and needy foreign "mi lor" when Mrs. Higginbottom's carriage stops the way with its tawdry, ill-fancied accompaniments. *Will* none of their "governors" tell our cits the Æsopean fable of the donkey that tried to imitate the gambols of the little dog?[1]

The wife of my nobleman is so well matched with him that she has no need to be the better half. She is his almoner, his counselor, and the priestess who keeps burning on the domestic hearth a fire from the fuel he collects in his out door work, whose genial heat and aspiring flame comfort and animate all who come within its range.

---

[1] Aesop's fable of the ass which tried to imitate a dog, even to the point of jumping into his owner's lap, showed the moral that to be satisfied with one's lot is better than to desire something which one is not fitted to receive.

His children are his ministers, whose leisure and various qualifications enable them to carry out his good thoughts. They hold all that they possess—time, money, talents, acquirements—on the principle of stewardship. They wake up the seeds of virtue and genius in all the young persons of their acquaintance, but the poorer classes are especially their care. There they seek for those who are threatened with dying mute, inglorious Hampdens and Miltons, but for their scrutiny and care.[2] Of these they become the teachers and patrons to the extent of their power. Such knowledge of the arts, sciences and just principles of action as they have been favored with, they communicate and thereby form novices worthy to fill up the ranks of the true American aristocracy.

And the house—it is a large one, a single family does not fill its chambers. Some of them are devoted to the use of men of genius, who need a serene home, free from care, while they pursue their labors for the good of the world. Thus, as in the palaces of the little princes of Italy in a better day these chambers become hallowed by the nativities of great thoughts, and the horoscopes of the human births that may take place there are likely to read the better for it. Suffering virtue sometimes finds herself taken home here, instead of being sent to the almshouse or presented with a half dollar and a ticket for coal, and finds upon my nobleman's mattresses (for the wealth of Crœsus would not lure him or his to sleep on down) dreams of angelic protection which enable her to rise refreshed for the struggle of the morrow.

The uses of hospitality are very little understood among us, so that we fear generally there is small chance of entertaining Gods and Angels unawares, as the Greeks and Hebrews did in the generous time of hospitality when every man had a claim on the roof of fellow man. Now, none is received to a bed and breakfast unless he come as "bearer of despatches" from his Excellency So and So.

But let us not be supposed to advocate the system of all work and no play, or to delight exclusively in the pedagoguish and Goody Two Shoes vein. Reader, if any such accompany me to this scene of my vision, cheer up, I hear

[2] John Hampden (1594-1643), English statesman considered a great champion of Parliament.

the sound of music in full band, and see the banquet prepared. Perhaps even they are dancing the Polka and Redowa in some of those airy, well lighted rooms. In another they find in the acting of extempore dramas, arrangement of tableaux, little concerts or recitations, intermingled with beautiful national or fancy dances, some portion of the enchanting, refining and ennobling influences of the arts. The finest engravings on all subjects attend such as like to employ themselves more quietly, while those who can find a companion or congenial group to converse with, find also plenty of recesses and still rooms with softer light provided for their pleasure.

There is not this side of the Atlantic, we dare our glove upon it, a more devout believer than ourselves in the worship of the Muses and Graces, both for itself and its importance no less to the moral than the intellectual life of a nation. Perhaps there is not one who has *so* deep a feeling or so many suggestions ready, in the fulness of time to be hazarded on the subject.

But in order to such worship what standard is there as to admission to the service? Talents of gold or Delphian talents? fashion or elegance? "standing" or the power to move gracefully from one "position" to any other?

Our nobleman did not hesitate; the handle to his door-bell was not of gold, but mother-of-pearl, pure and prismatic.

If he did not go into the alleys to pick up the poor, they were not excluded, if qualified by intrinsic qualities to adorn the scene. Neither were wealth or fashion a cause of exclusion more than of admission. All depended on the person; yet he did not *seek* his guests among the slaves of Fashion, for he knew that persons highly endowed rarely had patience with the frivolities of that class, but retired and left it to be peopled mostly by weak and plebeian natures. Yet all depended on the person. Was the person fair, noble, wise, brilliant, or even only youthfully innocent and gay, or venerable in a good old age, he or she was welcome. Still, as simplicity of character and some qualification positively good, healthy and natural was requisite for admission, we must say the company was select. Our nobleman and his family had weeded their 'circle' faithfully year by year.

Some valued acquaintances they had made in ball-rooms and boudoirs, and kept; but far more had been made through the daily wants of life, and shoemakers, sempstresses and graziers mingled happily with artists and statesmen, to the benefit of both. (N.B.—None used the poisonous weed in or out of our domestic temple.)

I cannot tell you what infinite good our nobleman and his family were doing by creation of this true social center where the legitimate aristocracy of the land assembled, not to be dazzled by expensive furniture (our nobleman bought what was good in texture and beautiful in form but not *because* it was expensive,) not to be feasted on rare wines and high seasoned dainties, though they found simple refreshments well prepared, (as indeed it was a matter of duty and conscience in that house that the least office should be well fulfilled,) but to enjoy the generous confluence of mind with mind and heart with heart, the pastimes that are not waste-times of taste and inventive fancy, the cordial union of beings from all points and places in noble human sympathy.— New-York was beginning to be truly American or rather Columbian, and money stood for something in the records of history. It had brought opportunity to genius and aid to virtue. But just this moment the jostling showed me that I had reached the corner of Wall-st. I looked earnestly at the omnibuses discharging their eager freight, as if I hoped to see my merchant. Perhaps he has gone to the Post Office to take out letters from his friends in Utopia, thought I. "Please ye give me a penny," screamed a ragged, half-starved little street sweep, and the fancied cradle of the American Utopia receded or rather proceded fifty years at least into the Future.

Darkness Visible*

We have had this book before us for several weeks, but the task of reading it has been so repulsive that we have been obliged to get through it by short stages with long intervals of rest and refreshment between, and have only just reached the end. We believe, however, we are now possessed of its substance, so far as it is possible to admit into any mind matter wholly uncongenial with its structure, its faith and its hope.

Meanwhile others have shown themselves more energetic in the task, and notices have appeared that express, in part, our own views. Among others an able critic has thus summed up his impressions:

"Of the whole we will say briefly, that its premises are monstrous, its reasoning sophistical, its conclusions absurd, and its spirit diabolic."

We know not that we can find a better scheme of arrangement for what we have to say than by dividing it into sections under these four heads:

1st. The premises are monstrous. Here we must add the qualification, they are monstrous *to us*. The God of these writers is not the God we recognize; the views they have of human nature are antipodal to ours. We believe in a Creative Spirit, the essence of whose being is Love. He has created men in the spirit of love, intending to develop them to perfect harmony with himself. He has permitted the temporary

---

* *A Defence of Capital Punishment, by Rev. George B. Cheever, D.D., and An Essay on the Ground and Reason of Punishment, with Special Reference to the Penalty of Death; by Tayler Lewis, Esq. With an Appendix, Containing a Review of Burleigh on the Death Penalty*. New York: Wiley & Putnam, 1846. In *New-York Daily Tribune*, 4 March 1846, p. 1.

existence of evil as a condition necessary to bring out in them free agency and individuality of character. Punishment is the necessary result of a bad choice in them; it is not meant by him as vengeance, but as an admonition to choose better. Man is not born totally evil; he is born capable both of good and evil, and the Holy Spirit in working on him only quickens the soul already there to know its Father. To one who takes such views the address of Jesus becomes intelligible:

"Be ye therefore merciful, as your Father also is merciful." "For with the same measure that ye mete withal, it shall be measured to you again."

Those who take these views of the relation between God and man must naturally tend to have punishment consist as much as possible in the inward spiritual results of faults, rather than a violent outward enforcement of penalty. They must, so far as possible, seek to revere God by showing themselves brotherly to man; and if they wish to obey Christ, will not forget that he came especially to call *sinners* to repentance.

The views of Messrs. Lewis and Cheever are the opposite of all this. We need not state them; they are sufficiently indicated in each page of their own. Their conclusions are the natural result of such premises. We could say nothing about either except to express dissent from beginning to end. Yet would it be sweet and noble, and worthy of this late period of human progress, if this might be done in a spirit of religious, of manly courtesy; if they had the soul to say—"We differ from you, but we know that so wide and full a stream of thought and emotion as you are engaged in could not, under the providential rule in which we believe, have arisen in vain. The object of every such manifestation of life must be to bring out truth; come, let us seek it together. Let us show you our view, compare it with yours, and let us see which is the better. If, as we think, the truth lie with us, what joy will it be for us to cast the clear light on the object of your aspirations!"

Of this degree of liberality we have known some, even, who served the same creed as these writers to be capable. There is, indeed, a higher form which, believing all forms of opinion which we hold in the present stage of our growth can be but approximations to truth, and that God has permitted to the multitude of men a multitude of ways by which they may approach our common goal, looks with reverence on all modes of faith sincerely held and acted upon, and while it rejoices in those who have reached the higher stages of spiritual growth, has no despair as to those who will grope in a narrow path and by a glimmering light. Such liberality is, of course, out of the question with such writers as the present. Their creed binds them to believe that they have absolute truth, and that all who do not believe as they do are wretched heretics. Those whose creed is of narrower scope are to them hateful bigots, but also those with whom it is of wider are latitudinarians or infidels. The spot of earth on which they stand is the only one safe from the conflagration, and only through spectacles and spy-glasses such as are used by them can the sun and stars be seen. Yet, as we said before, some such, though incapacitated for an intellectual, are not so for a spiritual tolerance. With them the heart, more Christ-like than the creed, urges to a spirit of love and reverence even toward convictions opposed to their own. The sincere man is always respectable in their eyes, and they cannot help feeling that, wherever there is a desire for truth, there is the spirit of God, and His true priests will approach with gentleness and do their ministry with holy care. Unhappily, it is very different with the persons before us.

We let go the first two counts of the indictment. Their premises are, as we have said, such as we totally dissent from, and their conclusions such as naturally flow from those premises. Yet they are those of a large body of men, and there must, no doubt, be temporary good in this state of things or it would not be permitted. When these writers say that to them moral and penal are coincident terms, they display a state of mind which prefers basing virtue on the fear of punishment rather than the love of right. If this be sincerely their state, if the idea of morality be with them entirely dependent on the retributions upon vice rather than the loveliness and joys of goodness, it is impossible for those who are in a different state of mind to say what they *do* need. It may seem to us, indeed, that, if the strait jacket was taken off, they might recover the natural energy of their frames, and do far better without it; or that, if no longer hurried along the road by the impending lash behind, they might uplift their eyes and find sufficient cause for speed in the glory visible before, though at a distance; however, it is not for us to say what their wants are. Let them choose their own principles of action, and if they lead to purity of life and benevolence and humanity of heart, we will not say a word against them.

But in the instance before us they do not produce these good fruits but the contrary, and therefore we have something to say on the other part of the criticism, to wit: that "the reasoning is sophistical and the spirit diabolic;" for indeed, in the sense of pride by which the angels fell, arrogance of judgment, malice and all uncharitableness, we have never looked on printed pages more deeply sinful.

We wish, however, to make all due allowance for incapacity in these writers to do better, and their disqualifications for their task, apart from a form of belief which inclines them rather to cling to the past, than to seek progress for the future, seem to be many.

From Mr. Lewis's hand we have read but little before these pages, but sufficient to show the quality of his mind. It seems to be what is vulgarly considered the mind of a lawyer, though, in fact, a great lawyer can no more have such an one than a great statesman; but a good advocate may, and the habit of pleading all of one side and seeking to carry a special object, rather than to elicit truth, is likely to give such a cast. It is a mind active, acute upon details, capable of scholarship, but incapable of broad views, or thorough reasoning, and in the last degree unspiritual,—that is to say, blind to the working of principles either in the main stream of life or in the mind of the individual. He has a sense only for rules and precedents and their application to special cases.

Mr. or Dr. Cheever has a mind of better quality and more real life, but that life all tainted by the heat and bitterness of his spirit. He had by nature some congeniality with the noble poetic spirit, but it is soured and checked by the excess of petty and local feelings. It is mournful to see him amid the sublime beauties of Switzerland, fretting himself into a polemical fever against the Roman Catholic Church, or full of anxiety lest he shall forget God, if he cannot put all the emotions such sights inspire into the form of a sermon. It is pitiful to see him in his preface to a work (Vestiges of Creation) which attempts to give a philosophical view of the facts of science, so wholly benighted by his fears as to the spirit and scope of what he treats of, and though, we believe, with a good intention, using the most unfair as well as ridiculous means to provide an antidote against a fancied bane.

The history of this preface is so amusing a specimen of the steps to which the arrogant notions held by some shepherds as to their duties in the care of men's souls may lead, that we must give it here, only premising that we give it, not as one having authority from the publishers or the prefatorial D. D. himself, but as the received version of the affair. If it be not true let it be corrected; if it be, let it figure in the annals of an age when, if Truth be still alive and bold, it is not the fault of Cant.

The book of the Vestiges was no sooner published in Great Britain than those reverend men and women who, with all their professions of honor to God evince an amazing skepticism as to his power of upholding truth against the invasions of error, stood up, each in his or her place, to hurl their anathema against the dangerous man who tried to show that God works by law. 'If he can only make out his case, cried they, he will get the helm of the Universe so completely in his hand, that he may perhaps steer it quite away from God. He professes, indeed, a reverence for God, and that he seeks to prove it by attempting to show the harmony which regulates the world. But that is very unlikely; it is too different from our way of going on. We have been contented to know that God made the world without caring to know the *how*. Such inquiries are dangerous—who knows whither they may lead? Is it not a horrible thought that men might even be *developed* to the life of angels, instead of being transported into it in an instant by the hand of Death?—Who can tell where this development is to stop? it might even substitute the study of laws and causes for regular attendance on Church service, perhaps! We'll none of it.'

Thus cried they, but each from his or her place. The Author of the Vestiges stood in his place and they in theirs and said their say. They made their critiques and he has answered them according to his judgment and ability in the "Explanations."

Of course a work which had caused so much mental excitement passed over to this country and was published here.
It was published, as a matter of business, because it was
written and because people wanted to read it. No sooner was
it out than our self-elected censors of the press, who, in their
vigilance and jealous care, vie with any officials of foreign
governments, declare that the book is most shocking, "blasphemous, atheistical," and, if suffered to go abroad will ruin
our nation, root and branch, with its insidious canker.

"But what is to be done?" replies the publisher "The book
is in the world, and people choose to read it. Some one
would publish it, if I gave up."

The answer was found in a commission to Rev. Dr.
Cheever to prepare a short prelude, which, being every
where played before the piece itself, should put the ear into
such a state as to repel all dangerous intoxication. A device
borrowed from the wise man of old, who stopped the ears of
his mariners with wax when they were exposed to the peril-
ous song of the Syrens.[1] This preface is, in itself, at once one
of the weakest and most unfair productions on which we ever
glanced. Like the productions before us (on Capital Punishment) it depends for its stress on appeals to passion and prejudice as to themes, where, if ever, they should be silent.
Like these, it shows a want of that power without which no
argument can ever be either honorable or cogent—the power
of comprehending the other side. The assault is principally
made by talking of the author groping amid dead matter and
similar remarks. The chief reliance as to prejudicing the
reader against the work he is about to read is upon addresses
to the author as *thou fool*, or a use of the term "dead" which
shows either an utter ignorance and misconception of the
work or a willing perversion of truth.

But what we would wish to lay emphasis upon as illustra-
tive of the state of this person's mind, is the indelicacy,
impertinence and arrogance of the position he assumes. Suppose a self-constituted master of ceremonies thus to introduce to a circle an *invited* guest, "Mr. —— is here; you have
invited him and I cannot help his entering the room. But I
wish first to give you the correct view of him, which you

---

[1] Ulysses; see note 10, p. 90 above.

must be careful not to lay aside for any other. *I know* that he is a wicked, unprincipled man, in fact an Atheist. If he says any thing that seems to imply the contrary, you are to infer that he adds the vice of hypocrisy to all his others. If you find that, in spite of what I say, his conversation and manners make a favorable impression on you, then, indeed, is your danger dreadful and imminent. Do not trust yourself to examine farther, but think of my words, turn in all haste and flee from the wrath to come."

Such is the position assumed by the Rev. Mr. Cheever in regard to this work; a position not unworthy the worst days of the class he most detests, the framers of golden bulls and expurgatory indexes. So inconsistent is man, and so sadly needful is it that he should, day by day, recall the precept, "Judge not that ye be not judged."

We know of no parallel yet to offer to the future D'Israeli of our literary history except the preface by another such self-elected guardian to Sir Humphrey Davy's Consolations in Travel, who charges the reader to attach no importance to the heretical views advanced in the book, as there is every reason to believe that the author recanted them and died a Christian.[2]

The Public, we suppose, have in the present case rejected the guardianship of Mr. Cheever, as the preface is dropt from the third edition, and we found it almost impossible now to procure a copy for the refreshment of our memory.

This position is more legitimately occupied in the book on Capital Punishment, but in the same spirit. We love an honest lover, but next best we, with Dr. Johnson, know how to respect an honest hater. But even he would scarce endure so bitter and ardent a hater as Mr. Cheever, and with so many and inconsistent objects of hatred—one who hates Catholics and thorough Protestants, hates materialists and hates spiritualists. His list is really too large for *human* sympathy.

Messrs. Lewis and Cheever profess to occupy the position

---

[2] Isaac D'Israeli (1766-1848) edited a number of collections of literary anecdotes, including *Curiosities of Literature*, beginning in 1791; Sir Humphrey Davy (1778-1829) published his *Consolations in Travel, or, The Last Days of a Philosopher* in 1830.

of defence; surely never was one sustained so in the spirit of offence.

The "reasoning is sophistical," and it would need the patience of a Socrates to ravel the weary web and convince these sophists against their will that they are exactly in the opposite region to what they suppose. For the task we have not space, skill or patience, but we can give some hints by which readers may be led to examine whether it is so or not.

1st. Mr. Lewis appeals either to the natural or regenerate man as suits his purpose. Sometimes all traditions and their literal interpretations are right; sometimes it is impossible to interpret them aright unless according to some peculiar doctrine, and the natural inference of the common mind would be an error.

2d. He strains, but vainly, to show the New Testament no improvement on the Old, and himself in harmonious relations to both. On this subject we would confidently leave the arbitration to a mind, could such an one be found, sufficiently disciplined to examine the subject, and new both to the New Testament and his essay, as that of Rammohun Roy might have been,[3] whether his views are not of the same strain that Jesus sought to correct and enlighten among the Jews, and whether he does not treat the teachings of the new dispensation most unfairly in his desire to wrest them into the service of the old.

3d. Wherever there is a weak place in the argument, it is filled up by abuse of the opposite party. The words 'absurd,' 'infidel,' 'blasphemous,' 'shallow philosophy,' 'sickly sentimentalism,' and the like, are among the favorite missiles of these *defenders* of the truth. They are of a sort whose frequent use is generally supposed to argue a want of a shield of reason and a heart of faith.

And this brings us to a more close consideration of the *spirit* of this book, characterized by our cotemporary as 'diabolic.' And we, also, cannot excuse ourselves from marking it as, in this respect, one of the worst books we have ever seen.

It is not merely bitter intolerance, arrogance and want of

---

[3] Rammohun Roy (*c*.1774-1833), great Indian religious thinker.

spiritual perception which we have to condemn in these
writers. It is a want of fairness and honor, of which we think
they must be conscious. We fear they are of those who hold
the opinion that the end sanctifies the means, and who, by
pretending to serve the God of Truth by other means than
strict truth, have drawn upon the 'professors of religion' the
frequent obloquy of 'priestcraft.' How else are we to construe
the artful use of the words 'dishonest' and 'infidel' wherever
they are likely to awaken the fears and prejudices of the
ignorant? How the studied introduction and coupling together of the names of Paine and Parker, and the relation in
which they stand? *Does* the writer here sincerely express any
conviction of his mind? If he does *not*, while daring to accuse
others of dishonesty, the words moral and penal should, indeed, be associated for him!

Of as bad a stamp as any is the part of the book headed
"Spurious Public Opinion." Here, as in the insinuations
against Charles Burleigh, we are unable to believe the writers to be sincere. Where we think they are, however poor and
narrow we may esteem their statement, we can respect it, but
here we cannot.

Who can believe that such passages as the following stand
for any thing real in the mind of the writer?

"Indeed there is nothing that can possibly check the spirit of
murder, but the fear of death! That was all that Cain feared; he
did not say, people will put me in prison, but, they will put me
to death; *and how many other murders he may have committed
when released from that fear, the sacred writer does not tell
us!!*"

Why does not the writer draw the inference and accuse
God of mistake, as he says His opponents accuse Him, whenever they attempt to get beyond the Jewish ideas of vengeance. He plainly thinks death was the only safe penalty in
this case of Cain!

"The reasoning from these drivelings of depravity in malefactors is to the last degree wretched and absurd.—Hard pushed
indeed must he be in argument, who can consent to dive down
into the polluted heart of a Newgate criminal,[4] in order to fish

---

[4] Newgate, English prison with an unsavory reputation.

up, from the confessions of his monstrous, unnatural obduracy, an argument in that very obduracy against the fit punishment of his own crimes."

We can only wish for such a man that the vicissitudes of life may break through the crust of theological arrogance and Phariseeism and force him to "dive down" into the depths of his own nature.—We should see afterward whether he would be so forward to throw stones at malefactors, so eager to hurry souls to what he regards as a final account.

But we have said enough as to the spirit and tendency of this book. We shall only add a few words as to the unworthy use of the word "infidel" in the attempt to fix a stigma upon opponents. We feel still more contempt than indignation at the desire to work in this way on the unthinking and ignorant.

We ourselves are of the number stigmatized by these persons as sharing an infidel tendency, as are all not enlisted under their own sectarian banner. They, on their side, seem to us unbelievers in all that is most pure and holy, and in the saving grace of love. They do not believe in God, as we believe; they seem to us utterly deficient in the spirit of Christ, and to be of the number of those who are always calling 'Lord, Lord,' yet never have known him. We find throughout these pages the temper of "Lord, I thank thee that I am not as other men are," hatred of those whom they deem Gentiles, and a merciless spirit toward the sinner, yet we do not take upon ourselves to give them the name of Infidels, and we solemnly call them to trial before the bar of the Only Wise and Pure, the Searcher of hearts, to render an account of this daring assumption. We ask them in that presence if they are not of the class threatened with "retribution" for saying to their brother "Thou fool," and that not merely in the heat of anger, but coolly, pertinaciously, and in a thousand ways.

We call to sit in council the spirits of our Puritan fathers, and ask if such was the right of individual judgment, of private conscience, they came here to vindicate. And we solicit the verdict of posterity as to whether the spirit of mercy or of vengeance be the more divine, and whether the denunciatory and personal mode chosen by these writers for carrying on this inquiry be the true one.

We wish most sincerely the book had been a wise and noble book. To ascertain just principles, it is necessary that the discussion should be full and fair and both sides ably argued. After this has been done, the sense of the world can decide. It would be a happiness for which it might seem that man at this time of day is ripe, that the opposing parties should meet in open lists as brothers, believing each that the other desired only that the truth should triumph, and able to clasp hands as men of different structure and ways of thinking, but fellow students of the Divine will. O had we but found such an adversary, above the use of artful abuse, or the feints of sophistry, able to believe in the noble intention of a foe as of a friend, how cheerily would the trumpets ring out while the assembled world echoed the signal words, 'GOD SPEED THE RIGHT!' The tide of Progress rolls onward, swelling more and more with the lives of those who would fain see all men called to repentance. It must be a strong arm, indeed, that can build a dam to stay it even for a moment. None such do we see yet, but we should rejoice in a noble and strong opponent, putting forth all his power for conscience' sake.—God speed the Right!

Consecration of Grace Church*

Whoever passes up Broadway finds his attention arrested by three fine structures, Trinity Church, that of the Messiah, and Grace Church.

His impressions are, probably, at first of a pleasant character. He looks upon these edifices as expressions, which, however inferior in grandeur to the poems in stone which adorn the older world, surely indicate that man cannot rest content with his short earthly span, but prizes relations to eternity. The house, in which he pays deference to claims which death will not cancel, seems to be no less important in his eyes than those in which the affairs which press nearest are attended to.

So far, no good! That is expressed which gives man his superiority over the other orders of the natural world, that consciousness of spiritual affinities of which we see no unequivocal signs elsewhere.

But, if this be something great when compared with the rest of the animal creation, yet how little seems it when compared with the ideal that has been offered to him, as to the means of signifying such feelings. These temples! how far do they correspond with the idea of that religious sentiment from which they originally sprung?

In the old world the history of such edifices, though not without its shadow, had many bright lines.—Kings and Emperors paid oftentimes for the materials and labor a price of blood and plunder, and many a wretched sinner sought by contributions of stone for their walls! to roll off that he had laid on his conscience. Still the community amid which they rose, knew little of these drawbacks. Pious legends attest the

* In *New-York Daily Tribune*, 11 March 1846, p. 1. Grace Church in New York had been consecrated on 7 March 1846.

purity of feeling associated with each circumstance of their building. Mysterious orders, of which we know only that they were consecrated to brotherly love and the development of mind, produced the genius which animated the architecture, but the casting of the bells and suspending them in the tower was an act in which all orders of the community took part; for when those cathedrals were consecrated it was for the use of all. Rich and poor knelt together upon their marble pavements, and the imperial altar welcomed the obscurest artisan.

This grace our Churches want, the grace which belongs to all religions, but is peculiarly and solemnly enforced upon the followers of Jesus. The poor to whom he came to preach can have no share in the grace of Grace Church. In St. Peter's, if only as an empty form, the soiled feet of travel-worn disciples are washed, but such feet can never intrude on the fane of the holy trinity here in republican America, and the Messiah may be supposed still to give as excuse for delay "The poor you always have with you."

We must confess this circumstance is to us quite destructive of reverence and value for these buildings.

We are told that at the late consecration the claims of the poor were eloquently urged, and that an effort is to be made, by giving a side chapel, to atone for the luxury which shuts them out from the reflection of sunshine through those brilliant windows. It is certainly better that they should be offered the crumbs from the rich man's table than nothing at all. Yet it is surely not *the* way that Jesus would have taught to provide for the poor.

Would you not then have these splendid edifices erected? We certainly feel that the educational influence of good specimens of architecture, (and we know no other argument in their favor) is far from being a counterpoise to the abstraction of so much money from purposes that would be more in fulfilment of that Christian idea which these assume to represent.

Were the rich to build such a church, and, dispensing with pews and all exclusive advantages, invite all who would to come in to the banquet, that were, indeed, noble and Christian. And, though we believe more, for our nation and time, in intellectual monuments than those of wood and stone, and, in opposition even to our admired Powers,[1] think that Michael Angelo himself could have advised no more suitable monument to Washington than a house devoted to the instruction of the people, and believe that that great master and the Greeks no less would agree with us if they lived now to survey all the bearings of the subject; yet we would not object to these splendid churches, if the idea of Him they call Master were represented in them. But till it is, they can do no good, for the means are not in harmony with the end. The rich man sits in state while 'near two hundred thousand' Lazaruses linger, unprovided for, without the gate. While this is so, they must not talk much, within, of Jesus of Nazareth, who called to him fishermen, laborers and artisans, for his companions and disciples.

We find some excellent remarks on this subject from Rev. STEPHEN OLIN, President of the Wesleyan University.[2] They are appended as a note to a discourse addressed to Young Men, on the text:

"Put ye on the Lord Jesus Christ, and make not provision for the flesh, to fulfill the lusts thereof."

This discourse, though it discloses formal and external views of religious ties and obligations, is dignified by a fervent, generous love for men, and a more than commonly catholic liberality, and though these remarks are made and meant to bear upon the interests of his own sect, yet they are anti-sectarian in their tendency and worthy the consideration of all anxious to understand the call of duty in these matters. Earnest attention of this sort will better avail than fifteen hundred dollars, or more, paid for a post of exhibition in a fashionable Church, where, if piety be provided with one chance, worldliness has twenty to stare it out of countenance.

[1] Hiram Powers (1805-1873), American sculptor who lived in Florence.
[2] *Resources and Duties of Christian Young Men* (1846) was delivered by Stephen Olin (1797-1851) to the graduating class at Wesleyan University in August 1845.

The Poor Man—
An Ideal Sketch*

The sketch of the Rich Man, made some three or four weeks since, seems to require this companion-piece, and we shall make the attempt, though the subject is far more difficult than the former was.

In the first place, we must state what we mean by a poor man, for it is a term of wide range in its relative applications. A pains-taking artisan, trained to self-denial and a strict adaptation, not of his means to his wants, but of his wants to his means, finds himself rich and grateful, if some unexpected fortune enables him to give his wife a new gown, his children cheap holiday joys, and to his starving neighbor a decent meal; while George IV. when heir apparent to the throne of Great Britain, considered himself driven by the pressure of poverty to become a debtor, a beggar, a swindler, and, by the aid of perjury, the husband of two wives at the same time, neither of whom he treated well. Since poverty is made an excuse for such depravity in conduct, it would be well to mark the limits within which self-control and resistance to temptation may be expected.

When he of the olden time prayed "Give me neither poverty nor riches," we presume he meant that proportion of means to the average wants of a human being which secures freedom from eating cares, freedom of motion, and a moderate enjoyment of the common blessings offered by earth, air, water, the natural relations, and the subjects for thought which every day presents. We shall certainly not look above this point for our poor man.—A Prince may be poor, if he has not means to relieve the sufferings of his subjects, or secure to them needed benefits. Or he may make himself so, just as

* In *New-York Daily Tribune*, 25 March 1846, p. 1.

a well-paid laborer by drinking brings poverty to his roof. So may the Prince, by the mental gin of horse-racing or gambling, grow a beggar. But we shall not consider these cases.

Our subject will be taken between the medium we have spoken of as answer to the wise man's prayer, and that destitution which we must style infamous, either to the individual or to the society whose vices have caused that stage of poverty in which there is no certainty, and often no probability, of work or bread from day to day,—in which cleanliness and all the decencies of life are impossible, and the natural human feelings are turned to gall because the man finds himself on this earth in a far worse situation than the brute. In this stage there is no Ideal, and from its abyss, if the unfortunates look up to Heaven, or the state of things as they ought to be, it is with suffocating gasps which demand relief or death. This degree of poverty is common, as we all know, but we who do not share it have no right to address those who do from our own standard, till we have placed their feet on our own level. Accursed is he who does not long to have this so,—to take out at least the physical Hell from this world! Unblest is he who is not seeking either by thought or act to effect this poor degree of amelioration in the circumstances of his race.

We take the subject of our sketch, then, somewhere between the abjectly poor and those in moderate circumstances. What we have to say may apply to either sex and to any grade in this division of the human family, from the hod-man and washerwoman up to the hard-working, poorly paid lawyer, clerk, schoolmaster or scribe.

The advantages of such a position are many. In the first place, you belong, inevitably, to the active and suffering part of the world. You know the ills that try men's souls and bodies. You cannot creep into a safe retreat, arrogantly to judge, or heartlessly to forget, the others. They are always before you; you see the path stained by their bleeding feet; stupid and flinty, indeed, must you be, if you can hastily wound or indolently forbear to aid them. Then as to yourself, you know what your resources are; what you can do, what bear; there is small chance for you to escape a well-tempered modesty. Then, again, if you find power in yourself to endure the trial, there is reason and reality in some degree of self reliance. The moral advantages of such training can scarcely fail to amount to something, and as to the mental, that most important chapter, how the lives of men are fashioned and transfused by the experience of passion and the development of thought, presents new sections at every turn, such as the distant dilettanti's opera-glasses will never detect,—to say nothing of the exercise of mere faculty, which, though insensible in its daily course, leads to results of immense importance.

But the evils, the disadvantages, the dangers, how many, how imminent! True, indeed, they are so.—There is the early bending of the mind to the production of marketable results, which must hinder all this free play of intelligence and deaden the powers that craved instruction. There is the callousness produced by the sight of more misery than it is possible to relieve; the heart, at first so sensitive, taking refuge in a stolid indifference against the pangs of sympathetic pain, it had not force to bear. There is the perverting influence of uncongenial employments, undertaken without or against choice, continued at unfit hours and seasons, till the man loses his natural relations with summer and winter, day and night, and has no sense more for natural beauty and joy. There is the mean providence, the perpetual caution to guard against ill, instead of the generous freedom of a mind which expects good to ensue from all good actions. There is the sad doubt whether it will *do* to indulge the kindly impulse, the calculation of dangerous chances and the cost between the loving impulse and its fulfilment. Yes: there is bitter chance of narrowness, meanness and dullness on this path, and it requires great natural force, a wise and large view of life taken at an early age, or fervent trust in God, to evade them.

It is astonishing to see the poor, no less than the rich, the slaves of externals. One would think that, where the rich man once became aware of the worthlessness of the mere trappings of life from the weariness of a spirit that found itself entirely dissatisfied after pomp and self-indulgence, the poor man would learn this a hundred times from the experience how entirely independent of them is all that is intrinsically valuable in our life. But no! The poor man wants dignity, wants elevation of spirit. It is his own servility that forges the fetters that enslave him. Whether he cringe to, or rudely defy, the man in the coach and handsome coat, the cause and effect are the same. He is influenced by a costume and a position. He is not firmly rooted in the truth that, only in so far as outward beauty and grandeur are a representative of the mind of the possessor, can they count for anything at all. Oh poor man! you are poor indeed, if you feel yourself so; poor if you do not feel that a soul born of God, a mind capable of scanning the wondrous works of time and space, and a flexible body for its service, are the essential riches of a man, and all he needs to make him the equal of any other man. You are mean, if the possession of money or other external advantages can make you envy or shrink from a being mean enough to value himself upon such. Stand where you may, oh Man, you cannot be noble and rich, if your brow be not broad and steadfast, if your eye beam not with a consciousness of inward worth, of eternal claims and hopes which such trifles cannot at all affect. A man without this majesty is ridiculous amid the flourish and decorations procured by money, pitiable in the faded habiliments of poverty. But a man who is a man, a woman who is a woman, can never feel lessened or embarrassed because others look ignorantly on such matters. If they regret the want of these temporary means of power, it must be solely because it fetters their motions, deprives them of leisure and desired means of improvement, or of benefiting those they love or pity.

I have heard those possessed of rhetoric and imaginative tendency declare that they should have been outwardly great and inwardly free, victorious poets and heroes, if Fate had allowed them a certain quantity of dollars. I have found it impossible to believe them. In early youth penury may have power to freeze the genial current of the soul and prevent it, during one short life, from becoming sensible of its true vocation and destiny. But if it *has* become conscious of these, and yet there is not advance in any and all circumstances, no change would avail.

No! our poor man must begin higher. He must, in the first place, really believe there is a God who ruleth, a fact to which few men vitally bear witness, though most are ready to affirm it with the lips.

2d.   He must sincerely believe that rank and wealth—

> —are but the guinea's stamp,
> The man's the gold,

take his stand on his claims as a human being, made in God's own likeness, urge them when the occasion permits, but, at all times, never be so false to them as to feel put down or injured by the want of mere external advantages.

3d.   He must accept his lot, while he is in it. If he can change it for the better, let his energies be exerted to do so. But if he cannot, there is none that will not yield an opening to Eden, to the glories of Zion and even to the subterranean enchantments of our strange estate. There is none that may not be used with nobleness.

> "Who sweeps a room, as for Thy sake
> Makes that and th' action clean."

4th.   Let him examine the subject enough to be convinced that there is not that vast difference between the employments that is supposed, in the means of expansion and refinement. All depends on the spirit as to the use that is made of an occupation. Mahomet was not a wealthy merchant, and profound philosophers have ripened on the benches, not of the lawyers, but the shoemakers.[1] It did not hurt Milton to be a poor school-master, nor Shakespeare to do the errands of a London play-house. Yes, the mind is its own place, and if it will keep that place, all doors will be opened from it. Upon this subject we hope to offer some hints at a future day, in speaking of the different trades, professions and modes of labor.

5th.   Let him remember that from no man can the chief wealth be kept. On all men the sun and stars shine; for all the oceans swell and rivers flow. All men may be brothers, lovers, fathers, friends; before all lie the mysteries of birth and death. If these wondrous means of wealth and blessing be likely to remain misused or unused, there are quite as many disadvantages in the way of the man of money as of the man who has none. Few who drain the choicest grape know the ecstacy of bliss and knowledge that follows a full draught

---

[1] Mahomet or Mohammed (*c*.570-632), founder of the Islam religion.

of the wine of life. That has mostly been reserved for those on whose thoughts society, as a public, makes but a moderate claim. And if bitterness followed on the joy, if your fountain was frozen after its first gush by the cold winds of the world, yet, moneyless men, ye are at least not wholly ignorant of what a human being has force to know. You have not skimmed over surfaces, and been dozing on beds of down during the rare and stealthy visits of Love and the Muses. Remember this, and, looking round on the arrangements of the lottery, see if you did not draw a prize in your turn.

It will be seen that our ideal poor man needs to be religious, wise, dignified and humble, grasping at nothing, claiming all; willing to wait, never willing to give up; servile to none, the servant of all, and esteeming it the glory of a man to serve. The character is rare, but not unattainable. We have, however, found an approach to it more frequent in woman than in man.

Woman, even less than Man, is what she should be, as a whole. She is not that self-centered being, full of profound intuitions, angelic love, and flowing poesy, that she should be. Yet there are circumstances in which the native force and purity of her being teach her how to conquer where the restless impatience of man brings defeat and leaves him crushed and bleeding on the field.

Images rise to mind of calm strength, of gentle wisdom learning from every turn of adverse fate, of youthful tenderness and faith undimmed to the close of life, which redeem humanity and make the heart glow with fresh courage as we write. They are mostly from obscure corners and very private walks; there was nothing shining, nothing of an obvious and sounding heroism to make their conduct doubtful, by tainting their motives with vanity. Unknown they lived, untrumpeted they died. Many hearts were warmed and fed by them, but, perhaps, no mind but our own ever consciously took account of their virtues.

Had Art but the power adequately to tell their simple stories, and to cast upon them the light which, shining through those marked and faded faces, foretold the glories of a second Spring! The tears of holy emotion which fell from those eyes have seemed to us pearls beyond all price, or rather whose price will be paid only when beyond the grave they enter those better spheres in whose faith they felt and acted here.

From this private gallery we will, for the present, bring forward only one picture. That of a Black Nun was wont to fetter the eyes of visitors in the Royal Galleries of France, and my Sister of Mercy too is of that complexion. The old woman was recommended as a laundress by my friend, who had long prized her. I was immediately struck with the dignity and propriety of her manner. In the depth of winter she brought herself the heavy baskets through the slippery streets, and when I asked why she did not employ some younger person to do what was so entirely disproportioned to her strength, simply said, "she lived alone and could not afford to hire an errand-boy." "It was hard for her?" "No! she was fortunate in being able to get work at her age, when others could do it better. Her friends were very good to procure it for her." "Had she a comfortable home?" "Tolerably so; she should not need one long." "Was that a thought of joy to her?" "Yes; for she hoped to see again the husband and children from whom she had long been separated."

Thus much in answer to the questions; but at other times the little she said was on general topics. It was not from her that I learnt how "the great idea of Duty had held her upright" through a life of incessant toil, sorrow, and bereavement, and that not only she had remained upright, but that the character had been constantly progressive. Her latest act had been to take home a poor sick girl, who had no home of her own, and could not bear the idea of dying in a hospital, and maintain and nurse her through the last weeks of her life. "Her eye-sight was failing, and she should not be able to work much longer, but then God would provide. *Somebody* ought to see to the poor motherless girl."

It was not merely the greatness of the act, for one in such circumstances, but the quiet, matter-of-course way in which it was done, that showed the habitual tone of the mind, and made us feel that life could hardly do more for a human being than to make him or her the *somebody* that is daily so deeply needed to represent the right,—to do the plain right thing.

"God will provide." Ay, indeed, it is the poor who feel

themselves near to the God of Love.—"Though he slay them, still do they trust him." "I hope," said I to a poor apple-woman who had been drawn on to disclose a tale of distress that almost, in the mere hearing, made me weary of life, "I hope I may yet see you in a happier condition." "With God's help," she replied, with a smile that Raphael would have delighted to transfer to the canvas, a Mozart to his strains of angelic sweetness. All her life she had seemed an outcast child, still she leaned upon her Father's love.

The dignity of a state like this may vary its form in more or less richness and beauty of detail, but here is the focus of what makes life valuable. It is this spirit which makes Poverty the best servant to the Ideal of Human Nature. I am content with this type, and will only quote, in addition, a ballad I found in a foreign periodical translated from Chamisso,[2] and which forcibly recalled my own laundress as an equally admirable sample of the same class, the Ideal Poor, which we need for our consolation so long as there must be real poverty:

THE OLD WASHERWOMAN.

Among you lines her hands have laden,
    A laundress with white hair appears,
Alert as many a youthful maiden,
    Spite of her five-and-seventy years.
Bravely she won those white hairs, still
    Eating the bread hard toil obtained her,
And laboring truly to fulfil
    The duties to which God ordained her.

Once she was young and full of gladness,
    She loved and hoped, was wooed and won;
Then came the matron's cares, the sadness
    No loving heart on earth may shun.
Three babies she bore her mate; she prayed
    Beside his sick-bed; he was taken;
She saw him in the church-yard laid,
    Yet kept her faith and hope unshaken.

The task her little ones of feeding
    She met unfaltering from that hour;

---

[2] Adelbert von Chamisso (1781-1838), German poet who created the hapless character of Peter Schlemihl.

She taught them thrift and honest breeding,
    Her virtues were their worldly dower.
To seek employment, one by one,
    Forth with her blessing they departed,
And she was in the world alone,
    Alone and old, but still high-hearted.

With frugal forethought, self-denying,
    She gathered coin, and flax she bought,
And many a night her spindle plying,
    Good store of fine-spun thread she wrought.
The thread was fashioned in the loom;
    She brought it home, and calmly seated
To work, with not a thought of gloom,
    Her decent grave clothes she completed.

She looks on them with fond elation,
    They are her wealth, her treasure rare,
Her age's pride and consolation,
    Hoarded with all a miser's care.
She dons the sark each Sabbath day,
    To hear the Word that faileth never;
Well pleased she lays it then away,
    Till she shall sleep in it for ever.

Would that my spirit witness bore me
    That, like this woman, I had done
The work my Maker put before me,
    Duly from morn till set of sun.
Would that life's cup had been by me
    Quaffed in such wise and happy measure,
And that I too might finally
    Look on my shroud with such meek pleasure.

Such are the noble of the earth. They do not repine; they do not chafe, even in the inmost heart.—They feel that, whatever else may be denied or withdrawn, there remains the better part, which cannot be taken from them. This line exactly expresses the woman I knew:

    "Alone and old, but still high-hearted."

Will any, Poor or Rich, fail to feel that the children of such a parent were rich, when

    "Her virtues were their worldly dower?"

Will any fail to bow the heart in assent to the aspiration—

"Would that my spirit witness bore me
That, like this woman, I had done
The work my Maker put before me,
Duly from morn till set of sun?"

May not that suffice to any man's ambition?

What fits a Man to be a Voter?
Is it to be White Within,
or White Without*

The country had been denuded of its forests, and men cried—"Come! we must plant anew, or there will be no shade for the homes of our children, or fuel for their hearths. Let us find the best kernels for a new growth."

And a basket of butternuts was offered.

But the planters rejected it with disgust. "What a black, rough coat it has," said they; "it is entirely unfit for the dishes on a nobleman's table, nor have we ever seen it in such places. It must have a greasy, offensive kernel; nor can fine trees grow up from such a nut."

"Friends," said one of the planters, "this decision may be rash. The chestnut has not a handsome outside; it is long encased in troublesome burrs, and, when disengaged, is almost as black as these nuts you despise. Yet from it grow trees of lofty stature, graceful form and long life. Its kernel is white and has furnished food to the most poetic and spendid nations of the older world."

"Do n't tell me," says another, "brown is entirely different from black. I like brown very well; there is Oriental precedent for its respectability. Perhaps we will use some of your chestnuts, if we can get fine samples. But for the present I think we should use only English walnuts, such as our forefathers delighted to honor. Here are many basketsfull of them, quite enough for the present. We will plant them with a sprinkling between of the chestnut and acorn." "But," rejoined the other, "many butternuts are beneath the sod, and

---

* In *New-York Daily Tribune*, 31 March 1846, p. 1.

you cannot help a mixture of them being in your wood at any
rate."

"Well! we will grub them up and cut them down wherever
we find them. We can use the young shrubs for kindlings."

At that moment entered the council two persons of a darker
complexion than most of those present, as if born beneath the
glow of a more scorching sun. First came a Woman, beautiful
in the mild, pure grandeur of her look; in whose large dark
eye a prophetic intelligence was mingled with infinite sweetness. She looked at the assembly with an air of surprise,
as if its aspect was strange to her. She threw quite back her
veil, and stepping aside made room for her companion. His
form was youthful, about the age of one we have seen in
many a picture, produced by the thought of eighteen centuries, as of one "instructing the Doctors." I need not describe the features; all minds have their own impressions of
such an image,

"Severe in youthful beauty."

In his hand he bore a little white banner on which was embroidered PEACE AND GOOD WILL TO MEN. And the words
seemed to glitter and give out sparks, as he paused in the
assembly.

"I came hither," said he, "an uninvited guest, because I
read sculptured above the door—'All men born Free and
Equal,' and in this dwelling hoped to find myself at home.
What is the matter in dispute?"

Then they whispered one to another, and murmurs were
heard—"He is a mere boy; young people are always foolish
and extravagant;" or "He looks like a fanatic." But others
said, "He looks like one whom we have been taught to
honor. It will be best to tell him the matter in dispute."

When he heard it, he smiled and said, "It will be needful
first to ascertain which of the nuts is soundest *within*." And
with a hammer he broke one, two, and more of the English
walnuts, and they were mouldy.

Then he tried the other nuts, but found most of them fresh
within and *white*, for they were fresh from the bosom of the
earth, while the others had been kept in a damp cellar.

And he said, "You had better plant them together, lest
none or few of the walnuts be sound. And why are you so

reluctant? Has not Heaven permitted them both to grow on
the same soil? and does not that show what is intended about
it?"

And they said, "But they are black and ugly to look upon."
He replied, "They do not seem so to me. What my Father has
fashioned in such guise offends not mine eye."

And they said, "But from one of these trees flew a bird of
prey who has done great wrong. We meant, therefore, to suffer no such tree among us."

And he replied, "Amid the band of my countrymen and
friends there was one guilty of the blackest crime, that of
selling for a price the life of his dearest friend, yet all the
others of his blood were not put under ban because of his
guilt."

Then they said, "But in the Holy Book our teachers tell us,
we are bid to keep in exile or distress whatsoever is black
and unseemly in our eyes."

Then he put his hand to his brow and cried in a voice of
the most penetrating pathos, "Have I been so long among ye
and ye have not known me?"—And the Woman turned from
them, the majestic hope of her glance, and both forms suddenly vanished, but the banner was left trailing in the dust.

The men stood gazing at one another. After which one
mounted on high and said:

"Perhaps, my friends, we carry too far this aversion to objects merely because they are black. I heard, the other day, a
wise man say that black was the color of evil—marked as
such by God, and that whenever a white man struck a black
man he did an act of worship to God.* I could not quite
believe him. I hope, in what I am about to add, I shall not be
misunderstood. I am no Abolitionist. I respect above all
things, divine or human, the Constitution framed by our
forefathers, and the peculiar institutions hallowed by the
usage of their sons. I have no sympathy with the black race in
this country. I wish it to be understood that I feel toward
negroes the purest personal antipathy. It is a family trait with
us. My little son, scarce able to speak, will cry out "Nigger!
Nigger!" whenever he sees one, and try to throw things at
them. He made a whole omnibus load laugh the other day by

* Fact, that this is affirmed. [Fuller's note.]

his cunning way of doing this.† The child of my political antagonist, on the other hand, says "he likes *tullared* children the best."‡ You see he is tainted in his cradle by the loose principles of his parents, even before he can say nigger or pronounce the more refined appellation. But that is no matter. I merely mention this by the way: not to prejudice you against Mr.——, but that you may appreciate the very different state of things in my family, and not misinterpret what I have to say. I was lately in one of our prisons where a somewhat injudicious indulgence had extended to one of the condemned felons, a lost and wretched outcast from society, the use of materials for painting, that having been his profession. He had completed at his leisure, a picture of the Lord's Supper. Most of the figures were well enough, but Judas he had represented as a black.§—Now, gentlemen, I am of opinion that this is an unwarrantable liberty taken with the Holy Scriptures and shows *too much* prejudice in the community. It is my wish to be moderate and fair, and preserve a medium, neither, on the one hand, yielding the wholesome antipathies planted in our breasts as a safeguard against degradation, and our constitutional obligations, which, as I have before observed, are, with me, more binding than any other; nor on the other hand forgetting that liberality and wisdom which are the prerogative of every citizen of this free Commonwealth. I agree then with our young visitor. I hardly know, indeed, why a stranger and one so young was permitted to mingle in this council, but it was certainly thoughtful in him to crack and examine the nuts. I agree that it may be well to plant some of the black nuts among the others, so that, if many of the walnuts fail, we may make use of this inferior tree."

At this moment arose a hubbub, and such a clamor of "dangerous innovation," "political capital," "low-minded demagogue," "infidel who denies the Bible," "lower link in the chain of creation," &c. that it is impossible to say what was the decision.

---

† Fact. [Fuller's note.]
‡ Fact. [Fuller's note.]
§ Fact. [Fuller's note.].

Melville's *Typee**

"Typee" would seem, also, to be the record of imaginary adventures by some one who had visited those regions. But it is a very entertaining and pleasing narrative, and the Happy Valley of the gentle cannibals compares very well with the best contrivances of the learned Dr. Johnson to produce similar impressions. Of the power of this writer to make pretty and spirited pictures as well of his quick and arch manner generally, a happy specimen may be seen in the account of the savage climbing the cocoa-tree, p. 273, vol. 2d. Many of the observations and narratives we suppose to be strictly correct. Is the account given of the result of the missionary enterprises in the Sandwich Islands of this number? We suppose so from what we have heard in other ways. With a view to ascertaining the truth, it would be well if the sewing societies, now engaged in providing funds for such enterprises would read the particulars, they will find in this book beginning p. 249, vol. 2d, and make inquiries in consequence, before going on with their efforts. Generally, the sewing societies of the country villages will find this the very book they wish to have read while assembled at their work. Othello's hairbreadth 'scapes were nothing to those by this hero in the descent of the cataracts, and many a Desdemona might seriously incline her ear to the descriptions of the lovely Fay-a-way.

* Herman Melville. *Typee*. New York: Wiley & Putnam, 1846. Part of a review of Wiley & Putnam's Library of American Books series in *New-York Daily Tribune*, 4 April 1846, p. 1; title supplied.

Mistress of herself,
though china fall*

Women, in general, are indignant that the satirist should have made this the climax to praise of a woman. And yet, we fear, he saw only too truly.—What unexpected failures have we seen, literally, in this respect! How often did the Martha blur the Mary out of the face of a lovely woman at the sound of a crash amid glass and porcelain![1] What sad littleness in all the department thus represented! Obtrusion of the mop and duster on the tranquil meditations of a husband and brother. Impatience if the carpet be defaced by the feet even of cherished friends!

There is a beautiful side and a good reason here; but why must the beauty degenerate and give place to meanness?

To Woman the care of home is confided. It is the sanctuary of which she should be the guardian angel. To all elements that are introduced there she should be the "ordering mind." She represents the spirit of beauty, and her influence should be spring-like, clothing all objects within her sphere with lively, fresh and tender hues. She represents purity, and all that appertains to her should be kept delicately pure. She is modesty, and draperies should soften all rude lineaments, and exclude glare and dust. She is harmony, and all objects should be in their places, ready for and matched to their uses.

We all feel that there is substantial reason for the offence we feel at defect in any of these ways. A woman who wants purity, modesty, and harmony in her dress and manners is

---

* In *New-York Daily Tribune*, 15 April 1846, p. 4.
[1] Fuller is comparing Martha, goddess of the household and symbol of the active life, with the Virgin Mary, symbol of the contemplative life.

unsufferable—one who wants them in the arrangements of her house disagreeable, to every one. She neglects the most obvious ways of expressing what we desire to see in her, and the inference is ready that the inward sense is wanting.

It is with no merely gross and selfish feeling that all men commend the good housekeeper, the good nurse. Neither is it slight praise to say of a woman that she does well the honors of her house in the way of hospitality. The wisdom that can maintain serenity, cheerfulness and order in a little world of ten or twelve persons, and keep ready the resources that are needed for their sustenance and recovery in sickness and sorrow, is the same that holds the stars in their places and patiently prepares the precious metals in the most secret chambers of the earth. The art of exercising a refined hospitality is a fine art, and the music thus produced only differs from that of the orchestra in this, that in the former case, the overture or sonata can be played twice in the same manner. It requires that the hostess shall combine true self-respect and repose,

"The simple art of not too much,"

with refined perception of individual traits and moods in character, with variety and vivacity, an ease, grace and gentleness that diffuse their sweetness insensibly through every nook of an assembly, and call out reciprocal sweetness wherever there is any to be found.

The only danger in all this is the same that besets us in every walk of life, to wit: that of preferring the outward sign to the inward spirit, whenever there is cause to hesitate between the two.

"I admire," says Goethe, "the Chinese novels; they express so happily ease, peace, and a finish unknown to other nations in the interior arrangements of their homes. In one of them I came upon this line: 'I heard the lovely maidens laughing, and found my way to the garden-house, where they were seated in their light cane chairs.' To me this brings an immediate animation, by the images it suggests of lightness, brightness and elegance."

This is most true, but it is also true that the garden-house would not seem thus charming unless its "light cane chairs" had "lovely laughing maidens" seated in them. And the lady who values her porcelain, that most exquisite product of the peace and thorough breeding of China, so highly, should take the hint, and remember, that, unless the fragrant herb of wit, sweetened by kindness, and softened by the cream of affability also crown her board, the prettiest teacups in the world might as well lie in fragments in the gutter, as adorn her social show. The show loses its beauty when it ceases to represent a substance.

Here, as elsewhere, it is only vanity, narrowness and self-seeking that spoil a good thing. Women would never be too good housekeepers for their own peace or that of others, if they considered housekeeping only as a means to an end. If their object was really the peace and joy of all concerned they could bear to have their cups and saucers broken easier than their tempers, and to have curtains and carpets soiled rather than their hearts by mean and small feelings. But they are brought up to think "it is a disgrace to be a bad housekeeper," not because they must, by such defect, be a cause of suffering and loss of time to all within their sphere, but because other women will laugh at them if they are so. Here is the vice—for want of a high motive, there can be no truly good action.

We have seen a woman otherwise noble and magnanimous in a high degree, so insane on this point as to weep bitterly because she found a little dust on her picture frames, and torment her guests all dinner time, with excuses for the way in which the dinner was cooked. We have known others join with their servants to backbite the best and noblest friends for trifling derelictions against the accustomed order of the house. The broom swept out the memory of much sweet counsel and loving kindness, and spots on the table cloth were more regarded than those they made on their own loyalty and honor in the most intimate relations.

"The worst of furies is a woman scorned," and the sex so lively, mobile, and impassioned, when passion is around at all, are in danger of frightful error under great temptation. The angel can give place to a mere subtle and treacherous demon, though one, generally, of less tantalizing influence, than in the breast of man. In great crises woman needs the highest reason to restrain her, but her besetting danger is that of littleness. Just because nature and society unite to call on

her for such fineness and finish, she can be so petty, so fretful, so vain, so envious and base! O women! see your danger.
See how much you need a great object in all your little actions. You cannot be fair, nor can your homes be fair, unless
you are holy and noble. Will you sweep and garnish the
house only that it may be ready for a legion of evil spirits to
enter in? For imps and demons of gossip, frivolity, detraction
and a restless fever about small ills? What is the house good
for, if good spirits cannot peacefully abide there? Lo! they
are asking for the bill in more than one well-garnished mansion. They sought a home, and found a work-house. Martha!
it was thy fault!

Hawthorne's *Mosses from an Old Manse**

We have been seated here the last ten minutes, pen in hand, thinking what we can possibly say about this book that will not be either superfluous or impertinent.

Superfluous, because the attractions of Hawthorne's writings cannot fail of one and the same effect on all persons who possess the common sympathies of men. To all who are still happy in some groundwork of unperverted Nature, the delicate, simple, human tenderness, unsought, unbought and therefore precious morality, the tranquil elegance and playfulness, the humor which never breaks the impression of sweetness and dignity, do an inevitable message which requires no comment of the critic to make its meaning clear. Impertinent, because the influence of this mind, like that of some loveliest aspects of Nature, is to induce silence from a feeling of repose. We do not think of any thing particularly worth saying about this that has been so fitly and pleasantly said.

Yet is seems unfit that we, in our office of chronicler of intellectual advents and apparitions, should omit to render open and audible honor to one whom we have long delighted to honor. It may be, too, that this slight notice of ours may awaken the attention of those distant or busy who might not otherwise search for the volume, which comes betimes in the leafy month of June.

So we will give a slight account of it, even if we cannot say much of value. Though Hawthorne has now a standard repu-

* Nathaniel Hawthorne. *Mosses from an Old Manse*. New York: Wiley & Putnam, 1846. In *New-York Daily Tribune*, 22 June 1846, p. 1; title supplied.

tation, both for the qualities we have mentioned and the beauty of the style in which they are embodied, yet we believe he has not been very widely read. This is only because his works have not been published in the way to insure extensive circulation in this new, hurrying world of ours. The immense extent of country over which the reading (still very small in proportion to the mere working) community is scattered, the rushing and pushing of our life at this electrical stage of development, leave no work a chance to be speedily and largely known that is not trumpeted and placarded. And, odious as are the features of a forced and artificial circulation, it must be considered that it does no harm in the end. Bad books will not be read if they are bought instead of good, while the good have no abiding life in the log-cabin settlements and Red River steamboat landings, to which they would in no other way penetrate. Under the auspices of Wiley and Putnam, Hawthorne will have a chance to collect all his own public about him, and that be felt as a presence which before was only a rumor.

The volume before us shares the charms of Hawthorne's earlier tales; the only difference being that his range of subjects is a little wider. There is the same gentle and sincere companionship with Nature, the same delicate but fearless scrutiny of the secrets of the heart, the same serene independence of petty and artificial restrictions, whether on opinions or conduct, the same familiar, yet pensive sense of the spiritual or demoniacal influences that haunt the palpable life and common walks of men, not by many apprehended except in results. We have here to regret that Hawthorne, at this stage of his mind's life, lay no more decisive hand upon the apparition—brings it no nearer than in former days.—We had hoped that we should see, no more as in a glass darkly, but face to face. Still, still brood over his page the genius of revery and the nonchalance of Nature, rather than the ardent earnestness of the human soul which feels itself born not only to see and disclose, but to understand and interpret such things. Hawthorne intimates and suggests, but he does not lay bare the mysteries of our being.

The introduction to the "Mosses," in which the old Manse, its inhabitants and visitants are portrayed, is written with even more than his usual charm of placid grace and many strokes of his admirable good sense. Those who are not, like ourselves, familiar with the scene and its denizens, will still perceive how true that picture must be; those of us who are thus familiar will best know how to prize the record of objects and influences unique in our country and time.

"The Birth Mark" and "Rappaccini's Daughter" embody truths of profound importance in shapes of aerial elegance. In these, as here and there in all these pieces, shines the loveliest ideal of love and the beauty of feminine purity, (by which we mean no mere acts or abstinences, but perfect single truth felt and done in gentleness) which is its root.

"The Celestial Railroad," for its wit, wisdom, and the graceful adroitness with which the natural and material objects are interwoven with the allegories, has already won its meed of admiration.—"Fire-worship" is a most charming essay for its domestic sweetness and thoughtful life. "Goodman Brown" is one of those disclosures we have spoken of, of the secrets of the breast. Who has not known such a trial that is capable indeed of sincere aspiration toward that only good, that infinite essence, which men call God. Who has not known the hour when even that best-beloved image cherished as the one precious symbol left, in the range of human nature, believed to be still pure gold when all the rest have turned to clay, shows, in severe ordeal, the symptoms of alloy. Oh hour of anguish, when the old familiar faces grow dark and dim in the lurid light—when the gods of the hearth, honored in childhood, adored in youth, crumble, and nothing, nothing is left which the daily earthly feelings can embrace—can cherish with unbroken Faith! Yet some survive that trial more happily than young Goodman Brown. They are those who have not sought it—have never of their own accord walked forth with the Tempter into the dim shades of Doubt. Mrs. Bull-Frog is an excellent humorous picture of what is called to be "content at last with substantial realities"!! The "Artist of the Beautiful" presents in a form that is, indeed, beautiful, the opposite view as to what *are* the substantial realities of life. Let each man choose between them according to his kind: Had Hawthorne written "Roger Malvin's Burial" alone, we should be pervaded with the sense of the poetry and religion of his soul.

As a critic, the style of Hawthorne, faithful to his mind,

shows repose, a great reserve of strength, a slow secure movement. Though a very refined, he is also a very clear writer, showing, as we said before, a placid grace, and an indolent command of language.

And now, beside the full, calm yet romantic stream of his mind, we will rest. It has refreshment for the weary, islets of fascination no less than dark recesses and shadows for the imaginative, pure reflections for the pure of heart and eye, and, like the Concord he so well describes, many exquisite lilies for him who knows how to get at them.

Brown's Novels*

We rejoice to see these reprints of Brown's novels, as we have long been ashamed that one who ought to be the pride of the country, and who is, in the higher qualities of the mind, so far in advance of our other novelists, should have become almost inaccessible to the public.

It has been the custom to liken Brown to Godwin.[1] But there was no imitation, no second hand in the matter. They were congenial natures, and whichever had come first might have lent an impulse to the other. Either mind might have been conscious of the possession of that peculiar vein of ore without thinking of working it for the mint of the world, till the other, led by accident, or overflow of feeling, showed him how easy it was to put the reveries of his solitary hours into words and upon paper for the benefit of his fellow men.

"My mind to me a kingdom is."[2]

Such a man as Brown or Godwin has a right to say that. It is no scanty, turbid rill, requiring to be daily fed from a thousand others or from the clouds! Its plenteous source rushes from a high mountain between bulwarks of stone. Its course, even and full, keeps ever green its banks, and affords the means of life and joy to a million gliding shapes, that fill its deep waters, and twinkle about its golden sands.

Life and Joy! Yes, Joy! These two have been called the dark Masters, because they disclose the twilight recesses of

* Charles Brockden Brown's *Wieland; Or, the Transformation* (1798) and *Ormond; Or, the Secret Witness* (1799) were both reprinted in New York by W. Taylor in 1846. In *New-York Daily Tribune*, 21 July 1846, p. 1; title supplied.
[1] William Godwin; see note 68, p. 129 above.
[2] Sir Edward Dyer (1543?-1607), "My Mind to Me a Kingdom Is."

375

the human heart. Yet their gravest page is joy compared with the mixed, shallow, uncertain pleasures of vulgar minds. Joy! because they were all alive and fulfilled the purposes of being. No sham, no imitation, no convention deformed or veiled their native lineaments, checked the use of their natural force. All alive themselves, they understood that there is no joy without truth, no perception of joy without real life. Unlike most men, existence was to them not a tissue of words and seemings, but a substantial possession.

Born Hegelians, without the pretensions of science, they sought God in their own consciousness, and found him.[3] The heart, because it saw itself so fearfully and wonderfully made, did not disown its Maker. With the highest idea of the dignity, power and beauty of which human nature is capable they had courage to see by what an oblique course it proceeds, yet never lose faith that it would reach its destined aim. Thus their darkest disclosures are not hobgoblin shows, but precious revelations.

Brown is great as ever human writer was in showing the self-sustaining force of which a lonely mind is capable. He takes one person, makes him brood like the bee, and extract from the common life before him all its sweetness, its bitterness, and its nourishment.

We say makes *him*, but it increases our own interest in Brown that, a prophet in this respect of a better era, he has usually placed this thinking royal mind in the body of a woman. This personage too is always feminine, both in her character and circumstances, but a conclusive proof that the term *feminine* is not a synonym for *weak*. Constantia, Clara Wieland, have loving hearts, graceful and plastic natures, but they have also noble thinking minds, full of resource, constancy, courage. The Marguerite of Godwin, no less, is all refinement, and the purest tenderness, but she is also the soul of honor, capable of deep discernment, and of acting in conformity with the inferences she draws.[4] The Man of Brown and Godwin has not eaten of the fruit of the tree of

---

[3] Hegelians, followers of the German idealistic philosopher Georg Wilhelm Hegel (1770-1831).

[4] Marguerite, heroine of Godwin's novel *St. Leon* (1799); see also p. 130 and note 70 above.

knowledge and been driven to sustain himself by the sweat of his brow for nothing, but has learned the structure and laws of things, and become a being, natural, benignant, various, and desirous of supplying the loss of innocence by the attainment of virtue. So his Woman need not be quite so weak as Eve, the slave of feeling or of flattery: she also has learned to guide her helm amid the storm across the troubled waters.

The horrors which mysteriously beset these persons, and against which, so far as outward facts go, they often strive in vain, are but a representation of those powers permitted to work in the same way throughout the affairs of this world. Their demoniacal attributes only represent a morbid state of the intellect, gone to excess from want of balance with the other powers. There is an intellectual as well as a physical drunkenness and which, no less, impels to crime. Carwin, urged on to use his ventriloquism, till the presence of such a strange agent wakened the seeds of fanaticism in the breast of Wieland, is in a state no more foreign to nature than that of the wretch executed last week, who felt himself drawn as by a spell to murder his victim because he had thought of her money and the pleasures it might bring him, till the feeling possessed his brain that hurls the gamester to ruin. The victims of such agency are like the soldier of the Rio Grande, who, both legs shot off and his life-blood rushing out with every pulse, replied serenely to his pitying comrades that "he had now that for which the soldier enlisted." The end of the drama is not in this world, and the fiction which rounds off the whole to harmony and felicity before the curtain falls, sins against truth, and deludes the reader. The Nelsons of the human race are all the more exposed to the assaults of Fate that they are decorated with the badges of well-earned glory.[5] Who but feels as they fall in death, or rise again to a mutilated existence, that the end is not yet? Who, that thinks, but must feel that the recompense is, where Brown places it, in the accumulation of mental treasure, in the severe assay by fire that leaves the gold pure to be used sometime—somewhere.

Brown, man of the brooding eye, the teeming brain, the

---

[5] Horatio Nelson (1758-1805), English admiral.

deep and fervent heart; if thy country prize thee not and has almost lost thee out of sight, it is that her heart is made shallow and cold, her eye dim, by the pomp of circumstance, the love of gross outward gain. She cannot long continue thus for it takes a great deal of soul to keep a huge body from disease and dissolution. As there is more soul thou wilt be more sought, and many will yet sit down with thy Constantia to the meal and water on which she sustained her full and thoughtful existence who could not endure the ennui of aldermanic dinners, or find any relish in the imitation of French cookery. To-day many will read the words, and some have a cup large enough to receive the spirit, before it is lost in the sand on which their feet are planted.

Brown's high standard of the delights of intellectual communion and of friendship correspond with the fondest hopes of early days. But in the relations of real life, at present, there is rarely more than one of the parties ready for such intercourse as he describes. On the one side there will be dryness, want of perception or variety, a stupidity unable to appreciate life's richest boon when offered to its grasp, and the finer nature is doomed to retrace its steps, unhappy as those who having force to raise a spirit cannot retain or make it substantial, and stretch out their arms only to bring them back empty to the breast.

We were glad to see those reprints, but angry to see them so carelessly done. Casting the eye lightly over the page we find *feign* for *fain*, *illegibility* for *eligibility* and the like. Under the cheap system, the carelessness in printing and translating grows to a greater excess day by day. Please, Public, to remonstrate, else very soon all your books will be offered for two shillings apiece and none of them in a fit state to be read.

Farewell*

Farewell to New-York City, where twenty months have presented me with a richer and more varied exercise for thought and life than twenty years could in any other part of these United States.

It is the common remark about New-York that it has, at least, nothing petty or provincial in its methods and habits. The place is large enough; there is room enough and occupation enough for men to have no need or excuse for small cavils or scrutinies. A person who is independent and knows what he wants, may lead his proper life here unimpeded by others.

Vice and Crime, if flagrant and frequent, are less thickly coated by Hypocrisy than elsewhere. The air comes sometimes to the most infected subjects.

New-York is the focus, the point where American and European interests converge. There is no topic of general interest to men that will not betimes be brought before the thinker by the quick turning of the wheel.

Too quick that revolution, some object. Life rushes wide and free, but *too fast*; yet it is in the power of every one to avert from himself the evil that accompanies the good. He must build for his study, as did the German poet, a house beneath the bridge, and, then, all that passes above and by him will be heard and seen, but he will not be carried away with it.

Earlier views have been confirmed and many new ones

* In *New-York Daily Tribune*, 1 August 1846, p. 2. A writer in the *National Anti-Slavery Standard* complained that when Fuller wrote that she had experienced more "thought and life" in twenty months in New York City than was possible in twenty years elsewhere in America, she was showing egotism and aloofness (VII [6 August 1846], 38).

opened. On two great leadings,—the superlative importance of promoting National Education by hightening and deepening the cultivation of individual minds, and the part which is assigned to Woman in the next stage of human progress in this country, where most important achievements are to be effected, I have received much encouragement, much instruction, and the fairest hopes of more.

On various subjects of minor importance, no less than these, I hope for good results from observation with my own eyes of Life in the Old World, and to bring home some packages of seed for Life in the New.

These words I address to my friends, for I feel that I have some. The degree of sympathetic response to the thoughts and suggestions I have offered through the columns of this paper has indeed surprised me, conscious as I am of a natural and acquired aloofness from many, if not most, popular tendencies of my time and place. It has greatly encouraged me, for none can sympathize with thoughts like mine who are permanently ensnared in the meshes of sect or party; none who prefer the formation and advancement of mere opinions to the free pursuit of Truth. I see, surely, that the topmost bubble or sparkle of the cup is no voucher for the nature of its contents throughout, and shall, in future, feel that in our age, nobler in that respect than most of the preceding, each sincere and fervent act or word is secure, not only of a final, but a speedy, response.

I go to behold the wonders of art, and the temples of old religion. But I shall see no forms of beauty and majesty beyond what my Country is capable of producing in myriad variety, if she has but the soul to will it; no temple to compare with what she might erect in the Ages, if the catch-word of the time, a sense of DIVINE ORDER, should become, no more a mere word or effigy, but a deeply rooted and pregnant Idea in her life. Beneath the light of a hope that this may be, I ask of my friends once more a kind Farewell.

American Literature;
Its Position in the Present Time, and Prospects for the Future*

Some thinkers may object to this essay, that we are about to write of that which has, as yet, no existence.

For it does not follow because many books are written by persons born in America that there exists an American literature. Books which imitate or represent the thoughts and life of Europe do not constitute an American literature. Before such can exist, an original idea must animate this nation and fresh currents of life must call into life fresh thoughts along its shores.

We have no sympathy with national vanity. We are not anxious to prove that there is as yet much American literature. Of those who think and write among us in the methods and of the thoughts of Europe, we are not impatient; if their minds are still best adapted to such food and such action. If their books express life of mind and character in graceful forms, they are good and we like them. We consider them as colonists and useful schoolmasters to our people in a transition state; which lasts rather longer than is occupied in passing, bodily, the ocean which separates the new from the old world.

We have been accused of an undue attachment to foreign continental literature, and, it is true, that in childhood, we had well nigh "forgotten our English," while constantly reading in other languages. Still, what we loved in the literature of continental Europe was the range and force of ideal man-

* From *Papers on Literature and Art* (New York: Wiley & Putnam, 1846), II, 122-143.

ifestation in forms of national and individual greatness. A model was before us in the great Latins of simple masculine minds seizing upon life with unbroken power. The stamp both of nationality and individuality was very strong upon them; their lives and thoughts stood out in clear and bold relief. The English character has the iron force of the Latins, but not the frankness and expansion. Like their fruits, they need a summer sky to give them more sweetness and a richer flavour. This does not apply to Shakspeare, who has all the fine side of English genius, with the rich colouring, and more fluent life, of the Catholic countries. Other poets, of England also, are expansive more or less, and soar freely to seek the blue sky, but take it as a whole, there is in English literature, as in English character, a reminiscence of walls and ceilings, a tendency to the arbitrary and conventional that repels a mind trained in admiration of the antique spirit. It is only in later days that we are learning to prize the peculiar greatness which a thousand times outweighs this fault, and which has enabled English genius to go forth from its insular position and conquer such vast dominion in the realms both of matter and of mind.

Yet there is, often, between child and parent, a reaction from excessive influence having been exerted, and such an one we have experienced, in behalf of our country, against England. We use her language, and receive, in torrents, the influence of her thought, yet it is, in many respects, uncongenial and injurious to our constitution. What suits Great Britain, with her insular position and consequent need to concentrate and intensify her life, her limited monarchy, and spirit of trade, does not suit a mixed race, continually enriched with new blood from other stocks the most unlike that of our first descent, with ample field and verge enough to range in and leave every impulse free, and abundant opportunity to develope a genius, wide and full as our rivers, flowery, luxuriant and impassioned as our vast prairies, rooted in strength as the rocks on which the Puritan fathers landed.

That such a genius is to rise and work in this hemisphere we are confident; equally so that scarce the first faint streaks of that day's dawn are yet visible. It is sad for those that foresee, to know they may not live to share its glories, yet it is sweet, too, to know that every act and word, uttered in the light of that foresight, may tend to hasten or ennoble its fulfilment.

That day will not rise till the fusion of races among us is more complete. It will not rise till this nation shall attain sufficient moral and intellectual dignity to prize moral and intellectual, no less highly than political, freedom, not till, the physical resources of the country being explored, all its regions studded with towns, broken by the plow, netted together by railways and telegraph lines, talent shall be left at leisure to turn its energies upon the higher department of man's existence. Nor then shall it be seen till from the leisurely and yearning soul of that riper time national ideas shall take birth, ideas craving to be clothed in a thousand fresh and original forms.

Without such ideas all attempts to construct a national literature must end in abortions like the monster of Frankenstein, things with forms, and the instincts of forms, but soulless, and therefore revolting. We cannot have expression till there is something to be expressed.

The symptoms of such a birth may be seen in a longing felt here and there for the sustenance of such ideas. At present, it shows itself, where felt, in sympathy with the prevalent tone of society, by attempts at external action, such as are classed under the head of social reform. But it needs to go deeper, before we can have poets, needs to penetrate beneath the springs of action, to stir and remake the soil as by the action of fire.

Another symptom is the need felt by individuals of being even sternly sincere. This is the one great means by which alone progress can be essentially furthered. Truth is the nursing mother of genius. No man can be absolutely true to himself, eschewing cant, compromise, servile imitation, and complaisance, without becoming original, for there is in every creature a fountain of life which, if not choked back by stones and other dead rubbish, will create a fresh atmosphere, and bring to life fresh beauty. And it is the same with the nation as with the individual man.

The best work we do for the future is by such truth. By use of that, in whatever way, we harrow the soil and lay it open to the sun and air. The winds from all quarters of the globe bring seed enough, and there is nothing wanting but preparation of the soil, and freedom in the atmosphere, for ripening of a new and golden harvest.

We are sad that we cannot be present at the gathering in of this harvest. And yet we are joyous, too, when we think that though our name may not be writ on the pillar of our country's fame, we can really do far more towards rearing it, than those who come at a later period and to a seemingly fairer task. *Now*, the humblest effort, made in a noble spirit, and with religious hope, cannot fail to be even infinitely useful. Whether we introduce some noble model from another time and clime, to encourage aspiration in our own, or cheer into blossom the simplest wood-flower that ever rose from the earth, moved by the genuine impulse to grow, independent of the lures of money or celebrity; whether we speak boldly when fear or doubt keep others silent, or refuse to swell the popular cry upon an unworthy occasion, the spirit of truth, purely worshipped, shall turn our acts and forbearances alike to profit, informing them with oracles which the latest time shall bless.

Under present circumstances the amount of talent and labour given to writing ought to surprise us. Literature is in this dim and struggling state, and its pecuniary results exceedingly pitiful. From many well known causes it is impossible for ninety-nine out of the hundred, who wish to use the pen, to ransom, by its use, the time they need. This state of things will have to be changed in some way. No man of genius writes for money; but it is essential to the free use of his powers, that he should be able to disembarrass his life from care and perplexity. This is very difficult here; and the state of things gets worse and worse, as less and less is offered in pecuniary meed for works demanding great devotion of time and labour (to say nothing of the ether engaged) and the publisher, obliged to regard the transaction as a matter of business, demands of the author to give him only what will find an immediate market, for he cannot afford to take any thing else. This will not do! When an immortal poet was secure only of a few copyists to circulate his works, there were princes and nobles to patronize literature and the arts. Here is only the public, and the public must learn how to cherish the nobler and rarer plants, and to plant the aloe, able to wait a hundred years for its bloom, or its garden will contain, presently, nothing but potatoes and pot-herbs. We shall have, in the course of the next two or three years, a convention of authors to inquire into the causes of this state of things and propose measures for its remedy. Some have already been thought of that look promising, but we shall not announce them till the time be ripe; that date is not distant, for the difficulties increase from day to day, in consequence of the system of cheap publication, on a great scale.

The ranks that led the way in the first half century of this republic were far better situated than we, in this respect. The country was not so deluged with the dingy page, reprinted from Europe, and patriotic vanity was on the alert to answer the question, "Who reads an American book?" And many were the books written, worthy to be read, as any out of the first class in England. They were, most of them, except in their subject matter, English books.

The list is large, and, in making some cursory comments, we do not wish to be understood as designating *all* who are worthy of notice, but only those who present themselves to our minds with some special claims. In history there has been nothing done to which the world at large has not been eager to award the full meed of its deserts. Mr. Prescott, for instance, has been greeted with as much warmth abroad as here.[1] We are not disposed to undervalue his industry and power of clear and elegant arrangement. The richness and freshness of his materials is such that a sense of enchantment must be felt in their contemplation. We must regret, however, that they should have been first presented to the public by one who possesses nothing of the higher powers of the historian, great leading views, or discernment as to the motives of action and the spirit of an era. Considering the splendour of the materials the books are wonderfully tame, and every one must feel that having once passed through them and got the sketch in the mind, there is nothing else to which it will recur. The absence of thought, as to that great picture of Mexican life, with its heroisms, its terrible but deeply significant superstitions, its admirable civic refinement, seems to be quite unbroken.

Mr. Bancroft is a far more vivid writer; he has great re-

[1] William Hickling Prescott; see note 52, p. 123 above.

sources and great command of them, and leading thoughts by whose aid he groups his facts.[2] But we cannot speak fully of his historical works, which we have only read and referred to here and there.

In the department of ethics and philosophy, we may inscribe two names as likely to live and be blessed and honoured in the later time. These are the names of Channing and of Emerson.

Dr. Channing had several leading thoughts which corresponded with the wants of his time, and have made him in it a father of thought. His leading idea of "the dignity of human nature" is one of vast results, and the peculiar form in which he advocated it had a great work to do in this new world. The spiritual beauty of his writings is very great; they are all distinguished for sweetness, elevation, candour, and a severe devotion to truth. On great questions, he took middle ground, and sought a panoramic view; he wished also to stand high, yet never forgot what was above more than what was around and beneath him. He was not well acquainted with man on the impulsive and passionate side of his nature, so that his view of character was sometimes narrow, but it was always noble. He exercised an expansive and purifying power on the atmosphere, and stands a godfather at the baptism of this country.

The Sage of Concord has a very different mind, in every thing except that he has the same disinterestedness and dignity of purpose, the same purity of spirit. He is a profound thinker. He is a man of ideas, and deals with causes rather than effects. His ideas are illustrated from a wide range of literary culture and refined observation, and embodied in a style whose melody and subtle fragrance enchant those who stand stupified before the thoughts themselves, because their utmost depths do not enable them to sound his shallows. His influence does not yet extend over a wide space; he is too far beyond his place and his time, to be felt at once or in full, but it searches deep, and yearly widens its circles. He is a harbinger of the better day. His beautiful elocution has been a

---

[2] George Bancroft (1800-1891), statesman and historian; the first volume of his monumental *History of the United States* appeared in 1834.

great aid to him in opening the way for the reception of his written word.

In that large department of literature which includes descriptive sketches, whether of character or scenery, we are already rich. Irving, a genial and fair nature, just what he ought to be, and would have been, at any time of the world, has drawn the scenes amid which his youth was spent in their primitive lineaments, with all the charms of his graceful jocund humour. He has his niche and need never be deposed; it is not one that another could occupy.

The first enthusiasm about Cooper having subsided, we remember more his faults than his merits.[3] His ready resentment and way of showing it in cases which it is the wont of gentlemen to pass by in silence, or meet with a good humoured smile, have caused unpleasant associations with his name, and his fellow citizens, in danger of being tormented by suits for libel, if they spoke freely of him, have ceased to speak of him at all. But neither these causes, nor the baldness of his plots, shallowness of thought, and poverty in the presentation of character, should make us forget the grandeur and originality of his sea-sketches, nor the redemption from oblivion of our forest-scenery, and the noble romance of the hunter-pioneer's life. Already, but for him, this fine page of life's romance would be almost forgotten. He has done much to redeem these irrevocable beauties from the corrosive acid of a semi-civilized invasion.*

[3] James Fenimore Cooper brought many successful lawsuits against the press for their attacks on his books and personal character.

* Since writing the above we have read some excellent remarks by Mr. W.G. Simms on the writings of Cooper. We think the reasons are given for the powerful interest excited by Hawk Eye and the Pilot, with great discrimination and force.

"They both think and feel, with a highly individual nature, that has been taught, by constant contemplation, in scenes of solitude. The vast unbroken ranges of forest to its one lonely occupant press upon the mind with the same sort of solemnity which one feels condemned to a life of partial isolation upon the ocean. Both are permitted that degree of commerce with their fellow beings, which suffices to maintain in strength the sweet and sacred sources of their humanity. * * * The very isolation to which, in the most successful of his stories, Mr. Cooper subjects his favourite personages, is, alone, a proof of his strength and genius. While the ordinary writer, the man of mere talent, is compelled to look around him among masses for his

Miss Sedgwick and others have portrayed, with skill and feeling, scenes and personages from the revolutionary time. Such have a permanent value in proportion as their subject is fleeting. The same charm attends the spirited delineations of Mrs. Kirkland, and that amusing book, "A New Purchase."[4] The features of Hoosier, Sucker, and Wolverine life are worth fixing; they are peculiar to the soil, and indicate its hidden treasures; they have, also, that charm which simple life, lived for its own sake, always has, even in rude and all but brutal forms.

What shall we say of the poets? The list is scanty; amazingly so, for there is nothing in the causes that paralyze other kinds of literature that could affect lyrical and narrative poetry. Men's hearts beat, hope, and suffer always, and they must crave such means to vent them; yet of the myriad leaves garnished with smooth stereotyped rhymes that issue yearly from our press, you will not find, one time in a million, a little piece written from any such impulse, or with the least sincerity or sweetness of tone. They are written for the press, in the spirit of imitation or vanity, the paltriest offspring of the human brain, for the heart disclaims, as the ear is shut against them. This is the kind of verse which is cherished by the magazines as a correspondent to the tawdry pictures of smiling milliners' dolls in the frontispiece. Like these they are only a fashion, a fashion based on no reality of love or beauty. The inducement to write them consists in a little

material, he contents himself with one man, and flings him upon the wilderness. The picture, then, which follows, must be one of intense individuality. Out of this one man's nature, his moods and fortunes, he spins his story. The agencies and dependencies are few. With the self-reliance which is only found in true genius, he goes forward into the wilderness, whether of land or ocean; and the vicissitudes of either region, acting upon the natural resources of one man's mind, furnish the whole material of his work-shop. This mode of performance is highly dramatic, and thus it is that his scout, his trapper, his hunter, his pilot, all live to our eyes and thoughts, the perfect ideals of moral individuality."

No IX. Wiley and Putnam's Library of American books. Views and Reviews by W.G. Simms. [Fuller's note.] William Gilmore Simms (1806-1870), South Carolina novelist whose *Views and Reviews in American Literature, History and Fiction* was published in 1845.

[4] Mrs. Caroline Kirkland (1801-1864), whose *A New Home—Who'll Follow?* was published in 1839.

money, or more frequently the charm of seeing an anonymous name printed at the top in capitals.

We must here, in passing, advert also to the style of story current in the magazines, flimsy beyond any texture that was ever spun or even dreamed of by the mind of man, in any other age and country. They are said to be "written for the seamstresses," but we believe that every way injured class could relish and digest better fare even at the end of long days of exhausting labour. There are exceptions to this censure; stories by Mrs. Child have been published in the magazines, and now and then good ones by Mrs. Stephens and others;[5] but, take them generally, they are calculated to do a positive injury to the public mind, acting as an opiate, and of an adulterated kind, too.

But to return to the poets. At their head Mr. Bryant stands alone. His range is not great, nor his genius fertile. But his poetry is purely the language of his inmost nature, and the simple lovely garb in which his thoughts are arranged, a direct gift from the Muse. He has written nothing that is not excellent, and the atmosphere of his verse refreshes and composes the mind, like leaving the highway to enter some green, lovely, fragrant wood.

Halleck and Willis are poets of society.[6] Though the former has written so little, yet that little is full of fire,—elegant, witty, delicate in sentiment. It is an honour to the country that these occasional sparks, struck off from the flint of commercial life, should have kindled so much flame as they have. It is always a consolation to see one of them sparkle amid the rubbish of daily life. One of his poems has been published within the last year, written, in fact, long ago, but new to most of us, and it enlivened the literary thoroughfare, as a green wreath might some dusty, musty hall of legislation.

Willis has not the same terseness or condensed electricity. But he has grace, spirit, at times a winning pensiveness, and a lively, though almost wholly sensuous, delight in the beautiful.

[5] Mrs. Anne Stephens (1813-1886) wrote over two dozen novels of English and American history.

[6] Fitz-Greene Halleck (1790-1867), New York poet; Nathaniel Parker Willis (1806-1867), New York newspaperman and poet.

Dana has written so little that he would hardly be seen in a more thickly garnished galaxy.[7] But the masculine strength of feeling, the solemn tenderness and refined thought displayed in such pieces as the "Dying Raven," and the "Husband and Wife's Grave," have left a deep impression on the popular mind.

Longfellow is artificial and imitative. He borrows incessantly, and mixes what he borrows, so that it does not appear to the best advantage. He is very faulty in using broken or mixed metaphors. The ethical part of his writing has a hollow, second–hand sound. He has, however, elegance, a love of the beautiful, and a fancy for what is large and manly, if not a full sympathy with it. His verse breathes at times much sweetness; and, if not allowed to supersede what is better may promote a taste for good poetry. Though imitative, he is not mechanical.

We cannot say as much for Lowell, who, we must declare it, though to the grief of some friends, and the disgust of more, is absolutely wanting in the true spirit and tone of poesy.[8] His interest in the moral questions of the day has supplied the want of vitality in himself; his great facility at versification has enabled him to fill the ear with a copious stream of pleasant sound. But his verse is stereotyped; his thought sounds no depth, and posterity will not remember him.

R. W. Emerson, in melody, in subtle beauty of thought and expression, takes the highest rank upon this list. But his poems are mostly philosophical, which is not the truest kind of poetry. They want the simple force of nature and passion, and, while they charm the ear and interest the mind, fail to wake far-off echoes in the heart. The imagery wears a symbolical air, and serves rather as illustration, than to delight us by fresh and glowing forms of life.

We must here mention one whom the country has not yet learned to honour, perhaps never may, for he wants artistic skill to give complete form to his inspiration. This is William Ellery Channing, nephew and namesake of Dr. C., a volume

---

[7] Richard Henry Dana, Sr. (1787-1879), poet and founder of the *North American Review*.

[8] For more on Lowell and Fuller, see pp. 27, 59 above.

of whose poems, published three or four years ago in Boston, remains unknown, except to a few friends, nor, if known, would they probably, excite sympathy, as those which have been published in the periodicals have failed to do so.[9] Yet some of the purest tones of the lyre are his, the finest inspirations as to the feelings and passions of men, deep spiritual insight, and an entire originality in the use of his means. The frequently unfinished and obscure state of his poems, a passion for forcing words out of their usual meaning into one which they may appropriately bear, but which comes upon the reader with an unpleasing and puzzling surprise, may repel, at first glance, from many of these poems, but do not mar the following sublime description of the beings we want, to rule, to redeem, to re-create this nation, and under whose reign alone can there be an American literature, for then only could we have life worth recording. The simple grandeur of this poem as a whole, must be felt by every one, while each line and thought will be found worthy of earnest contemplation and satisfaction after the most earnest life and thought.

> Hearts of Eternity! hearts of the deep!
> Proclaim from land to sea your mighty fate;
> How that for you no living comes too late;
> How ye cannot in Theban labyrinth creep;
> How ye great harvests from small surface reap;
> Shout, excellent band, in grand primeval strain,
> Like midnight winds that foam along the main,
> And do all things rather than pause to weep.
> A human heart knows naught of littleness,
> Suspects no man, compares with no man's ways,
> Hath in one hour most glorious length of days,
> A recompense, a joy, a loveliness;
> Like eaglet keen, shoots into azure far,
> And always dwelling nigh is the remotest star.

A series of poems, called "Man in the Republic," by Cornelius Mathews, deserves a higher meed of sympathy than it has received.[10] The thoughts and views are strong and noble, the exhibition of them imposing. In plastic power this writer

---

[9] Ellery Channing, married to Fuller's sister Ellen; see note 157, p. 216 above. "Sonnet. IV." is quoted from his *Poems* (1843).
[10] Cornelius Mathews (1817-1889), New York editor, novelist, and poet.

is deficient. His prose works sin in exuberance, and need consolidating and chastening. We find fine things, but not so arranged as to be seen in the right places and by the best light. In his poems Mr. Mathews is unpardonably rough and rugged; the poetic substance finds no musical medium in which to flow. Yet there *is* poetic substance which makes full chords, if not a harmony. He holds a worthy sense of the vocation of the poet, and worthily expresses it thus:—

> To strike or bear, to conquer or to yield
> Teach thou! O topmost crown of duty, teach,
> What fancy whispers to the listening ear,
> At hours when tongue nor taint of care impeach
> The fruitful calm of greatly silent hearts;
> When all the stars for happy thought are set,
> And, in the secret chambers of the soul,
> All blessed powers of joyful truth are met;
> Though calm and garlandless thou mayst appear,
> The world shall know thee for its crowned seer.

A considerable portion of the hope and energy of this country still turns towards the drama, that greatest achievement when wrought to perfection of human power. For ourselves, we believe the day of the regular drama to be past; and, though we recognize the need of some kind of spectacle and dramatic representation to be absolutely coincident with an animated state of the public mind, we have thought that the opera, ballet, pantomime and briefer, more elastic forms, like the *vaudeville* of the French theatre, or the *proverb* of the social party, would take the place of elaborate tragedy and comedy.

But those who find the theatres of this city well filled all the year round by an audience willing to sit out the heroisms of Rolla,[11] and the sentimentalism and stale morality of such a piece as we were doomed to listen to while the Keans were here,[12] ("Town and Country" was its name,) still think there is room for the regular drama, if genius should engage in its creation. Accordingly there have been in this country, as well as in England, many attempts to produce dramas suitable for

[11] *Rolla*, a verse tale by Alfred de Musset (1810-1857), published in 1833.
[12] The Keans were a famous English acting family best-known for their productions of Shakespeare's plays.

action no less than for the closet. The actor, Murdoch, about to devote himself with enthusiasm and hope to prop up a falling profession, is to bring out a series of plays written, not merely *for* him, but because his devotion is likely to furnish fit occasion for their appearance. The first of these, "Witchcraft, a tragedy," brought out successfully upon the boards at Philadelphia,[13] we have read, and it is a work of strong and majestic lineaments; a fine originality is shown in the conception, by which the love of a son for a mother is made a sufficient *motiv* (as the Germans call the ruling impulse of a work) in the production of tragic interest; no less original is the attempt, and delightful the success, in making an aged woman a satisfactory heroine to the piece through the greatness of her soul, and the magnetic influence it exerts on all around her, till the ignorant and superstitious fancy that the sky darkens and the winds wait upon her as she walks on the lonely hill-side near her hut to commune with the Past, and seek instruction from Heaven. The working of her character on the other agents of the piece is depicted with force and nobleness. The deep love of her son for her, the little tender, simple ways in which he shows it, having preserved the purity and poetic spirit of childhood by never having been weaned from his first love, a mother's love, the anguish of his soul when he too becomes infected with distrust, and cannot discriminate the natural magnetism of a strong nature from the spells and lures of sorcery, the final triumph of his faith, all offered the highest scope to genius and the power of moral perception in the actor. There are highly poetic intimations of those lowering days with their veiled skies, brassy light, and sadly whispering winds, very common in Massachusetts, so ominous and brooding seen from any point, but from the idea of witchcraft, invested with an awful significance. We do not know, however, that this could bring it beyond what it has appeared to our own sane mind, as if the air was thick with spirits, in an equivocal and surely sad condition, whether of purgatory or downfall; and the air was vocal with all manner of dark intimations. We are glad to see this mood of nature so fitly characterized.

[13] Fuller included more comments on "The Tragedy of Witchcraft" and reprinted a review of the play from the New York *Evening Post* as an "Appendix" to *Papers on Literature and Art* (II, 177-183).

The sweetness and *naiveté* with which the young girl is made to describe the effects of love upon her, as supposing them to proceed from a spell, are also original, and there is no other way in which this revelation could have been induced that would not have injured the beauty of the character and position. Her visionary sense of her lover, as an ideal figure, is of a high order of poetry, and these facts have very seldom been brought out from the cloisters of the mind into the light of open day.

The play is very deficient as regards rhythm; indeed, we might say there is no apparent reason why the lines should begin with capital letters. The minor personages are mere caricatures, very coarsely drawn; all the power is concentrated on the main characters and their emotions. So did not Shakspeare, does not ever the genuine dramatist, whose mind teems with "the fulness of forms." As Raphael in his most crowded groups can put in no misplaced or imperfect foot or hand, neither neglect to invest the least important figure of his backgrounds with every characteristic trait, nor could spare the invention of the most beautiful *coiffure* and accessories for the humblest handmaid of his Madonnas, so doth the great artist always clothe the whole picture with full and breathing life, for it appears so before his mental eye. But minds not perfectly artistical, yet of strong conceptions, subordinate the rest to one or two leading figures, and the imperfectly represented life of the others incloses them, as in a frame.

In originality of conception and resting the main interest upon force of character in a woman, this drama naturally leads us to revert to a work in the department of narrative fiction, which, on similar grounds, comes to us as a harbinger of the new era. This book is "Margaret, or the Real and Ideal," a work which has appeared within the past year; and, considering its originality and genuineness, has excited admiration and sympathy amazingly soon.[14] Even some leading reviews, of what Byron used to speak of as the "garrison" class, (a class the most opposite imaginable to that of Garrison abolitionists,) have discussed its pretensions and done

---

[14] *Margaret*, by Sylvester Judd (1813-1853), was reviewed by Fuller in the 1 September 1845 *New-York Daily Tribune*.

homage to its merits. It is a work of great power and richness, a genuine disclosure of the life of mind and the history of character. Its descriptions of scenery and the common people, in the place and time it takes up, impart to it the highest value as a representative of transient existence, which had a great deal of meaning. The beautiful simplicity of action upon and within the mind of Margaret, Heaven lying so clearly about her in the infancy of the hut of drunkards, the woods, the village, and their ignorant, simply human denizens, her unconscious growth to the stature of womanhood, the flow of life impelled by her, the spiritual intimations of her dreams, the prophecies of music in the character of Chilion, the *naive* discussion of the leading reform movements of the day in their rudimental forms, the archness, the humour, the profound religious faith, make of this book an aviary from which doves shall go forth to discover and report of all the green spots of promise in the land. Of books like this, as good, and still better, our new literature shall be full; and, though one swallow does not make a summer, yet we greet, in this one "Yankee novel," the sufficient earnest of riches that only need the skill of competent miners to be made current for the benefit of man.

Meanwhile, the most important part of our literature, while the work of diffusion is still going on, lies in the journals, which monthly, weekly, daily, send their messages to every corner of this great land, and form, at present, the only efficient instrument for the general education of the people.

Among these, the Magazines take the lowest rank. Their object is principally to cater for the amusement of vacant hours, and, as there is not a great deal of wit and light talent in this country, they do not even this to much advantage. More wit, grace, and elegant trifling, embellish the annals of literature in one day of France than in a year of America.

The Reviews are more able. If they cannot compare, on equal terms, with those of France, England, and Germany, where, if genius be rare, at least a vast amount of talent and culture are brought to bear upon all the departments of knowledge, they are yet very creditable to a new country, where so large a portion of manly ability must be bent on making laws, making speeches, making rail-roads and canals. They are, however, much injured by a partisan spirit, and the fear of censure from their own public. This last is always slow death to a journal; its natural and only safe position is *to lead*; if, instead, it bows to the will of the multitude, it will find the ostracism of democracy far more dangerous than the worst censure of a tyranny could be. It is not half so dangerous to a man to be immured in a dungeon alone with God and his own clear conscience, as to walk the streets fearing the scrutiny of a thousand eyes, ready to veil, with anxious care, whatever may not suit the many-headed monster in its momentary mood. Gentleness is dignified, but caution is debasing; only a noble fearlessness can give wings to the mind, with which to soar beyond the common ken, and learn what may be of use to the crowd below. Writers have nothing to do but to love truth fervently, seek justice according to their ability, and then express what is in the mind; they have nothing to do with consequences, God will take care of those. The want of such noble courage, such faith in the power of truth and good desire, paralyze mind greatly in this country. Publishers are afraid; authors are afraid; and if a worthy resistance is not made by religious souls, there is danger that all the light will soon be put under bushels, lest some wind should waft from it a spark that may kindle dangerous fire.

For want of such faith, and the catholic spirit that flows from it, we have no great leading Review. The North American was once the best. While under the care of Edward Everett,[15] himself a host in extensive knowledge, grace and adroitness in applying it, and the power of enforcing grave meanings by a light and flexible satire that tickled while it wounded, it boasted more force, more life, a finer scope of power. But now, though still exhibiting ability and information upon special points, it is entirely deficient in great leadings, and the *vivida vis*, but ambles and jogs at an old gentlemanly pace along a beaten path that leads to no important goal.

Several other journals have more life, energy and directness than this, but there is none which occupies a truly great and commanding position, a beacon light to all who sail that way. In order to do this, a journal must know how to cast

---

[15] Edward Everett (1794-1865), politician and author who edited the *North American Review* from 1820 to 1824.

aside all local and temporary considerations when new convictions command, and allow free range in its columns, to all kinds of ability, and all ways of viewing subjects. That would give it a life, rich, bold, various.

The life of intellect is becoming more and more determined to the weekly and daily papers, whose light leaves fly so rapidly and profusely over the land. Speculations are afloat, as to the influence of the electric telegraph upon their destiny, and it seems obvious that it should raise their character by taking from them in some measure, the office of gathering and dispersing the news, and requiring of them rather to arrange and interpret it.

This mode of communication is susceptible of great excellence in the way of condensed essay, narrative, criticism, and is the natural receptacle for the lyrics of the day. That so few good ones deck the poet's corner, is because the indifference or unfitness of editors, as to choosing and refusing, makes this place, at present, undesirable to the poet. It might be otherwise.

The means which this organ affords of diffusing knowledge and sowing the seeds of thought where they may hardly fail of an infinite harvest, cannot be too highly prized by the discerning and benevolent. Minds of the first class are generally indisposed to this kind of writing; what must be done on the spur of the occasion and cast into the world so incomplete, as the hurried off–spring of a day or hour's labour must generally be, cannot satisfy their judgment, or do justice to their powers. But he who looks to the benefit of others, and sees with what rapidity and ease instruction and thought are assimilated by men, when they come thus, as it were, on the wings of the wind, may be content, as an unhonoured servant to the grand purposes of Destiny, to work in such a way at the Pantheon which the Ages shall complete, on which his name may not be inscribed, but which will breathe the life of his soul.

The confidence in uprightness of intent, and the safety of truth, is still more needed here than in the more elaborate kinds of writing, as meanings cannot be fully explained nor expressions revised. Newspaper writing is next door to conversation, and should be conducted on the same principles. It has this advantage: we address, not our neighbour, who forces us to remember his limitations and prejudices, but the ideal presence of human nature as we feel it ought to be and trust it will be. We address America rather than Americans.

A worthy account of the vocation and duties of the journalist, is given by Cornelius Mathews. Editors, generally, could not do better than every New Year's day to read and insert the following verses.

As shakes the canvass of a thousand ships,
    Struck by a heavy land-breeze, far at sea,
Ruffle the thousand broad sheets of the land,
    Filled with the people's breath of potency.

A thousand images the hour will take,
    From him who strikes, who rules, who speaks, who sings,
Many within the hour their grave to make,
    Many to live, far in the heart of things.

A dark-dyed spirit he, who coins the time,
    To virtue's wrong, in base disloyal lies,
Who makes the morning's breath, the evening's tide,
    The utterer of his blighting forgeries.

How beautiful who scatters, wide and free,
    The gold-bright seeds of loved and loving truth!
By whose perpetual hand, each day supplied,
    Leaps to new life the empire's heart of youth.

To know the instant and to speak it true,
    Its passing lights of joy, its dark, sad cloud,
To fix upon the unnumbered gazer's view,
    Is to thy ready hand's broad strength allowed.

There is an inwrought life in every hour,
    Fit to be chronicled at large and told.
'Tis thine to pluck to light its secret power,
    And on the air its many-colored heart unfold.

The angel that in sand-dropped minutes lives,
    Demands a message cautious as the ages,
Who stuns, with dusk-red words of hate his ear,
    That mighty power to boundless wrath enrages.[16]

This feeling of the dignity of his office, honour and power in fulfilling it, are not common in the journalist, but, where

[16] "The Poet," *Poems on Man, in His Various Aspects Under the American Republic* (London: Wiley and Putnam, 1843).

they exist, a mark has been left fully correspondent to the weight of the instrument. The few editors of this country who, with mental ability and resource, have combined strength of purpose and fairness of conduct, who have never merged the man and the gentleman in the partisan, who have been willing to have all sides fully heard, while their convictions were clear on one, who have disdained groundless assaults or angry replies, and have valued what was sincere, characteristic and free, too much to bend to popular errors they felt able to correct, have been so highly prized that it is wonderful that more do not learn the use of this great opportunity. It will be learned yet; the resources of this organ of thought and instruction begin to be understood, and shall yet be brought out and used worthily.

We see we have omitted honoured names in this essay. We have not spoken of Brown, as a novelist by far our first in point of genius and instruction as to the soul of things. Yet his works have fallen almost out of print. It is their dark, deep gloom that prevents their being popular, for their very beauties are grave and sad. But we see that Ormond is being republished at this moment. The picture of Roman character, of the life and resources of a single noble creature, of Constantia alone, should make that book an object of reverence. All these novels should be republished; if not favorites, they should at least not be lost sight of, for there will always be some who find in such powers of mental analysis the only response to their desires.

We have not spoken of Hawthorne, the best writer of the day, in a similar range with Irving, only touching many more points and discerning far more deeply. But we have omitted many things in this slight sketch, for the subject, even in this stage, lies as a volume in our mind, and cannot be unrolled in completeness unless time and space were more abundant. Our object was to show that although by a thousand signs, the existence is foreshown of those forces which are to animate an American literature, that faith, those hopes are not yet alive which shall usher it into a homogeneous or fully organized state of being. The future is glorious with certainties for those who do their duty in the present, and, lark-like, seeking the sun, challenge its eagles to an earthward flight, where their nests may be built in our mountains, and their young raise their cry of triumph, unchecked by dullness in the echoes.

Since finishing the foregoing essay, the publication of some volumes by Hawthorne and Brown have led to notices in "The Tribune," which, with a review of Longfellow's poems, are subjoined to eke out the statement as to the merits of those authors.[17]

[17] Fuller's reviews of Hawthorne's *Mosses from an Old Manse*, Brown's *Wieland* and *Ormond*, and Longfellow's *Poems* which follow are here omitted; they are printed following the text of their appearance in the *New-York Tribune* on pp. 371-74, 375-78, 317-24 above. The *Tribune* texts contain these substantive variants from the *Papers on Literature and Art* texts:

372.14   no] an
372.30   lay] lays
*374.9   Ciacord] Con-/cord
377.1   by the sweat] by sweat
378.25– [¶] We . . . read.] [*not present*]
378.32
318.3   Meantime] Meanwhile
320.10   Dandy] dandy
321.36   substances] substance
322.2   these] those
324.10   Plan] Plans
324.17   those] these
* See "Textual Note," p. 46.